SPECIAL EDITION

American Reading Instruction

NILA BANTON SMITH

INTERNATIONAL
**Reading
Association**

800 Barksdale Road, PO Box 8139
Newark, Delaware 19714-8139, USA
www.reading.org

Director of Publications   Joan M. Irwin
Editorial Director, Books and Special Projects   Matthew W. Baker
Senior Editor, Books and Special Projects   Tori Mello Bachman
Permissions Editor   Janet S. Parrack
Production Editor   Shannon Benner
Acquisitions and Communications Coordinator   Corinne M. Mooney
Assistant Editor   Charlene M. Nichols
Administrative Assistant   Michele Jester
Editorial Assistant   Tyanna L. Collins
Production Department Manager   Iona Sauscermen
Supervisor, Electronic Publishing   Anette Schütz
Senior Electronic Publishing Specialist   Cheryl J. Strum
Electronic Publishing Specialist   R. Lynn Harrison

Project Editor   Janet S. Parrack

Cover Design   Linda Steere

Library of Congress Cataloging-in-Publication Data
Smith, Nila Banton.
    American reading instruction / Nila Banton Smith.— Special ed.
       p.   cm.
Includes bibliographical references (   ) and index.
    ISBN 0-87207-348-3 (alk. paper)
1. Reading (Elementary)—United States—History.   2. Readers—United States—History.   I. International Reading Association.   II. Title.
    LB1573 .S765 2002
    372.4'0973--dc21   2002009116

Nila Banton Smith

CONTENTS

CHAPTER EIGHT

The Period of International Conflict 247

CHAPTER NINE

The Period of Expanding Knowledge and Technological Revolution

Richard D. Robinson

University of Missouri-Columbia

Reading is an affirmation of the future by an ability to use the past—
Harry Golden (1964)

The history of reading education has been one that clearly reflects George Santayana's comment, "Those who cannot remember the past are condemned to repeat it" 1905–1906, p. 284). In what seems to be an almost endless pendulum swing from one extreme position to another, the search for answers to various philosophical or pedagogical questions in reading education has continued almost unabated for more than 100 years. Viewed from a historical perspective, this sequence of events reflects a circular pattern of repeated periods of emphasis on various reading topics and then invariably a subsequent time of a lack of interest in these ideas. Often there has been little learned from former experiences with a particular reading issue. Thus, each new "innovation" in reading education has been met with almost the same repeated debate and discussion, while ignoring much of the acquired knowledge and experience of the past. Unfortunately, the inevitable consequence of this continuing dilemma has simply been the fact that real progress in reading education has frequently been of a very limited nature.

What then must we do as educators to effectively build for the future on this common ground of acquired knowledge about reading practices and issues that have stood the test of time? Perhaps in answering this question there is no better beginning than to simply know and appreciate the rich historical background of this profession. For those educators who truly desire to understand this reading legacy of the past, a most promising beginning is simply to read and value this volume, *American Reading Instruction*, by Nila Banton Smith.

Smith was a public school teacher and administrator as well as a university professor. Although her professional record as a researcher and writer was extensive and varied, she is most remembered today for her work in the area of the history of reading. It was here that Smith has had her most lasting effect, especially in relation to the publication of this foundation study, *American Reading Instruction*. From its initial printing in 1934 by Silver Burdett as an extension of Smith's doctoral dissertation, and through subsequent revisions in 1965 and 1986 by the International Reading Association, this volume has had a continuing influence on the research and writing in the field of reading history.

There has been significant progress made in the field of the history of reading education since the initial publication of *American Reading Instruction*, but this in no way detracts from the fundamental importance of this volume. Educators at all levels will find in the pages of this book an enlightening discussion of the important trends and issues in past literacy education as well as descriptions of the prominent individuals who played major roles in American reading instruction. Illustrating much of this history are references made to reading materials as well as teaching behaviors that typified these developments.

Because *American Reading Instruction*, throughout its many revisions, had never been subject to a formal editing process, it was decided that it was time to make the necessary editorial changes to make the book more professional and reader friendly for today's scholars. This edition has been edited lightly to address issues of accuracy, clarity, conciseness, and sentence and paragraph structure to name a few. In several instances, reference citation and documentation remains confusing because of the different forms used and the limited sources to check for accuracy. However, great care has been taken to maintain and preserve the integrity of the author in terms of her meaning, style, and voice. At times, readers may encounter terms and viewpoints that do not reflect current standards of political correctness, but these have been retained to document and portray the social and cultural norms of the times, and to authenticate the era in which the book was written.

Several changes have been made to update this edition: A new epilogue by Norman A. Stahl; a chapter-by-chapter list of endnotes to take the place of footnotes in the previous edition; and the Selected Bibliographies, while maintaining their unusual numbering and dating system, have been reformatted in a more familiar and customary "humanities" style used by researchers and scholars. Also, a new appendix contains an annotated bibliography of resources on the history of reading published since 1986, and a short biography of Nila Banton Smith.

The publication of this revised edition of *American Reading Instruction* by the International Reading Association clearly reaffirms the importance of this book as a foundational study of the history of reading instruction. Equally significant for today's teachers is the fact that this work is also an opportunity to learn of effective reading practices of the past as well. It is hoped that this knowledge of our reading profession's rich historical legacy will be a significant first step in breaking the ever-present pendulum swing from one reading extreme to another.

REFERENCES
Golden, H. (1964). *So what else is new? How to read a book and why.* New York: Putnam.

Santayana, G. (1905–1906). *The life of reason, or, the phases of human progress.* New York: Scribner and Sons.

Nila Banton Smith

Reading was the most important subject in our early American schools, and it has continued to be the most important subject all through the years of our national growth. It therefore seems fitting that a story of the developments in reading instruction should be made available, not only as a matter of information and for the light it throws on the history of education, but also as an aid in giving a clearer perspective on current practices in this significant field.

In surveying the successive movements in American reading instruction, one finds more changes taking place during the last five and a half decades of the 20th century than during the entire span of time preceding. Moreover, for the actual improvement of classroom instruction, it is of greater moment to be informed about recent changes. Hence, the major emphasis in this book is given to developments within the present century.

At any given time, and particularly during a period of transition in teaching practices such as we are now passing through, it is not uncommon to find within a single school different teachers whose procedures exemplify the outstanding characteristics of several of the more recent movements. Furthermore, one teacher may be using some of the techniques and materials associated with three or four different movements. In either case, it is advantageous that the teacher know about these movements and that she understand the one toward which she is primarily tending. Therefore, one of the practical uses of this book is that of serving teachers and consultants in analyzing their own techniques and materials of instruction from the standpoint of the time periods represented.

It is hoped that the perspective on movements in the field of reading instruction, which may be obtained from a study of this book, will be of value also to committees preparing courses of study and to those in charge of textbook selection. The recent developments described and analyzed in these pages may afford a basis for criteria in selecting and in preparing reading materials and techniques for present and future classroom use. It is also hoped that students of both the history of American education and of reading methods may find herein some contribution to their primary fields of interest.

In order that those who read these pages may have some information in regard to the authenticity of statements made, it may be advisable to state the sources of the data that the book contains. The facts were obtained through a careful study of reading materials published in America from 1607 to 1965. These materials included hornbooks; spellers; readers; courses of study; yearbooks and proceedings of national societies; articles in periodicals; histories and diaries; professional books; teachers' manuals; and reports and bulletins of school boards, commissioners of education, and superintendents. Reports of research in reading were carefully perused.

Many dangers of misinterpretation were confronted in organizing and presenting the data upon which this book is based. Perhaps some of these should be mentioned as a safeguard against possible wrong impressions.

First there was the tantalizing problem of selecting representative materials from the great wealth of historical data on reading instruction. Probably everyone who reads this book will think of a favorite reader that he, his parents, or perhaps his child has used and that seemingly has been neglected in this account. Each decade of history has brought forth a harvest of reading materials in ever-increasing numbers. It was impossible to mention all of them in this one book. Most of the books described in the first five periods were selected on the basis of their popularity as determined by ascertaining the number of copies sold or, when this information was lacking, the number of editions published. In later periods, the reading series that were recommended most often in school board reports or courses of study of the various states, and that also showed the highest number of copies or editions published, were selected for description as the leading and representative readers of the period.

The criteria described above were not used in selecting the readers for the last four periods because so many excellent texts have been produced recently that the different series are more evenly distributed in sales than was the case in preceding periods, when one or two books, such as the "Blue-Back Speller" or McGuffey's Readers, overtopped all others. The recent readers were selected, as historical materials usually are selected, it seems, with no better guide than human judgment. The writer conscientiously culled from the great masses of materials in present use those that to her seemed representative in that they conveyed ideas that were found again and again in many different and contemporary sources.

The second problem was that of organizing the unwieldy body of historical facts collected into a structure that would function in pointing up trends and in drawing fairly clear lines of demarcation between successive periods of development. It was finally decided that the fundamental influences which, themselves, were responsible for bringing about change would serve in the most functional way as guidelines for dividing the continuous flow of evolutionary progress into significant growth stages.

Third, there was the problem of setting dates for the periods. The marking of any historical period with definite initial and closing dates is a precarious undertaking. There are overlappings and mergings from one period to another, and there are certain continuous strands that extend through all periods. In spite of these difficulties, it seemed desirable to give some idea of when certain aspects of reading development were most in evidence. For this reason, approximate dates were set for the purpose of delineating the periods of strongest emphasis, but with no suggestion that change took place suddenly on the specific dates indicated in the chapters.

A fourth problem in preparing this book was that of characterizing reading instruction during the different periods of emphasis without conveying the impression that all reading aims, methods, and materials of the time conformed to the general characterization. Although it is true that the leading readers of a given period exhibit certain general characteristics, it is equally true that every period, after the period of religious emphasis, was marked by random shots in different directions, and that there were always some authors whose convictions varied from the great body of opinion. An attempt has been made to indicate this by describing different developments within a period, by pointing out exceptions, and occasionally by describing materials that were unique rather than representative.

The pleasantest mission of this preface is that of extending recognition to those who have rendered services to me. I wish to extend first acknowledgments to Dr. Milo B. Hillegas for his stimulating encouragement, helpful advice, and aids of many kinds; to Dr. Edward H. Reisner for invaluable assistance in historical research; and to Dr. William A. McCall and Dr. Clyde J. Tidwell for many helpful criticisms and suggestions.

Acknowledgment is due also to the many librarians who have graciously and efficiently supplied me with materials in Chicago; Detroit; Ann Arbor, Michigan; New York; New Haven, Connecticut; Philadelphia; and Washington, DC. I am especially grateful to the many publishers who have supplied me with information about the early and current editions of their reading programs.

And finally, an incalculable debt of gratitude is due my mother for her constant and inexhaustible supply of help, faith, and inspiration.

CHAPTER ONE

The Beginnings of Reading Instruction

The story of American reading instruction is a fascinating one to pursue. It is a story of old readers which have moved in long procession from the schoolroom to the garret, from noisy popularity to silent oblivion. It is a story which reflects the changing religious, economic, and political institutions of a growing and progressive country. It is a story shot through with glimpses of advancing psychologies, of broadening and more inclusive philosophies, of ever-increasing attempts to apply science to education.

This evolutionary progress in reading has been marked by a series of emphases, each of which has been so fundamental in nature as to have controlled, to a large extent, both the method and the content of reading instruction during the period of its greatest intensity. This book has been written for the purpose of pointing out these periods of emphasis, tracing the background influences, which have brought them about, and briefly discussing their effects upon reading instruction.

The long pilgrimage of reading instruction began with the invention of characters for use in expressing and recording thought; consequently the beginnings of reading must be traced in conjunction with the development of written symbols and the materials upon which they were inscribed.

In this modern age we stand on the sidewalk and gaze upward with interest as a sky pilot unfolds a message in the heavens by puffing white smoke characters against a blue sky. As we gaze, we marvel at this product of 20th-century genius, and perhaps it does not occur to us that this seeming innovation had its prototype in the very first writing done by man. To be sure, primitive man had no airplane and no alphabet, but his messages were drawn in the air and his fellow men read them element by element as they were revealed. His hand was his writing instrument, gestures were his characters, and the air was the medium upon which they were written.

The use of gestures as a means of communication was either supplemented or followed by the use of picture symbols. Drawing pictures on sand, bark, or stone would seem to be a natural transition from drawing them in the air. However, authorities on paleography are not agreed as to whether the picture language was derived from the gesture language or whether the two developed together. In discussing these mediums of communication, E.B. Tyler says in his *Early History of Mankind,*

> There is, indeed, a very close relation between these two ways of expressing and communicating thought. Gesture can set forth thought with much greater speed and fullness than picture writing, but it is inferior to it, having to place the different elements of a sentence in succession in single file, so to speak; both belong to similar conditions of the human mind. (1: 62)

Picture writing had its origin so far back in the dim mists and myths of antiquity that no one can say when it began. Nevertheless, we have abundant proof of its existence in the more permanent types of materials which nature has so faithfully treasured for us. In *The Story of the Alphabet*, Edward Clodd says,

> On fragments of bone, horn, schist, and other materials, the savage hunter of the Reindeer Period, using a pointed flint-flake, depicted alike himself and the wild animals which he hunted. From cavern

---

[Numbers in parentheses throughout the book refer to the titles listed by number in the Selected Bibliography on pages 399–411 and the volume and page numbers of the quoted passage.]

floors of France, Belgium, and other parts of Western Europe, whose deposits date from the Old Stone Age, there have been unearthed rude etchings of naked, hardy men brandishing spears at wild horses, or creeping along the ground to hurl their weapons at the urus, or wild ox, or at the woolly-haired elephant. A portrait of this last named, showing the creature's shaggy ears, long hair, and upwardly curved tusks, its feet being hidden in the surrounding high grass, is one of the most famous examples of paleolithic art. (2: 22)

At first these pictures represented only single objects, but gradually they came to embody ideas and feelings. When they have reached this latter stage, they are called ideograms. Primitive pictographers were very skillful in expressing thought through ideograms and primitive readers interpreted them with keen insight. Nevertheless, the time arrived when picture writing was unable adequately to cope with the complexity of the languages of progressive peoples. It became necessary to represent the sounds of these languages; as Clodd says, "to select from the big and confused mass of ideograms, phonograms, and all their kin, a certain number of signs to denote, unvaryingly, certain sounds" (2: 124).

By degrees words and syllables were analyzed into letter sounds and symbols were evolved to represent them. The Egyptians are said to have developed such symbols very early, perhaps 25 centuries before Christ. The Phoenician alphabet was developed from these early signs or letters, and from them sprang the Greek letters and their offshoot, the Roman alphabet.

As the symbols for writing and reading were evolving into systematic sets of characters, a more definite provision was also made for materials on which to place them. Instead of limiting their inscription only to the scraps of bark, bone, stone, or skin which in the exigency of the situation were found convenient, men began to prepare tablets of stone or wood and pieces of tile for the express purpose of providing mediums on which symbols might be inscribed.

During a visit to the Ashmolean Museum at Oxford, the writer had an opportunity to examine what is said to be the oldest alphabet writing in existence. It consists of a series of characters engraved on a tablet of stone, prepared during the reign of Sent, an Egyptian monarch who ruled about the year 4700 B.C. None of the characters resembled the letters of our alphabet except one, this one being almost an exact duplicate of the *N* that we use.

In many of the museums of Europe, one sees pieces of old tiles on which characters had been incised or impressed before baking. In the earliest of these, the words appeared in cursive writing; in the later ones the separate letters of the alphabet were stamped in with clay of a color different from that of the foundation. Various color combinations were used, but red and black predominated. The characters were artistically arranged on the tiles and it is evident that they were intended to be decorative as well as useful.

Tablets on which characters were scratched or incised are also exhibited in many European museums. Some of these were made of stone, others of wood. The wooden ones often had a rim around them. This rim formed a receptacle for wax, which was poured into it to harden, later to provide a surface upon which the letters could be impressed. Such tablets were usually accompanied by an instrument called a stylus, made of either bone or ivory. The stylus always had one pointed end for use in writing and one flat end for use in smoothing over the wax, when one wished to place new symbols upon it. The Greek and Roman tablets were sometimes double, and sometimes they were made up of several separate tablets held together with ring hinges.

Although we are skipping centuries of history to do so, it may be interesting incidentally to note that as late as 1853 the Society of Antiquaries of London reported the following practice in India.

4

In the native schools of Surat, and elsewhere in our Indian posses-
sions, the floor of the room where the children assemble is thickly
strewn with dust swept up from the street. In lieu of a slate, the
·pupil is provided with a wooden boar and also a pointed stick. He
scatters dust over the board and on that traces letters or tacks in
verses dictated by the master. Careless little Hindoo boys do not
escape scot free. The master looks at the work submitted to him on
the dust-boards; if it is satisfactory, he strikes the board with the end
of a rod, when the figures disappear; if he disapproves, he strikes
again, but this time it is not the board.

The British Museum contains a splendid collection of tablets
which the Egyptians used in teaching their children. Quintilian,
the great Roman educator of the first century, mentioned wooden
tablets with letters for teaching children reading and writing.
From all evidences it would appear then that these old tiles and
tablets were the first "reading textbooks" prepared for children.

The hornbook was undoubtedly the next link in the chain of
textbook developments. Just when the first hornbook was made
and by whom it was made are mysteries that probably always will
remain unsolved. Andrew White Tuer in his *History of the Horn
Book* offers the suggestion that

> [I]n days far behind the invention of paper and printing, the horn-
> book was the happy thought of some overtaxed scribe, who, hastily
> detesting the profitless labor of rewriting the ABC, fastened the
> skin to a slab of wood and covered it with horn. For in those days, as
> in these, children's fingers were smudgy and their ways were care-
> less. (3: I: 14)

Hornbooks were made of wood, iron, pewter, ivory, silver, and
even gingerbread! This latter medium was perhaps the first attempt
to motivate reading instruction. In the 16th century, gingerbread was
a most delectable and popular dainty. Shakespeare in *Love's Labour's
Lost* said, "An I had but one penny in the world, thou shouldst have
it to buy gingerbread!" Since gingerbread was so highly prized,

someone must have conceived the idea of bribing children to engage in the unpleasant task of learning the alphabet by offering them the gingerbread letters to eat when they had learned to name them. Matthew Prior, in Canto II of *Alma*, describes the nurse's use of this device for teaching Master John to read.

> I mention'd diff'rent Ways of Breeding,
> Begin We in our Children's Reading.
> To Master John the English Maid
> A Horn Book gives of Ginger-bread:
> And that the Child may learn the better,
> As he can name, he eats the Letter;
> Proceeding thus with Vast Delight,
> He spells, and gnaws from Left to Right.

Basedow, a German educator of the 18th century, was so enthusiastic about the gingerbread method of teaching the alphabet that he recommended the employment of a school baker for every school. He figured that the cost of shaping the dough into letters would amount to less than half a penny daily for each child, and since no child would need to eat the alphabet for more than three weeks "the acquisition is surely worth so much and is possible even to poor children."

Although this unique hornbook material is interesting, it should not be given undue emphasis because it was not a universal or enduring practice. The typical hornbook consisted of a sheet of paper about 3 by 4 inches in size, fastened on a thin paddle-shaped board. The name "hornbook" came from the fact that a translucent sheet of horn was used to cover the paper, in order "to save from fingers wet the letters faire." A narrow strip of metal was fastened around three sides of the horn while the fourth side was left open to permit the insertion of the sheet of paper. At one end of the board was a handle, usually with a hole through which a string was passed, for use in suspending the hornbook from the child's neck. The earlier hornbooks contained only the alphabet; the later ones usually contained syllables and religious selections.

We have now reached the point of considering that piece of reading material whose name, at least, has persisted throughout the centuries and is still applied to the first reading book—the primer. Early in the history of religious instruction priests came to believe that certain religious selections were so fundamental that all adults and children should memorize them. In the year 813, it was decreed in the 44th Canon of the Council of Mainz that children should be taught the "fidem Catholicam et orationium dominicans."

Because children were to receive universal instruction in this material, it became necessary to make it available to the laity; hence the appearance of the first books containing religious selections to be taught to children. In the Middle Ages, this book came rather generally to contain the Creed, the Lord's Prayer, the Ten Commandments, and a few Psalms. It was called a primer not because it was the first book of reading instruction, but because it was primary or fundamental in containing the "minimum essentials" deemed necessary for one's spiritual existence. Eventually and gradually the alphabet and lists of syllables and words were added to this simple religious manual, and it became the standard book for instruction in reading.

Coexistent with the primer was an entirely separate development of a type of book known as "the ABC." The authorized primer in its early conception was not a schoolbook; it was a manual of church services, handsomely printed, and very expensive. There was need also for a different type of book, a schoolbook that would serve the demands of reading instruction as well as religion, and which could be sold at a moderate price. The ABC came into existence in response to this need. The earliest ABC of which the writer found any record was *The Enschude*

Abecedarium (4: 8). This book, made in the 15th century, was used as the elementary book of the Catholic Church. It contained the alphabet, the Pater Noster, the Ave Maria, the Credo, and two prayers. The function of the ABC is neatly summed up in a quotation from Tuer:

> They were to be the first books placed in the hands of the child and to contain all that it was necessary for him to know, to enable him to understand the rudiments of the Christian Religion and to join in the services of the Church and even to serve at Mass, or, as it is called, "to help a priest sing." (3: II: 198)

In this brief review, an attempt has been made to touch on the different types of reading materials most widely used up to the end of the 16th century. The important point to note is that the hornbook, the primer, and the ABC were all cognates and contemporaries, and all were progenitors of our modern reading textbooks.

CHAPTER TWO

The Period of Religious Emphasis
in Reading Instruction

I. Motives for Teaching Reading

The threads of early American history are so inextricably interwoven with the warp and woof of English institutions and customs that one who studies any phase of colonial civilization must constantly seek explanation in its antecedent and contemporary in England. Consequently, in describing the motives, methods, and materials which characterized the earliest period of American reading instruction (1607–1776), it is necessary to examine the status of each of these aspects of reading in England, and then to trace the English influences as they entered into the more truly American products.

As the Church of England gradually changed its aims from Catholicism to Protestantism, the right of the church to control the schools continued to be an undisputed claim. In fact, fresh impetus was given to this already well established precedent of church control over education, in that the church now felt that it must tighten its grip on the schools in order to maintain the doctrines of the new religion and to implant them irrevocably in the minds of oncoming generations.

One of the most important of these doctrines was that each individual was directly responsible to God for his own salvation. He must not depend upon the interpretation of any mass or prayer, priest or pastor, but must read the Word of God directly and draw his own conclusions. If he were illiterate, he would be compelled to rely upon someone else for this Biblical information and in so doing he would thwart the most fundamental concept of Protestantism. Thus it was that the new religion, for its own sake, was compelled to foster reading instruction. It may be of interest to note Luther's recommendation in regard to the course in reading:

> Above all things, let the Scriptures be the chief and most frequently used reading book, both primary and high schools and the very young should be kept in the gospels. Is it not proper and right that every human being, by the time he has reached his tenth year, should be familiar with the holy gospels, in which the very core and marrow of his life is bound? (5: 321)

The extent to which this religious motive affected classroom instruction in England, and family life as well, is summed up by Foster Watson in *English Grammar Schools to 1660*:

> The whole school round of religious observances, Catechisms, primers, and Bible reading shows the permeation of the school work with religious instruction. The ecclesiastical organization of the school in the Middle Ages had prepared the ground for a theological discipline in the seventeenth century. The old objective influences of a picturesque ceremonial religion gave way to a subjective Biblical atmosphere, and the school was continuously cast in a religious mould....
>
> The Bible was the center of family religious life, known by all members of the family, read aloud morning and evening at family prayers, the sign and seal of the profession of religion, in a religious age. Family and school education were at one, in recognition of the importance of religion. (6: 60)

In *New Discovery of the Old Art of Teaching School* printed in London in 1660, the author, Charles A. Hoole, states the underlying motive of the English schools during this period.

> Now because all our teaching is but mere trifling unless withal we be careful to instruct children in the grounds of true religion, let them

be sure to get the Lord's Prayer, the Creed, and the Ten Commandments. (7: 109)

We have seen, then, that the English Protestants considered one of the most pressing of their national duties to be that of providing school training which would give children a thorough grounding in their religious faith and such reading ability as would enable them to read the Word of God for themselves. This religious motive was the one that directed and controlled reading instruction in England at the time the early settlers migrated to America.

The pioneers of America were, in general, deeply religious. Many of these early settlers came from among those people and from those lands that had embraced some form of the Protestant faith, and their purpose in coming to America was to enjoy a religious freedom not possible in their own country. It was their religious convictions that caused these pioneers to face the dangers attendant upon the establishment of colonies in the wilderness of a new country, and it was these same religious convictions that caused them so courageously to endure the hardships with which they were confronted in the early years. As the religious motive was the all-controlling force in their lives, it is quite natural that one should find it permeating and directing the instruction in their schools.

Massachusetts was the leader in shaping the policies of early American schools. No better statement of the purpose for teaching reading in America during this period can be found than in a quotation from the famous law of 1647 passed by the General Court of Massachusetts:

It being one chief point of that old deluder, Satan, to keep men from the knowledge of the Scriptures, as in former times, by keeping them in an unknown tongue, so in these latter times, by persuading from the use of tongues, that so at last the true sense and

11

meaning of the original might be clouded by false glosses of saint-seeming deceivers, that learning might not be buried in the grave of our fathers in church and commonwealth, the Lord assisting our endeavors. It is therefore ordered that every township in this jurisdiction, after the Lord hath increased them to the number of fifty householders, shall then forthwith appoint one within their town to teach all such children as shall resort to him to write and read. (8: 60)

II. Materials of Reading Instruction

The materials that constituted the reading course in England during the 16th and 17th centuries are described in the following paragraph in a way that not only instructs us as to the materials used, but at the same time gives us an appreciation of the religious atmosphere with which reading instruction was saturated at that time.

> We have the ABC for children, and because there is no grace therein, lest we should lack prayers, we have the Primer and the Ploughman's prayer and a book of other small devotions, and then the whole Psalter, too. After the Psalter, children were wont to go straight to their Donat and their Accidence, but now they go straight to Scripture, and for this we have as a Donat the book of the Pathway to Scripture in a little book, so that after these books are learned well we are ready for Tyndale's Pentateuchs and Testament. (6: 33)

Hoole gives a more concise but less picturesque statement when he says,

> The Primer, the Psalter, the Bible are to be used in teaching spelling and reading. Writing and casting accounts are to be taught. The Lord's Prayer, the Creed, the Ten Commandments and the Catechism are to be known by all. (7: 21)

It is evident that several different types of material for reading instruction were in use in Europe at the time the early colonists migrated to America. Whether they brought any of these reading materials with them is a matter of conjecture. Since the New England settlers came from sections of the country where hornbooks, primers, ABCs, and Psalters were commonly used, it seems quite likely that they would equip themselves with these materials in the prudential anticipation of instructing their young Johns and Priscillas. Although we cannot prove that the colonists actually conveyed reading materials to America with them, we have ample proof that they imported English reading materials rather generously throughout the colonial period. Some records bear evidence to this effect:

> Just imported from London, and to be Sold by the Printer hereof, Bibles of several sorts, Testaments, Psalters and Primers.
>
> (From *New York Weekly Post-Boy*, December 24, 1744)

> H. Gaine at the Bible & Crown, in Queen-Street, has just imported in the Snow Irene, Captain Jacobson, from London, the following Books, viz...Bibles, Testaments, Common-Prayers of all Sizes, Psalters, Primmers, several sorts of School Books &c.
>
> (From *New York Mercury*, June 7, 1756)

> Just imported in the last vessels from London and Bristol, and to be sold by WRIGHT and YOUNG, at their store in the corner house opposite Doctor Murray's, near the Meat Market...testaments, psalters, spelling books, primers, shaded crewels, knitting needles, &c.
>
> (From *New York Mercury*, July 18, 1757)

Having shown that English reading materials were used in America during colonial times, we may now proceed to a discussion of the different types of materials, both English and American, which characterized this period of reading instruction.

The hornbook is the first piece of instructional material specifically mentioned in American records. This mention appears in a bill that Charles Liggett made out for cash, paid to his wife in 1678 (9: 264). The following item appeared among several articles listed in his bill:

> May 1678 / for 1 horning book and paper—.8

The writer found no evidence of any hornbooks having been actually constructed in this country. In light of frequent references to importation from England, it is reasonably safe to assume that the English hornbooks were the ones commonly used. (See page 15 for the content of one hornbook of the period.)

The hornbook seems to have been very popular throughout the colonial period. It was used in two capacities: for catechizing in church, and for giving children their first reading instruction in school. The following few items of interest are typical of those found rather generously distributed throughout the records of this period. In the "Diary of Samuel Sewell" (10: 344) under the date of April 27, 1691, is this entry:

> This afternoon had Joseph to school to Capt. Townsend's mother's, his cousin Jane accompanying him, carried his hornbook.

In the records of the Old South Church in Boston for 1708 is the following entry:

> Paid 1£ 10S. for horns for catechising.

Andrew Bradford advertised "Horn books for sale" in the *American Weekly Mercury* in 1727, 1730, and 1734. After he died, his wife advertised them frequently in the same paper from 1744 to 1746.

The hornbook was used for catechizing in church and for giving children their first reading instruction in school.

The last advertisement of hornbooks that the writer has been able to find in colonial newspapers appeared in the *Pennsylvania Gazette* of December 4, 1760. It advertised "Primers, Gilt Hornbooks or Plain Hornbooks." Since apparently it was not profitable to advertise hornbooks after this date, it seems quite likely that the use of this kind of reading material died out in American classrooms somewhere near the middle of the 18th century.

The ABC

The ABC seems not to have been popular for instructional purposes in America. We know that its use as a separate piece of reading material was continued in England throughout the first half of the 18th century, and undoubtedly some copies of the English ABCs found their way to this country. No mention, however, is made of the ABC in the advertisements of the times; so it would appear that the frugal American saw no need for this separate piece of material and was satisfied with the combined ABC and primer.

Psalters

Psalters were frequently mentioned as materials of instruction during this period. The following voluminous title on one Psalter published in 1760 is perhaps more enlightening than any other description that could be given:

THE NEW ENGLAND PSALTER

Improved by the addition of a variety of lessons in spelling, accented and divided according to rule. Likewise, rules for reading and particularly of the emphasis belonging to some special word or words in the sentence. Instructions for reading verse; as also of the different letters used in printed books, and particularly of the use of capitals, notes and points, made use of in writing and printing. Likewise, some account of the books of the old testament: of the books of the prophets: of the Apocryphal books, and of the books of the new testament. The whole being a proper introduction, not only to learning, but to the training of children in the reading of the holy scriptures in particular. (11: 1)

Primers Printed in America

The American Antiquarian Society of Worcester, Massachusetts, has a copy of *The Protestant Tutor*, printed by Sam Green and sold by John Griffin in Boston in 1685. Undoubtedly, this was the first reading textbook printed in America. To understand its significance, one must turn back to its origin in England.

On February 27, 1679, Benjamin Harris, a printer by trade, advertised in his London newspaper a book called *The Protestant Tutor*. The preface is addressed "to all Protestant Parents, Schoolmasters, and School Mistresses of Children." This book was reissued in England in 1680 and again in 1695. In the meantime, the 1685 edition was printed in Boston. The principal contents were the "Roman Small Letters," the syllabarium, the Lord's Prayer, the Creed, the Ten Commandments, John Rogers's biography and verses, words of from two to seven syllables, the "Proper Names" (from Scripture), a catechism, and other religious selections.

The first reading textbook specifically designed for the American colonies was *The New England Primer*, and the first edition of this book was probably printed in England. In the *Stationer's Register* in London under the date of October 5, 1683, a certain John Gaine entered a title in accordance with the statute requiring the registration of all books for sale. This entry (12) reads:

Mr. John Gaine
  Eodem Die et Anno. Entred then for his Book or Coppy Entituled the New England Primer or Milk for Babes with Win. Scoresby.

Jno. Gaine

The next mention of *The New England Primer* is found in an advertisement appearing in Newman's *News from the Stars*, Boston, 1690 (see page 18).

The book swept into wide popularity with Americans and succeeded in winning and holding their support as the standard textbook of reading instruction throughout the colonial period.

The New England Primer *was advertised in an almanac entitled* News from the Stars, *published in Boston in 1690.*

The earliest extant copy of *The New England Primer* is from an edition printed in Boston by S. Kneeland and T. Green in 1727. This copy is now in the Lenox Collection of the New York Public Library. The second earliest copy that has been preserved came to view as the result of an auction sale. The Labach family in Labachsville, Pennsylvania, died out after a residence of 200 years in America, and in 1903 their library was sold at public auction. M.D. High, a neighbor, bought this rare old book for 12 cents and later sold it to the publishing company Dodd, Mead, for the sum of $2,500. Paul Leicester Ford presents a vivid picture of *The New England Primer* with the following description:

Here was no easy road to knowledge and to salvation; but with prose as bare of beauty as the whitewash of their churches, with poetry as rough and stern as their storm-torn coast, with pictures as crude and unfinished as their own glacial-smoothed boulders, between stiff oak covers which symbolized the contents, the children were tutored, until, from being unregenerate, and as Jonathan Edwards said, "young vipers, and infinitely more hateful than young vipers" to God, they attained that happy state, when as expressed by Judge

Sewall's child, they were afraid they "should goe to hell," and were "stirred up dreadfully to seek God." (4: 1)

The mechanical make-up of *The New England Primer* is quite evident in Ford's description. We might add that the shape and size of the book varied with its numerous editions. Sometimes it was square, sometimes oblong; but always it was a small book. The standard form in which it appeared most frequently was an oblong about 2 ½ by 4 ½ inches.

The stiff oak covers mentioned by Ford must have persisted far into the 18th century. The 1727 edition had wooden covers. The 1735 edition is thus described in the *Boston Evening Transcript*, June 15, 1904: "The book contains 104 pages and is bound in oak and leather. It is 3 ½ inches long and 3 inches wide."

The 1750 edition is described by the same newspaper (November 8, 1901) in this manner: "It is a small octavo in size, and the copy sold by Dodd, Mead is a fine complete example in the original wooden boards, leather back, flowered paper sides." The frontispiece was usually a portrait of the British monarch reigning at the time the edition was printed. Each book contained also a series of small pictures about 1 by ⅔ inches in size, each accompanied by a verse designed to teach a letter of the alphabet. The picture often accentuated the gloomy message of the verse. For example, the verse for *R* was

> Rachel doth mourn
> For her first born. (13: 10)

This verse was illustrated with the picture of a woman standing at the foot of a cot upon which a child reposes, apparently stiff and dead. For *Y* we find this verse:

> Youth forward slips,
> Death soonest nips.

EASY SYLLABLES FOR CHILDREN.

Ab	eb	ib	ob	ub
ac	ec	ic	oc	uc
ad	ed	id	od	ud
af	ef	if	of	uf
ag	eg	ig	og	ug
aj	ej	ij	oj	uj
al	el	il	ol	ul
am	em	im	om	um
an	en	in	on	un
ap	ep	ip	op	up
ar	er	ir	or	ur
as	es	is	os	us
at	et	it	ot	ut
av	ev	iv	ov	uv
ax	ex	ix	ox	ux
az	ez	iz	oz	uz

In The New England Primer, *the child started off with columns of two–letter syllables and within the next four pages progressed rapidly to words of five syllables.*

The illustration accompanying this verse shows a hideous figure holding in his hand a huge spear which he is directing toward the head of a little child who stands near by. The illustrative features of the book were concluded with a picture of John Rogers about to be burned at the stake or, in some editions, actually being

20

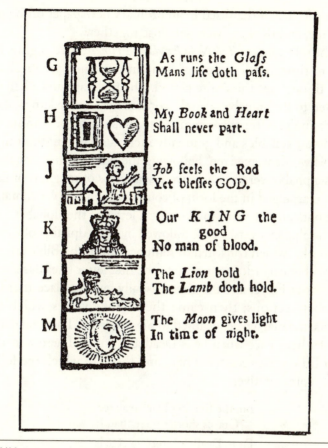

G As runs the *Glafs*
Mans life doth pafs.

H My *Book* and *Heart*
Shall never part.

J *Job* feels the Rod
Yet bleffes GOD.

K Our *K I N G* the good
No man of blood.

L The *Lion* bold
The *Lamb* doth hold.

M The *Moon* gives light
In time of night.

The child was encouraged to learn to read by the use of a series of alphabet rhymes and pictures in The New England Primer. *This page is from an edition of 1729.*

consumed by the flames while "his Wife with nine small Children and one at her breast" stands gazing at the "sorrowful sight."

All these pictures were woodcuts in black and white, crudely drawn, poorly proportioned, and altogether unattractive and inartistic. The paper was rough and heavy. The type was small, about the size of that used in an ordinary newspaper of the present time, and the lines were set close together.

The selections in *The New England Primer* varied slightly from time to time, but its standard content remained practically the same throughout this entire period. The first page and a half were devoted to the alphabet, vowels, consonants, double letters, italics, and capitals. After these came the syllabarium, beginning with two-letter syllables and gradually increasing in length until six-syllable words were given. Following the syllabarium came the famous alphabet verses. These were sentences of religious or moral import, arranged in the form of couplets, each couplet containing some outstanding word to illustrate a letter of the alphabet.

The alphabet verses were followed by "An Alphabet of Lessons for Youth," which consisted of sentences from the Bible arranged in alphabetical order according to the first letter of each sentence. The Lord's Prayer and the Creed usually found a place after these alphabet sections; then came the famous verses which John Rogers, the martyr, bequeathed to his children, "That you may see your Father's Face when he is Dead and gone." There were a few other little verses scattered here and there, of which the following is representative:

> I in the Burying Place may see
> Graves shorter there than I;
>
> From Death's Arrest no Age is free,
> Young children too may die;
>
> My God, may such an awful sight,
> Awakening be to me!
>
> Oh, that by early Grace I might
> For death prepared be. (13: 22)

The authorship of *The New England Primer* is generally ascribed to Benjamin Harris, the Englishman who also first printed *The Protestant Tutor*. Harris's trade as a printer, coupled with his propensity for scribbling verse and his devotion to the Protestant religion, apparently constituted the right combination for the production of just such a book as *The New England Primer*. Although much of the material was taken directly from the Bible, Harris paraphrased the biblical content of the alphabet verses and probably originated some of the other verses. The two catechisms most generally used were "The Shorter Catechism" composed by the Reverend Assembly of Divines at Westminster, and "Milk for Babes" written by Cotton Mather, the famous New England minister. *The New England Primer* was by far the most popular textbook of the period.

> In 1747 Z. Fowle printed in a single edition 10,000 copies of the New England Primer.
> Accounts of Franklin and Hall show that that firm, between the years 1749 and 1766, printed and sold 37,100 copies. (4: 84)

A careful count of all editions recorded reveals the fact that 22 editions were printed between 1727 and 1776, a period of 49 years.

Spellers

In spite of the popularity of *The New England Primer*, its career did not pass unchallenged. The chief books with which it had to compete were spellers whose function was not only to teach spelling, but also to teach reading, religion, and morals. One of the first spellers to gain admission to American schools was *England's Perfect School-Master* by Nathaniel Strong. The following description of this book in the *Boston News Letter*, August 12, 1706, is revealing not only as to the nature of this particular book, but also in respect to the motives, methods, and contents of reading instruction in general.

> The following books to be sold by Benjamin Elliot in his shop under the West-End of the Town-House in Boston, Viz.

England's Perfect School-Master: or, Directions for exact spelling, reading and writing: Showing how to spell or read any Chapter in the Bible, by four and twenty words only; with Examples of most words, from one to six syllables, both in whole words and also divided; with Rules how to spell them: also how to spell all such words which are alike found, yet differ in their sense and spelling. Together with the true meaning and use of all stops and points to be observed by all that would Read and Write well; with a table of Orthography, shewing how to write true English: Also a variety of Pieces, both English and Latin Verse, on the most remarkable passages mentioned in Scripture, very useful for Writing Schools.

This speller, entitled *England's Perfect School-Master*, was first printed in America by B. Green in Boston in 1710, according to Charles Evans's *American Bibliography of Printing* (14: ¶1487). Several editions were printed after that time, but by the middle of the century it had retired in favor of other popular spellers.

Instructions for Right Spelling by George Fox, an English clergyman, was used in America throughout the first three quarters of the 18th century. It first appeared from the American press in 1702 and was printed in this country repeatedly during the 75 years (14: ¶1049).

The copy of Fox's speller that the writer examined was one of an edition printed in 1760 (15). This little book was about 4 by 6 inches. It was bound in brown leather, was made of rough, unglazed paper, and contained no pictures. The lines of print were close together, but the type was a little larger than that of other schoolbooks of the period, being about the size found in the usual third reader of the present time.

The aims of this speller were clearly stated in its title, which read thus: "Instructions for right spelling and plain directions for reading and writing true English." In later editions the following lines were added: "With several delightful things very useful and necessary for both young and old to read and learn." An examination of the book revealed the following "delightful things":

three pages of small letters and capital letters; three pages of syllables, increasing in length; several "Child's Lessons" composed of short religious sentences; proper names in Scripture with their "Syllables and their Significance"; a few pages of information regarding weights and measurements and many "memorable passages mentioned in Scripture, necessary and delightful for children to read and learn." The first "Child's Lesson," which appeared following the syllabarium, is given below:

> Christ is the Truth. Christ is the Light. Christ is the way. Christ is my life. Christ is my Savior. Christ is my Hope of Glory. (p. 9)

Perhaps the most successful of the spellers of this period was Thomas Dilworth's *A New Guide to the English Tongue*. The first edition of this book was issued in England in 1740. The first American reprint was made by Benjamin Franklin in 1747. Fourteen additional reprints were made in America between this date and 1778. The 1770 edition (16) was 4 by 6 inches in size and was bound in leather. The typographical features were the same as in all other books of the period. This speller, however, had one feature which none of the contemporary spellers displayed— a series of 12 crude little woodcuts, 2¾ by 3 inches.

From the standpoint of content, this book is important in that it contained a considerable amount of secular material. Several pages were given over to rules for the correct spelling and writing of English. A still greater innovation was the inclusion of twelve fables. They were highly moral in tone, but at least the fables were a departure from the strictly religious material of the past. Forty-eight pages of the book were devoted to the usual lists of words ranging from one to seven syllables. As if he dared not break with the precedent of the past, Dilworth devoted all the remaining pages in his speller to religious materials. There were many lessons for beginners consisting of short sentences taken from the Psalter; there were "Public Prayers for Use in Schools in the Morning"; and in some editions, the Shorter Catechism also was included. The first lesson following the syllabarium read as follows:

LESSON 1

The eye of God is on them that do ill.
Go not from me, O God, my God.
The Lord will help them that cry to him.
My Son, if thy Way is bad, see that you mend it.

Another popular speller that made its appearance toward the middle of the 18th century was *The Child's New Plaything* also published in England. It had gone through two editions in England before it was printed in America. According to Evans, the first American edition was printed by Joseph Edwards in Boston in 1744, and by 1765 there were four more editions.

The 1750 edition (17) was a paper-covered volume measuring 3 by 6 inches. It contained no pictures and had the same typographical features as other schoolbooks of the time. Its complete title read thus:

Child's New Plaything: or, Best Amusement: Intended to make the learning to read a diversion instead of a task. Consisting of Scripture-Histories, Fables, Stories, Moral and Religious Precepts, Proverbs, Songs, Riddles, Dialogues, etc.

From the title it is immediately obvious that this book further emphasized the tendency to include secular material. The greater part of its secular text consisted of moralistic fables, precepts, and admonitions. There were, however, two pages of riddles on such subjects as the year, the age, and a reflection in a mirror; and for the first time we find three real stories that were entitled "Earl of Warwick," "St. George and the Dragon," and "Reynard, the Fox." The first four pages of the book were devoted to the alphabet. The succeeding 45 pages contained lists of syllables interspersed with moral and religious precepts and the history of Noah's flood. Following is a sample from the first reading lesson:

LESSON 1

MORAL PRECEPTS

Only by pride cometh Contention.
He loveth Transgression that Loveth Strife.

The fables were followed in each case by a paragraph pointing out the moral implication. There were two dialogues, of which the following excerpt is representative:

A. What is the usefullest thing in the world?
B. Wisdom

A. What is the pleasantest thing in the world?
B. Wisdom.

There were two other English spellers that came into wide use during the second half of the 18th century. One of these was Fenning's *The Universal Spelling-Book*, which appeared in 1755 and contained "Tables of words, Lessons both moral and divine, Fables and pleasant Stories, and a very easy and approved Guide to English Grammar." The other popular speller was William Perry's *The Only Sure Guide to the English Tongue*, which offered the usual lists of words; religious selections consisting of stories, hymns, the Ten Commandments, and some prayers; a chapter on manners; and a few illustrated fables.

These spellers by Dilworth, Fenning, and Perry, along with *The Child's New Plaything*, foreshadowed two changes that gradually and rather generally took place during the last quarter of the 18th century. These changes were the transition from strictly religious to moralistic content and the inclusion of other secular materials such as stories, riddles, and dialogues.

The controlling principle governing the vocabulary selection in all the readers of this period was that of proceeding from the simple to the complex in respect to the number of letters and syllables in words. The individual letters always came first, then lists of one-syllable words, followed by lists of two-syllable words, and so on up to words of five and six syllables. No provision was made for the repetition of words to insure adequate practice, and a great many words occurred only once throughout the reader; nor was any attention given to the distribution of words by pages. One finds the rate of introduction in the first five pages of the primers of this period ranging all the way from twenty to one hundred new words per page.

III. Methods of Teaching Reading

Direct references to the methods used in teaching reading during the period of colonization are very rare. However, the arrangement of materials in books used by the colonists, as well as the voluminous titles with which these books were endowed, bear out the assumption that the methods described as being generally practiced in England at that time were the ones used also in America. So it would seem that in treating the reading methods of the period one could do no better than to describe the entire course of teaching reading in Hoole's picturesque words, from his *New Discovery of the Old Art of Teaching School*, with an incidental reference to other English or American authors, when it seems that such reference will add interest and clarity to the description.

In 1612, Brinsley in his "Ludus Literarius" suggested a new method of teaching the alphabet. In this treatise he pointed out the desirability not only of having the child learn the ABC by rote, forwards and backwards, but also of requiring him to point out which is *a, b, c, d,* or any other letter, first in the alphabet, then "in any other place." He also suggested that one letter be learned at a time, whereas the custom appears to have been to learn the entire alphabet first. Brinsley's suggestion must have been rather generally adopted, as is shown in a statement in Hoole's book, published in 1660.

The usual way to begin a child when he is first brought to Schoole is to teach him to know his letters in the Horn-book, where he is made to run over all the letters in the Alphabet or Christ-cross row both forwards and backwards, until he can tell any of them, which is pointed at, and that in the English character....

The greatest trouble at the first entrance of children is to teach them how to know their letters one from another, when they see them in a book altogether....

Some have therefore begun but with one single letter, and after they have shewed it to the childe in the Alphabet, have made him to find the same anywhere else in the book, till he knew that perfectly; and then they have proceeded to another in like manner, and so gone through the rest.....

Some have contrived a piece of ivory with twenty-four flats or squares, in every one of which was engraven a single letter, and by playing with a childe in throwing this upon a table, and shewing him the letter only which lay uppermost have in a few days taught him the whole alphabet.

Some have made pictures in a little book or upon a scroll of paper wrapt upon two sticks within a box of iceing-glass and by each picture have made three sorts of that letter, with which its name beginneth; but those being too many at once for a childe to take notice on, have proved not so useful as was intended.

Some likewise have had pictures and letters printed in this manner on the back side of a pack of cards, to entice children, that naturally love that sport, to the love of learning their books. (7: 35, 36, 37)

After having mastered the alphabet, the child was inducted into the syllabarium. In regard to this phase of the work, Hoole says,

The common way to teach a child to spell, is, after he knows the letters in the Alphabet, to initiate him into those few syllables, which consist of one vowel before a consonant, *as, ba, be, bi, bo, bu,* etc., in the Horn Book, and thence to proceed with him little and little to the bottom of the book, hearing him twice or thrice over till he can say his lesson and then putting him to a new one. (7: 39)

Clifton Johnson in *Old-Time Schools and School-Books* affords us an additional glimpse of the customary use of memorization and spelling methods in his description of the dame schools of the period. He says that while the dame "heard the smaller pupils recite their letters, and the older ones read and spell from their primers, she busied her fingers with knitting and sewing, and in the intervals between lessons, sometimes worked at the spinning-wheel."[1] Learning the alphabet and the syllabarium was a preparation for the real business of reading, which began when the child attacked the primer itself. Hoole thus describes the method used in the teaching of the primer:

After they have got some knowledge of their letters and a smattering of some syllables and words in the horn book, to turn them into the ABC or Primer and therein to make them name the letters, and spell the words, till by often use they can pronounce (at least) the shortest words at first sight. (7: 41)

The Lord's Prayer, the Creed, the Ten Commandments, and other religious materials were to be memorized by the child, and as Hoole suggests:

[W]hich he will do the more cheerfully, if he be also instructed at home to say them by heart....

When he is thus well entered in the Roman characters, I would have him made acquainted with the rest of the characters now in use, which will be easily done by comparing one with another, and reading over those sentences, Psalms, Thanksgivings and Prayers till he have them pretty well by heart. (7: 50, 52)

Among the few direct references to method is a statement in *The New England Primer* that follows the syllabarium and alphabet verses. It verifies the method of memorizing as described by Hoole.

> Now the child being entered in his Letters and Spelling, let him learn these and such like Sentences by heart, whereby he will be both instructed in his Duty, and encouraged in his Learning. (13: 16)

Having been "graduated" from the primer, a child was permitted to read from the Bible, resorting to spelling as the only technique he knew for solving new words. Many passages of the Bible also were memorized. Let us turn to Hoole's interesting description of this phase of reading instruction.

> When he can read any whit readily, let him begin the Bible, and read over the book of Genesis (and other remarkable Histories in other places of Scripture which are most likely to delight him) by a chapter at a time; but acquaint him a little with the matter beforehand, for that will entice him to read it, and make him more observant of what he reads. After he has read, ask him such general questions out of the Story as are most easie for him to answer, and he will the better remember it. I have known some, that by hiring a child to read two or three chapters a day, and to get so many verses of it by heart, have made them admirable proficients, and that betimes, in the Scriptures. (7: 52)

It is quite obvious that the subject matter of early reading instruction was a much more important consideration than was the method of teaching reading. Method was considered incidentally as a tool in furthering the fundamental aim of acquainting children with the content needed in their early religious life and equipping them to read the Bible in meeting the needs of their later religious life.

The techniques used were those of learning the alphabet, spelling syllables and words, memorizing sections of content, and reading orally. All children were inducted into the reading process through the alphabetical method because that was the only reading approach known at that time. Memorization was perhaps a natural correlate of the religious materials used and the religious motive for teaching them. The Lord's Prayer, the Ten Commandments, the Creed, and other articles of faith were so important in the religious life of the early settlers that they deemed it necessary for all children to memorize them in their "green and tender years." The catechism, which made up the bulk of *The New England Primer*, was to be learned verbatim, so that when that eventful day arrived on which the child was catechized by the minister, he would deport himself commendably by answering every question unfalteringly and unerringly. As for the Bible, it was quite customary to memorize long passages of Scripture, so that they could be quoted with ease and fluency whenever the occasion called for them.

Oral reading also played an important role in the lives of these people. There was a great dearth of reading materials during the colonial period. The Bible, generally speaking, was the only book the home libraries contained, and many families did not have even a Bible. Furthermore, illiteracy was highly prevalent at that time; so it was customary for the uneducated members of the family or the community to gather in little groups in the evenings and on Sabbaths to listen to the oral reading of the Scriptures by one who had mastered the art of reading. Thus we see that oral reading met a real social need in our earliest period of reading instruction.

CHAPTER THREE

The Period of Nationalistic-Moralistic Emphasis in Reading Instruction

I. Motives and Aims of Reading Instruction

By the latter part of the 18th century, the vividness of the early strife for religious freedom had been dimmed in the birth of new generations, who had learned of the ardent efforts and bitter struggles of their forbears only through hearsay, and whose own hearts and minds were completely occupied with the new struggle for political freedom and the business of developing a young nation, strong, unified, and harmonious.

The mental horizon of these people had been broadened by the growth which had taken place in commerce and industry and by the development of facilities for communication and transportation. The expansion of the press and the increase in literacy had extended the range of esoteric knowledge. These and several lesser influences gradually brought about a weakening in religious control over education. The break with Great Britain and the establishment of an independent nation were the final incidents which caused politics to replace theology as the center of intellectual interest. The movement toward the secularization of education reached its fruition during the first half of the nineteenth century, when in the more progressive states the great system of public education was founded.

State control of education was accompanied, as one would expect, by new motives for classroom instruction. While the greatest concern of the church had been that of saving souls and making good communicants, the foremost goal of the state was that of building national strength and making good citizens. We find this general change in educational goals accompanied by a new era in reading instruction, which began about 1776 and extended to about 1840. Reading content now had several new functions to perform: it was expected to purify the American language; to develop loyalty to the new nation, its traditions and institutions, its occupations and resources; and to inculcate the high ideals of virtue and moral behavior which were considered so necessary a part of the general program of building good citizenship.

One finds the nationalistic motive of reading instruction manifesting itself in the new texts in a variety of ways. The most obvious evidence of this trend is in the names of the readers, many of which were of a strongly patriotic tone. We find, for instance, numerous titles such as these: *The American Spelling Book*, *An American Selection of Lessons in Reading and Speaking*, *The Columbian Orator*, *The American Preceptor*, *American Popular Reader*, *Class Book of American Literature*, *A History of the American Revolution*, *National Preceptor*, and *American Manual*.

On examining these and other readers of the period, one finds that the nationalistic aim had a strong influence in the selection of their contents. Lyman Cobb gives this new emphasis as a keynote in the preface to *The North American Reader*, as we may note in the following paragraph.

> The pieces in this work are chiefly American. *The English Reader* so largely used in our country does not contain a single piece or paragraph written by an American citizen. Is this good policy? Is it patriotism? Shall the children of this great nation be compelled to read, year after year, none but the writings and speeches of men whose views and feelings are in direct opposition to our institutions and government? Certainly, pride for the literary reputation of our own country, if not patriotism and good policy, should dictate to us the propriety of inserting in our school readers specimens of our own literature; and it is certainly no disparagement to English

reading books to assert that they are not adapted to American schools. The United States has political and civil institutions of its own; and how can these be upheld, unless the children and youth of our country are early made to understand them by books and other means of instruction? (19: v)

Not only did the nationalistic aim exert an influence over the content of the new readers, but to a large extent it also shaped the methods used in teaching reading during this period. Great stress now came to be laid upon rules and exercises in correct pronunciation and enunciation for the purpose of overcoming the diversity of dialects and promoting greater unity in the American language. Noah Webster, the author of the most popular readers of the period, was gravely concerned with the language situation and in the preface of his famous speller he expressed his foremost aim in this way:

> To diffuse a uniformity and purity of language in America—to destroy the provincial prejudices that originate in the trifling differences of dialect, and produce reciprocal ridicule—to promote the interest of literature and harmony of the United States—is the most ardent wish of the Author; and it is his highest ambition to deserve the approbation and encouragement of his countrymen. (21: x)

The stress on nationalism is so startling and conspicuous at first sight that it overshadows a second and independent point of emphasis which is revealed upon closer study. This second emphasis is moralism, an influence which permeated reading instruction quietly and unassumingly but so persistently and universally as to claim an equal rank with nationalism in our characterization of the period. In some instances the moral aim of reading instruction constituted a part of the more inclusive nationalistic aim of making good citizens for the United States. On the whole, however, the moralistic influence seems to have been a development entirely apart from national purposes. In fact, it appears that the moral emphasis in reading would have come to fruition during this period even though there had been no Revolution and the people had continued peaceably to abide under British rule.

For generations reading had been looked upon as an instrument for promoting "the good life." The broadened interests of the people of this period led them to forsake strictly religious reading instruction as too narrow a program to meet their expanding needs. Many of them, however, still believed that one of the most important functions of education was to make children "good"—in other words, to build character. The method which they considered the most effective in promoting this aim was that of impressing on young minds the ideals of virtue and moralism; hence, the readers were eagerly seized upon as carriers of moralistic content. This was but the natural transition from the religious motive of the colonial period to the secularized motives of succeeding periods.

Owing to this dual emphasis in reading instruction, we find, in addition to the nationalistic readers, a series of other texts devoted entirely to moralistic content. In some of these readers the titles plainly convey the authors' intentions, as in the case of "The American Moralist" by George Chipman and "The Franklin Primer containing a new and useful selection of Moral Lessons." Not only did such books as these devote themselves to moralistic content, but many readers of nationalistic import also contained a considerable amount of material based on the subject of morals. The moralistic attitude toward education at this time is clearly revealed by Leavitt in one of the opening pages of his *Easy Lessons in Reading*. Leavitt's expression is representative of the viewpoint of several other authors of the period.

> Let not the faithful teacher consider the time spent in learning his scholars to read with spirit and force, as wholly wasted or lost. In addition to the important practical use of good reading, he may be

assured that the great end of education, that of forming the younger and tender minds to virtue and usefulness, is promoted by no branch of science, more effectually than by learning to read. (25: 7)

In considering the more immediate and specific classroom aims of reading instruction, we find that the aim of developing eloquent oral reading was paramount to all others. Perhaps the most effective means of describing this purpose is to state it in the language of the writers of the time.

Caleb Bingham says in the preface of *The Columbian Orator*:

The art of oratory needs no encomium. To cultivate its rudiments, and diffuse its spirit among the Youth of America is the design of this book. (26: iii)

Lyman Cobb gives a succinct summary of the specific reading objectives of the times when he says:

A just delivery consists in a distinct articulation of words pronounced in proper tones, suitably varied to the sense, and the emotions of the mind; with due attention to accent, to emphasis, in its several gradations; to rests or pauses of the voice, in proper places and well-measured degrees of time; and the whole accompanied with expressive looks, and significant gestures. That the pupil may be assisted in forming a correct method of reading and speaking, a few rules shall be laid down, pointing out a proper use of each of those necessary parts of a just delivery. (19: 12)

An additional glimpse of the aims of reading instruction is given by Leavitt in the following advice to the child:

Try to read as if you were telling a story to your mother or talking to some of your playmates. Reading is talking from a book. (25: 2)

II. The New Materials

The emphasis upon nationalism and moralism was immediately apparent in the content of the new readers which came from the American press. The nationalistic materials made their advent rather suddenly following the Revolution and manifested themselves in the following ways:

1. Exercises and rules for pronunciation and enunciation designed to overcome the diversity of dialects and to promote greater unity in the American language.

2. Patriotic selections intended to instill within the young a love for their country. Even the titles of readers assumed a patriotic character.

3. Literary productions of American authors designed to awaken within children an appreciation of the talent in their own country.

4. Historical selections intended to acquaint children with the history of America and Europe in so far as it had affected America and American policies.

5. Informational selections designed to inform children concerning objects in their immediate environment and concerning the affairs of state, so that they might become better enlightened regarding their own country.

6. Oratorical selections intended to develop elocutionary ability, which was considered to be an important factor in social life under a democratic government.

The moralistic materials began to work their way into readers somewhat earlier than did the nationalistic materials. It will be recalled that a sprinkling of moral precepts and admonitions appeared in some of the later readers of the colonial period. It was not until the period following the Revolution, however, that moralistic materials came to replace the religious content of readers. It is rather surprising to note how sharply and completely this change came about. We saw in chapter two that the most widely used readers of the colonial period devoted the bulk of their content to strictly religious materials. In checking three of the most popular readers of this later period, one finds that the emphasis on religious materials had all but disappeared. Noah Webster in *The American Spelling Book* devoted 2 pages out of a total of 158 pages to religious content, while he gave 29 pages in the same book to moral admonitions and advice. Bingham's *The Columbian Orator* used 4 pages out of a total of 228 for religious materials and 95 pages for moralistic content. Cobb in *The North American Reader* devoted 75 pages out of 350 pages to moralistic materials and only 3 pages to religious selections. Several readers of the period, however, continued to use some religious selections. The moralistic reading materials of the period took such forms as these:

1. Admonitions, proverbs, and advice on good behavior and virtuousness.

2. Realistic stories of children or grown-ups who had received a coveted reward for good behavior or suffered a severe punishment for bad behavior.

3. Poems exalting desirable qualities of character.

4. Fables of a strongly moral tone, followed in each case by a paragraph in which the lesson was pointed out.

As a natural correlative of the changes in subject matter, we find also a different literary type in the new content. Owing to the emphasis upon oratory and moralism, the expository type of literature came to predominate in all readers of the period. One of the interesting developments at this time was the emergence of the series idea. It is true that isolated readers appeared in large numbers during these years, but some of the prominent authors were evolving the idea of a set of readers, the earliest of which would lay the foundation for the others. Thus we find that the materials that generally constituted the course in reading consisted of a speller or primer and a more advanced reader intended for use in academies. Sometimes an intermediate reader was used between the speller and the advanced reader, but this was the exception rather than the rule. Having observed the significant characteristics of the new content, we may now examine some of the most popular readers of the period as typifying the materials of instruction at this time.

Noah Webster's Readers

Noah Webster received his B.A. from Yale College in 1778. He had intended to become a lawyer, but as the country was impoverished by war and the outlook for a young lawyer was discouraging, he resorted to teaching school. The interruption of commerce with England during the war had caused a shortage in reading texts in America. This condition was aggravated by the antipathy which the Americans felt toward English books, even those that had been printed in America for many years previously.

Noah Webster became keenly aware of the need for school books in the course of his teaching experience, and since he had a natural propensity for writing and a strongly patriotic attitude toward the new nation, he arose to the emergency and produced the first set of readers written by an American author. He gathered his selections while teaching in Orange County, New York, in 1782. They were published the following year under the title *A Grammatical Institute of the English Language*. This book was made up of three sections. Section I consisted of a spelling book for use in teaching beginning reading; Section II contained a treatise on grammar; and Section III contained "An American Selection of Lessons in Reading and Speaking." This third section was designed for advanced reading instruction in academies. In 1790, the three parts were printed separately and Section I became known as *The American Spelling Book*. Feeling the need of an intermediate reader, Webster also prepared *The Little Reader's Assistant*, which was designed to bridge the gap between the other two readers. These three books constituted the first set of consecutive readers in the history of American reading instruction.

The American Spelling Book proved to be the most popular of the three readers. It did not sweep into immediate favor, but it gradually won wide acceptance and came to enact in this period the stellar role which *The New England Primer* had enacted in the preceding period. It is said that the royalty from this book provided the entire support for Webster's family during the twenty years (1807–1827) when he was writing his dictionary, even though he received only a cent a book as his share of the profits. In a letter regarding *The American Spelling Book* that Webster wrote to Termel Shattuck in 1833, he said,

> This book gradually superseded Dilworth; but the number of editions published cannot be ascertained; for since 1804 it has been printed on standing types or on stereotype plates, and this by several proprietors, in different and distant parts of the United States... But for nearly thirty years, returns of the numbers printed with an estimate of what had been before printed, enable me to state, with tolerable certainty, that the whole number published cannot fall much short of ten millions of copies. (28: IV: 475)

The book is said to have reached a total distribution of 24,000,000 copies.

This famous old "Blue-Back Speller" as it was affectionately called by millions of users, had 158 pages encased in wooden covers, was 4 by 6 ½ inches in size, and covered with pale blue paper. The pages were held together by two pieces of tape drawn through slits in the leaves. A strip of leather formed the backbone of the book and the leaves were glued into it. The paper was deep cream in color, of rough finish and medium weight. The type varied in size in different portions of the book. The rules were printed in type about the size found in a modern newspaper; the word lists and reading selections were in type of a size approximating that in a modern fifth reader. All the lines were closely crowded, and one feels considerable eye strain after reading the book for any length of time.

The pictures were black and white woodcuts, small and so crudely drawn as to be almost unintelligible at times. The first picture in an early edition was supposed to be a likeness of Noah Webster, showing him with hair standing upright in little horn-like spikes, which gave him a most uncouth appearance. This portrait brought so much derision upon the author that it threatened for a time to ruin the future of his books. The speller, however, had so much merit that the public soon forgot the strange-looking author who appeared in the frontispiece and accepted the book on its own worth. The other pictures in the speller were used to illustrate fables and were of a highly moral character. The pictures occupied approximately 1 1/2 percent of the total space of the book.

The first 25 pages of the book were given over to rules and instructions. Page 26, the first page that a child was supposed to read, contained the alphabet, syllables, and consonant combinations. The second page for a child to read contained 197 syllables. The succeeding several pages were devoted to lists of words arranged in order by their number of syllables, and further organized into lists according to the similarity of phonetic elements. In checking the new words and syllables introduced on the first 10 pages, one finds the number ranging all the way from 86 to 197 per page. There were no repetitions of the same word from page to page on these first 10 pages. This would make very difficult reading for beginners, as judged by our present standards.

The bulk of the book was made up of lists of words and syllables, 74 pages out of 158 being devoted to this type of content. Rules for correct reading and speaking occupied a total of 39 pages, and moralistic advice and admonitions occupied 29 pages. There were 4 pages of fables, 4 pages of realistic stories, 2 pages of dialogues, and a half page of poetry. The following excerpts give

FABLE I. *Of the Boy that stole Apples.*

AN old Man found a rude Boy upon one of his trees stealing Apples, and desired him to come down; but the young Sauce-box told him plainly he wou'd not. Won't you? said the old Man, then I will fetch you down; so he pulled up some tufts of Grass, and threw at him; but this only made the Youngster laugh, to think the old Man should pretend to beat him out of the tree with grass only.

Well, well, said the old Man, if neither words nor grass, will do, I must try what virtue there is in Stones; so the old Man pelted him heartily with stones; which soon made the young Chap, hasten down from the tree and beg the old Man's pardon.

MORAL.
If good words and gentle means will not reclaim the wicked, they must be dealt with in a more severe manner.

H

Webster's Blue-Back Speller provided reading lessons that aimed at moral instruction. This page is from an 1800 edition.

a glimpse of the nature of the moralistic material that constituted most of the actual reading content of Noah Webster's speller.

> Be a good child; mind your book; love your school; strive to learn.
> Tell no tales; call no ill names; you must not lie, nor swear, nor cheat, nor steal.
> Play not with bad boys.
> Play no tricks on those that sit next to you; for if you do, good boys will shun you as they would a dog they knew would bite them. (21: 56, 65)

The religious catechism found in *The New England Primer* was replaced in this book with a moral catechism.

> Q. Is pride commendable?
> A. By no means. A modest self-approving opinion of our own good deeds is very right—it is natural—it is agreeable and a spur to good actions. But we should not suffer our hearts to be blown up with pride; for pride brings upon us the ill-will of mankind, and the displeasure of our Maker. (21: 78)

It was largely through the methods of teaching the material in this book that Webster intended to achieve his nationalistic aim of purifying the American language. There was little in the actual reading content that was patriotic in tone. On the other hand, *An American Selection of Lessons in Reading and Speaking* was designed to further nationalism through a direct presentation of patriotic materials. Perhaps the most concise description which can be given of the materials included in this book is Webster's own statement in the preface:

> The design of the Third Part of the *Grammatical Institute* is to furnish Scholars with a variety of exercises for Reading and Spelling. Colleges and academies are already supplied with excellent collections for this purpose.... But none of these, however judicious the selection, is calculated particularly for the American Schools: The essays reflect dis-

tant nations and ages, or contain general ideas of morality. In America it will be useful to furnish schools with additional essays containing history, geography, and transactions of the United States. Information on these subjects is necessary for youth, both in forming habits and improving their minds. A love of country, and an acquaintance with its true state are indispensable: They should be acquired early in life.

In the following works, I have undertaken to make such a collection of essays as should form the morals as well as improve the knowledge of youth.

In choice of pieces, I have been attentive to the political interests of America. I consider it as a capital fault in all our schools, that the books generally used, contain subjects wholly uninteresting to our youth; while the writings which marked the revolution, which are perhaps not inferior to Cicero and Demosthenes and which are calculated to impress interesting truths upon youthful minds, lie neglected and forgotten. Several of these masterly addresses of Congress written at the commencement of the late revolution contain such noble sentiments of liberty and patriotism, that I cannot help wishing to transmute them into the breasts of the rising generation. (22: A2)

In addition to the patriotic speeches and moralistic selections, Webster devoted 66 pages of this book to historical and geographical information concerning the United States as a whole and the individual states that had been formed up to this time; 6 pages to the First Petition to Congress; and 6 pages to the Declaration by Representatives of the United Colonies.

Webster's *The Little Reader's Assistant* is an interesting book. Its contents are divided into four sections:

I. A number of stories, mostly taken from the history of America and adorned with Cuts.

II. Rudiments of English Grammar.

III. A Federal Catechism, being a short and easy explanation of the Constitution of the United States.

IV. General Principles of Government and Commerce. (23: 1)

The first lesson in *The Little Reader's Assistant* is representative of both the stories and the cuts included in Section I. It describes the voyage of Columbus and is accompanied by a crude picture of a boat rocking on a choppy sea. One has to glance twice to be sure whether the figures on the surface of the water are meant to represent waves or fish. The Federal Catechism in Section III asks and answers such questions as these:

> What is a constitution of government? How many kinds of constitutions are there? Which is the best?

In Section IV we find the famous "Farmer's Catechism," designed to inculcate an admiration for the great agrarian industry of America and to give valuable information concerning it. It begins in this way:

> Q. What is the best business a man can do?
> A. Tilling the ground, or farming.
> Q. Why is farming the best business?
> A. Because it is the most necessary, the most innocent and the most agreeable employment of men.

Caleb Bingham's Readers

Caleb Bingham received an A.M. degree from Dartmouth College in 1782. He taught in private and public schools in Boston until 1796, when he purchased a bookshop there, which came to be a center of educational interests. It is said that the idea of the primary school had its origin in the discussions held in Bingham's bookstore. An anecdote from *The New England Magazine* sheds light on both his professional activities and his personality.

> Few authors can present a list of more popular works than Caleb Bingham, although he suffered pecuniary embarrassment in his profession as one of the public professors and was not always promptly

46

paid. At a certain time being unable to procure the money for a town order, as a draft on the treasury was then called, he advertised it in the public papers for sale at a large discount. At a town meeting which was held soon after, an order was passed, that Master Bingham be sent for to answer for the insult thus offered to the town in publicly attacking its character and credit. On his appearance he was sharply reprimanded, and required to give a reason for his outrageous conduct. Taking off his hat, he answered in his usual dignified manner:

"Fellow citizens, I did not come before you in obedience to your illegal message, but solely to inform you that want, sheer want, compelled me to advertise your order, and to assure you, that if your future payments are more punctual, I will never advertise your orders again." (28: II: 477)

Bingham's books, together with the figures showing their distribution, up to 1832, are listed below:

Young Lady's Accidence	20 Editions	100,000	copies
Child's Companion	20 Editions	180,000	copies
The American Preceptor	64 Editions	640,000	copies
The Columbian Orator	23 Editions	190,000	copies
Grog Caticulan	22 Editions	100,000	copies
Juvenile Letters	7 Editions	25,000	copies
		1,235,000	(28: II: 477)

It is evident from these data that *The American Preceptor* and *The Columbian Orator* were the most popular of his books.

The American Preceptor was a small book, 6 1/2 by 4 inches in size. It was bound in wooden covers which, like Webster's speller, were covered with pale blue paper, and it had a leather strip down the backbone. The sheets were held together by two leather tapes drawn through the leaves. The book was glued into the cover. The paper was heavy, rough, and of a deep cream color. The print was of the size usually appearing in contemporary readers, which was about like that in our present-day newspapers. As was customary at the time, the lines were very close together. There were no illustrations in the book. One can do no better in describing the contents of this reader than to quote from the author's preface:

> In making selections for the following work, preference has been given to productions of American genius. The compiler, however, has not been entirely confined to Americans; but has extracted from approved writers of different ages and countries. Convinced of the impropriety of instilling false notions into the minds of children, he has not given place to romantic fiction. Although moral essays have not been neglected, yet pleasing and interesting stories, exemplifying moral virtues were judged best calculated to engage the attention and improve the heart. Tales of love have not gained admission. (27: ii)

An analysis of the book shows the following proportions of different types of content. Ninety-five pages were devoted to moralistic selections; 63 pages, historical selections designed to inculcate patriotism; 22 pages, literary productions of American authors; 16 pages, information on national affairs; 9 pages, religious materials; and 8 pages, female education and the place of women in society in general. There were 3 or 4 pages each devoted to stories of adventure, geographical information, and rules for reading and speaking.

The different types of literature were represented in the following proportion: 52 pages of realistic stories with moral implications, 44 pages of dialogues, 42 pages of moral admonitions, 40 pages of orations, 21 pages of old tales (heroic, legendary, etc.), 11 pages of description of objects and places of interest, 11 pages of poems and verse, 3 pages of rules, 2 pages of Biblical quotations, and 1 page of fable. An excerpt typical of the moralistic content of the book is given below:

ON THE DUTY OF SCHOOL-BOYS
1. Quintilian says, that he has included almost all the duty of scholars in this one piece of advice which he gives them: to love

those who teach them, as they love the science they learn of them; and to look upon them as fathers from whom they derive not the life of body, but that instruction which is in a manner the life of the soul....

3. Docility, which consists in submitting to directions, in readily receiving the instructions of their master, and reducing them to practice, is properly the virtue of scholars, as that of masters is to teach well. (27: 13)

The Columbian Orator devoted itself entirely to dialogues and elocutionary selections suitable for declamations. The following quotation is representative:

LINES SPOKEN AT A SCHOOL-EXHIBITION, BY A LITTLE BOY SEVEN YEARS OLD

> You'd scarce expect one of my age,
>
> To speak in public, on the stage;
>
> And if I chance to fall below
>
> Demosthenes or Cicero,
>
> Don't view me, with a critic's eye,
>
> But pass my imperfections by. (26: 57)

Lyman Cobb's Readers

Lyman Cobb is frequently mentioned as one of the great educators of his time. He was a prolific writer of reading texts, having produced a *First Book*, a *Spelling Book*, *Juvenile Readers*, Numbers I, II, and III, and *The North American Reader*. He sets forth clearly his motive for preparing these various books in the following statement:

The author has long considered that a series of elementary Reading-Books, which shall contain a greater variety of subjects, better adapted to the capacities and tastes of children than any now in use, would be an acquisition to our already extended list of Class-Books. (20: 1)

Cobb's *First Book* and *Spelling Book* consisted of lists of syllables and words with no illustrations of any kind. A description of the content of his Juvenile Readers is best given in the words of the author:

> No. 1 contains short and easy lessons, in which there are no words of more than two syllables... The first eleven lessons contain words of one syllable only; the remaining 47, words of one and two syllables.
>
> No. 2 contains lessons composed of words of one, two, and three syllables, and No. 3 of a greater number of speeches and a greater variety of compositions, both in prose and poetry, selected from writings of the best America and English authors. (20: v)

The most popular of Cobb's books was *The North American Reader*, which appeared in 1835. This book was 4 1/2 by 7 inches in size, somewhat larger than other books of the period. Its leaves were sewed together in four places with twine and were stuck into the cover with glue. The cover was made of cardboard covered with brown leather. The paper was creamy white, smooth but not glossy, and of medium weight. The type was small but was clearer and better spaced than that in the earlier readers.

The book contained but one illustration, a black and white reproduction of "Washington's Head-Quarters, Newburg, New York." About 350 of the 498 pages of this reader were given to selections by American authors; of these, 119 pages dealt with historical material designed to instill patriotism, and 75 pages with subject matter chosen for its moral or character-building qualities. There were 16 pages devoted to governmental policies and 12 pages of geographic information. Education seems to have been an important concern at the time, for we find 23 pages of the book devoted to this topic. Rules for correct reading and speaking occupied 36 pages. The remaining content covered a variety of topics, such as the Declaration of Independence, the Constitution of the United States, Indians, the place of women, and religion. It is interesting to note that only 7 pages were given to religion.

A Class engaged in Reading.

Reading instruction in the 1840s is pictured in this frontispiece from Cobb's Juvenile Reader, No. 1 *(1841).*

The literary structure of this book was predominantly expository, only 17 pages having a narrative element. Of the approximately 350 pages of expository material, 100 pages were devoted to orations and the remainder largely to essays on the subjects mentioned in the paragraph above. There were 76 pages of poetry and 15 pages of dialogues. The titles of some of the selections give us a further insight into the nature of the content. The patriotic selections bore such names as these:

The Love of Country and Home
My Country
Speech in United States Senate (Van Buren)
Extent of Country Not Dangerous to the Union (Madison)

The Danger of Altering the Constitution (Gouverneur Morris)
Address of the President to Lafayette (J.Q. Adams)
Effects of the Dissolution of the Federal Union Government
Political Definitions
The Debt Due to the Soldiers of the Revolution

The moralistic selections appear under such titles as these:

Moral Sublimity Illustrated	Charity to Orphans
Moral Effects of Intemperance	Little Things Destroy Character
Intellectual and Moral Education by a People	Advice to the Young
	Danger of Bad Habits
Decisive Integrity	

George Hillard's Readers

George Hillard was another author of the times who conceived the idea of preparing a set of readers. His literary efforts produced *The Franklin Primer*, *The Improved Reader*, *The General Classbook*, and *The Popular Reader*. These last three books devoted about half of their contents to poetry and half to prose. The author's summary of *The Improved Reader* gives a representative idea of the nature of the materials in that book as well as in the other two advanced readers.

> *The Improved Reader* provides for the instruction of the learner in regard to the using of many words, which are likely to occur in the books he will read, and the exercises he may be required to attend; while it entertains him with moral tales and many sketches in natural history. (29: 1)

Hillard describes the special contribution of *The Popular Reader* in this manner:

> One of the peculiarities of this book will be found in the number of dialogues amounting to twenty, which have been collected with the greatest pains and which it is believed will increase the value of

the work, affording, as they will, the best expression for the voice in reading, while they will give the same thoughts a livelier interest than if they were delivered in a didactic manner. (29: 4)

The most distinctive of Hillard's readers was *The Franklin Primer*, which was a little book, 3 by 5 inches, bound in pasteboard covered with mottled blue paper. It was described by the author as being "A new and useful selection of moral lessons adorned with a great variety of elegant cuts calculated to strike a lasting impression on the tender minds of youth." The "elegant cuts" consisted of a portrait of Benjamin Franklin and about a dozen crude black and white illustrations intended to reinforce the moral implications of the text.

In common with other beginning books of the period, we find the first several pages of this reader given over to lists of syllables and words grouped according to their number of syllables. Page 8, which is the first page intended for the child, contained the alphabet, as one would expect. The second page for the child to read contained 178 syllables. A check of the first 10 pages reveals a range of from 63 to 178 new syllables or words introduced per page, with no provision for repetition. The first reading content, which appeared directly after the word lists, consisted of short sentences composed of words of two, three, and four letters. In the latter part of the book one finds short moralistic poems and expositions composed of longer words. Here is a stanza which touches on one method of learning to read:

> Then wish a good morning to all in your view,
> And bow to your parents, and bid them adieu;
> Salute every person as to school you go;
> When at school, to your master due reverence show.
> And if you can't read, pray endeavour to spell,
> For by frequently spelling you'll learn to read well.

Lindley Murray's Readers

There was one reader published in England that not only survived after the Revolution, but proved so successful that it passed through several American editions during this period. This was the English Reader or "Pieces in prose and poetry, selected from the best writers" by Lindley Murray. The author was a native-born American, but upon retiring from business he moved to England where he wrote this reader and several others which were not so popular.

Murray stated in the preface of his English Reader that the book "aims at the attainment of three objects: to improve youth in the art of reading; to elevate their language and sentiments; and to inculcate some of the most important principles of piety and virtue." In order to achieve these aims, he distributed the content about equally between moralistic materials and literary selections, many of the latter being designed "to give exercise to a great variety of emotions." There were also a few religious selections. Half of the book was devoted to poetry and half to prose. The prose was classified under these headings: narrative pieces, didactic pieces, argumentative pieces, descriptive pieces, pathetic pieces, dialogues, public speeches, promiscuous pieces. A part of the first lesson in the book is quoted as representative of its moralistic type of content:

> Diligence, industry, and proper improvement of time are material duties of the young.
> The acquisition of knowledge is one of the most honorable occupations of youth.
> Whatever useful or engaging endowments we possess, virtue is requisite, in order to their shining with proper lustre.
> Virtuous youth gradually brings forward accomplished and flourishing manhood. (31: B2)

An example of the literary selections in the book is found in Addison's description of the importance of a good education. An excerpt is given below:

I consider a human soul, without education, like marble to the quarry; which shows none of its inherent beauties, until the skill of the polisher fetches out the colours, makes the surface shine, and discovers every ornamental cloud, spot, and vein that runs through the body of it. Education, after the same manner, when it works upon a noble mind, draws out to view every latent virtue and perfection, which, without such helps, are never able to make their appearance.

The book itself had the usual features of mechanical make-up. It was 7 by 4 inches in size, was bound in cardboard covered with brown leather, had exceedingly fine type, and was printed on rough, deep cream paper. Murray eventually followed the example of other writers of the time and supplemented this advanced reader by three others: *Sequel to the English Reader*, which appeared in America in 1818; *Introduction to the English Reader*, published in New York in 1818; and *A First Book for Children*, which made its first appearance in this country in 1821. These supplemental books never proved to be so popular as the original *English Reader*.

Primers

The readers described on the preceding pages were the ones most widely used during this period. A variety of other readers, however, enjoyed more or less popularity. A number of miscellaneous primers appeared under such names as these: *The Child's Guide*, *Union Primer*, *The Child's Instructor*, Gallaudet's *The Child's Picture Defining and Reading Book*, *The Child's Instructor and Moral Primer*, and *The Christmas School Primer* (see page 56). Each of these had some distinctive feature, yet there was a dreary sameness about them all.

Perhaps the most entertaining of these readers is *The Christmas School Primer*. No author is named on this interesting little book, which was published in 1839. It was a paper-covered

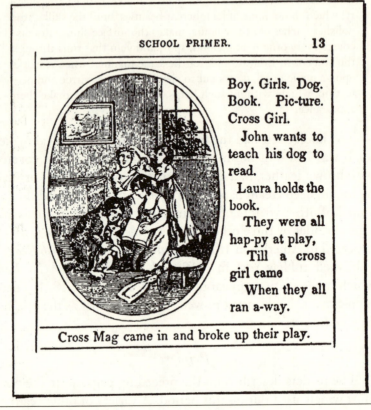

Boy. Girls. Dog. Book. Pic-ture. Cross Girl.

John wants to teach his dog to read.

Laura holds the book.

They were all hap-py at play,

Till a cross girl came

When they all ran a-way.

Cross Mag came in and broke up their play.

The Christmas School Primer had an illustration for every story, and the stories were for the most part realistic with strong moral applications.

volume, 4 $^1/_2$ by 6 inches. One of its unique features was that it was printed throughout in blue ink, both text and illustrations. The early pages of the book were given over to a pictured alphabet. For example, we find *w* illustrated by a picture of a well, with the word "well" and the separate letter *w* under the picture. The bulk of the content was devoted to realistic stories of a moral tone, each illustrated by a small picture. This was a lavish use of illustrations at that time. One representative story from the book is quoted:

IDLE TOM

Here goes Tom Truant down to the pond to play with the ducks, instead of going to school as he told his poor mother he would. But Tom has got to be a bad boy. He has kept the company of bad boys so long that he don't mind telling lies now. See how ragged and dirty he looks, and it is all because he don't love to go to school and be a good boy. Tom will surely come to a bad end. Ignorance and vice always go hand in hand. If Tom does not die in the prison, or poorhouse, it will be a wonder. (32: 34)

The illustration for this story shows Tom's home in the background. His mother is milking a cow near the house, and she is seated with her back toward Tom, who is slinking off to the duck pond. The pond appears to be a puddle in the front yard within plain sight of the house.

Any description of the materials of this period would be incomplete without further mention of the famous reader of the preceding period, *The New England Primer*. This book continued to survive throughout the nationalistic-moralistic period, but in rapidly decreasing popularity.

In order to meet the demands of the new emphasis on nationalism, the primer was several times reprinted under the titles of "The American Primer" and "The Columbian Primer." Its contents also were changed in many respects to meet the demands of the new republic.

In 1776 the frontispiece portrait of George III was relabeled and came forth as John Hancock. Fortunately, the likeness between the two men was extraordinary. In 1777, the correct portrait of Hancock was substituted. The 1777 Hartford edition used the picture of Samuel Adams as its frontispiece. By the end of the Revolution, the standard portrait came to be that of George Washington. Many of the religious verses also were replaced with other verses of patriotic import. In the 1727 edition the alphabet verse for *o* was

> The Royal Oak, it was the tree
> That Sav'd His Royal Majestie.

A Hartford edition printed sometime in the early part of the 19th century substituted this verse:

> The Charter Oak, it was the tree
> That saved to us our Liberty.

Similar changes were made in the verses for *w*. The original lines for this letter are given first below, followed by the verse substituted in a New York edition of 1794; then the form used in the edition printed in Brattleboro, Vermont, in 1825.

> Whales in the sea
> God's voice obey.

> By Washington
> Great deeds were done.

> George Washington brave
> His country did save.

The 1727 edition of *The New England Primer* used this verse for *k*:

> Our King the good
> No man of blood.

The printer of the Boston edition of 1791 evidently was not so sure that a king was good, so he replaced the original verse with this one:

> Kings should be good
> Not men of blood.

In the Philadelphia edition of 1797, the printer dispensed with all pretense of reverence for kings and boldly said:

The British King
Lost States Thirteen.

Other patriotic gestures of this type were made from time to time in an earnest attempt to hold the prestige which the primer had gained during the preceding period. Such overtures, however, were generally in vain. The book was too narrowly confined to a religious content to meet with the approval of the expanding interests of this new generation.

Sets of Readers

Among the sets of readers, in addition to those previously described, we find a most ambitious undertaking in the American Class Books, compiled by A. Pickett and J.W. Pickett, and published in New York in 1818. The seven books covered the subjects of reading, geography, and grammar.

John Pierpont was an outstanding educator of his time and it was entirely fitting that he should produce a series of readers that vied in popularity with Bingham's, Cobb's, and Murray's readers. The series consisted of four books that appeared between 1823 and 1830. They were called the *Young Reader*, the *Introduction*, the *National Reader*, and the *American First Class Book*. These readers were decidedly patriotic in tone and contained selections of a much higher literary quality than most of the other readers of the period. The content was drawn largely from the speeches and writings of American statesmen, poets, and scholars, including such men as Patrick Henry, Everett, Jefferson, Webster, Irving, and Bryant.

In 1828, a series of three readers by Putnam was published: *Introduction*, the *Analytical Reader*, and the *Sequel*. In the latter readers, the text was placed on the left-hand page in each case, and the facing page was devoted to definitions of words and phrases so that the book served the double purpose of reader and dictionary.

It is not surprising to find that the prolific Peter Parley (Samuel G. Goodrich) produced a series of readers between 1834 and 1840. The series consisted of the *Picture Book* or *First Reader*, *The Little Reader*, *The Common School Reader*, and *The Universal Reader*. These books contained many charming poems and interesting stories for children.

Samuel Worcester published a *Primer of the English Language for the Use of Schools and Families* in 1828. *A Second Book for Reading and Spelling* appeared in 1830, and *A Third Book for Reading and Spelling* was published in 1848. There was nothing unusual about the content of Worcester's books, but the method he mildly suggested was quite revolutionary. To Worcester belongs the distinction of being the first American author to advocate the word method.

Spellers

Several spellers were published during the period between 1776 and 1840. In those times, of course, the speller served in the same capacity as the basic reader does today. One of the earliest was *The Child's Spelling Book*, compiled by a Hartford, Connecticut, printer in 1798. This book was exceptional in providing content of a more entertaining nature and in using more illustrations than other spellers of the period. It opens with the following paragraph:

Come hither, Charles, come, tell me your letters; do you know how many there are? Where is the pin to point with? Here is the pin. Now read your book.

A spelling book by Caleb Alexander, published in 1799, bore the polite title of *The Young Ladies' and Gentleman's Spelling Book*.

The outstanding feature of this book was a series of illustrated poems by Isaac Watts, all of a highly moral nature. *The New England Spelling Book* was published in Brookfield, Massachusetts, in 1803. It contained the usual lists of words to be spelled, some "Moral Tales," the Constitution of the United States, the Declaration of Independence, the Constitution of Massachusetts, and Washington's Farewell Address.

Other spelling books, all largely given over to moral selections, were Comly's *A New Spelling Book* (Philadelphia, 1806); Jones's *Analytical Spelling Book* (New York, 1823); Bolles's *Spelling Book* (New London, 1831); *The Young Tyro's Instructor* (New York, 1834); Parsons's *Analytical Spelling Book* (Portland, Maine, 1836).

III. Methods of Teaching Reading

READING

1. And so you do not *like* to *spell,*
   Mary, my dear? *O very well;*
   'Tis *dull* and *troublesome,* you say,
   And you had rather be at *play.*

2. Then bring me all your *books* again;
   Nay, Mary, why should you complain?
   For as you do not choose to *read,*
   You should not have your *books, indeed.*

3. So as you wish to be a dunce,
   Pray go and fetch me them at once.
   For as you will not learn to *spell,*
   'Tis vain to think of *reading* well.

4. Now don't you think you'll *blush* to own,
   When you become a woman grown,
   With out *one good* excuse to plead,
   That you have never *learnt* to *read?*

5. "O dear Mamma," said Mary then,
   "*Do* let me have my books again,

I'll not fret *any* more, indeed,
If you will *let* me learn to read." (25: 34)

The poem above appears in Leavitt's *Easy Lessons in Reading*, published in 1829. It is reprinted here as an interesting bit of evidence to the effect that spelling was still used as the foundation method for inducting children into the mysteries of reading. Incidentally, we may glean from the poem that the spelling method was not altogether enjoyable to the little boys and girls who were obliged to spend many weary hours naming the letters in syllables and words before reading sentences of any textual content.

A description of the method used at this time in teaching reading is found in "The District School as It Was." The author's delightful account of one child's first experience in reading is given:

"Come and read" says the mistress to the little flaxen-headed creature of doubtful gender, for the child is in petticoats and sits on the female side as close as possible to its guardian sister. But then those coarser features, tanned complexion, and close-clipped hair, with other minutia of aspect, are somewhat contradictory to the feminine dress. "Come and read." It is the first time that he-or-she was ever inside of a school-house and in the presence of a schoolma'am, according to recollection; and the order is heard with shrinking timidity. But the sister whispers an encouraging word and helps "tot" down from the seat, who creeps out into the aisle, and hesitates along down to the teacher, biting his fingers, or scratching his head, perhaps both, to relieve the embarrassment of the novel situation.

"What is your name, dear?" "Tholomon Icherthon," lisps the now discovered he, in a choked voice scarce above a whisper. "Put your hands down by your side, Solomon, and make a bow." He obeys, if a short and hasty jerk of the head is a bow.

The alphabetical page of the spelling-book is presented and he is asked, "What's that?" But he cannot tell. He is but two years and a half old, and has been sent to school to relieve his mother from trouble, rather than to learn. No one at home has yet shown or named a letter for him. He has never had even that celebrated character, round *o*, pointed out to his notice. It was an older beginner, most probably, who being asked a similar question about the first letter of the alphabet, replied, "I know him by sight, but can't call him by name." But our namesake of the wise man does not know the gentleman even by sight, nor any of his twenty-five companions.

Solomon Richardson has at length said, "A, B, C" for the first time in his life. He has *read*. "That's a nice boy; make another bow and go to your seat." He gives another jerk of the head and whirls on his heel and trots back to his seat, meeting the congratulatory smile of his sister with a satisfied grin, which, put into language would be, "There, I've read ha'n't I?" (28: IV: 519)

This account of a child's first reading lesson illustrates the usual method of initiating the pupil into the reading process. Learning the alphabet was considered the most important first step throughout this period. Some fresh techniques, however, were introduced with the advent of the nationalistic emphasis, and while they did not interfere with the memorization of the alphabet, they did affect the later stages of reading instruction. The two changes in method for which this new emphasis was responsible were:

1. Emphasis upon articulation and pronunciation as a means of correcting the numerous dialects that had sprung up in different sections, and of bringing about a greater unity in the American language.
2. Increasing attention to elocution, an art which was considered highly necessary in the life under a democratic, representative form of government.

The emphasis upon articulation and pronunciation is significant from the standpoint of method, in that it brought about the practice of teaching the sounds of letters as well as their names. Noah Webster was the chief heralder of this change in reading method. In the preface of *The American Spelling Book* he said:

Among the defects and absurdities found in books of this kind hitherto published, we may rank the want of a thorough investigation of the sounds in the English language, and the powers of the several letters—the promiscuous arrangement of words in the same table....

In attempting to correct these faults it was necessary to begin with the elements of the language and explain the powers of the letters. (21: vi)

Webster put this intention into effect by setting forth an analysis of the sounds in the English language, a treatise covering several pages at the front of his speller. He then proceeded to organize the syllable and word lists for the pupils, not only according to the number of letters, but also according to similarity of sounds. The first lesson in the book is given below, together with Webster's note of instruction:

LESSON 1

ba	be	bi	bo	bu	by
ca	ce	ci	co	cu	cy
da	de	di	do	du	dy
fa	fe	fi	fo	fu	py
pa	pe	pi	so	su	sy

N.B. The following columns are to be read downwards: all the words in the same columns being sounded alike, when a child has a sound of the first, the others will naturally follow. They may also be read across the page. (21: 36)

In the lists that followed, these words were preceded by a dagger: *human, negro, angel.* At the bottom of the page, this instruction was given in regard to their pronunciation: *not yuman, negur, anegle.*

The emphasis upon elocutionary reading had an even more spectacular effect upon method than did the emphasis upon articulation. Let us examine a few of the instructions given to teachers by textbook writers of the period. Leavitt says in the introduction to his *Easy Lessons in Reading,*

Great pains should be taken to make reading appear like real life. The reader should place himself exactly in the circumstances supposed by the writer, and endeavor to possess the same feelings and passions. Children should never be allowed to pronounce a sentence or even a word, in that dull, monotonous humdrum style, which so often disgraces our common schools. Such reading is as fatigueing to the reader as it is painful to the hearer, while good reading affords equal delight and improvement to both.

It is a very useful practice for the teacher to read over a sentence before the scholar, giving it the proper pauses, inflection and emphasis, and then to require the scholar to repeat it, until he can pronounce it with propriety. (25: 6)

Bingham, in common with other authors of the time, went to great length in explaining various points of method which must be put into practice if one were to become a good reader or, in other words, an eloquent oral reader. He boldly states:

The first object of a reader or speaker is to be clearly understood by his hearers. In order for this to be possible, it is necessary that he should pronounce his words distinctly and definitely; and that he should carefully avoid the two extremes of uttering either too fast or too slow; and that the tone of his voice should be perfectly natural....

Perhaps nothing is of more importance to a reader or speaker, than a proper attention to accent, emphasis, and cadence. Every word in our language, of more than one syllable, has, at least, one accented syllable. This syllable ought to be really known, and the word should be pronounced by the reader or speaker in the same manner as he would pronounce it in ordinary conversation. Some rules and principles of these ideas will, however, be found useful, to prevent erroneous and vicious modes of utterance, to give the young reader some taste of the subject, and to assist him in acquiring the just and accurate mode of delivery. The observations which we have to make for these purposes, may be compressed under the following heads: proper loudness of voice; distinctness; slowness; propriety of pronunciation; emphasis; tones; pauses; and mode of reading verse. (27: A2)

Owing to its strong demands upon elocutionary ability, Lindley Murray places reading on the basis of inherited talents. He does think, however, that by the use of his rules and by practice everyone can improve his reading ability. He expresses the thought in this way:

> The perfect mastery of it [reading] doubtless requires great attention and practice, joined to extraordinary natural powers; but as there are many degrees of excellence in the art, the student whose aims fall short of perfection, will find himself amply rewarded for every exertion he may think proper to make. (31: A2)

The marked tendency toward the use of readers for developing eloquent delivery caused a few authors of this period to go to the extreme of dividing all the lines in the reader into metrical feet and marking them with a system of notation which would make discourse like music and would, according to the authors, cause the pupils to read "with perfect ease and rhythm." Jonathan Barber's *Exercises in Reading and Recitation*, which appeared in 1825, was a book of this type.

A few words should be added concerning the method used for teaching the lengthy sets of rules which occupied so large a proportion of space in the readers. Cobb's "Note to Teachers" in this regard is both enlightening and representative:

> Every teacher is respectfully requested to require of each of his pupils thoroughly to read all the preceding "Observations on the Principles of Good Reading," and to commit to memory the Rules for the right use of the Stops, or Points, and Other Characters Used in Writing and Printing.
>
> In order to test the knowledge of each scholar, it may be well frequently to exercise him, by requiring him to answer the following or similar questions:
>
> > What is the use of a Comma?
> > What is the use of a Semicolon?

What is the use of a Colon?
What is the use of Crotchets?
What is the use of an Obelisk, etc. (19: xxii)

A general summary of those aspects of method which were deemed most desirable during this period is given by Leavitt in a set of rules addressed to the child:

If you wish to know how to read *well*, you must learn these rules by heart.

RULES

1. Be careful to *call* your words right.

2. Learn to *pronounce* them properly.

3. Speak with a *clear* and *distinct* voice.

4. Do not read too *fast*. Read *slow* and *carefully* so as not to make any *mistakes*.

5. Be very particular to observe all the *stops*.

6. Learn to use the proper *Emphasis* and Inflection of voice. Ask your teacher to show you what these mean and how to do it.

7. Try to understand every word as you go along. *Study* your reading lessons very carefully before you read.

8. Try to read as if you were telling a story to your mother or talking with some of your playmates. *Reading is talking from a book.*

9. Take pains to read poetry, not to sing it.

10. The emphatic words are printed in *Italick letters*.

If you learn these rules and attend to them, I think you will soon read very prettily, and be able to read books aloud to your parents and friends at home. (25: 2)

The above summary would seem to constitute a fitting conclusion to this section on method. In the course of the writer's searches, however, a few more lines came to view which are so significant that they are added here. These lines were embedded in one of the dialogues in Webster's speller. They not only afford a glimpse into the memoriter repetitional method of learning to read, but they also serve to project one into the general atmosphere of the classroom of a century and a half ago.

> Have you learned your lesson?
> I am almost master of it.
> It is almost time to repeat it.
> I shall be ready in half an hour.
> Who took my penknife?
> Did it lie near your inkhorn?
> It lay on the table by my papers.
> Will you hand me a ruler, please?
> Do not blot your paper.
> Sit in your place and be silent.
> Indeed, I will not speak a word. I think of the ferule.
> Will you please to make me a pen?
> Make your pen yourself, if you please. (24: 127)

CHAPTER FOUR

The Period of Emphasis on Education for Intelligent Citizenship

I. Motives and Influences That Affected Reading Instruction

The period following the years marked by the patriotic-moralistic emphasis is less clearly defined than any other in the history of American reading instruction. For that reason, one hesitates to fix its bounds by specific dates or to characterize it with a particular title. Stating a date for any historical period is a precarious undertaking, but particularly so when the changes described are the product of slow evolutionary growth rather than the result of a sudden revolutionary movement, such as the American war for independence. The period of reading instruction under consideration was of the evolutionary type. Some of the characteristics of the preceding period were retained throughout this period; many of the new trends had been creeping in for a quarter of a century previously. There were, nevertheless, marked changes in most of the reading materials that began to come from the press about 1840. For this reason it seems advisable to use 1840 as the approximate initial date of this period of reading emphasis, which continued about 40 years.

We noted in the preceding period that the birth of our nation was followed by an emotional outburst of patriotism. Educators were gravely concerned with the task of bringing about unity and harmony among the various states and instilling a strong feeling of love and loyalty for the nation. During the first half of the new century the effort to inculcate this intense type of patriotism had subsided to a saner program, that of preparing the great masses to discharge their duties of citizenship. Educators came to realize that the success of the new democracy depended not so largely upon arousing patriotic sentiment as upon developing the intelligence of the people, whose ballots were to choose its leaders and determine its policies. The speeches and writings of the times are saturated with this underlying motive of education. This quotation from an article published in 1839 is typical:

> Of the importance of popular education, and I mean by that phrase the education of all the people, we need not speak. It is evidently necessary to our political well-being, and therefore what every class of men may justly claim at the hands of the government, that all should receive that amount and kind of instruction which will fit them for the intelligent discharge of all their duties to the state. (34: 468)

The nature of the period as well as this general aim of education is apparent in the following paragraphs from a speech delivered before the state legislature in 1841 by a governor of Ohio:

> It is in times of profound tranquility, when the people are undisturbed by the tumult of war, that the duties of enlightened patriotism unite us to the grateful task of giving depth and permanency to our free institutions. It is only at such periods that a Commonwealth can hope to deliberate calmly and successfully upon systems of policy, calculated to stimulate industry, by giving it legal assurance that it shall be protected in the enjoyment of its acquisitions; to strengthen general morality, by laws which shall tend to suppress vice and crime in all their forms; to give energy and independence of character to all classes, by measures which will promote, as far as practicable, equality of conditions and thus establish a rational liberty for ourselves, and give hope of its continuance for ages to come.

Of measures which contribute to these ends, education, comprehending moral as well as intellectual instruction, is of the first importance. Under a constitution like ours, which imparts to every citizen the same civil rights, education must ever remain a subject of vital interest, in reference to the general welfare of the State. If we are to trust the lessons of history, we are brought to the conclusion that the government is, and always has been, the most efficient of all the causes which operate in forming the character and shaping the destinies of nations. Where the right of suffrage is so unrestricted as with us, government is necessarily the offspring of all people, and will reflect the moral and intellectual features of its parents, with unvarying fidelity. (35: 23)

The aim of promoting intelligent citizenship was the underlying motive for improving the educational methods and materials of the period. In seeking to implement this motive in reading educators turned their attention to new sources for principles that would broaden the content of readers intellectually and new methods that might make reading instruction more effective. The German Pestalozzean principles and methods seem to have been the prime source from which ideas for reforms were obtained. Many American educators at this time were visiting Prussia and returning with enthusiastic reports of the work they had seen. This information was diffused by the addresses and articles that one finds generously distributed through the publications of the time. Horace Mann was one of the most influential leaders of the period; perhaps he did more than any other one individual to shape its educational policies. In his Seventh Annual Report to the Board of Education of Massachusetts, he describes some of the Prussian practices in regard to reading and the principles which controlled them. He opens his discussion thus:

In regard to this as well as other modes of teaching, I shall endeavor to describe some particular lessons that I heard. The Prussian and Saxon Schools are all conducted substantially upon the same plan, and taught in the same manner. About twenty years ago teachers in Prussia made the important discovery that children have five senses, — together with various muscles and mental faculties, —all of which, almost by necessity of their nature, must be kept in a state of activity.... It is much easier to keep the eye and hand and mind at work together, than it is to employ any one of them separately from the others. (36: VI: 116)

Following this introduction, Mann describes a reading lesson that he saw in a Prussian school:

The teacher first drew a house upon the blackboard; and here the value of the art of drawing, —a power universally possessed by Prussian teachers, —became manifest. By the side of the drawing and under it, he wrote the word *house* in the German script hand, and printed it in the German letter. With a long pointing rod, —the end being painted white to make it more visible, —he ran over the form of the letters, —the children, with their slates before them and their pencils in their hands, looking at the pointing rod and tracing the forms of the letters in the air. In all our good schools, children are first taught to imitate the forms of letters on the slate before they write them on paper; here they were first imitated on the air, then on slates, and subsequently, in older classes, on paper.

The next process was to copy the word *house*, both in script and in print, on their slates. Then followed the formation of the sounds of the letter of which the word was composed, and the spelling of the word. Here the *names* of the letters were not given as with us, but only their powers, or the sounds which those letters have in combination. The letter *A* was first selected and set up in the reading-frame, and the children, instead of articulating our alphabetic *h* (aitch), merely gave a hard breathing,—such a sound as the letter really has in the word house. Then the diphthong *au* (the German word for *house* is spelled *haus*) was taken and sounded by itself in the same way. Then the blocks containing *h* and *a* were brought together and the two sounds were combined. Lastly, the letter *s* was first sounded by itself, then added to the others, and then the whole word was spoken.

Sometimes the last letter in a word was first taken and sounded, —after that the penultimate, and so on until the word was completed. The responses of the children were sometimes individual and sometimes simultaneous, according to the signal given by the master.

In every such school, also, there are printed sheets or cards containing the letters, diphthongs, and whole words. The children are taught to sound a diphthong, and then asked in what words that sound occurs. On some of these cards there are words enough to make several short sentences, and when the pupils are a little advanced, the teacher points to several isolated words in succession, which when taken together make a familiar sentence, and thus he gives the man agreeable surprise, and a pleasant initiation into reading. (36: VI: 116)

Now let us turn to Mann's scathing denunciation of American reading instruction as contrasted with this Prussian lesson:

Compare the above method with that of calling up a class of abecedarians, —or, what is more common, a single child,—and while the teacher holds a book or card before him, with a pointer in his hand, says, *a*, and he echoes *a*; then *b*, and he echoes *b*; and so on until the vertical row of lifeless and ill-favored characters is completed, and then of remanding him to his seat, to sit still and look at vacancy. If the child is bright, the time which passes during the lesson is the only part of the day in which he does not think. Not a single faculty of the mind is exercised excepting that of imitating sounds; and even the number of these imitations is limited to twenty-six. A parrot or an idiot could do the same thing.... As a general rule, six months are spent before the twenty-six letters are mastered, though the same child would learn the names of twenty-six playmates or twenty-six playthings in one or two days. (36: VI: 117)

How could one possibly expect the old type of instruction to persist under such rapid-fire criticism as this? This discussion by Horace Mann is but one example of the great body of evidence in regard to general Prussian influence on American reading instruction. Another line of evidence is found in the similarity between German and American readers. In examining several German readers published between 1840 and 1880, one finds that they have many features in common with our readers of that period, such as the following: abundant provision for materials on the subjects of science, nature study, geography, history, and general informational content; the inclusion of much script in primers and first readers; emphasis upon teaching the sounds of letters; much attention to the arrangement of subject matter on the basis of the principle of proceeding from the simple to the complex.

As a specific illustration of the nature of content we might refer to Hornung's *Lesebuch für die weibliche Jugend* (Erlangen, 1841), in which the subject matter is organized into four sections as follows: "First Section—Something from Natural History; Second Section—The Seasons; Third Section—Wanderings and Travel; Fourth Section—Human Life from the Cradle to the Grave."

Lesebuch zum Gebrauch in Volksschulen (Oldenburg, 1851) contained more stories and tales than our readers of the period did, but was like them in treating of informational subjects. The selections in this book fall under the following heads: stories, fairy tales and folk lore, fables and parables, informational material, natural history and technological material, historical stories, geographical stories, poetry. In the preface of the book the author says, "We are proceeding from the more simple to the more difficult, and the organization of the book is keeping this in mind."

A German primer by Beckman and Sertzog entitled *Deutsches Lesebuch* (printed in Berlin in 1860, reprinted in Philadelphia in 1867) devoted itself largely to didactic nature stories on such topics as grapes, a tiger, the rose, dogs, the horse, and the cat. Much attention was given to learning the sounds of the letters as well as their names and combining them into phonetic syllables. Script was liberally used throughout the book.

This brief description of German readers should serve to point out many of the earmarks of content and method which also characterized our readers during this period, as will be evident in the account of American readers given later in the chapter. The Prussian influences discussed above reflected the Pestalozzian principles in some respects. One finds, however, many evidences of changes in American practices which are more directly attributable to the great educator himself. Let us first note the general attitude of American educators toward Pestalozzi as revealed in their abundant discussions of him during this period and the years leading up to it. The following quotation comes from an article headed "The Pestalozzian System of Education," appearing in the *American Annals of Education* in 1837:

> The new views [on education] usually have for a long period only a partial or local influence, and often fall back into forgetfulness. They are like the springs and rivulets of the mountains, fertilizing here and there the fields of an individual or village. It is only when they are embodied by some of those master-spirits, which Providence from time to time sends forth for this work, that they unite in one broad stream of improvement, which becomes the highway of nations and conveys rich blessings to extensive regions.
> Such a spirit appeared in Henry Pestalozzi. (37: 7)

Now let us consider some evidence of the more direct application of Pestalozzian theories to reading materials and methods. Again we turn to Horace Mann in a discussion which engages our attention not only because of its reading content but also because within it we find a statement of the origin of Pestalozzi's famous method of object teaching.

> In teaching children words, in the earlier stages of education, the objects they designate should, as far as possible, be presented. When the object is familiar to the child, but is one which is not or cannot be presented or in sight, then let it be referred to, so that there shall be in the mind of the child a conscious union of the name and object as in the case of the words river, boat, moon, etc. If the object itself cannot be exhibited, and is not familiar so as to be referred to, then some representation or model of it should be presented.

In the school of Pestalozzi, a series of engravings were prepared, representing a variety of objects, whose names, structure, and use the children were to learn. One day the master having presented to his class the engraving of a ladder, a lively little boy exclaimed, "But there is a real ladder in the courtyard: why not talk about that rather than the picture?" "The engraving is here," said the master, "and it is more convenient to talk about what is before the eyes than to go out into the yard and talk about the other." The boy's remark, thus eluded, was for that time disregarded. Soon after the engraving of a window formed the subject or examination. "But why," exclaimed the same little objector,—"why talk of this picture of a window, when there is a real window in the room, and there is no need to go into the courtyard for it?"

In the evening, both circumstances were mentioned to Pestalozzi. "The boy is right," said he; "the reality is better than the counterfeit; put away the engravings, and let the class be instructed in real objects."

This was the origin of a better mode of instruction, suggested by the wants and pleasures of an active mind. "Put away the engravings," we respond when the real objects can be had as referred to. If it is impracticable to exhibit the real object, as it is to show a boat to an inland child, then present the picture, or what is better the model....

If children should be introduced to a knowledge of written language, by means of the most attractive and impressive objects and ideas of objects, then those names which are the names of the most striking and agreeable things, the adjectives descriptive of the most brilliant and pleasing qualities, and the verbs expressive of agile and graceful motions, should be presented to them, at first without the encumbrances of articles, prepositions, and conjunctions. There are many single words which represent an entire picture; while for other pictures we must use sentences. (36: IV: 44)

From this report and others regarding Pestalozzi, it seems quite likely that there was a close connection between the principles advocated by him and such innovations in reading as the introduction of the word method, the appearance of many pictures in primary readers, and the inclusion of material dealing with objects and experiences familiar to children. This discussion of German-Pestalozzian influences has perhaps proceeded far enough to make clear the factors which contributed so largely to the changes in the readers appearing after 1840. We will now pass on to a brief consideration of the specific reading aims of the period.

Specific Reading Aims

Expressive oral reading and elocutionary delivery continued to be outstanding aims in reading instruction. These aims were reiterated by authors in such statements as the one below, quoted from *Tower's Third Reader*:

> A just and distinct articulation is the first and most important requisite of good reading or speaking.... Correct articulation is the basis of this art [reading], and we must look well to the foundation before we can safely raise the superstructure; it is, therefore, necessary that, in the order of teaching, it should take precedence of the other elements. (38: 3)

Additional reading aims were summed up by Alonzo Potter in the *American School Journal* for August 1856, in which he said that the "objects" of reading should be as follows:

> 1st, to acquire knowledge both for its own sake and its uses: 2ndly, to improve the intellectual powers: 3rdly, to refine taste: 4thly, to strengthen the moral and religious sentiments. (40: 215)

II. The New Materials

Professional books and teachers' manuals did not appear in the field of American reading instruction during this period although such developments were quite general in England at the time. The only courses of study in reading were occasional meager outlines in reports of superintendents or school boards, usually stating the amount of material to be covered but giving no hints as to method. So, as in earlier periods, we are limited to a discussion of textbooks as the chief materials of the period.

One of the outstanding features of the new materials was the appearance of carefully graded series of readers. We noted in chapter three some indication of this trend. We saw that authors were preparing several books, each intended to be more advanced than the preceding one. It was not until this period, however, that series appeared in which a book was definitely prepared for each of the different school grades. Between 1840 and 1860, graded series of readers were published by Worcester, McGuffey, Swan, Russell, Tower, Sanders, Town and Holbrook, Hillard, Parker and Watson, and others. It was during this period, of course, that our graded school was evolving, largely as a result of the reports concerning German-Pestalozzian schools, in which the children were "divided according to age and attainments, and a single teacher had charge only of a single class." Graded series of readers were a natural development of the new graded school system.

The subject matter of readers also underwent considerable change. We find the intense patriotic type of materials all but disappearing in the new readers; to be sure, there remained a few selections which might be termed patriotic, but no more than appear in our readers at the present time. The moral selections continued to retain their hold, but with the introduction of new materials they steadily decreased until by the end of the period they had dwindled to a small fraction of the total contents. With the new emphasis upon reading as means of obtaining information, we find the upper grade readers increasingly given over to a wider range of informational subjects in science, history, art, philosophy, economics, and politics (see figure, page 79). Some space was devoted to literature in the upper grades, but such material was included chiefly because it was the type that would lend itself to elocutionary delivery. Primers and first readers came more generally to contain realistic materials. Stories of nature occupied a large

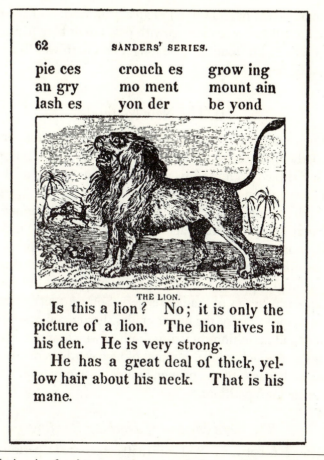

SANDERS' SERIES.

pie ces	crouch es	grow ing
an gry	mo ment	mount ain
lash es	yon der	be yond

THE LION.

Is this a lion? No; it is only the picture of a lion. The lion lives in his den. He is very strong.

He has a great deal of thick, yellow hair about his neck. That is his mane.

In Sanders's series of readers, we see the new emphasis on reading as a means of obtaining information. This page is from the first reader, the 1849 edition.

proportion of these texts, probably because of the Pestalozzian emphasis upon science and object teaching, which gave nature materials an important place in the primary curriculum.

The pictures in readers for beginners became more plentiful and more directly representative of objects familiar to children and experiences of child life. Practically all readers of the period had cardboard covers adorned with pale tan or blue paper. They varied in size but tended to be longer and narrower than in the preceding period.

III. The New Methods

There were two ramifications of method during this period, so distinctly different as to require separate treatment. Before discussing these two methods, we will consider some of the new features common to both methods.

With the increased emphasis upon words and phonetics, we find that the syllabarium disappeared as a means of inducting children into reading. Heightened attention to the principle of "proceeding from the simple to the complex" was generally and painstakingly applied, not only in the new primers but throughout an entire series of graded readers. Some attention was now called to meanings in the upper grades through questions on the content and definitions of words, both of which were specified in the book. A much smaller number of new words were introduced in the early pages of the primer, and definite provision was usually made for repetition.

The Word Method of Teaching Reading

The years between 1840 and 1850 constituted a period of vigorous protest against the ABC method by educational leaders who had glimpsed a more sensible procedure for initiating the child into reading. Let us examine some of the evidence of the times in regard to this reversal of opinion.

In the preceding chapter we noted that Worcester mildly advocated the use of the word method in his *Primer of the English Language* published in 1828. Here is the remarkably sensible suggestion which Worcester advanced at that time:

It is not, perhaps, very important that a child should know the letters before he begins to read. It may learn first to read words by seeing them, hearing them pronounced, and having their meanings illustrated, and afterwards it may learn to analyze them or name the letters of which they are composed.

Although Worcester's suggestion was prophetic, it received scant attention. It was not until the popular readers by Bumstead and Webb appeared in the 1940s, bearing their vigorous arguments for the word method, that this innovation was given any serious consideration. Josiah Bumstead's *My Little Primer*, which appeared in 1840, was the first reader to be based specifically on the word method. Bumstead expressed his policy in regard to this book:

In teaching reading, the general practice has been to begin with the alphabet, and drill the child upon the letters, month after month, until he is supposed to have acquired them. This method, so irksome and vexatious to both teacher and scholar, is now giving place to another, which experience has proved to be more philosophical, intelligent, pleasant, and rapid. It is that of beginning with familiar and easy *words*, instead of *letters*. (41: 1)

Bumstead's next reader, *My First School Book*, was presented to the teaching public with a spirited explanation and defense of its method and contents:

TO THE TEACHER

A little boy, who had been a long time plodding his dreary way through the alphabet and had finally reached the columns of three-letter syllables, one morning (the first snow of winter having fallen during the night), on rising from his bed, and looking out at the window, exclaimed with ecstasy,

"Hurrah there's a sleigh ! S-l-a, sleigh!"

"John," said his father, "that doesn't spell sleigh."

"Don't it! What does it spell, sir?"

"O, I don't know—it don't spell anything."

"Why, father! What is it in my book for?"

In preparing this little book, it has been the intention to make it strictly a suitable book for children in their first efforts at learning to read and spell; and to have it contain only what is, in some degree at least, intelligible and useful —only that concerning which a child, on making inquiry, *What is it in my book for?* would at once receive, from a teacher or parent, a satisfactory answer.

For this reason, there is here an exclusion of that chaotic mass of fragments of words, which it has been usual to present to the eyes and ears of children in their first exercises. Such lessons, it is believed, are as unnecessary as they are uninteresting. They convey no thought; they rather teach a child not to think.

Children are delighted with ideas; and in school exercises, if nowhere else, they are disgusted with their absence. The present selection of words has been made with reference to this fact; and it is hoped that no one can be found which is not, partially at least, intelligible to the young scholar, or capable of being made so. No regard whatever has been paid to *length*, or to the popular opinion that a word is *easy* because it is *short*. This is a great error. A word is not easy tread and spell simply because it is short; nor difficult, because it is long; it is easy or difficult, chiefly, as it expresses an idea easy or difficult of comprehension. (42: 3)

John Russell Webb published a primer in 1846 entitled *The New Word Method*. In the preface of the book one finds this amusing account:

THE ORIGIN OF THE WORD METHOD

(The following brief history of the Word Method is published at the request of many friends of this system of teaching. Its author, Mr. Russell, is a nephew of the man after whom our author was named. —PUBLISHERS)

On an early summer morning of 1846, a young man, barely twenty-one years of age, was reading a newspaper in the sitting-room of his boarding place. He was the teacher of the village school.

From early boyhood he had been regarded as "odd." He did not do, he did not think, as boys of his age generally did. Often he was reproved for finding fault with what others considered "well enough." He would reply: "If we could see no defects, we would make no improvements." Many were the little devices, to save labor and give better results, seen on the home farm.

While awaiting breakfast, as already mentioned, a little girl, four or five years old, climbed into his lap as she had often climbed before. Her mother was in the kitchen preparing the breakfast; her father, in the yard milking the cow.

The teacher laid down his paper and began to talk to the child. The father was mentioned, what he was doing, and the cow was talked about. Just then his eye caught the word *cow*, on the paper he had laid down. He took it up and pointed out the word to the child, again calling attention to the cow, and to this word as the name of the animal her papa was milking. Soon she looked up into the teacher's face; her eyes kindled with intelligence; she caught the paper, jumped out of his lap and ran to her mother, exclaiming as she ran: "I know what it means; I know what it means. It is a cow, just like what papa is milking!" and she pointed out the word to her mother.

Many a boy and many a man before Newton had seen an apple fall. It may be that many a teacher had done just what this teacher did; but into him the circumstances had flashed an idea. He at once began to experiment, not only with the little four-year-old girl, but with the beginners in the school. The lessons were prepared in the evening, and in the morning printed on the blackboard, and he, himself, taught them to the children with the most marked—the most wonderful success. There were no unpleasant tones, no drawling. On the contrary, the children read in pleasant natural tones, giving the emphasis and inflections of the playground.

From time to time these lessons were printed and formed page or hand cards. The children became very much interested in reading them. They read them in and out of school. They read them anywhere—everywhere one would listen. They took their cards with them to the table—to bed, as little girls sometimes do their dolls.

At first all the parents were very much pleased. But, alas! there was trouble ahead. It was soon discovered that the children could not spell the words—that they did not even know the names of the letters! Some of the parents "waited on the teacher," and left with him unpleasant memories. Others had faith that "That teacher knows what he is about." There was a good deal of talking, and what "the teacher" was doing became noised abroad.

That fall a Teachers' Institute was held at Watertown, twelve miles away. Our teacher was sent for. They wanted to know what the "new thing" was. For a week it was explained, illustrated, discussed. Then the following resolution was passed:

Resolved, That having heard an exposition of a new method of teaching children to read, by J. Russell Webb, we are of opinion that the interests of our schools require its publication, and we pledge ourselves to use efforts to introduce its use into our schools should it be published.

Resolved, That a copy of this resolution be signed by our chairman and secretary and presented to Mr. Webb.

Watertown, N.Y.,   E.S. Barnes, *Chairman*
October 20, 1846   J. L. Montgomery, *Secretary*

A Watertown bookseller (Joel Greene) was present. He offered to publish an edition at his own expense—and he did, that fall, 1846. This edition bore the title: "John's First Book; or, The Child's First Reader."

The New York *School Journal* says: "That book was the means of a great reform. Millions of children have been saved years of drudgery by the use of the method it proposed, and Mr. Webb is entitled to unlimited praise."

And this is how the Word Method originated, and how it was born into the world. Since then it has written its own history.

Jay Russell (44: ii)

Webb was not wholly deserving of the great distinction which "the nephew of the man after whom he was named" confers upon him. Worcester had previously advocated the word method and Bumstead had already published his primer based on this method. Webb may have developed his ideas independently of the others, but at least he did so contemporaneously with them. The account, nevertheless, is enlightening in that it shows the seriousness with which this change of method was regarded.

The advent of the word method was so startling that a cursory examination of the writings on this subject would leave one with the impression that the entire procedure for teaching reading was revolutionized by its introduction. As a matter of fact, it affected only the beginning stages of reading instruction and was not felt at all in the methods used in connection with the advanced grades. The greatest innovation was that the child learned entire words during his first weeks of reading instruction. As soon as this task was achieved, however, spelling and phonetics were employed in the same capacity and with emphasis equal to that found in the alphabet-phonetic methods, which will be described later. Script also was usually correlated with the teaching of beginning reading in the word methods as well as in the alphabet-phonetic methods. In the upper grades we still find an emphasis on elocutionary delivery and expressive oral reading.

There seems, however, to have been a greater tendency to give attention to meanings in methods advocated for advanced reading in word method series than in the alphabet-phonetic series. As an illustration of this increased attention to meanings, we may note the five points around which Webb organized the rules in his third reader:

To read well, the following particulars are essential, viz.:

1. A full comprehension of the matter to be read
2. Correct position or action
3. Knowledge of the forms and force of words
4. Perfect control over the voice
5. Judgment (45: 3)

Another statement from Webb's introduction not only sums up the method he advocated, but gives evidence of a new trend creeping into the field of reading method—the notion of *silent* reading.

The reading lesson should be carefully read, silently, previous to the class exercise, at which time every word not understood should be examined in the dictionary, and these definitions, or their import, given at the *spelling* exercise from the *reading* lesson. (45: 9)

Bumstead's Readers. Josiah Bumstead is recorded in history as a Boston merchant and a writer of textbooks. For several years prior to the Civil War he was superintendent of a Negro Sunday School. This is the only mention of teaching experience which one finds in his biography. The full title of Bumstead's first book was *My Little Primer going before My First School Book to get me ready for it* published in 1840. The distinctive feature of this primer was that it departed from the usual introductory pages given over to the alphabet and syllabarium and devoted itself entirely to lists of words. These words were selected on the basis of child experience and were organized according to related meanings. Lesson 1 enumerated parts of the human head; Lesson 2 listed parts of the human body, and so on. A little further on in the book one finds the words arranged in a manner intended to convey, more or less, the thought of a complete sentence. An illustration follows.

Another	did	raised
boy	that	hand
very	which	struck
angry	he	own
because	did not	sister
his	like	shame
sister	raise	shameful (41: 11)

The book was bound in cardboard covered with dull tan paper. The pages were held together with two white tapes and were glued into the cover. Down the backbone there was a brown leather strip. The book contained 36 pages of medium weight paper, cream in color and unglazed, much better paper than that in earlier readers; and it had smooth edges, which was a real innovation at the time. The type also was improved in this reader. On most of the pages the type was about the size used in a modern second reader; the type on the first five pages was slightly larger and heavier than that on the other pages. There was only one illustration in the book—a picture printed on the cover and repeated on the title page. It was a crude little drawing of children entering the primary school. The only other illustrative feature of the book was an ornate border enclosing each list of words. Sometimes there were three of these "boxes" on a page. There were 38 new words on the first page. On the succeeding nine pages the number of new words per page ranged all the way from 3 to 41.

Bumstead's *Third Reading Book* will be described briefly as representative of all of his advanced readers, which appeared at the very edge of the preceding period. Method did not figure largely in the readers after the first year. Consequently, one finds little change in his readers for the upper grades. In common with these other readers, the subject matter of the third reader is predominantly moralistic, 87 pages being filled with this type of content. The remainder of the book, however, departs from the customary patriotic and elocutionary selections and is devoted to such subjects as experiences in child life, family relationships, and nature material (plants, clouds, seasons, etc.). Only 7 pages are used for religious material, and only 1 page contains anything which might be characterized as patriotic. Paragraphs representative of the moralistic and nature types of content in this book are given as follows:

> These things, though they may seem to be trifles, are full of instruction. They teach us to beware of impatience; —to wait till the fruit is ripe. They teach us that the cup of pleasure seized before the proper time, may be a cup of poison.
>
> Spring, Summer, Autumn, and Winter, —Morning, Noon, and Night, —all bring with them a pleasant change, making the country like a large picture-book, the leaves of which you may turn over, continually, and always find something new. (43: 26, 86)

In examining the literary types in the book, we find that realistic narratives are most prominent. There are 35 pages of poetry. No dialogues appear, unless one counts a 4-page selection in which a bird begs a man not to shoot him, and gives his reasons. There are only 4 pages of old tales, and 8 pages each of admonitions and informational material. The third reader has a page slightly larger than the beginning book in the series. In cover, binding, endpaper, it is similar to the first reader. The type is clear, black, and varying in size. At the front of the book the type is about the size used in an average fifth reader today; beginning with page 126 the type becomes as small as that found in newspapers. An unusual typographical feature of the book is that the pages are divided into two columns, each only 1 $^1/_2$ inches wide.

The frontispiece is the only illustration in the book. It is a full-page picture showing a schoolroom. "Love, Industry, Order" are the words in the border at the top of the room and below the picture is a quotation—"And school to make us wise."

Webb's Readers. John Russell Webb was a graduate of the New York State Normal School in Albany. He taught in country schools until 1851, when he went to Indianapolis, Indiana, to teach, but he did not remain there long because of ill health. He apparently devoted his time to writing during the rest of his life. In 1846 Webb published *John's First Book*, or, *The Child's First Reader*. By 1855 he had completed his entire series of Normal Readers.

John's First Book now became *Webb's Normal Reader, No. 1.* In its make-up, this little reader had the usual characteristics of the period. It was bound in blue cardboard covers, 4 by 6 $^1/_2$ inches; the paper was somewhat thinner than that seen in previous readers, and the type somewhat larger. The book contained 12 black and white illustrations, about 2 inches square, occupying a total of 3 pages out of 90. They depicted familiar objects and child life.

read-ing, like´ to look off, and see what is going on a-bout them.

Such lit-tle boys and girls are try-ing to do
more than one thing at a time, and will not do
a-ny thing well.

I hope when you read, you will let oth-er
things a-lone.

QUESTIONS.—How many things should you try to learn at a
time ? Should you look around the house when read´ng ? Why
not ? What word has two f's in it ?

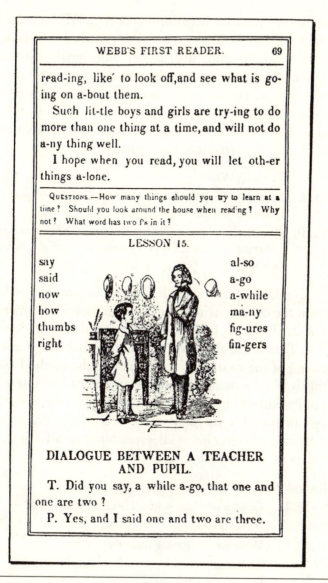

LESSON 15.

say	al-so
said	a-go
now	a-while
how	ma-ny
thumbs	fig-ures
right	fin-gers

DIALOGUE BETWEEN A TEACHER AND PUPIL.

T. Did you say, a while a-go, that one and
one are two ?

P. Yes, and I said one and two are three.

In Webb's primary readers, special attention was given to words and their meanings.

Owing to the increased attention to method, Webb devoted the first eight pages of the book to carefully prescribed "Directions for Teachers" and liberally distributed additional instructions throughout the text. This was an unusually large provision for teaching directions in connection with first readers. Perhaps it was a harbinger of the quantity of instructions which in the next period became so bulky as to require a separate teachers' manual. The book was organized into three parts:

Part I.   Teaching Words

Part II. Teaching New Words, Reading, Spelling, the Alphabet, Sounds of Letters

Part III. A Speller as Well as a Reader, Teaching Children to Spell Columns of Words and Pronounce at Sight before Reading

Practically all the content in each of these parts was derived from objects in the child's environment or from experiences representative of child life. Let us consider a characteristic selection from Part III. This particular excerpt is chosen because it conveys something of the content of the hook and the method used in teaching it. Furthermore, this sample of content is of interest because of its evident intention to promote a wider use of the book through an appeal to its young readers. Can it be that this dialogue depicting a clever bit of salesmanship is an offspring of the Catechism in *The New England Primer*?

Dialogue Between Peter and James

PE-TER.   Good morn-ing, James; where are you go-ing?

JAMES.   To school.

P.   What are you go-ing there for?

J.   To learn.

P.   What do you learn there?

J.   To read and to spell.

P.	What book do you read in?
J.	John's First Book.
P.	Is it a good book?
J.	Yes it is a ve-ry good book, there are so ma-ny fine sto-ries in it.
P.	But what do you spell in?
J.	O! I spell in that too, for the words are all in spell-ing les-sons over the read-ing les-sons, and when I have learned the spell-ing les-sons, I can read the read-ing les-sons right off.
P.	Well, James, you know I nev-er liked to go to school, but I think I should like to read THAT book. I will go right home, and ask pa to get me one, and then I will go to school and read it with you. (44: 75)

As representative of Webb's books for the upper grades, we may examine his fourth reader (46), which was bound more substantially than was customary for other readers at that time. The cardboard foundation was covered with an unusually heavy grade of brown paper with a slightly rough surface. It contained a table of contents, and was printed from type somewhat larger than that used in other fourth readers of the period.

The reader is so diversified in content and the different types of subject matter overlap so frequently that a clear-cut analysis is impossible. The subject matter, however, may be classified approximately as follows: 51 pages of narrations with no particular subject matter content; 20 pages of science material; 30 pages of various informational materials; 34 pages of history; 10 pages based on economics; 10 pages of religious content; 15 pages of prose literature; 83 pages of poems on a variety of subjects; and 80 pages of moralistic material. It is interesting to note that only 12 pages are devoted to rules for speaking and reading. The remainder of the book can be classified only as miscellaneous.

As for literary types, we find the narrative predominating with 145 pages; poetry comes next with 83 pages; and exposition last with 74 pages. An unusual feature is that much of the poetry is accompanied with music so that the children may sing it. Perhaps a few representative titles from the book will be sufficient to characterize its contents: The Pet Lamb, Anecdote of Washington, Universal Education, Beware of Bad Books, The Carrier Pigeon, Typography, Self-Culture, and Europe and America.

Alphabet-Phonetic Methods

One frequently encounters in educational writings the statement that the alphabet method was abandoned about 1840. This is far from the truth. In spite of all the agitation in behalf of the word method, the majority of teachers continued to use the alphabet method. The word method was conspicuous because of its newness, but the alphabet method was persistent because of the years of tradition behind it. Many statements such as the one quoted below bear evidence to this effect. The statement from Gideon Thayer's "Letters to a Young Teacher"(1857) is particularly convincing in that it comes from one who was advocating the word method:

> The first step in teaching children to read has usually been that of making the pupils familiar with the alphabet, and *the large majority of teachers* at the present time pursue that course. There is, however, a better mode.... It is that of teaching by words. (47: 221)

Perhaps one reason why teachers continued to use the alphabet method was because the majority of textbooks advocated it. Some few authors adroitly dodged the issue by stating that either the word method or the alphabet method could be used with their materials; others openly scoffed at the new plan, as we shall see in the following paragraphs from Town and Holbrook's *Progressive Primer:*

92

No time is here to be wasted in fruitless experiment on some *exploded* theory, boldly set forth as a *new* discovery. The book is merely and strictly as it purports to be, —*progressive*. The child is called upon to learn words of two or three syllables first; then those of more than two or three.

Each reading exercise is followed by words arranged for a *spelling* lesson; and these, on the first few pages, are in *larger type*. Thus the pupil learns to spell more than six hundred words besides those in the reading lessons. (48: 3)

There was, however, a strong tendency during this period to teach the sounds of the letters, either together with their names or instead of their names. Hence we are characterizing this procedure as the alphabet-phonetic method. One main feature of the method is thus expounded by Gideon Thayer:

The method of spelling the words should be by the *sounds* of the letters which combine to form them and not by the *names*. No difficulty will be found in giving the several sounds of the vowels, and after a little practice those of the consonants will be easily made; and the pupil will be agreeably surprised to discover of what simple elements the consonants are composed. (47: 220)

David B. Tower also advocated the teaching of the sounds of the letters in *The Gradual Primer*. His method is indicated in the following quotation:

How easy the task, comparatively, to learn to spell and read, when a child *knows* all the *powers* of the letters, and can *execute* them, clearly, forcibly, and distinctly!...

Sound the *short vowel*, then the syllable, prolonging the sound so as to observe the positions of the organs, and then, with the tongue and lips retaining the same position, sound *l alone*. Do this repeatedly. In sounding *l* the tip of the tongue presses the upper gums, near the *teeth*; hence it is called a *dental*. (39: 23, 32)

We have seen that spelling and reading were closely tied together during this period. Furthermore, an attempt was made to correlate writing with the reading by having the children copy the script sentences that appeared in most of the primers. In some books, the children were told to copy the letters and phonetic combinations from the blackboard as they were taught. In other primers the script sentences were accompanied by more lenient instructions, such as these:

> To TEACHERS. —The child should have slate and pencil, and use them in trying to make letters, almost as soon as he begins to go to school. Let him draw anything,—it keeps him from being idle, if nothing more. But the teacher will find that he will learn to print and write, and will do better in his other studies, and will be more orderly, if so employed a part of the time. (39: 104)

In the upper readers, elocution continued to be stressed. A glimpse of its importance and requirements from the author's standpoint may be gained from a statement by William H. McGuffey, which appeared in his *Eclectic Fourth Reader*.

> To read with a loud and full tone, to pronounce every syllable properly and distinctly, and to mind the pauses; —are the three most difficult points to be gained in making good readers. If these three things are attained, the various intonations that express sentiment will generally follow, as soon as pupils have knowledge enough to understand the sense, and will give their attention to it. (50: xi)

The various exercises required of pupils in connection with each lesson in McGuffey's upper readers are representative of the different points of method emphasized during this period of German-Pestalozzian emphasis. One of these typical lessons is given as an illustration:

LESSON II

RULE. —Be careful to pronounce every syllable distinctly, and not to join the words together.

Exercise under the Rule. To be read over several times by all the pupils.

The *ribs of death.*

Can you *cry crackers, crime, cruelty, crutches?*

The *orb'd moon.*

It was the worst *act* of all *acts.*

It is a *mixed government.*

The *idle spindle.* Long *droves of cattle.*

It was *highly and holily* done.

THE MANIAC—Anonymous

I. A gentleman who had traveled in Europe, relates that he one day visited the hospital of Berlin, where he saw a man whose exterior was very striking.... [A page and a half is given to this story.]

QUESTIONS—You may sketch the circumstances here narrated. How do you account for the *unhinging* of this man's mind? Is it common that one idea keeps possession of a maniac's mind?

ERRORS—Hosp-tal for hos-pi-tal; as-sid-di-ous for as-sid-u-ous; de-fi-cit for def-i-cit, (pronounced def-e-cit).

SPELL AND DEFINE.—1. Hospital, commanding, melancholy; 2. measured; 3. contemplation, traveler; 4. assiduous, finance; 6. defaulter, secretaries, miscalculation, multiplying; 7. Imprisonment; 8. solicited ; 9. experimental. (50: 17–19)

In one of Russell and Goldsbury's readers we find the following story, which not only serves to sum up the different phases of reading method, but also points out rather vividly the new trend of paying some attention to meanings and withal has a refreshing touch of humor.

The most extraordinary spelling, and, indeed, reading machine, in our school, was a boy whom I shall call Memorus Wordwell. He was mighty and wonderful in the acquisition and remembrance of words; of signs without the ideas signified. The alphabet he acquired at home before he was two years old. What exultation of parents, what exclamation from admiring visitors! "There was never anything like it!" He had almost accomplished his Abs before he was thought old enough for school. At an earlier age than usual, however, he was sent; and then he went from Ache to Abomination, in half the summers and winters it took the rest of us to go over the same space.

Astonishing how quickly he mastered column after column, section after section, of obstinate orthographies! Those martial terms I have just used, together with our hero's celerity, put me in mind of Caesar. So I will quote him. Memorus might have said, in respect to the hosts of the spelling-book, "I came, I saw, I conquered." He generally stood at the head of a class, each one of whom was two years his elder. Poor creatures! They studied hard, some of them; but it did no good; Memorus Wordwell was born to be above them, as some men are said to have been "born to command."

At the public examination of his first winter, the people of the district, and even the minister, thought it marvellous, that such monstrous great words should be mastered by "such a leetle mite of a boy!" Memorus was mighty also in saying those after-spelling matters, the Key, the Abbreviations, the Punctuation, &c. These things were deemed of great account to be laid up in remembrance, although they were all very imperfectly understood, and some of them not understood at all.

Punctuation! How many hours, days, and even weeks have I tugged away, to lift, as it were, to roll up into the storehouse of my memory, the many long, heavy sentences comprehended under this title! Only survey, (we use this word when speaking of considerable space and bulk) only survey the first sentence, a transcript of which I will endeavor to locate in these narrow bounds. I would have my readers of the rising generation know what mighty labors we little creatures of five, six, and seven years old were set to perform.

"Punctuation is the art of pointing, or of dividing a discourse into periods by points, expressing pauses to be made in the reading thereof, and regulating the cadence or elevation of the voice."

There, I have labored weeks on that; for I always had that lamentable defect of mind not to be able to commit to memory what I did not understand. My teachers never aided me with the least explanation of the above-copied sentence, nor of other reading of a similar character, which was likewise to be committed to memory. But all this was nothing, as it were, to Memorus Wordwell. He was a very Hercules in this wilderness of words.

Master Wordwell was a remarkable reader too. He could rattle off a word as extensive as the name of a Russian noble, when he was but five years old, as easily as the schoolmaster himself. "He can read the hardest chapters of the Testament as fast ag'in as I can," said his mother. "I never did see nothin' beat it," exclaimed his father; "he speaks up as loud as a minister." But I have said enough of this prodigy. I have said thus much, because, although he was thought so surpassingly bright, he was the most decided ninny in the school.

The fact is, he did not know what the sounds he uttered meant. It never entered his head, nor the heads of his parents, and the most of his teachers, that words and sentences were written, and should be read, only to be understood. He lost some of his reputation, however, when he grew up toward twenty-one; and it was found that *numbers*, in more senses than one, were far above him in arithmetic. (52: 235)

McGuffey's Readers. We have seen that *The New England Primer* was the favorite reader during the period of religious emphasis, and we have noted that Webster's famous "Blue-Back Speller" held sway in the classrooms of the nationalistic-moralistic period. Now we are about to consider the characteristics of the reading text that outstripped all others in sales and popularity during this new period. It was none other than the famous McGuffey series.

McGuffy's complete set of readers first appeared between 1836 and 1844. The readers came into immediate popularity and continued their strong hold on the American public for the next 40 years, after which they were gradually replaced by the more attractive new books. There has been a demand for these readers, however, until recent times. The last editions intended for general school use were printed by the American Book Company in 1896 and 1907. Still more interesting is the fact that Henry Ford had a private edition printed in 1925. In that year, Mr. Ford opened a new experimental school on his estate at Dearborn, Michigan. Evidently his interest in restoring various features of

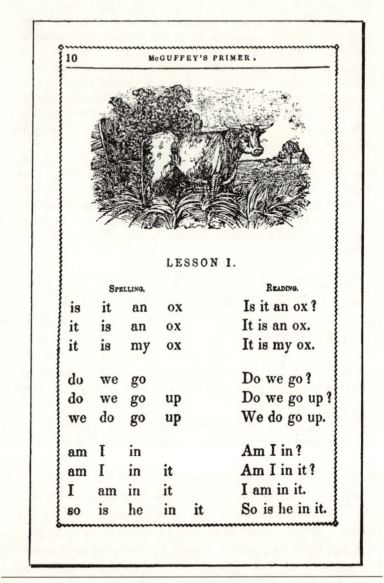

LESSON I.

SPELLING.					READING.
is	it	an	ox		Is it an ox?
it	is	an	ox		It is an ox.
it	is	my	ox		It is my ox.
do	we	go			Do we go?
do	we	go	up		Do we go up?
we	do	go	up		We do go up.
am	I	in			Am I in?
am	I	in	it		Am I in it?
I	am	in	it		I am in it.
so	is	he	in	it	So is he in it.

The children who were drilled on Lesson I of McGuffey's Primer *would be sure to know these two-letter words.*

98

the past led him to supply the school with McGuffey's Readers. In other respects, the equipment of the school was ultra-modern, and it was staffed with highly trained personnel, including a psychiatrist and a dietitian. McGuffey's Readers and a school psychiatrist seem a bit inconsistent; nevertheless, Mr. Ford's selection bears testimony to the fact that McGuffey's Readers still retain their grip on at least one of America's distinguished citizens.

The author of the books, William H. McGuffey, had an illustrious educational career. He was graduated from Washington College in Pennsylvania in 1826. He served as professor in Miami University, Ohio, for a time, then became President of Cincinnati College, and a few years later President of Ohio University at Athens. It was while holding this high position that he wrote his famous readers. McGuffey must be given the credit of being the first author to produce a clearly defined and carefully graded series consisting of one reader for each grade in the elementary school. As typical of the series, the first reader and the fourth reader will now be described.

Some of McGuffey's books appeared in a rather substantial binding of cardboard covered with light brown leather; others were covered with blue paper. His first reader was 5 by 7 1/2 inches, which is approximately the standard size of today's readers. It contained 84 pages of smooth, glazed paper of medium weight and of a cream color somewhat lighter than that used in the books of the preceding period. The type showed improvement in being clear, deep black, and well spaced. It varied in size; at the front of the book it was about the size of the type in a present-day second reader, and in the latter part the type became smaller and more closely set.

There are 140 one-inch pictures and 11 half-page pictures in the book, occupying approximately 20 percent of the space in the reader. The pictures are fairly well drawn. On the first page of the book is the alphabet in large and small letters; then comes

LESSON LXIV.

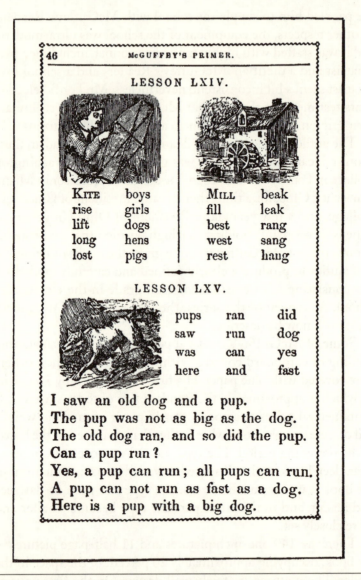

KITE	boys	MILL	beak
rise	girls	fill	leak
lift	dogs	best	rang
long	hens	west	sang
lost	pigs	rest	hang

LESSON LXV.

pups	ran	did
saw	run	dog
was	can	yes
here	and	fast

I saw an old dog and a pup.
The pup was not as big as the dog.
The old dog ran, and so did the pup.
Can a pup run?
Yes, a pup can run; all pups can run.
A pup can not run as fast as a dog.
Here is a pup with a big dog.

At Lesson LXV of McGuffey's Primer, *the children had apparently not advanced beyond words of three or four letters.*

the picture-alphabet, which occupies three pages; and then Lesson I, followed by reading matter similar to that shown on pages 98 and 100.

There is one page of religious material in this first reader and only five pages are devoted to moralistic content. The book consists chiefly of sentences about children and animals. These sentences are usually subservient to the phonetic elements that McGuffey selected for drill purposes. At intervals they are arranged in various combinations with the additional motive of reviewing words previously introduced. With such a basis of selection and organization, the content is very dull and so altogether senseless that it is difficult for an adult to read.

In spite of this objection to the content, one feels a relief to find at last an author who recognized the necessity of repetition for fixing new words. McGuffey was the first who definitely provided for repetition. He also made an innovation in decreasing the number of new words introduced per page. In his lessons in the first reader, the new words range in number from 10 to 12 per page; in the review lessons, there are no new words at all.

There are two pages of poetry in this first reader, but otherwise we cannot say that any particular type of literature is represented. The content consists mostly of choppy, isolated sentences; even the few selections that might be classed as realistic stories have little of real narrative interest.

McGuffey's fourth reader has much the same type of content as the readers of the earlier period. He devotes 135 pages to moralistic material, a great deal of which refers to death and its horrors. For example, here is the conclusion to a story about a girl who died while showing her vanity:

> Indeed, it was a most humiliating and shocking spectacle. Poor creature! struck *dead* in the very *act* of sacrificing at the shrine of female vanity!... I have seen many hundreds of corpses, as well in the calm composure of natural death, as mangled and distorted by

violence; but never have I seen so startling a satire upon human vanity, so repulsive, unsightly, and loathsome a spectacle, as a *corpse dressed for a ball!* (51: 64)

Forty-five pages of this book are devoted to material designed to inspire patriotism. The following quotation, for instance, is from a selection exalting the Puritans and inspires admiration for the Puritan fathers: "Every settler's hearth was a school of independence; the scholars were apt, and the lessons sunk deeply; and thus it came that our country was always free; it could not be other than free" (51: 303). Forty pages out of the total 336 contain selections from or about the Bible. This is a larger allotment of space to religious material than was found in the prominent readers of the preceding period.

McGuffey was not entirely neglectful of American literature, for the book devotes 22 pages to this type of material. Thirteen pages are given to educational interests, and 8 pages to geographical material, and 32 pages are of miscellaneous character. In common with his predecessors, he uses considerable space for rules on reading, 41 pages in all. His upper grade readers in general, however, were of a high literary standard. Mark Sullivan in his *America Finding Herself* says that

> to millions, to probably nine out of ten average Americans, what taste of literature they got from McGuffey's was all they ever had; what literature the children brought into the home in McGuffey's readers was all that ever came. Broad classical reading was not general. McGuffey, in short, because of the leverage of his readers, had a large part in forming the mind of America. (p. 15)

Tower's Readers. David B. Tower wrote many popular schoolbooks during the period under discussion, among which were his *Gradual Readers*, a series of grammars, and his *Intellectual Algebra*. Tower was for a time principal of the Eliot Grammar School in Boston and later principal of the Pennsylvania Institution for the

Blind. During the latter part of his life he evidently retired from active school work and devoted his time to writing.

Tower's series are the first reading textbooks, among the many examined, which were written by a school principal. Perhaps this was a forecast of a well-defined tendency of a later period, that of having reader authorship associated with persons working directly in the elementary teaching field. Tower's primer, designated by the author as *The Child's First Step Taken in the Right Place*, was a small book bound in cardboard on which tan paper was pasted. Its leaves were taped and glued in, in the usual fashion. The paper was unglazed, creamy, and slightly rough. The size of type varied considerably; in the early part of the book one frequently finds six different sizes of type on a page, but in most of the book type of a uniform size was used, approximately that found in our present-day second readers. Tower was one of the authors who attempted to make some adjustment between the alphabet method and the word method. In *The Gradual Primer*, he says,

> Amid the conflicting opinions of the best methods of teaching a child to read,—whether *letters* or *words* shall take precedence,—the author hopes that his *new plan*, while it escapes the objections advanced against either, will be found to embody the advantages of both....
>
> The wisdom of forcing down a whole unmeaning alphabet at once may be well questioned; but that the remedy hitherto applied is less objectionable, needs practical confirmation.
>
> The *new feature* in this little book consists in giving the child only a *few letters* before he is called upon to read *words* composed of those *few letters*. Thus the child is taught words long before he has mastered the whole alphabet; and yet no words are given him, of which he has not *previously* learned the *letters*. (39: 6)

In spite of Tower's conciliatory attitude, the organization of his reading content as well as his statement shows that his method was predominantly alphabetic in nature. The book contains a few small black and white pictures. They represent such objects as horses, cows, and dogs, and often depict a childish experience, such as wading in a brook. The figures of the children are badly proportioned, the heads being too large for the body and the legs too short.

The content of *The Gradual Primer* falls into three groups. The first 17 pages are devoted to letters and words gradually increasing in length. There is a range of from 3 to 10 new words on each page, with considerable repetition. The next 43 pages are made up of words containing a certain number of letters and arranged in lists or short sentences, with grouping by similarity of phonetic elements. On the last 40 pages of the book, there are short stories, some based on nature, some on moralistic content, and some on child life. Typical lessons are shown here and on page 105.

LESSON XVII

The short *sound of* E, *as in* MET *marked* ĕ *or* è.

ĕ	Pen	Led	Let	Bell
ĕ	men	bed	pet	tell
ĕ	ten	red	yet	well

I met ten men.
I have a bad pen.
Let men set a net. (39: 22)

The predominating type of literature is the realistic narrative, although a large portion of the reader is devoted to sets of stilted, unrelated sentences, which have not enough of the story element to be classified as narrative.

The third reader in Tower's series had a larger page than his primer. Like the primer, it had a cardboard cover, but the paper on the cover was pale blue instead of tan, as on the primer cover. The paper of the book was of the same quality as in the primer, but the type was much smaller. There were no illustrations. The first 50 pages contain the usual exercises in articulation. The

LESSON LXXXVIII.
A Time to write.

Here is a nice school room.
See the girls at their desks.
One, two, three, four, five,
Six girls sit at the desks.
The teach-er stands near them
She looks on to see that they
write with care.
They write with pens and ink.
She tells them to sit up, and not
to lean this way or that.
How clean and neat the desks
all look !
Girls do not bring in so much
dirt as boys do.

Tower's Gradual Readers were popular in the middle years of the nineteenth century and later.

remainder of the book consists of "Reading Lessons" based on various types of subject matter. There are a few pages each of natural history, scientific discussions, general information, realistic stories, and poetry on various subjects. The remainder of the reader is devoted to moralistic content. Some of the lesson titles give a further glimpse into the nature of the topics treated: How the Fly Walks on the Wall, A Wasp the First Paper Maker, Even a Child Is Known by His Doings, The Use of Learning, and Susan's Dream. A short excerpt may give some idea of one of the pages in this book.

LESSON XXVI

THE PHILOSOPHER, THE NATURALIST,
AND THE POLITICIAN

1. Perhaps some of you can tell me what a philosopher is.
2. "A philosopher is the same thing with a very wise man, — is it not?"
3. That is pretty near the meaning. Philosopher means a person who loves wisdom; and such a person will always be trying to get knowledge; and a man who is always trying to get knowledge, is apt to be a wise and learned man.
4. You know what the word *naturalist* means, —do you not?
5. "I think it means a man who loves to study about animals and insects."
6. It means a man or woman either who loves to study the things in nature, whether they are animals, stones, grass, or flowers, or any of the things which God has made. Observe, I said to study the *things*, and you said to study *about* the things. (38: 106)

It is somewhat difficult to classify the contents of this book according to literary types because there is so much overlapping of materials. An approximate estimate, however, shows the following proportion of literary types: 65 pages of narrative material, 102 pages of expository and informational material, 24 pages of poetry, and 1 page of fable.

Willson's Readers. We may now glance at one of the exceptional series of readers of this period, just for the purpose of noting the fact that all readers did not run in the same channels. The School and Family series by Marcius Willson, published in New York in 1860, was distinctive in that it specialized in scientific content. The series contained a variety of types of literature, such as incident, anecdote, and poetry, but all these were subordinated to the author's intent to convey scientific information. The following lesson headings are found in Number Five of the series: elocution, reptiles, physiology and health, botany, fishes, architecture, natural philosophy, physical geography, chemistry, geology, general history, and geometry.

This chapter has demonstrated the many applications of German-Pestalozzian principles to American reading instruction during the years between 1840 and 1880. We shall now turn to a discussion of the next change that became apparent in this field.

CHAPTER FIVE

The Period of Emphasis on Reading as a Cultural Asset

I. Motives and Influences That Affected Reading Instruction

Sometime in the early 1880s, a new movement began to shape itself in the field of reading instruction. At this time in history, the United States had reached a status of tranquility and security. Previously, we had experienced a period of strong effort to develop patriotism for and unity in a new nation. Following this period, we had lived through a transition stage in which the major focus was to develop the intelligent citizenship deemed necessary in casting ballots for leaders in the new democracy. Both objectives continued, but in greatly subdued emphases. With the success of the American democracy assured, with threats of major wars no longer impending, and with a population comfortable in a prosperous economy, a new trend emerged that affected the nature of reading instruction. The nation now had the leisure and peace of mind to turn to cultural pursuits in music, art, and literature. This concern for cultural development resulted in an emphasis on the use of reading as a medium for awakening a permanent interest in literary material that would be a cultural asset to the individual in adult life. It is true that some literature had been included in upper-grade readers previous to this time, but it was designed to serve as a vehicle for elocutionary or drill exercises and not to promote literary appreciation and interest. It was not until the beginning of the period now under discussion that one finds well-defined aims, methods, and materials all directed toward the goal of developing permanent interest in literature.

The major portion of this chapter will be devoted to a discussion of ways in which the cultural influence changed reading instruction. In the latter part of the chapter, however, mention will be made of the studies in reading conducted by investigators during this period. These studies, while few in number, are significant from the historical standpoint in that they represent beginnings in reading research. A slight beginning was also made during this period in regard to giving special attention to reading disability cases. This matter as well as reading investigations will be discussed toward the end of the chapter.

The Cultural Emphasis

Perhaps it would be well at the beginning of this discussion to quote some of the educators of the times in regard to this new emphasis. In the introduction of a state report made by the Superintendent of Public Instruction in Indiana in 1880, we find this statement:

> The public school teaches the child to read, but it does not teach him what to read or how to read. It gives him the ability to interpret the printed page, but it fails in a great measure to cultivate in him a taste for that which is pure, elevating, and instructive. In view of the attractive garb in which vicious literature is clothed, he will be more likely to read to his injury than to his profit. The person, then, who teaches children to read and fails to cultivate in them a taste for good literature, puts an instrument into their hands which may possibly be used by them to their own destruction. (53: 5)

Sarah Louise Arnold expressed similar views in her *Reading: How to Teach It*, which appeared later in the period (1889):

> Learning to read is an important part of the child's training, but learning *what* to read is quite as important. A child's mastery of

the printed page may leave him with the key to that which is base and ignoble in literature, or it may open to him that which is noble and inspiring. His newly gotten power may unlock to him the dime novel or the Iliad. Whether he turns to the one or the other depends largely upon his early associations. It is determined especially by his early teaching. (54: 25)

We have examined evidence from a school report and a professional book. Now let us see what one of the courses of study has to say, turning to the course published in Rochester, New York, in 1901:

Constantly in all grades the teacher should bear in mind the importance of cultivating a taste for good literature. Giving the child possession of the art of reading, without the power to discriminate between good literature and bad, is like giving him a sharp tool without instruction as to its proper use.

In tracing the cause of this new emphasis, it would have been much more convenient if one had found that it began in 1890 instead of 1880, because then it would have been obvious that this emphasis was a direct product of the wave of Herbartianism that swept the country in the 1890s through the influence of American educators who returned from study in Germany and published reports of Herbart's philosophy between 1889 and 1897. As a matter of fact, there is abundant evidence that the new emphasis in reading instruction was well under way in America in the 1880s. Even so, it seems more than likely that the movement later was accentuated by Herbartian principles emanating from Europe. Herbart's doctrines first became popularized in Germany through a book published in 1865, which in turn led to the formation of a society in 1868 for the purpose of studying the principles advocated by the great educator. In 1874, the pedagogical seminary and practice school was established at Jena. This school attempted to put the Herbartian principles into effect and became a center of inspiration for educators from all over the world. Charles De Garmo studied in Germany about 1886 and published *The Essentials of Method* in 1889.

Charles A. McMurry studied at Jena about 1887 and published *General Method* in 1892. Frank M. McMurry studied at Jena in 1889 and published, with Charles A. McMurry, *The Method of the Recitation* in 1897. The National Herbartian Society was organized in 1892. These combined influences were most important in bringing Herbartian pedagogy to a focus in America.

Now let us see how the Herbartianism may have accentuated the already existing emphasis on literary interest and appreciation in the teaching of reading. One of Herbart's most important goals was that of developing character through the use of literary and historical stories. In his own words, Herbart expressed his ideas in this regard.

The intent to teach spoils children's books at once; it is forgotten that everyone, the child included, selects what suits him from what he reads, and judges the writing as well as the writer after his own fashion. Show the bad to children plainly, but not as an object of desire, and they will recognize that it is bad. Interrupt a narrative with moral precepts and they will find you a wearisome narrator. Relate only what is good, and they will find it monotonous, and the mere charm of variety will make the bad welcome. Remember your own feelings on seeing a purely moral play. But give to them an interesting story, rich in incidents, relationships, characters, strictly in accordance with the psychological truth, and not beyond the feelings and ideas of children; make no effort to depict the worst or the best, only let a faint, half-unconscious moral tact secure that the interest of the action tends away from the bad towards the good, the just, the right; then you will see how the child's attention is fixed upon it, how he seeks to discover the truth and thinks over all sides of the matter, how the many-sided material calls forth a many-sided judgment, how the charm of change ends in preference for the best, so that the boy who perhaps feels himself a step or two higher in moral judgment than the hero or the author, will cling to his view with inner approbation, and so guard himself from a coarseness he already feels beneath him.

The story must have one more characteristic, if its effect is to be lasting and emphatic; it must carry on its face the strongest and cleanest stamp of human greatness.... I know of only one place where such a written story may be found—the classical age of childhood among the Greeks, and I consider the Odyssey ranks in the first place....

The earliest cultivation of the child's feelings will have been a failure, if, after his taking full pleasure in the characters, the moral impression left from these old stories is doubtful....

Periods which no master has described, whose spirit no poet breathes, are of little value to education. (55: 73, 89)

After reading only this one quotation, it becomes quite evident that there was a similarity between Herbart's principles and the new type of reading instruction. This account of influences would be incomplete without some reference to the vigorous campaign of Charles W. Eliot, president of Harvard University, to bring about changes in school reading with respect to literature. Whether Eliot's efforts were the outgrowth of his own independent viewpoint or whether they too reflected Herbartianism, it is impossible to say. Be that as it may, he was a strong factor in bringing about changes in school practices. In 1890 in an essay entitled "An Average Massachusetts Grammar School," President Eliot described a study in reading that he had made, the gist of which is embodied in the following quotation:

I turned next to an examination of the quantity of work done in the grammar school under consideration—and, first, of the amount of reading. The amount of time given to reading and the study of the English language through the spelling book and the little grammar which are used in that school, and through a variety of other aids to the learning of English, is thirty-seven per cent of all school time during six years. But what is the amount of reading in this time? I procured two careful estimates of the time it would take a graduate of a high school during six years, including the history, the reading lessons in geography, and the books on manners. The estimates were made by two persons reading aloud at a moderate rate, and reading everything that the children in most of the rooms of that school have been supposed to read during their entire course of six years. The time occupied in doing this reading was forty-six hours. These children had, therefore, been more than two solid years of school time in going through what an ordinary high-school graduate can read aloud in forty-six hours.... How small an acquaintance adults would make with English literature if their reading during six years were limited in amount [to this extent].... This test...is, of course, a very rough and inadequate one,.... but it gives some clue to the very limited acquaintance with literature which the children get in the entire course of six years. (56: 185)

In a magazine article, Eliot even went so far as to advocate literature in place of readers:

It would be for the advancement of the whole public school system if every reader were hereafter to be absolutely excluded from the school. I object to them because they are not real literature; they are but mere scraps of literature, even when the single lessons or materials of which they are composed are taken from literature. But there are a great many readers that seem to have been composed especially for the use of children. They are not made up of selections from recognized literature, and as a rule this class is simply ineffable trash. They are entirely unfit material to use in the training of our children. The object of reading with children is to convey to them the ideals of the human race; our readers do not do that and are thoroughly unfitted to do it. I believe that we should substitute in all our schools real literature for readers. (57: 497)

Much more could be written on the influences back of the literary emphasis in reading, but perhaps enough has been said to point out the chief factors which were instrumental in bringing it about. Let us now turn to the more specific reading aims of the period.

Specific Reading Aims

With the advent of courses of study in reading, one finds reading aims more frequently and more specifically stated. In examining the representative statements below, it may be of interest to note that developing an appreciation for and a permanent interest in literature is prominent; that the aim of getting the thought from the printed page is beginning to occupy an important place; and that expressive oral reading is still "the order of the day." The course of study for the public schools of Rochester, New York, published in 1901, states the reading aims in this way:

> The objects of reading lessons are two: First, to give the pupil the power to secure from the written or printed pages an intelligent and appreciative knowledge of the thoughts of the authors as recorded and expressed in literature. Second, to give the pupil the power to impart to others the knowledge thus obtained in a clear, sympathetic, pleasing manner. The teacher should always bear it in mind that the content of the reading lesson is of more value than its form, and that an appreciation of good literature is worth more than the mechanical ability to read. Careful attention should be paid in all grades to correct enunciation, and pronunciation, to proper use of the vocal organs and of the organs employed in breathing and the carriage of the body; and vocalization of both vowels and consonants should be employed when needed.

In a course of study from Flint, Michigan (1902–1903), this statement is made:

> The purpose of the courses in reading is threefold: first, to teach children to read; second, to cause children to like to read; third, to enable them to know and prefer good literature.

A course of study for the public schools of Kansas (1907) gives its purposes in such terse statements as these:

THIRD GRADE: *Purpose*

(a) To gather thought

(b) Expression

(c) Word Study

George L. Farnham, author of one of the first teachers' manuals in reading (1905), expressed reading aims in this way:

> Reading consists: first, in gaining the thoughts of an author from written or printed language; second, in giving oral expression to these thoughts, in the language of the author, so that the same thoughts are conveyed to the hearer. (58: 11)

II. The New Reading Materials

Professional Books

This is the period in which professional books in reading first came into prominence. With the issuance of new materials and the formulation of new methods, it was natural that entire treatises should appear, devoted to the discussion of reading instruction. The first book of the period to exert any particular influence on the teaching of reading was Scudder's *Literature in the Schools*, published in 1888. Scudder argued at length for the teaching of complete English classics in the elementary school and disparaged the scrappy bits of moralizing materials found in readers.

Sarah Louise Arnold's *Reading: How to Teach It* was another important book of the period. One finds this book recommended to teachers again and again in the courses of study during the decade following its publication in 1899. Although Miss Arnold gave many suggestions for teaching the mechanics of reading, one feels, after examining the book, that by far the strongest emphasis is directed toward the development of an appreciation of literature.

In 1899, Charles A. McMurry published *Special Method in the Reading of Complete English Classics*, which was the outstanding contribution to reading made by a protagonist of Herbartianism. It might be worth while to quote from this book a passage describing the improved conditions brought about under the new regime:

> With the increasing tendency to consider the literary quality and fitness of the reading matter used in school, longer poems and stories like "Snow Bound," "Rip Van Winkle," "Hiawatha," "Aladdin," "The Courtship of Miles Standish," "The Great Stone Face," and even "Lady of the Lake" and "Julius Caesar" are read and studied as complete wholes. Many of the books now used as reading books are not collections of short selections and extracts, as formerly, but editions of single poems or kindred groups, like "Sohrab and Rustum" or the "Arabian Nights" or "Gulliver's Travels" or a collection of complete stories or poems by a single author, as Hawthorne's "Stories of the White Hills" or Lowell's "Vision of Sir Launfal" and other poems. Even the regular series of readers are often made up largely of longer poems and prose masterpieces. (59: 48)

It was during this period also that Edmund Burke Huey produced his well-known *The Psychology and Pedagogy of Reading*, which does not advocate any particular method or take sides on any issue. It gives an entirely scientific treatment of such topics as the psychology of reading, the history of reading, the hygiene of reading, and it also includes an impartial discussion of the pedagogy of reading. This book was the first scientific contribution to reading instruction and is still considered a standard reference in the field. Other popular professional books of the period devoted exclusively to reading instruction are *Reading in the Public Schools* by Thomas H. Briggs and L.D. Coffman, and *Children's Reading* by Frances J. Olcott.

Courses of Study

Separate courses of study in reading appeared for the first time during this period. Until about 1890, the courses were but meager outlines in reports of a school board or a superintendent of schools. While this condition prevailed generally throughout the period, there was a new development in the way of separate publications containing the course of study for all elementary grades and covering all subjects. As an example of this development, one might refer to the Utah course of study for the public schools published in 1897. Here we find about nine pages devoted to reading and six pages to phonics. There are some "General Suggestions" about reading, "A Few Helpful Rules for Questioning for Thought and Expression," and finally outlines for each grade stating the material to be covered. The outlines for Class A of the first grade will serve as an example:

SECOND HALF—CLASS A

Readers.—Werner's and Finch's Primers; also the first half of *Stepping Stones to Literature*, No. 1.

Although the great majority of courses in reading during this period were included in the general course of study as described above, a few separate reading courses appeared. One outstanding piece of work was "The Teaching of Reading" by George A. Mirick of the New Jersey Department of Public Instruction, published in 1914 near the close of this period. This book devoted 90 pages entirely to the subject of reading. There were background discussions on phonetics, voice training, and the use of the blackboard. Following these sections came rather full assignments of work by grades, together with "Plans for Reading Lessons." The entire treatment was a superior piece of work and in advance of its time in many respects. One quotation from this course is given here because it points to the coming trend, that of emphasis on silent reading, a feature that characterizes the next period to be described. Mirick says,

> By far the larger part of the reading done in the world is silent reading. This common, everyday sort of reading is a very different process from oral reading, and has a different purpose. The great

majority of people seldom have occasion to read aloud. And yet for many years the only kind of reading recognized as *reading* in the schools has been *oral* reading. This almost exclusive practice of oral reading in school has produced several results which students of school practice have adversely criticized.

Supplemental Materials

It was during this period that the reading of materials other than those included in the basic reader came to be a popular practice. This enrichment of the reading course was undoubtedly an outgrowth of the aim of developing an interest in literature, particularly as applied to the reading books each of which contained a single classic. One finds many interesting arguments in support of the new plan, as well as suggestions of method for putting it into effect in the classroom. The following quotation from an article in the New York *School Journal* embodies both points and is characteristic of the general discussion of the subject during the early 1880s, when it seems first to have commanded attention.

> Now it is very evident that the advantages which the readers have as exercises in elocution and drill-books prevent them in most cases from inspiring any love of good reading and from giving the power of sustained interest. It is to promote these two objects that supplemental reading has been introduced into many of our schools. Books and magazines are brought forward to do what the reading books from their nature cannot do.
>
> Then, some day when the reading has dragged, the readers are shut, "Evangeline" is brought out and the children are allowed to read their favorite passages aloud. The school has perhaps two or three or more copies of the book, and while one is reading others are getting ready for their turn.

After discussing the desirability of using supplemental books of a literary type, the writer goes on to say,

Take the two books already named, *American Poems* and *American Prose*, and consider that the children who under the guidance of a teacher have gone through them, have made the acquaintance of Longfellow, Whittier, Bryant, Lowell, Thoreau, Hawthorne, Holmes, Irving, and Emerson, and that the works of these authors, pure and lofty in character, constitute a body of literature distinctly American, and rich and powerful in influence; consider further that the children have been led on and on in their interest and the gentle compulsion of school work, and see if they have not already been given unconsciously at school just what we want them to have, a love of good literature, an interest in their home authors, a taste for the high and enduring form of art, and a shield more or less protective against meaner literature and associates. (53: 28)

The materials used for supplemental reading in the upper grades took the form, as one would naturally expect, of classic literature in books devoted to that type of content and developed entirely apart from any purpose as a systematic reader. In the primary grades, the usual practice was to equip each classroom with two or three sets of additional readers, providing enough copies so that each child might have one, and to prescribe in the course of study the proportion of these readers that should be covered in a given term. In addition to this, the children were sometimes provided with books containing fairy tales, such as "The Three Bears" and "Jack and the Beanstalk." A few excerpts from the Rochester, New York, course of study (1901) will illustrate the trend of the times:

First Grade
  During the semester *Stepping Stones* No. 1, and at least two other first readers, should be completed.
Third Grade
  Pupils should read an equivalent of half of *Stepping Stones* No. 3 and two other Third Readers and much supplemental matter.
Seventh Grade B Class
  Seventh Reader, Stepping Stones, and other literature, especially by American authors, and relating to periods of American history.

Combined Alphabetic and Phonetic Systems

One new feature in reading materials that developed during this period was the contrivance of certain alphabetic and phonetic systems, which it was thought would make reading easier for beginners. One such system was the "Scientific Alphabet." This alphabet reduced the number of characters needed in representing the sounds in the English language by respelling words and by omitting silent letters. Some diacritical markings also appeared in this alphabet (see example below).

Another alphabetic and phonetic system that appeared during this period was known as "The Shearer System." In this system, a letter's sound where it might be equivocal is represented by a mark that constantly stands for that sound and for that sound only, irrespective of what the letter may be. Comparatively few marks are needed and the constant value of the marks is supposed to give an easy guide to pronunciation. The silent letters are indicated by a dot.

Wuns, Rip Van Win'-kl went up
    a-mung' thẹ hilz, hwār hĩ sō
    cwîr lit'-l men plê'-ing bōl.
Thê gêv Rip sum -thing tū drink,
    hwich put him tū slîp.
Hĩ slept twen'-ti yîrz, and hwen hĩ wōk up
    hĩ wez an ōld man with grê hār and bîrd.
Hĩ went hōm.   Nō wun niū him at fẹrst.
Hĩ wez tōld hwet had hap'-nd
    hwail hĩ wez a-slîp' a-mung' thẹ hilz.

The "Scientific Alphabet" was used by the authors in the first reader of their Standard Reading Series published in 1902 (60:70).

The enthusiastic inventors of the early alphabetic and phonetic methods held out great promise for their respective inventions as means of teaching beginning reading more speedily and effectually. As an example, in the *Combination Speller* (see page 122), Shearer states that by his method

> A child may be taught the art of reading, not fluently, but well both in phonetic and in ordinary books, in three months—aye, often in twenty hours of thorough instruction, a task which is rarely accomplished in three years of toil by the old alphabet. (61: 3)

Neither system described enjoyed wide or permanent usage. They evoked some excitement for a short time but were not used generally. The Scientific Alphabet, however, was revived with several changes in 1960 when it appeared as the "Augmented Roman Alphabet" (see chapter nine of this volume).

III. General Features of the New Methods

There were three important new developments in method during this period. The first two applied particularly to the primary grades: (1) the sentence method and the story method, both of which were an outgrowth and expansion of the word method so strongly agitated during the preceding period; and (2) the elaborate phonetic methods, which stressed and extended the previous practices in regard to teaching children the sounds of letters and combinations of letters. The practice of learning the alphabet and spelling words as an initial step came generally to be abandoned early in this period. The third development in method, and the one which affected the upper grades particularly, was the use of new techniques to arouse appreciation for literature and to establish permanent interest in literature. These techniques were of the defining-dissecting type, which we now look upon with disapproval; but even so, they marked a real step in advance of the

I. ALPHABETIC NAMES, SOUNDS AND SYMBOLS.
KEY TO CONSONANT AND VOWEL SOUNDS

p,	as pėt, tŏp.	**sh, ch, ṣ,** } as	show, chaiṣe, ṣůrę.
b,	" bėt, rŏb.	**ọ, ṭ,** } "	ȧppreçlatę, ȧetiŏn.
t,	" tėn, nėt.	**ṣ, ẓ, g,** "	viṣiŏn, ȧzůrę, rŏụgę.,
d,	" dėn, ėnd.	**x,** "	ȧx, bŏx.
ch,	" chėss, whĭch.	**x̣,** "	ėxȧmplę.
j, g̣,	" jėt, g̣ĭn.	**wh,** "	whėn, whȧt.
k, e, q,	" kĭt, eȧt, pīqụę.	**w,** "	wėn, wȧṣ.
g,	" gŭn, pėg.	**h,** "	hȧt, hŏt.
f, ph, gh,	" fŭn, phiz, tŏụgh.,	**y,** "	yŏn, yėt.
v,	" vinę, hȧvę.	**l,** "	lėt, tālę.
th,	" thĭn, hȧth.	**r,** "	rȧt, tár.
th,	" thėn, lāthę.	**m,** "	mȧt, ȧm.
c, ṣ,	" cėnt, sėnt.	**n,** "	nėt, fȧn.
z, ọ, ṣ, x̣,	" zero, diṣçėrn, x̣ebėe.	**ṇ, ng,** "	sĭṇk, riṇg.

—	as, lātę, theỹ.	(C	as, prûnę, mŏvę, mȯon, dręẇ.
|	" lėt, sȧịd, (bȧrỹ).	))	" fůll, bȯok, wŏmȧn.
)S	" fár, (sérgęȧnt).	(O	" bûrn, wȯrd, hȇrd, bĭrd, myrr̄ḥ.
(\	" fȧst.		" bŭn, sŏn.
)<	" fárę, thérę.		
(\	" fȧt.		**DIPHTHONGS.**
{::	as, fẹẹt, pīqụę, (qụȧỹ).		
	" fĭt, bẹẹn, bụṣy, (wŏmėn).	ſ	as, fĭnę, tỹpę.
<	as, nŏtę, sėẇ, (hȧụtboy).	ſC	" eow, loud.
)Λ	" eȧụght, wȧll.	Λ:	" oĭl, boy.
)Y	" eŭt, wȧtch.	C	" fůṣę, nęẇ.

II. A SAMPLE OF ALPHABETIC REFORM PRINT

Bỹ the *phonėtĭe ȧlphabėt a chĭld maỹ be tȧụght the ȧrt ŏf
reading, nŏt fluėntlỹ, bŭt wėlḷ, both ĭn phonėtĭe ȧnd ĭn ŏrdĭnȧrỹ
bȯoks, ĭn three mŏnths—ȧỹę, ŏftẹn ĭn twėntỹ hoụrṣ ŏf thŏroụgh
ĭnstrŭeṭiŏn, a tȧsk whĭch ĭṣ rȧrelỹ ȧeeŏmplĭshẹd ĭn three yęarṣ ŏf toĭl
bỹ the old ȧlphabėt.. Whȧt fȧthȇr ȯr teȧchȇr will nŏt glȧdlỹ haĭl
ȧnd ėarnėstlỹ wȯrk fȯr this great boọn tŏ ėdueaṭiŏn —thĭs puwȇrfůl.
mȧchinȇ fȯr the dĭffusiŏn ŏf knŏwlėdg̣ę.

*Dots above g and y, and below other letters indicate silent letters. The signs are omitted for
the alphabetic sounds of a, e, i, o and u, except for exact representation.,

As copyrighted, 1894, by Rev. James W. Shearer, St. Louis, Mo.

This page from Shearer's Combination Speller.

122

emphasis upon elocutionary delivery, which had long held sway in the intermediate and upper grades.

The first two of the developments mentioned above—the sentence and story methods, and the elaborate phonetic methods—took a course so widely different from each other that separate and rather complete treatment is necessary. The procedure for teaching literary selections in the upper grades was common to both methods, and one discussion of this procedure should suffice for this phase of reading method.

George P. Brown, President of the Indiana Normal School, urged that several recitations be given over to each lesson from classical literature, and then recommended steps to take in such a series of lessons. This outline of procedure is presented because it represents a composite of the different techniques so largely used during the period.

1. There are biographical, historical, geographical, scientific, and literary allusions in nearly every piece, which must be studied, discussed, and understood before the selection can be read intelligently.

2. There are words of peculiar orthography and pronunciation that must be learned.

3. There are many words and phrases having a special meaning in the lesson, which should be sought out and defined by the pupil *in language of his own*. Mere dictionary synonyms will not serve. This must be done before the pupil is prepared to read at all.

4. Before the piece is finally left, the pupil should be required to write a paraphrase of certain portions or all of it, expressing the thoughts in his own language, and then his style of composition compared with the author's, and its defects noted.

5. If the selection is a gem worthy to be remembered, it should be committed to memory. No one who has ever experienced it will be able to estimate the values of a large store of classic pieces thus fixed in memory. They are valuable for the grandeur of the thoughts, for their excellence of style, and for the increased vocabulary they give. (53: 23)

Elaborate Phonetic Methods

After the word method had been in use for a few years, a growing dissatisfaction sprang up in some quarters because children who had been taught by this method were not able to read well in the upper grades. The following quotation from one of the school journals of the time exemplifies this trend of thought:

> There is quite a general complaint among teachers, principals, and superintendents that pupils in the higher grades are not able to read with ease and expression; they have so little mastery over words that an exercise in reading becomes a laborious effort at word-calling. Pupils read usually very well through the first three readers, according to our present standard of reading in these grades. But the trouble begins in the fourth reader, and by the time the class is in the fifth, the reading recitation is torture to the teacher and a hateful task to the pupil. There can be no good reading without the ability to call words readily, and it may be well to consider whether the methods of teaching primary reading, which seem productive of such good results in the primary grades, are not at fault in preparing the pupil for the advanced reading.
>
> We are inclined to think the inability of pupils in the higher grades to call words is the legitimate outgrowth of the teaching of the word method. By this method the word is presented to the child as a whole, and the teacher either tells the child the word, or by skillful questioning leads him to use the word. Later, when phonics have been introduced, the teacher writes the new and difficult words on the blackboard and marks them. The general results of these methods on the mind of the pupil are about the same. He soon learns to think he can do nothing with a new word without the help of the teacher in some way. While he should be learning independence in making out his words, he has learned dependence, and his dependence increases with the increase of difficulties. (62: 203)

As a result of such complaints, several writers of textbooks took the opposite position of advocating an extremely synthetic method. Rebecca Pollard was one of the first and strongest influences in bringing about this emphasis. Pollard's *Synthetic Method* was published in 1889. The following quotations from her manual reveal her position on reading method:

> Make reading of the first importance. As in music, let there be scales to practice; drills in articulation; a *thorough preparation* for reading before the simplest sentence is attempted.
>
> Instead of teaching the word as a whole and afterward subjecting it to phonic analysis, is it not infinitely better to take the sounds of the letters for our starting point, and with these sounds lay a foundation firm and broad, upon which we can build whole families of words for instant recognition?...
>
> There must be no *guess work*; no reference to pictures; no waiting for a story from the teacher to develop thought. If the instructions of the Manual are carefully followed (in inflection as well as pronunciation), the child's own voice will give him a perfect understanding of what he reads. (62: 3, 4)

The general procedure advocated by Pollard was as follows:

> First: Oral instructional excerpts from Johnny Story, using stencils and songs when teaching sounds; talk about the new sound; developing words by families; reasons for marking, etc.
>
> Second: Blackboard drill, which should include the marking on the board by pupils, in turn, of all the letters, words, and sentences given in the lesson.
>
> Third: Independent marking of the lesson by pupils at their seats.
>
> Fourth: Writing, from the teacher's dictation, the letters, family names, words, and keys of the lesson.
>
> Fifth: Recitation; pupils pronouncing the words and reading the sentences of the lesson. (62: 24)

One new feature of Pollard's method, which should be noted, is that she considered the children's interests and levels of maturity more carefully than anyone else had up to this time. Instead of teaching the sounds each as an isolated bit, she used, as a vehicle for teaching them, a story of several chapters in which she recounted the experiences of two little children who came in contact with different animals and objects, which suggested the sounds she wished to teach. For example, the two children saw a steamboat in the distance and heard it making a puffing sound like *p! p! p!* After hearing this part of the story, the pupil was told that he might draw *p* and a steamboat on the board, and was given this further instruction: "You may puff as you draw the curve to the right at the top, and think that the steamboat is coming nearer as you make the letters larger, as *p! P! P!*" Drawings of ladders and clock faces were frequently recommended for blackboard drill in order to make the work interesting.

We look on this at the present time as being artificial, but at that time, any attempt to make the work interesting and child-like was an innovation. This method marked the turning point from the teaching of reading largely from the adult point of view to a procedure that made use of the child's interest.

The Pollard method was the forerunner of several other reading systems that heavily stressed phonetics. None, however, went to such extremes as Pollard did. Most advocated the teaching of some whole words before giving practice in sounding letters and phonetic elements. Nevertheless, the foundation of the method in each case rested on an elaborate and highly organized system of phonetics. Chief among these systems were the Ward series, the Beacon Readers, and the Gordon Readers.

IV. Basal Readers

The outstanding changes in readers during this period may be briefly summarized as follows:

Elocutionary rules disappeared from the readers. Moralistic and information selections lost their foothold in basic readers. The new content for the upper grades consisted almost wholly of literary selections. Mother Goose rhymes and folktales were for the first time used in beginning readers.

126

Cloth covers replaced the cardboard covers of the preceding period. The type became clearer and larger. Colored pictures were used for the first time.

Ward's Readers

The Ward Rational Method in Reading was developed by Edward G. Ward, Superintendent of Public Instruction, Brooklyn, New York. Published in 1894 by Silver Burdett, the basic material consisted of a primer and six readers. Teacher's instructions were presented in prefatory material and notes in the children's readers. The primer is a good example of the improved mechanical make-up characteristic of the period. The covers were of strong binder's board, but instead of being covered with paper, they were covered with cloth of a neutral tan color. The end leaves had heavy cloth at the joints. The book was glued into the cover and also side wired with four staples. The paper was glazed and so thin that it showed printing on the reverse side of the sheet. The type was clear and of good size.

The greatest innovation was two full-page colored illustrations. This was probably the first school reader in which colored pictures were used. One of these showed two children walking down the road with their mother, and the other depicted four children riding in a little carriage drawn by two goats. Both illustrations were labeled "A Picture for a Story." There were several small uncolored pictures; some occupied the upper half of the page; others were set into the reading text at various places on the page. The animals were drawn very well, but the human figures were stiff, expressionless, and often out of proportion. Approximately 16 percent of the book was made up of pictures— a decided increase in picture space.

Ward was one of the authors who tried to reconcile the word method and the phonetic method by using the word method in connection with the early pages of his primer. Hence we find three pages filled with unrelated sentences designed to give drill on the new words introduced. These sight words were often those necessary in making stories but which do not lend themselves readily to phonetic sounding—does, do, you, and so forth. It was a convenience to have these words memorized in the beginning stages. Following is a sample of content designed to give drill on such sight words:

> I see a dog.
> Do you see a dog?
> Does the dog see me?
> Look at the dog.
> Does the dog look well?
> The dog looks well.
> You and I look well.
> Look well at the dog. (63: 13)

After the author had equipped the child with the stock of sight words that he thought necessary, he plunged him into intensive training in phonetics, which carried over to the reading materials by means of diacritical marks. One finds such marks freely used throughout the entire set of readers. An excerpt from Part II of the primer will give an idea of the appearance of these pages:

Rōs̸e is a good mit̸t māk er. She n<u>e</u>ver f<u>ails</u> to f<u>it</u>.

What is she k̸n<u>it</u> t̸ing now? That is not a mit̸t. See, it has a h<u>ee</u>l. What a k̸n<u>it</u> t̸er you are, Rōs̸e! (63:103)

The subject matter in general was based on children's pets and activities. A few pages on subjects such as locks, work, and snakes might be considered as informational. The sentences were sometimes arranged in paragraphs, but they might or might not have any connection. Often the transition from one idea to another was so abrupt as to be confusing to an adult. The word range on the first 10 pages of the primer varied from two to five new words per page, with a high percentage of repetition.

Ward's third reader may be considered as representative of his more advanced books. It embodied the same features of mechanical make-up as his primer, except that the book was of an odd size, measuring 7 ¼ by 6 inches. An unusual feature was that it contained type of the same size as that used in the latter part of the primer. The book was much more abundantly illustrated than had heretofore been customary in readers above the first grade. Approximately 13 percent of the space was given to illustrations. With the exception of nine full-page illustrations, the pictures were generally small and many of them were set into the type.

The subject matter reveals some interesting trends. There was a noted decline in patriotic and moralistic material, only 11 pages being devoted to the former and 31 pages to the latter type of subject matter. The new emphasis is apparent in several pages of old tales and fables. The remainder of the book is mainly devoted to nature selections, largely in the form of poetry. A stanza from Alice Cary's "Three Bugs" shows the way in which poetry was subjected to diacritical marking:

> Three little bugs in a băskĕt,
>   And härdly room for two!
> And one was yĕllōẃ and one was black,
>   And one like me, or you.   (64:25)

The following history story of George Washington seems to have made its first entrance into readers at this time:

> George's mother, knowing they had come from
> the fields, began to ask about the horses. . . .

Then George said, "The sŏrrel is dead, mădám; I killed him."

His mother looked grīēvd . . . .

When he had finishd she said gĕntly, "I rēgrĕt the loss of my sorrel, but I rējoiç in my son, who always speaks the truth." (64:77)

The types of literature found in this third reader also reflect the new emphasis. There are 55 pages of fables, folktales, and fairy stories; 47 pages of poetry; 42 pages of realistic stories; and the remainder is given over to miscellaneous materials.

The Beacon Readers

One of the later series of readers that made use of a highly systematized method of phonetics was the Beacon series, prepared by James H. Fassett, Superintendent of Schools at Nashua, New Hampshire. The primer appeared in 1912 and the first reader in 1913. These books were accompanied by a reading chart and a phonetic chart. The other readers for grades two to six were published successively by Ginn, and within a few years, the entire set was complete. No manual was published at that time, but as late as 1922, a manual by Fassett and Norton appeared. The authors make this statement:

> Just as carefully prepared and graded exercises are necessary for practice in playing the piano or any other musical instrument, so such exercises are necessary for practice in acquiring our spoken language.

In discussing their phonetic method, they explain that the chief features that distinguish their method from others:

> (1) Careful attention to the blending of consonant and *following* vowel; (2) ample practice in the short vowel sounds in ideal syllables;

(3) clear differentiation between words that are phonetic and words that are unphonetic; (4) adequate preparation for natural syllabification and spelling and the use of the dictionary; (5) the inculcation of the best standard of pronunciation. (65: x)

In examining the primer, one finds a well-made, gray, cloth-bound book containing 128 pages of unglazed, cream-colored paper, printed in large clear type. The pictures are plentiful but irregular in shape as are their position on the pages. One sees in this book a trend toward the use of colored pictures throughout the text yet it had not quite arrived. All pictures on the first 80 pages are printed in color, blue and brown together with black; but from page 80 onward the pictures are in black and white. Approximately 18 percent of the book is made up of illustrations. The predominating picture is one third of a page in size, stretching across the top; there are, however, several small pictures placed in various positions on the page.

The first 15 pages are made up of phonetic tables, which contain lists of words of from three to five letters organized according to certain vowel or consonant combinations, such as *camp, lamp, damp, bump, jump, pump.* Subject matter based on nature had suffered a sharp decline as evidenced in this primer, where we find only two pages devoted to this topic. There are a few pages of folktales and poems, and the rest of the book is given over to sentences on children's toys, pets, and activities. These sentences are arranged for drill purposes and are often choppy and difficult to read. The following is a typical example of this content:

> I have a doll
> I have a doll, mamma.
> See my doll,
> See my doll, mamma.
> See my doll, kitty.
> I like my doll.
> I like my kitty. (66: 19)

It is obvious from this sample that repetition is well provided for. The number of new words in the wordlist is rather high; there are, for example, 35 new words in the first list, but, of course, chart work has preceded the presentation of this list. On the first page of sentences, there are only three new words: *mamma, see,* and *kitty.* The highest number of words introduced on any of the first 10 pages of reading is five.

Literature is represented in three pages of poems and six pages of old tales. Other than this, one cannot say that any type of literature is included. The fourth reader of the series is representative of the upper-grade readers. It has the same mechanical features as the primer, with these exceptions: the page size is smaller; the book contains more pages, a total of 314; the type is not as heavy and only about half as large as that in the primer.

One finds many pictures in this book, without color but rather large in size for a fourth reader: 4 of them occupy a full page; 16 cover three fourths of a page; and several others range from two thirds to one half page. In addition, there are a few smaller pictures, making an approximate total of 14 percent of the book. The pictures show a great deal of action, and emotion is well expressed in the faces of the characters.

The predominating subject matter is fairy tales and supernatural events. Patriotism, once so prominent, has dwindled in this book to a half page on "Saluting the Flag," by Edward Everett Hale. It is interesting, however, to find that the character-building aim is still prominent in this book, because 37 pages deal with child and animal life seemingly with a distinctly moral intent. In addition to this subject matter, we find several pages on animal life and child life without moralistic design. There are 32 pages of classics by American authors and other miscellaneous material. The types of literature represented are only two: poems, 17 pages; and narratives, which make up the rest of the book. The unusual feature of this fourth reader is the length of the selections; for example, an adaptation of Thackery's "The Rose and the Ring," 56 pages long, and obviously another evidence of the new movement to emphasize the reading of entire classics.

Sentence and Story Methods

Contemporaneously with the elaborate phonetic systems, we find another, larger group of authors expanding the word method into the sentence method or the story method with phonetics receiving a subordinate emphasis. George L. Farnham was the earliest crusader for this new analytic method, and the following quotation gives some idea of his viewpoint:

> The first principle to be observed in teaching reading is that things are recognized as wholes. Language follows this law. Although it is taught by an indirect process, still, in its external characteristics, it follows the law of other objects.
>
> The question arises, "What is the whole? or what is the unit of expression?" It is now quite generally conceded that we have no ideas not logically associated with others. In other words, thoughts, complete in their relations, are the materials in the mind out of which the complex relations are constructed.
>
> It being admitted that the thought is the unit of thinking, it necessarily follows that *the sentence is the unit of expression....*
>
> A second principle is: we acquire a knowledge of the *parts* of an object by first considering it as a whole.... Repeated recognitions reveal the characteristics of the whole, so as to separate it from other things.... The sentence, if properly taught, will in like manner be understood as a whole, better than if presented in detail. The order indicated is, first the sentence, then the words, and then the letters. The sentence being first presented as a whole, the words rediscovered, and after that the letters composing the word. (58: 17)

Following publication of Farnham's manual, *The Sentence Method*, several reading systems appeared based on his theory. A method that made use of entire sentences or even whole stories as a starting point offered a happy opportunity to introduce cumulative folktales from literature into readers for beginners. It is small wonder, then, that this method was readily seized on as a means of furthering the general goal of the period, that of developing interest in literature. Stepping Stones to Literature and the Graded Literature series, which appeared in 1897 and 1899, respectively, made moderate use of the method. It was not, however, until 1909 to 1918 that the method enjoyed the height of its popularity, as applied in such well-known series as Baker and Carpenter's Language Readers (Macmillan), Burchill-Ettinger-Shimer's The Progressive Road to Reading (Silver, Burdett), Free and Treadwell's Reading Literature (Row, Peterson), Bryce and Spaulding's The Aldine Readers (Newson), Coe and Christie's Story Hour Readers (American Book), Dyer and Brady's The Merrill Readers (Charles E. Merrill), Hervey and Hix's The Horace Mann Readers (Longmans, Green), Baker and Thorndike's Everyday Classics (Macmillan), and the Elson Readers (Scott Foresman).

The essential steps of method advocated in these series were first, the teacher would tell a story or rhyme to the children until they had memorized it or had become very familiar with it; the selection was then read and analyzed into separate words and phrases; and eventually phonetics was applied in sounding the words. The emphasis on phonetics, however, was not marked. The authors of the Reading-Literature series of readers say in regard to this phase of reading:

> It is not the purpose here to set forth a "scientific system" of phonetics. It is not believed desirable that children in these early grades have even "a complete system" of phonics. It is the aim to give, in this manual, only such work as experience has shown necessary to train children into independent power over words in their reading vocabulary. There have been complete and scientific systems used for drill in the past. There are such systems yet in use in some sections of the country. But these systems have proved generally unsat-

isfactory. Their failure may be clearly traced to the fact that they are too complex and elaborate. (67: 6)

The general procedure commonly used in teaching reading with the use of the sentence or story methods is given clearly in outline form by the authors of the Story Hour Readers:

Method of Teaching

I. Telling the story
II. Dramatization
III. Blackboard work
IV. Analysis
   1. Thought groups
   2. Sentences
   3. Words in groups
   4. Sight words
   5. Phonetics
V. Reading from the book (69: 11)

There can be no doubt that the pioneers in literary readers were Arnold and Gilbert's Stepping Stones to Literature (Silver Burdett, 1897) and Judson and Bender's Graded Literature Readers (Maynard, Merrill, 1899). These series probably have not been surpassed in influence or sale by any other modern readers. One distinctive feature of these books was that they were the first to introduce cumulative tales and rhymes into primary readers. Incidentally, it is interesting to note that it was in Graded Literature that the Little Red Hen first scratched her name across the pages of readers for beginners (see example, page 136). This story proved to be so admirably adapted to the capacities of little children and to the repetitional needs of a beginning vocabulary that it readily found its way into several other primers of the period. It frequently was said that all first grade teachers of the country, East and West, had one bond in common—that of teaching "The Little Red Hen."

114

scrătched   grāin   bĭll   āte   mĭll
thrĕsh   flour   whēat   nor   bāked

As Little Red Hen scratched the ground, she found a grain of wheat.
"Who will plant this?" she asked.
"I will not do it," said the cat.
"Nor I," said the dog and the pig.
"Then I will," said Little Red Hen.
So she buried the wheat in the ground. It grew up yellow and ripe.

"The wheat is ripe now," said Little Red Hen. "Who will cut and thresh it?"
"I will not," said the pig.
"Nor I," said the cat and dog.
"Then I will," said she.
So she cut it with her bill and threshed it with her wings.
Then she asked, "Who will take this wheat to mill?"
"I will not," said the dog.
"Nor I," said the cat and the pig.

It was in the Graded Literature Readers: First Book *that the popular story of "The Little Red Hen" first appeared in readers.*

Stepping Stones to Literature, the earlier of these two pioneer series, will be described somewhat fully. It was prepared by Sarah Louise Arnold, who had been supervisor of schools in Boston, and Charles B. Gilbert, then superintendent of schools in Rochester, New York. The authors claimed two special features for their readers: first, that they aimed to include nothing but good literature; and second, that the books were better adapted to the modern graded school because eight readers were provided, whereas other series up to this time had included only five or six books.

The books were bound in grayish-green cloth and were printed on paper with a dull finish and a creamy tint. The typographical features were similar to those in present-day readers, except that less regard for regular left-hand margins was shown in the first reader. There are six beautifully colored full-page pictures in the first reader. With the exception of two half-page colored illustrations, all the other pictures are in black and white. Many of them are exceptionally well drawn for first reader pictures at that time.

The literary selections in the *First Reader* consist of the nursery rhymes of Jack and Jill; Baa, Baa, Black Sheep; Mary Had a Little Lamb; Little Boy Blue; and Rock-a-bye Baby. There are some short poems such as "The Cow" by Stevenson and "The Morning Song" by Tennyson. The old stories of the tortoise and the hare, the fox and the goat, and the mouse who lost her tail were other innovations in literary material for a first reader. Much of the content of this book, however, still consists of sets of related sentences such as the following

> See my Kitty.
> See Kitty.
> This is my Kitty.
>
> Kate likes Kitty.
> Kate likes Ben.
> Kate likes Fan.
> Kate likes me. (70: 7)

Later in the book, this type of material at times assumes a style approaching real literature more nearly than that found in most present-day primers and first readers. Consider, for instance, the following quotation:

> Here is the old mill by the brook.
> See the great wheel!
> How it turns around, around, around!
> The water falls upon the wheel and turns it around.
> Hear the splash, splash, splash of the water!
> It sings from morning till night. It sounds like a song.
> The brook sings as it works,—the merry, laughing brook! (70: 94)

The authors' description of the content of their advanced readers is especially interesting in that it clearly reflects the Herbartian emphasis upon literature and history. The following explanation is given in their preface:

> In the Fourth Book, the child is given his first distinct introduction to mythology. In the earlier books, fables and fairy stories have been used, and there has been a little suggestion of mythology; but in the Fourth, myth and wonder—those subjects which appeal to the child's imagination and carry him out of his limited environment into a larger world—are emphasized. We believe that this is in accord with whatever truth exists in the culture epoch theory of education....
>
> In the Fifth Book the use of the myth which is found in the Fourth is continued, but the myths here used are mainly historical, leading directly to the study of history....
>
> In the Sixth Book the pure myth does not appear, but in its place is much of history, especially of the legendary lore which appeals to the developing imagination of the child,—such as the tales of ancient Rome and Scott's poems.
>
> There is a large increase of matter which tends to stimulate patriotism, including particularly national songs. Here appear several selections from that sort of literature which requires thought and develops taste, such as "The Voyage to Lilliput." Here also are

found some appeals to the child's natural love of adventure and sports. The ethical motive is plainly evident throughout this book.

The Seventh Book is made entirely of selections from American authors. It is intended for the grade in which most stress is usually laid upon the study of the history of the United States, and can very appropriately be used in connection with this study. The literature of a country cannot be separated from its history, and the natural connection between these two should be emphasized in all study of either. This book is especially rich in matter intimately connected with history, and tending to stimulate patriotism.

Here, more than in some of the other books, selections have been made from longer works, and it is hoped that the teachers will urge the children to read the works entire.

The Eighth Book is made wholly from the writings of English authors. In many schools the study of English history is introduced in this grade. In such schools the selections here given will be found appropriate. Even in those schools in which the history of England is not specifically studied, it is of necessity studied incidentally in connection with the history of our own country, and a familiarity with the writings of the best English authors is essential to a comprehension of the writings of our own. (71: vi)

The Aldine Readers

In our discussion of the reading materials of this period, we come next to the Aldine Readers (Newson & Company, 1907), which enjoyed wide popularity for many years. This series was prepared by Frank E. Spaulding, at that time superintendent of schools at Newton, Massachusetts, and Catherine T. Bryce, then supervisor of primary schools in Newton. The original series consisted of a primer and five readers, bound in dark green cloth. It was one of the first sets of readers in which the primer had the same size cover as the advanced readers, and it was probably the first to employ the decorative feature of end papers in its primer. The books all have excellent typographical features. The left-hand margins in the primer are kept in a regular line, and at no place do the pictures cut into the text on the left or right side of the page.

The pictures throughout the series are artistically drawn; in general they are small in size, and color is used in delicate tones.

The distinctive feature of the primer and first reader is that the content is based on a series of rhymes, which the children learned by heart and later used as a self-help reference in looking up any word they might have forgotten. For example, they learned the Little Boy Blue rhyme and then read several pages based on this rhyme:

> Little Boy Blue, little Boy Blue!
> Come to me.
> Bring your horn.
> See, the sheep are in the meadow.
> The cows are in the corn.
> Blow your horn, Boy Blue. (72: 74)

If the child failed to recognize *sheep* or *horn* or any of the other rhyme words on these pages, he then referred to the rhyme previously learned as a means of recalling the word. A few of these rhymes were from Mother Goose, but the majority were composed by the authors, such as the following:

> Little squirrel, run around,
> Look for acorns on the ground. (72: 47)

The advanced readers consist largely of stories from literature. In the preface of the fifth-grade reader, the authors make this statement: "This book is a basal reader suitable for fifth and sixth grades. It is made up chiefly of selections from the writings of leading American and English authors." The first nine selections in this reader are

The Princess's Escape from the Goblins	George Macdonald
The Bugle Song	Alfred Tennyson
Song of Marion's Men	William Cullen Bryant

The Blue and the Gray	Francis M. Finch
The Pixy People	James Whitcomb Riley
The Indian Tale of Winter and Spring	Henry R. Schoolcraft
Song of the Fairy	William Shakespeare
Sweet Peas	John Keats
The Greenwood Tree	William Shakespeare

Poetry is given considerable space throughout the series. In the fifth-grade reader, 70 pages of a total 237 are devoted to poetry.

The Reading-Literature Series

Margaret Free and Harriette Taylor Treadwell were the first authors to prepare beginning readers with a content consisting wholly of adaptations from the old folktales. Miss Treadwell was principal of the West Pullman School, Chicago, and Miss Free was a primary teacher in the Forestville School, Chicago.

The primer of the Reading-Literature Series (Row, Peterson, 1910) is bound in tan cloth attractively decorated with figures of the story characters marching along at the top and bottom of the front cover. On the inside covers there is a warm tan paper covered with figures of little chicks.

The illustrations, drawn by Frederick Richardson, are artistically the best that had yet appeared in school readers. The figures are large, irrelevant details are omitted, and actions are well portrayed. The large number of illustrations gives evidence of the trend to an increase in picture space in primers and first readers. A total space of approximately 37 pages of 120 is devoted to illustrations, an unprecedented 31 percent of the book. The majority are quarter-page illustrations, although some are smaller. The pictures are variously placed across the top, bottom, or middle of the page, always extending straight across and never cutting into the

not

my

I hăve

bĭg

I have a red sled.

Is it not a big sled?

See my big red sled!

I see a sled

The teacher may direct the children to write the idiom "I see" four times more, substituting for "sled" the words they have already learned to write — "cat," "rat," "hat," "bed."

This page from Swinton's Readers (Ivision, Blakeman & Co.) Primer *and* First Reader *illustrates the appearance of reading texts in the early 1880s.*

text at the side. There are nine full-page illustrations, one introducing each story. All the pictures are printed in two colors, brown and blue in rather light tones, together with black. The type is clear and bold with wide spaces between the lines. The paper is light cream in color and sufficiently opaque to prevent any trace of printing or pictures showing through from the reverse side.

The subject matter is wholly concerned with adaptations from the following folktales: The Little Red Hen, The Gingerbread Boy, The Old Woman and the Pig, The Boy and the Goat, The Pancake, Chicken Little, Three Billy Goats Gruff, Little Toppers, and Little Spider's First Web. The word range is small. Four words (the, little, red, hen) appear on the first page of the primer, and on the second page there are six new words—the largest number introduced on any of the first 10 pages. The cumulative features of the folktales provide abundant repetition. Samples from this primer are as follows:

> The little red hen found a seed.
> It was a little seed.
> The little red hen found a seed.
> It was a wheat seed.
>
> A little boy had a goat.
> The goat ran away.
> He ran into the woods.
> He found some grass.
> He wanted to eat the grass. (68: 2, 40)

The *Fourth reader* of the series has the same tan cloth cover as the primer, with a different design, and is the same in mechanical make-up, except that it is slightly narrower and shorter than the primer. A new feature is four pages of glossary and notes at the back. The illustrations have but one color, a light, warm, brown, used in a variety of tones to give a pleasing effect. The majority of the illustrations are one half to two thirds of a page in size, occupying a total space of approximately 6 percent of the entire book. Frederick Richardson's fantastic representations seem especially well suited to the fairy tales and myths that the book contains.

Poems and tales are the two types of literature represented, with 82 pages of poems, and the remainder of the book devoted to tales. The subject matter predominantly consists of 182 pages of Greek and Scandinavian myths, 52 pages of American literature such as "Rip Van Winkle" and "Hiawatha," 33 pages of "The King of the Golden River," 26 pages of child life stories, and 16 pages of nature stories.

The Elson Readers

Late in this period of emphasis on reading appeared the Elson Readers (Scott Foresman, 1909–1914). These readers definitely reflected the cultural point of view, but with a distinct swing toward children's interests. William H. Elson, the leading author of the series, believed that "interesting material is the most important factor in learning to read" and that if American boys and girls "are ever to have their taste and judgment of literary values enriched by familiarity with the classics of our literature, the schools must provide the opportunity." Elson, however, was not only concerned with the development of an appreciation of literature as such, but he also glimpsed the valuable possibilities of a broader reading program and selected and organized literary materials that would cover the following range of topics: cultural background, nature and science, transportation and communication, history, biography, citizenship, industry, invention, adventure, humor, travel, and world friendship.

In the first edition, the books appeared in grayish white covers that were popular at that time. A later edition was encased in yellow covers, and since 1920, the series has been bound in dark blue.

The primer of the original edition is attractively illustrated in two colors, and the majority of the pictures are a third of a page in size. They are arranged variously at the top and bottom of the pages, and the total picture space amounts to a third of the book. The content is made up of modern stories from children's literature together with some of the simple Mother Goose rhymes and folktales. In the fourth reader of this early edition, the pictures are printed without color and occupy a total of 13 pages out of 320. The content of this reader is organized under the following themes: home and country, fairyland and adventure, nature, famous world heroes, and great American authors.

Looking ahead to the period of broadened objectives, we may note that this series of readers has been revised (1929–1932) under the coauthorship of William S. Gray for the purpose of taking advantage of later developments in the field of reading instruction.

This concludes our discussion of the cultural emphasis as it affected readers and methods of instruction during this period. Both the readers and methods of this period continued to be used widely during the 1910–1920 decade but eventually were replaced as a result of the new emphasis discussed in the next chapter.

V. The Beginnings of Reading Research [1]

During this period, interest in reading research emerged in the United States. These studies were preponderantly of the laboratory type and were few in number, but they must be recognized as the budding of an interest that burgeoned forth in great volume during succeeding periods.

Interest in the scientific study of reading began in Europe in the mid-18th century. Most of the early studies were conducted in France and Germany. A few investigations, however, were made in the United States by Americans who, stimulated by reports from abroad, undertook studies in this country. By 1910 only 34 studies had been reported by investigators in England and the United States. The following chart indicates the number of studies reported within successive 5-year periods from 1884 to 1910. Most of these were conducted by investigators in the United States.

1884–85	— 1
1886–90	— 1
1891–95	— 2
1896–1900	— 10
1901–05	— 6
1906–10	— 14 (75: 5)

Investigations of this period were mainly psychological and physiological in nature and had to do with such aspects of reading as eye-movements, visual perception, and inner speech. Among the American investigators who conducted early studies of these types were I.O. Quantz, Walter F. Dearborn, Edmond B. Huey, R.S. Woodworth, and E.B. Holt. Although these studies were not sufficient in number or practical enough in application to have an impact on classroom instruction during this period, they are historically important because they were first to call attention to rate in reading, distinctions between silent and oral reading, and individual differences in reading.

VI. Beginning Attention to Reading Disability

During the decade 1900 to 1910, considerable interest developed in regard to "congenitalalexia" or "word blindness" as the cause of retardation in reading. This writer's research revealed that these reports represented the first attempt to assign a specific cause for reading disability. The reports were made by men in the medical profession who, finding nothing wrong with the vision of children deficient in reading, pronounced the difficulty as being that of "congenital alexia." They arrived at this conclusion by reasoning from analogy using pathological cases of loss of reading ability in adults who had suffered brain injury by accident. Several experimenters tried teaching these brain-injured individuals using the alphabetic-spelling method.

The first report of congenital alexia as the cause of a child's disability in reading, which came to the attention of the writer, appeared in the *British Medical Journal* in 1896. The author was W.P. Morgan and the article was "Congenital Word Blindness." Several similar reports followed between 1900 and 1910, many of which came from France, Germany, and England. Some, however, were reported by American investigators prominent in the field, such as E.B. McCready, C.J. Thomas, Sidney Stephenson, and E. Nettleship.

The historical significance of these studies lies in the fact that they called attention to children who were not learning to read and to the possibility of doing something to help them in acquiring this skill.

CHAPTER SIX

The Period of Emphasis
on Scientific Investigation in Reading

I. Influences That Called Forth Innovations

The dramatic period beginning in 1910 ushered in the first truly great break-through in American reading instruction. Although there was no strong nationalistic aim for education or reading at this time, a new development suddenly shaped up that had startling effects in changing reading methods and materials.

This era in the history of reading was marked by the birth of the scientific movement in education. In 1909, Thorndike made the initial presentation of his handwriting scale before a meeting of the American Association for the Advancement of Science, and in 1910 it was published. Generally speaking, the publication of the Thorndike scale has been recognized as the beginning of the contemporary movement for scientifically measuring educational products. In the immediately ensuing years, scales and tests appeared rapidly: the Courtis arithmetic tests; the Hilligas Composition Scale; the Buckingham Spelling Scale; and then a reading test—the Gray Standardized Oral Reading Paragraphs, published in 1915. Other reading tests, mostly silent reading tests, followed shortly.

With the advent of instruments of measurement, it was possible for the first time to obtain scientific information about the effectiveness of reading methods and materials, and of administrative arrangements for teaching reading in the classroom. As a result, more innovations in reading instruction issued forth during this period than in all the past centuries. The initial period of emphasis on scientific investigation in reading, described in this chapter, extended from 1910 up to, but not including, 1925. This was, indeed, an eventful moment in the history of reading.

Although the development of scientific measurement was the most forceful influence in bringing about change during this period, the effects of World War I are not to be ignored. During the years the United States was involved in this war (1917–1918), it was discovered that thousands of U.S. soldiers could not read well enough to follow printed instructions used in connection with military life. Speeches of educators, newspapers, and educational periodicals published during the war and following it contained many spirited discussions lamenting this situation and vigorously urging that reading instruction should be improved.

Major innovations of this period include the change from oral to silent reading, rapid expansion of reading research, and the development of remedial reading techniques. There were other "firsts" that operated only in a very limited way during the period, but which also are worthy of mention because of later developments. These firsts were the initial use of experience charts in teaching beginning reading, the introduction of individual instruction in reading, and a growing concern about improvement of the teaching of reading. Each of these developments will be discussed in turn.

II. The Transition From Oral to Silent Reading

What Brought About the Change?

From the beginning of reading instruction, oral reading had maintained its supreme and undisputed claim over classroom methods. In marked contrast to this traditional practice, we find a period of years, approximately between 1918 and 1925, marked with an exaggerated and, in some cases, almost exclusive emphasis on silent reading procedures. What brought about this sharp reversal of practice? One factor that had a bearing on the silent reading emphasis was the ever-increasing attention directed toward meanings in all phases of education. This was a cumulative movement that continually gained in momentum as each of the great leaders—Rousseau, Pestalozzi, Herbart, and Froebel—successively added his influence to a further application of the principle. It was, however, left to one of our own educators, Francis W. Parker, to apply the principle in the most helpful way to reading instruction.

"Colonel" Parker improved on Froebel's practice in that he reduced its mechanical and imitative elements and also connected thought with motor expression. Parker stressed these points: expression helps thought, and thought is necessary for expression. Applying these ideas to language expression, he distinguished clearly between speech, silent reading, and oral reading. He considered speech and oral reading to be forms of expression, and he said that ordinary reading (silent reading) was not a form of expression but a matter of attention. Then he went on to say,

> Many of the grossest errors in teaching reading spring from confounding the two processes of attention and expression. Reading in itself is not expression any more than observation or hearing-language is expression. The custom of making oral reading the principal and almost the only means of teaching reading has led to the many errors prevalent today. (79: 93)

Dr. Edmund Huey discussed silent reading in his professional book, which was published in 1908 but widely quoted throughout the period under discussion. The following quotation gives an indication of his thinking on this subject:

Reading as a school exercise has almost always been thought of as reading aloud, in spite of the obvious fact that reading in actual life is to be mainly silent reading. The consequent attention to reading as an exercise in speaking, and it has usually been a rather bad exercise in speaking at that, has been heavily at the expense of reading as the art of thought getting and thought manipulating. (78: 359)

No doubt the pronouncements of Parker, Huey, and many other advanced thinkers concerning the need for meaningful education, called attention to the desirability of thought-getting in reading rather than considering the reading process as one primarily concerned with the pronunciation of words.

It was research, however, that revealed the most convincing evidence in regard to the superiority of silent reading over oral reading. The educational philosophers had been emphasizing meanings, and the laboratory studies of the preceding period had revealed differences between silent and oral reading. It is not surprising then that the spirit of investigation, which evolved with the new scientific movement, led several interested educators to probe further into the differences between silent and oral reading. During the years 1915 to 1918, Mead, Oberholtzer, Pintner and Gilliland, Schmidt, and Judd, all conducted investigations that indicated the superiority of silent reading over oral reading, both in speed and in comprehension. The objective evidence obtained by these investigators added substantially to the rapidly growing body of opinion in favor of silent reading.

Reading was the last of the tool subjects to yield itself to the testing movement. A few attempts were made to test vocabulary recognition, but no standardized reading test was published until 1915. One reason for this delay probably lay in the fact that oral reading procedure was the only one in general use, and oral reading proved to be an unwieldy and uneconomical product to measure by means of standardized group tests. Furthermore, the entire subject of reading was so complicated that it was difficult to analyze it into elements that seemed sufficiently significant to warrant testing. This very complication challenged the test makers, who directed their attention to this subject and succeeded eventually in making rather clear-cut analyses, in which speed and comprehension in silent reading stood out as highly important and, at the same time, testable features of the reading process.

In the Fourteenth Yearbook of the National Society for the Study of Education (1915), Courtis reported the first attempt to determine standard scores in some of the measurable elements of reading. In 1915, Starch reported a silent reading test that he had devised, and in this report we find the following analysis:

> The chief elements in reading are: (1) the comprehension of the matter read, (2) the speed of reading, and (3) the correctness of the pronunciation. The first two are the most important so far as reading strictly is concerned since we learn to read for our own individual use. For this reason such factors as intonation, expression, pauses, and the like are relatively insignificant. We use silent reading rather than oral reading in practical life. (80: 2)

Once such analyses as these had been made, we find numerous silent reading tests coming from the press: The Brown Silent Reading Test, the Kansas Silent Reading Test, Courtis's Silent Reading Tests, and Monroe's Standardized Silent Reading Test, all had appeared by 1918. Many additional tests of this nature were published in the immediately ensuing years. The wide use of these tests was a powerful factor in stressing silent reading in the classroom. A common inference is that as soon as school officials begin to test some phase of instruction, teachers begin to emphasize that phase in their teaching. This was undoubtedly the case in regard to silent reading.

Another influence back of this new emphasis is traceable to reports in the yearbooks of the National Society for the Study of Education between 1916 and 1920. In the Sixteenth Yearbook,

William S. Gray made a report on "The Relation of Silent Reading to Economy in Education." In the Eighteenth Yearbook, he made a report on "Principles of Method in Teaching Reading, as Derived from Scientific Investigations" in which he again emphasized the advantages of silent reading:

> First, rapid silent readers can be developed much earlier in the grades than is usually done at the present time. Second, silent reading exercises can be substituted to advantage for oral reading by the end of the third grade, since pupils have reached the point in their development where silent reading is a more economical and rapid process than oral reading.
>
> The results of practically every investigation of this problem [comprehension] indicate clearly the appropriateness of emphasizing the content of what is read, persistently and consistently, throughout the grades. (83: 29)

The climax came with the appearance of the Twentieth Yearbook (1921), Part II of which was devoted entirely to the report of the National Society for the Study of Education's Committee on Silent Reading. The report dealt with such topics as "Controlling Factors in the Measurement of Silent Reading," "Individual Differences in Silent Reading," "Development of Speed in Silent Reading," and "Motivated Drill Work in Silent Reading." W.W. Theisen effectively summed up the situation in regard to silent and oral reading in a report in this yearbook:

> For many years, oral reading has played a lone part in our schools, particularly in the primary grades. The growing dissatisfaction with reading progress and the evident superior merit of practice in silent reading is now resulting in a movement to introduce a larger proportion of the latter into all grades. To what extent silent reading can be profitably substituted for oral in the primary grades is a matter that should be determined by careful experimentation. In the light of the evidence we now possess, there is nothing that would justify the amount of oral reading commonly found....

The tenacity with which primary teachers have clung to oral reading is probably due to two causes. They know of no way to bring about improvement in oral reading except through oral reading, and they have not known how to conduct silent reading exercises. (93: 7, 8)

At about the time that the Twentieth Yearbook was published, textbook writers began to produce readers based on silent reading procedures; other authors prepared professional books treating some of the phases of silent reading; teachers racked their brains to think of exercises that would check children's comprehension in silent reading; and publishers began to issue quantities of seat work materials consisting of silent reading exercises in which children were to make some response in the way of drawing, construction work, true-false statements, and completion sentences. The entire school public seemed, for a time, to be obsessed with the idea of teaching silent reading of the type that would lend itself to an objective checking of comprehension and speed.

Specific Reading Aims

The specific aim of reading instruction overshadowing all others during this period was that of teaching efficient silent reading in order to enable the individual to meet the practical needs of life. Harry Grove Wheat (1923) presents this viewpoint and its supporting arguments clearly in the first chapter of his book *The Teaching of Reading*:[1]

> Society insists that reading be taught in order to meet certain definite social needs. Since society makes the necessary provisions that reading be taught, it has the right to make such a demand. Therefore instruction in reading should be so organized—should so aim—as best to meet the needs of society. (94: 6)

Wheat then asks, "What are the needs of society with respect to the teaching of reading and the outcomes of reading instruction?"

Following this question, he gives Professor S.C. Parker's answer and his chief arguments:

> (1) The social needs of former days required the teaching of expressive oral reading; (2) the social needs of the present require the teaching of effective rapid silent reading.

The Former Need for Expressive Oral Reading	The Present Need for Effective Rapid Silent Reading
1. Reading material *was* scarce.	1. Reading material *is* abundant.
2. Only a few *were* able to read.	2. Reading *is* universal; only a few *are* unable to read.
3. Communication *was* very slow.	3. Communication *is* very rapid.
4. Spoken language *was* the chief means of communication.	4. Written language *is* the chief means of communication. (93: 6)

After discussing these contrasted social needs for reading, Wheat states as his conclusion that "the aim of reading instruction which should now prevail is to develop ability in *effective rapid silent reading*."

The aims specified in the courses of study of this period also usually emphasized the thought-getting processes. The following statement from a Rhode Island Normal School course, published in 1919, is characteristic of the general expression of aims in courses of study:

> It appears at the present time that the pendulum which regulates these matters [methods of teaching reading] has swung away from the elaborate and fanciful schemes of songs, stories, games, jingles, and dramatics, which for the past few years have encumbered reading procedures and obscured reading purposes.
>
> It ought to be the aim of an efficient teacher of primary reading to assist the child to the ability to interpret a printed page with reasonable accuracy and facility. (95: 18)

155

When the aims were listed in courses of study, mastery of the mechanics of reading was almost always given first place, as, for example, in a course in phonics and reading prepared in Mitchell, South Dakota (1921):

First Grade

Aim:
   While the aim of all reading is apprehension of the thought and feeling expressed on the printed page, the realization of the aim depends upon
   1. The thoro mastery of the mechanics of reading
   2. The ability to get the thot rapidly, accurately, and comprehensively

Fifth Grade

Aim:
   a. Mastery of mechanics of reading
   b. Pupils should be able to read intelligently anything within the range of their experience
   c. Cultivation of a natural reading tone
   d. Rapid silent reading

Silent Reading Materials

Professional Books and Monographs. Nowhere else is the emphasis on silent reading more marked than in the professional books published during this period. J.A. O'Brien was the first to make a contribution of this type in 1921 with *Silent Reading, With Special Reference to Speed*, which the title indicates was concerned largely with a discussion of the various investigations concerning speed, but also gave suggestions for classroom procedures to teach silent reading.

   The year 1922 was particularly productive of books that treated different phases of silent reading. C.E. Germane and E.G. Germane published *Silent Reading; A Handbook for Teachers*, which summed up investigations having a bearing on silent reading and suggesting classroom procedures. Emma Watkins's *How to Teach Silent Reading to Beginners* was published at this time. The book was devoted almost entirely to a description of action-response silent reading exercises that Watkins had used in teaching primary pupils. Clarence R. Stone's *Silent and Oral Reading* was another product of this year. Stone recognized oral reading but placed emphasis on silent reading.

Wheat's *The Teaching of Reading* appeared in 1923. The title of the book does not indicate an emphasis on silent reading; nevertheless, this subject constitutes the main tenor of the author's discussion. In the first chapter he points out the importance of silent reading in meeting present social needs, and then says, "Skillful silent reading for meaning being the art to be developed through reading instruction, succeeding chapters will describe its nature and trace its development through the grades."

Educational periodicals contained several articles on silent reading. One of the earliest articles was by R. Pintner (1913) on "Oral and Silent Reading for Fourth Grade Pupils" (*Journal of Educational Psychology, 4,* 333–337). Another article was by A.S. Mead (1915) on "Silent Reading Versus Oral Reading With One Hundred Sixth Grade Pupils" (*Journal of Educational Psychology, 6,* 345–348). Additional articles on the subject appeared in the immediately ensuing years, and by the latter part of the period, such articles were very numerous.

As an outgrowth of the several scientific investigations in reading that took place during this period or just preceding it, we find an accumulation of literature embodying the results of these studies. Among the most prominent were monographs published by the University of Chicago: *Reading: Its Nature and Development* by Charles H. Judd; *Fundamental Reading Habits: A Study of Their Development* by Guy T. Buswell; and *Silent Reading: A Study of the Various Types* by Charles H. Judd and Guy T. Buswell. All had a profound effect on teaching methods. These reports presented objective evidence in photographic reproductions of eye movements, showing differences between the processes of silent and oral reading, and the effect on reading habits of changes in the content of and purpose for reading.

Additional professional books published during this period that dealt with topics other than silent reading were *Teaching Children to Read* by Paul Klapper (1914); and *The Psychology and Pedagogy of Reading* by Edmund Huey (1908), revised in 1912 and 1915, which continued to serve as a standard reference during this period. William A. Smith's *The Reading Process* summarized investigations, described tests, and discussed the history of reading and reading methods. It also appeared in the fruitful year of 1922. Willis F. Uhl's *The Materials of Reading* embodied a description and interpretation of investigations and standards in regard to reading materials.

Two other popular books that appeared at this time but do not fall into any of the classifications above were *How to Teach Reading* by Mary E. Pennell and Alice M. Cusack, containing practical suggestions for teaching both silent and oral reading; and *Essential Principles of Teaching Reading and Literature* by Sterling A. Leonard, the only book of the period that dealt with methods of developing literary appreciation.

Courses of Study. The emphasis on silent reading is reflected in materials published by boards of education during this period. Several important school systems prepared courses of study or bulletins specifically on silent reading. *The Maryland School Bulletin* on "Silent Reading" was an outstanding piece of work of this type. Other examples are "Silent Reading Exercises" by the Board of Education, Detroit, Michigan; "Courses of Study in Silent Reading," from Monessen, Pennsylvania; and "Silent Reading Exercises," New Castle, Pennsylvania. These and all similar publications gave practical suggestions to teachers for applying the new silent reading techniques.

The reading courses in general at this time were included in the course of study in English, which usually contained composition, grammar, spelling, and penmanship, as well as reading. The smaller school systems frequently included a brief outline of reading content and method in one general course covering all subjects in the elementary grades.

Even though the majority of reading courses took such forms as those described above, an increasing number of school systems published separate courses entirely devoted to the subject of reading. Seattle, Washington; Philadelphia; Montclair, New Jersey; and St. Cloud, Minnesota, were among the cities that produced a separate reading course during this period. The St. Cloud publication was by far the most ambitious undertaking in a course of study in reading. It was a large book with 300 pages devoted to background discussions of reading theory, scientific investigations, objectives, detailed procedures for each grade, and testing materials. This course recognized and treated the many different phases of reading instruction characterizing the period of broadened objectives, which will be discussed in the next chapter.

Teachers' Manuals. Emphasis on the new silent reading procedures was responsible for bringing teachers' manuals into general use during this period. Every author of new reading textbooks furnished generous instructions for the use of his material. Furthermore, authors of texts that had appeared during the preceding period without detailed instructions now came forth with manuals emphasizing silent reading and suggesting procedures to be used with their literary readers. The technique of teaching silent reading was so novel that authors evidently felt it incumbent upon them to furnish rather definitely prescribed instructions. For example, in The Silent Readers, Lewis and Rowland say,

> As this Manual is a *silent reading* manual, the method of presenting the work is quite different from that of the usual basic text. To

insure the correct application of the method, the teacher should read carefully the full directions for teaching a lesson before presenting the lesson. This is especially necessary for the lessons given for speed and comprehension tests. For these lessons she must master the entire plan of teaching and testing before presenting even a page of a lesson. (96: viii)

This manual, however, as well as the others, offered the teacher some leeway in respect to such features as supplemental silent reading exercises, seat work, phonetics, oral reading, and correlation of reading with other subjects.

A paper-covered booklet, one for each grade, was the most popular form in which the new manuals appeared. They varied in size but in general seemed to be a standard size of $7\frac{1}{2}$ by $5\frac{1}{4}$ inches, with 50 to 150 pages.

Some of the readers were accompanied by manuals containing both the content of the children's readers and also the instructions to the teacher. The Learn to Study Readers by Ernest Horn and Grace Shields (Ginn), and The Silent Reading Hour by Guy T. Buswell and William H. Wheeler (Wheeler Publishing) both used this form for their teachers' manuals. Emma M. Bolenius was a pioneer in setting a new standard for separate and detailed teachers' manuals for each grade. Miss Bolenius's first-grade manual for The Boys' and Girls' Readers (Houghton Mifflin) had all the appearance of a professional book, with neat gray cloth binding decorated with an attractive design, and contained 511 pages. In addition to giving instructions for procedure by lessons, it provided many helps to teachers in the way of discussion of scientific investigations, suggestions for optional and supplemental work, directions for home-made equipment, and bibliographies. Such a wealth of material in a teachers' manual was unprecedented at this time.

Supplemental Materials. Supplemental reading received a strong impetus as the new silent movement swept its way into popularity. The contrast between the former practices and those made possible by the new method is drawn clearly by Buswell:

> In the schools where oral reading prevails, it has been customary to read a very small number of readers each school year. Many schools have been limited to one reader per year. Short lessons are assigned and each pupil stands and reads orally a part of the selection which has been previously studied by every member of the class. The teacher's attention is centered upon small details of pronunciation and the whole process is barren of intellectual interest for the child.
>
> In contrast with this, in the modern school which emphasizes silent reading, a great many books are read in each grade. A typical example of the reading in a modern school is furnished by the report of a third-grade teacher in one of the elementary schools in Rockford, Illinois. This report, which covers one semester's work, shows that during the class period seven entire books were read by every member of the class of 43 children, while in addition to this, every member of the class read an average of eight books outside of class time. This means that the average number of books read both in and out of class during this semester was 15. The pupil who read the least, read eight books, while one pupil in the class read 42 books. This large amount of reading was possible only because the pupils read silently instead of orally. The value of the training in reading received in this class is greater beyond measure than that obtained in those schools which are still clinging to an oral method and are reading only a few books per grade. (99: 7)

Several of the silent readers of the period were supplemental in that they were to be used at the same time that a basal system was in use. These readers usually embodied factual materials and various types of exercises in which the child made some response to his silent reading. Many supplemental readers of a patriotic character appeared as an aftermath of the World War. There were also several new readers of the informational type, such as *Home Life Around the World* by George A. Mirick, The Twins Series by

Lucy Fitch Perkins, and *Little American History Plays for Little Americans* by Eleanor Hubbard.

The silent reading movement brought in its train a host of supplemental materials other than readers. The need for seat work had always been an urgent one with primary teachers. The use of silent reading materials was readily seized on as a solution to the problem, and publishers issued a generous supply of seat work materials in which the children were to read silently and follow directions for drawing or construction work, or were to answer true-false questions, complete sentences, mark opposites, classify words, dramatize, or make some other silent reading response.

The scientific movement was responsible for the publication of perception cards to increase eye span; flashcards containing silent reading exercises; remedial materials; and tests, both diagnostic and achievement. Flash cards for phonetics and word drill came very generally to be furnished with basal reading methods.

The New Readers. The effect of the silent reading emphasis was highly apparent in the new readers, as may be seen if we examine some of the features that distinguished these readers. The content came to consist largely of factual and informational selections that closely approximated the type of material frequently met in practical life reading. Lewis and Rowland in their fourth reader sound the new note in this way:

> In selecting the material for these books the authors have purposely avoided the established paths of literary reputation, and have selected from a wide variety of sources interesting material representative of the printed matter the child will inevitably read. (98: iv)

Buswell elaborates further on the current situation and explains the need of a new type of material:

Practically all the primary readers which are in common use at the present time (1923) are made up of fairy tales, folklore, myths, Mother Goose rhymes, and similar fanciful material. It has been assumed that such selections will stimulate the imagination of the child and also that they have literary value. There is no disposition on the part of the writer to deny that there is a certain element of truth in this assumption. On the other hand, it is becoming increasingly clear that to feed the child on an exclusive literary diet that is entirely divorced from the actual situations in the world in which he lives, will defeat one of the fundamental purposes of teaching reading. A certain amount of fanciful material may be legitimate. But at the present time the supply of "Little Red Hen" and "Gingerbread Boy" type of material, largely used in the schools, needs to be supplemented by a suitable proportion of factual material, in order that the child's thinking may be more directly related to the actual experiences which he daily encounters.

This series of readers provides selections which, with a very few exceptions, principally poems, are true to actual or possible experiences in the world in which the child lives. Many of the selections are informational in character and will stimulate conversation and thinking about the facts presented. (99: 10)

Much of this new factual material was well written and was presented in a direct and sincere style. For example, in the second reader of The Silent Reading Hour, we find this narrative:

THE PAPER BOY

Every morning Robert sat in the window to watch for the morning paper. He did not care much about the paper, but he did care about the paper boy. The paper boy was not much bigger than Robert, and his name was Joe.

Joe did not lay the paper on the doorstep. He stood off on the sidewalk and threw the paper. It went through the air in a big curve and then fell right down on the doorstep! (100: 73)

Authors, however, had depended for so long on cumulative folktales as a means of motivating the reading interest of young children, that some of them seemed afraid to trust the factual materials for this purpose and sometimes "dressed up" this type of content in the primary readers by endowing inanimate objects with life and linguistic ability, or by using fairies or other imaginative beings as a medium for transmitting the information.

Much of the content in the new readers consisted of exercises requiring children to make some reaction that would furnish a check on their comprehension. These exercises took the form of thought questions on the story, directions for drawing, construction work, or dramatization, true-false exercises, and completion sentences. A few illustrative examples of this type of content are as follows:

1. Find a blue crayon.   I am white.
2. Hold up the blue crayon.   I am good to drink.
3. Draw a blue balloon. (97: 7)   The cows give me to you.
                                      I am —. (101: 27)

MIXED SENTENCES

1. for gasoline fuel use automobiles
2. trees on grow oak apples
3. feet overshoes wet prevent
4. houses is electricity light used to (98: 104)

Some fanciful stories were included in the new readers, the purpose which, as usually explained by the author, was to provide easy, interesting text, the reading of which would contribute to the development of speed in silent reading. Such stories were usually accompanied by checks of comprehension, as illustrated:

RED RIDING HOOD [2]

Once there was a little girl. She lived with her mother. She was called Little Red Riding Hood.

Her grandmother lived on the other side of a big woods. Little Red Riding Hood often went to visit her.

1. What was the little girl's name?

2. Where did her grandmother live?

3. Did she see her grandmother often? (104: 98)

In general, the readers continued to be bound in somber gray or tan covers decorated with black designs. The pictures were usually printed in two colors, such as blue with orange, or green with brown. The shades were deeper and more vivid than in the preceding period. In primers, about the same amount of space (30 percent) was devoted to pictures as in the literary readers of the preceding period, but the upper readers showed a decrease in that only about 5 percent of the space was occupied by pictures.

Miss Bolenius's The Boys' and Girls' Readers and Lewis and Rowland's The Silent Readers were the first textbooks to employ the silent reading techniques. These were followed by several other series, notably The Progressive Road to Silent Reading by Ettinger, Shinier, et al.; The Silent Reading Hour by Buswell and Wheeler; Lippincott's Silent Reading for Beginners by Watkins; and The Learn to Study Readers by Horn and Shields.

Some of these readers were designed to constitute a complete and well-graded course in silent reading, which was to supplement a basic system; others were basic in that they were intended to constitute the foundation course in reading instruction. One of each type of reader will be described in order to present a representative sampling. William Dodge Lewis and Albert Lindsay Rowland were the first authors to produce a complete set of readers devoted to silent reading, under the title The Silent Readers (John C. Winston). The authors were well prepared for their work; both had had practical school experience and both held doctor's degrees. At the time the books appeared, Lewis was Deputy Superintendent of Public Instruction in Pennsylvania, and Rowland was Director of the State Bureau of Teacher Training of Pennsylvania.

The readers for grades four to eight appeared in 1920. Those for the lower grades were published in 1923 and 1924. Ethel Maltby Gehres collaborated with Lewis and Rowland in preparing several of the readers. The books of the original series are bound in three different colors of a neutral shade, some in tan, some in gray, and some in blue. Each cover is decorated with a border design in black. In typographical features the books are similar to the literary readers. A uniform type is used throughout each of the primary readers, but in the upper grades, a smaller type is used for the silent reading instructions than for the main text. All the books are of one standard size.

The illustrations in the readers for the primary grades are in varying shades of blue, green, and brown. The pictures in the intermediate readers are in black and white. There are no illustrations in the seventh and eighth readers. Pictures of half-page size predominate in the first reader; there are nine illustrations, however, which occupy three-fourths of a page each. An approximate 17 percent of the book is devoted to illustrations. The pictures are well drawn and artistic.

The bulk of the subject matter in this first reader is devoted to child life. In addition to this, there are a few pages given to the following subjects: nature, old tales, fairies, and health. There are two pages about the flag and one from Mother Goose.

From the literary standpoint, the content may be described as being made up of sentences related in thought but often having so little plot that they can hardly be called narratives. Owing to the emphasis on responses to check comprehension, one finds a large proportion of imperative and interrogative sentences. Dialogue is not represented in this book, but nearly all the longer stories are followed by suggestions for dramatizing the story. The dramatization was intended to furnish an indication of comprehension.

A check of the range of new words on the first 10 pages shows that the first page that a child reads contains 18 new words, page 6 contains 30 different words, the remaining 8 pages use a much smaller number, and on page 8 there are only 2 new words. The following quotation is from the first page that a child reads in the first book of The Silent Readers:

> Good-morning!
> Polly wants a cracker.
> 1. Have you heard a parrot talk?
> 2. What did the parrot say?
> 3. Do all birds talk?
> 4. What can all birds do? (97: 1)

The following quotation is typical of the dramatization checks at the end of the longer stories:

> MAKING OTHERS HAPPY
> Playing A Story
> Children in the kindergarten like to see little plays.
> They do not know the story of "The Lead Soldier."
> Let us play it for them.
> 1. Who can name the players in the story?
> 2. Who can be a good lead soldier?
> 3. If you think you can, raise your hand.
> 4. The lead soldier may choose/a rag doll/a tin horse/a woolly dog/ a paper lion. (97: 24)

As representative of the upper books in the Lewis and Rowland series, we may now examine the fourth reader. This book contains 20 full-page illustrations in black and white. This picture space constitutes approximately 9 percent of the entire 225 pages in the reader. Realistic subject matter predominates in this reader. An approximate estimate shows the following proportion of content: 57 pages of old tales, such as "The Great White Feather"; 45 pages of modern tales, such as "Tom's Trip on a Dream Cloud"; 30 pages of historical stories, such as "Leif, the Lucky"; 16 pages of information materials, such as "Artificial Silk"; 17 pages of Biblical stories about Joseph; 7 pages of poems, mostly from Stevenson; 20 pages of silent reading exercises entitled "Opposites," "Mixed Sentences," "True or False"; and the remaining pages are realistic stories, such as "The Red Rubber Ball." Much material in the nature of silent reading instructions and checks is not included in the previous analysis. Every lesson is either preceded or followed by such exercises, which taken in their entirety occupy considerable space.

The literary type is largely narrative, although the silent reading exercises and informational material constitute a considerable amount of expository content. The following excerpts illustrate some of the types of content and silent reading instructions in the fourth reader:

SIR WALTER RALEIGH

You will here learn of a man whose name is still famous although he has been dead many, many years. Read the story silently and as rapidly as you can without missing any of it, and find the answers to the following questions:

1. Why did Raleigh want to go to sea?
2. Was he well educated?
3. How did he prove he was gallant?
4. What did he have to do with America?
5. Why was he put in prison?
6. How did he die?

More than three hundred years ago when Elizabeth was queen of England, there lived a boy named Walter Raleigh. He went to school like other boys. As his home was near the sea-coast, he saw the ships going and coming and had many talks with the sailors. They told him about strange lands and people beyond the seas.

Little Walter soon made up his mind that he would some day sail away and see these things for himself. (98: 86)

ARE YOU QUICK TO UNDERSTAND?

Arrange your paper with your name, grade, etc., in the usual way. Beginning with the third, number the lines from 1 to 6.

This is an exercise to test your understanding of what you read. Perform each problem as rapidly as possible but also very carefully. You will be marked for both speed and correctness.

1. The river in front of my house is blocked with ice in winter, but in summer it flows freely by. As I look out of my window I see boys walking on the river.

If it is summer, draw a tree on the first line. If it is winter, write the word *ice* there. (98: 174)

Another widely used series of readers that should be recognized is The Lincoln Readers by Isobel Davidson and Charles J. Anderson (Laurel Book Company). The primer and eight readers of this series appeared between 1922 and 1926. According to the authors, "The selections are predominantly informational and testable and are designed as directly preparatory to the reading of such informational material as that met in history, geography, and other informational courses of the elementary school." These readers make considerable use of such silent reading checks as yes and no exercises, directions for making things, finding answers to questions, dramatizing stories, and organizing materials.

Methods of Teaching Silent Reading

The practice of reading to oneself without saying the words aloud is probably as old as is the process of reading. The new methods of teaching silent reading, however, implied activities far more directive and responsive than those generally involved in such casual silent reading, and decidedly different from those employed in the usual oral reading method. Buswell says,

Silent reading is more than noiseless reading. Silent reading is not mere non-vocal reading. It is the complex process of getting thought from the printed page and involves an entirely new pedagogy. Silent reading objectives will never be attained by oral reading methods. (101: 21)

The development of comprehension was one of the major concerns of the new silent reading methods. The procedure generally recommended was that of asking children to make certain definite responses to their reading which would require a thorough understanding of the subject matter. Courtis and Heller sounded this new note in the following statement from a 1921 report of "Experiments Developed at Detroit for Making Reading Function":

> In attempting to train children to read, schoolmen have usually made the mistake of beginning with the type of reading whose effect is most difficult to trace; namely, reading involving aesthetic appreciation. The coming of exact measurement, however, has revealed the inefficiency of past training and led to a desire for lesson material which shall both emphasize the need for comprehension of what is read and furnish the teacher a measure of the success or failure of the child to comprehend.
>
> The belief is steadily growing that a large part of children's reading in the early grades should be reading for a more direct and simple purpose than interest or appreciation; that, important as these elements are, they themselves must not be considered as the direct product of comprehension of meaning, and that all meaning comes from experience and action. (85: 153)

The method frequently used in teaching silent reading to first-grade children was that of presenting sentences that required action response. The first lesson recommended by Miss Watkins in using her silent reading method[3] is as follows:

> The children are in their usual seats. Print on the blackboard COME TO CLASS. (This is the *first step* in teaching a child to *receive an idea*—in this case, the idea of following directions.)

Pointing to the words, talk informally to the pupils. Waste no words. Say something like this: "What I have printed here (indicating) means that all of you are to rise whenever you see this and come to this place where the little chairs are. I call this place 'the class.'"

Before the children can comply with the request and COME TO CLASS, the teacher erases the request, saying nothing more. She then prints it again, still saying nothing, and looks at the class. Those pupils less timid than others will do as the words indicate. Tell the timid pupils just what it means.

When all the pupils are seated "in class," turn to the board and print GO TO YOUR SEATS. Tell the pupils that when that is printed it means: go and sit in your own seat.

The children return to their original seats. The teacher erases all words from the board. Again print COME TO CLASS. Say nothing, but look at the children. They rise, come to the class, and seat themselves. Now erase the words and re-print GO TO YOUR SEATS, and if necessary explain again. Repeat the exercise of coming to the class and returning to the seats as many times as necessary.

It is important that in the first lesson, as well as in the succeeding ones, the pupils shall obey *promptly*. You can insure this by insisting upon it. Never relax the rule. Do not give an oral command. (The writer has frequently conducted an entire recitation with not more than ten spoken words, and occasionally with none at all.) (104: 31)

A slightly different procedure was suggested in the reading course of study of St. Cloud, Minnesota (1924):

The teacher prints short action sentences (one word at first) such as

RUN

JUMP

RUN AND JUMP

These cards are used as follows: The teacher shows a card on which is printed "Run." She introduces the card by saying that it tells them to do something. If any child in the class can read it, he is permitted to do so silently and perform the action. If no one can read it, the teacher whispers it to some child, who performs the action, thus showing the other children what it says. The teacher then uses "Run" in combination with different children's names as:

Run, Jack.　　Run, Anna.　　Run, Mary.

A set of directions for drawing and construction work was another favorite technique used with beginners. It frequently took the form of seat work based on a story the children were reading. For example, if the story was about a pig and a cow, the seat work might be this:

1. Draw the pig.　　　　2. Draw the pig.
   Draw the cow.　　　　　Color the pig red.

In teaching phonetics, the usual method was to introduce the sounds of letters and combinations by oral exaggeration of similar sounds in rhymes and jingles and later have the children sound separate letters, diphthongs, and families, consisting of vowels attached to their succeeding consonant. Phonetics was usually introduced during the first 3 or 4 weeks of reading instruction, and considerable attention was given to it throughout the primary grades.

There were a few advocates of the silent reading method who went so far as to urge that no oral reading be taught. These, however, were very much in the minority. Practically all the professional books, courses of study, and textbooks emphasized silent reading, but at the same time they recognized oral reading and recommended its use, particularly in the primary grades. The general attitude was reflected by Buswell in the teachers' manual accompanying the second reader of The Silent Reading Hour:

> The recent reaction against the exclusive teaching of oral reading has caused some individuals to take the position that oral reading should no longer be taught at all. Such an extreme view is entirely unwarranted. Both oral reading and silent reading have a value, but the two processes are not at all the same. It is not the thought of the writer that silent reading should *supplant* oral reading in the

primary grades, but rather that it should in an increasing degree *supplement* oral reading. (99: 3)

The new emphasis on utilitarian reading overshadowed the development of literary appreciation in the reading methods so widely used at this time. Nevertheless, the use of silent reading for the enjoyment of literature was never entirely lost sight of. A statement from the *Maryland School Bulletin* on silent reading was typical of the attitude of some educators on this matter.

> One of the principal aims in the teaching of reading is to develop appreciation and enjoyment of what is fine in classical and current literature. The silent reading lesson should by no means always be conceived of as a training lesson. There should be frequent silent reading lessons when the main purpose is to have pupils experience the content values without specific reference to silent reading training. (105: 76)

Horn said in his introduction to Watkins's *How to Teach Silent Reading to Beginners* (104):

> It must not be thought that Miss Watkins would limit the teaching of reading to this sort of exercise. It is not intended that these exercises take the place of instruction in literary appreciation. There is also a necessity of reading, silently, a great deal of easy material such as is found in our best primers and first readers.

The appearance of tests that could be used in revealing individual weaknesses and also the large number of publications on the subject of diagnostic and remedial work combined to direct attention to individual needs. Some such procedure as that described in the *Maryland School Bulletin* was frequently used:

> As a preparation for remedial work, every teacher was asked by her supervisor to analyze carefully the errors made by her class in using the Paragraph Meaning test. To facilitate the work, a suggestive list of typical errors was furnished the teacher, who listed illustrations under each type and added other types.

The frequency of errors seemed to fall under the following heads, in the order in which they are given below:

1. Lack of comprehension due to inadequate vocabulary
2. Lack of comprehension due to inability to understand difficult sentences
3. Careless expression of pupils' answers
4. Preconceived ideas
5. Introduction of irrelevant facts and ideas
6. Overpowering suggestiveness of certain elements
7. Using words not synonymous, as if they were
8. Disregard of modifying elements
9. Failure to follow directions

This diagnosis of errors enabled the teacher to determine what factors produced the difficulties of most of the pupils in her class, and served as a basis for remedial work with certain groups of children. It also served as a basis for remedial work designed to overcome the difficulties of individual pupils. (105: 10)

Ability grouping in reading was recommended for the first time during this period. A few courses of study and teachers' manuals made recommendations similar to the following from the St. Cloud bulletin on reading:

During the early part of the first grade, the Detroit First Grade Intelligence Tests are given to all children entering school for the purpose of grouping them according to ability into a fast-moving group, an average-rate group, and a slow-moving group. The classification made on the basis of these tests is only tentative. If a teacher, after careful consideration, believes that a pupil belongs in a different group from the one in which the test placed him, she should feel free to give him a trial elsewhere. In the fast-moving group, the pupils are naturally more resourceful and self-reliant and are capable of covering a large amount of reading work. The average-rate group can, under ordinary conditions, cover the required amount of reading work with a reasonable amount of study and effort. The slow-moving group should confine their energies to the minimum essentials. The seat-work given them and the books used should be simple enough to be within their ability so that they will not be faced by failure and discouragement.

In the following grades, a similar grouping may be made on the basis of the results of the Haggerty Reading Tests, Sigma I, given at the end of each year, and the unstandardized tests sent out from the office. In seat-work assignments and class reading, provision should be made for individual differences. Each group should be stimulated to cover the maximum amount of work of which it is mentally capable.

With the introduction of factual material and silent reading exercises based on children's experiences, the possibilities of integration became much stronger than had been the case when the content consisted almost wholly of literary material. Reading, however, continued to be taught as the central subject with attempts to correlate hand work, language, and number work with the reading. All these subjects were to be subservient to the reading lessons. As Miss Bolenius said,

The correlation of first-grade activities with reading: number work, hand work, language, rhythm, etc.—all these are woven with the reading. In fact the whole day is made to revolve around the reading exercises. (106: iii)

We have seen that the emphasis on silent reading controlled, to a large extent, the methods and the materials of reading during this period. We shall now pass on to a consideration of other innovations of the period.

III. Reading Research Expands Rapidly [4]

As stated in the preceding chapter, only 34 studies in reading had been reported in the English language up until 1910. From 1910 to July 1, 1924, a total of 436 accounts of reading studies had been published by investigators in the United States. The peak year of this period in numbers of studies was 1923, during which accounts of 63 investigations were reported. This spurt in scientific investigation did not begin until standardized tests were available. It increased phenomenally, however, as soon as such tests were released. As would be expected, the majority of the first studies had to do with tests. From 1914 to 1915 two thirds of the studies conducted concerned themselves with the standardization and application of reading tests. The remaining third dealt primarily with reading time-allotments, methods of primary reading, and phonics.

As the period proceeded, broader interests were reflected in the problems chosen for investigation. The principal topics studied were: silent reading, speed, classification of pupils, phonics, methods in primary grades, appropriate materials, hygiene of reading, and uses of reading in school and adult life. A few studies, which were forerunners of investigations that were to appear in voluminous numbers in future periods, had to do with the topics of diagnosis and remedial instruction, and with correlations between reading achievement and achievement in other subject areas. Although the great majority of studies now had their settings in schools, some laboratory research continued. (See page 146 for the most important of these laboratory studies.)

The first doctoral dissertations in reading that came to the attention of this writer were conducted in 1917 at the University of Chicago: *Studies of Elementary-School Reading through Standardized Tests* by William S. Gray; *Types of Reading Ability as Exhibited through Tests and Laboratory Experiments* by C.T. Gray; and *An Experimental Study of the Psychology of Reading* by William Anton Schmidt. Between 1917 and 1924, 13 additional doctoral dissertations on reading were reported. These dissertations, like the published accounts of research, covered a wide range of topics such as reading interests, silent reading, speed, content of readers, measurement of reading ability, and sensory factors.

IV. Practice in Speed Receives Initial Attention

The laboratory studies of the preceding period called attention to differences in rates when reading silently and orally. It was not until this period, however, that rate was singled out as a special and an important reading skill that should be developed through classroom practice. Uhl, for example, said, "laboratory investigations have shown that an alertness and speed are the prime requisites of proficiency in reading" (111: 211).

The focus on the teaching of silent reading carried with it an emphasis on speed. In fact, one chief reason for teaching silent reading was because of its superiority in rate. Most investigators who reported studies on silent reading during this period included rate as one of their considerations. Even in the earliest studies of reading, attention was given to rate as a separate aspect of the reading process. The first study was a laboratory study reported by Romanes (112) in 1884 that had to do with rate of adult reading. One nonlaboratory study was reported by Abell (113) in 1894, and another by Quantz (114) in 1897. Abell tested Wellesley College girls and found that some of them read six times faster than others, and Quantz tested 50 men students at the University of Wisconsin and found that the number of words per second that they read varied from 3.5 to 8.8. Reports, however, did not begin to surface until 1915 in regard to rate standards and procedure for developing rate in the classroom. Courtis (115) presented "Standards in Rates of Reading" in 1915, Huey (78) discussed ways of improving rate in the 1915 revised edition of his professional book. As for one specific method, Gray (116) said as early as 1916, "Speed can be encouraged by limiting the amount of time given to the reading." Courses of study and teachers' manuals appearing in the latter part of the period suggested timed practice periods. The Twentieth Yearbook of the National Society for the Study of Education, Part II (85), contained an entire chapter on "The Development of Speed in Silent Reading."

The first doctoral study reported on this topic, *Some Factors in the Development of Speed in Silent Reading*, was conducted by J.A. O'Brien and completed in 1920 at the University of Illinois. A common procedure for increasing speed was one described in the *Maryland School Bulletin* on silent reading (1924):

> Have a series of lessons twenty or thirty minutes daily for a week or two. Direct the pupils to start reading the selection; have them stop at the end of two minutes, marking the end of the line they are reading when told to stop. The period should consist of alternate reading and reproduction. Reproduction should consist sometimes of free paraphrase—orally or in writing—and sometimes of answers to specific questions based on the text. Not more than one fourth of the total time should be allowed for reproduction. Emphasize the advantage of rapid rate of reading, and the fact that lip movement slows up rate.
>
> Direct the pupils as follows: "Read this selection as fast as you can. While reading do not move your lips or tongue. Do not pronounce the words to yourself, as that will cause you to read more slowly than you otherwise would. I want to see how much you can read in two (or three) minutes. But do not skip anything, as I am going to ask you to tell me about the story you have read. Try to read faster today than you did yesterday."
>
> Each pupil should keep an account of the number of lines and pages he reads each day. By knowing the average number of words per line and dividing by the total number of minutes used in reading, a pupil may get his score in number of words read per minute. If these scores are kept on individual class charts, the children will be stimulated to beat their own records and to raise their class score. (105: 67)

Flash cards of various types were also used in increasing rate. Perception cards were shown for brief intervals of time to increase eye span. Other cards containing words, phrases, and in some cases, silent reading exercises were exposed for decreasing lengths of time as a means of increasing rate of recognition.

V. Remedial Reading Extends to Public Schools

As indicated in the preceding chapter, the first reports of work with reading disability cases were made by men in the medical field who believed that congenital word blindness was the cause of these difficulties. During the period under present discussion, several psychologists concerned themselves with reading deficiency, and in the latter part of this period, personnel in the public schools joined in the new movement directed toward helping children who were having difficulty in learning to read.

Two early pioneers in this field were psychologists Augusta F. Bronner and Leta S. Hollingworth. Bronner began experimenting with deficient readers in 1910, and Hollingworth started to study reading disabilities in 1915. They and others made strong contributions in regard to the broadening of perspective relative to the causes of reading disability. As an example of this expanded viewpoint a quotation from Bronner is presented:

> Although we agree that there sometimes does exist a special defect or disability in reading, yet in our own discussions we have avoided the term word-blindness. At the present time it is questionable and much more experimentation is necessary in this field before other defects can be ruled out as possible explanations of disability for reading. In any case, there is no particular value in the term congenital word blindness. What is needed in every case is study of all mental processes, careful, thorough, and of as wide a range as possible—with thoughtful analysis of the results. (117: 88)

With the advent of standardized reading tests, school superintendents began conducting surveys in their systems to ascertain the status of their pupils in reading achievement. They were appalled to find that large numbers of children were deficient in reading. At this point in history (about 1920–1924), the public schools really became concerned about reading disability, and

179

many of them initiated some form of reading improvement for retarded readers.

The term *remedial reading* did not appear until the middle of this period. All early investigators used terms such as *inferiority in reading, reading disability*, and *reading deficiency*. The first use of the term *remedial reading* encountered by this writer was in "The Use of the Results of Reading Tests as a Basis for Planning Remedial Work" by W.L. Uhl (118: 265) in 1916. Anderson and Merton (119) used the term in an article published in 1920, and Gray (120) used it in a monograph in 1922. The term came into quite general usage during 1923 and 1924.

Two outstanding pioneers in developing diagnostic and remedial techniques during this period were William S. Gray and Arthur I. Gates. Both published articles and prepared monographs on this subject in the early 1920s. Two of the most notable monographs released by them at this time were Gray's (1922) *Remedial Cases in Reading: Their Diagnosis and Treatment* (Supplemental Educational Monograph No. 22), University of Chicago; and Gates's (1922) *The Psychology of Reading and Spelling: With Special Reference to Disability* (Contributions to Education, No. 129), Columbia University Teachers College. The first book on remedial reading was *Deficiencies in Reading Ability: Their Diagnosis and Treatment* by Clarence T. Gray (1922), who was also an early leader in this field and made many contributions to the emerging movement in remedial reading. According to the writer's researches, the first master's thesis on this subject, *Special Training and Tests for Elementary Pupils Deficient in Reading*, was presented by Katherine McLaughlin (August, 1917) at the University of Chicago. Later in the period, remedial reading increasingly became a topic both for master's theses and doctoral dissertations.

Diagnosis during this period usually involved the compilation of a case history (school, home, medical); the administration of standardized reading tests; and observation of such motor factors as eye movements, vocalization, extraneous bodily movements, and breathing. Remedial measures lagged far behind diagnostic techniques. Three different types were in use: (1) some workers in the medical profession were still using the alphabet-spelling method with children whom they termed "dyslexiacs"; (2) some psychologists were using special devices in phonics, and others were experimenting with the kinesthetic method; (3) the third and larger group of educators who were concerned with instruction for retarded readers in the classroom were using a variety of procedures to improve oral reading, silent reading, word recognition, and rate. Much emphasis was placed on methods designed to remedy such motor aspects of reading as inadequate eye movements, extraneous bodily movements, vocalization, and improper breathing. The status of methods for correcting reading deficiencies is well summarized by C.T. Gray (1922) in the following quotation:

> A survey of the literature upon remedial measures shows that the development of methods and devices for this type of work has not kept pace with the development of methods for diagnosis. Some authors are content to make general suggestions upon the problems, while others give the results of certain types of training but do not give the technique insufficient detail to be of benefit to teachers who may desire to attempt the same type of work. This probably means that a definite and refined technique was not developed for the training reported. (121: 365)

The first clinic for remedial instruction that came to the attention of the writer was established in 1921 at the University of California, Los Angeles. Grace M. Fernald who had previously been working with deficient readers was given a room in the University Training School that became The Clinic School, which later became a part of the university's psychology department. Special reading clinics at other universities had not been developed yet but became numerous from 1950 to 1965. Some public school systems, however, were laying the groundwork for later developments, which Gray reported in 1922:

> In order to provide classroom teachers with expert help, several cities have established educational clinics where detailed diagnostic studies are made and have also provided a special room where remedial instruction is given. (120: 3)

VI. Experience Charts Are Initiated

The Twentieth Yearbook of the National Society for the Study of Education, Part I (85), devoted itself to "New Materials of Instruction." In this yearbook, emphasis was on reading materials that could be developed in the classroom through the cooperative efforts of teachers and children. One chapter described charts for beginning reading based on children's experiences.

In preparing an experience chart, the teacher invited discussion of experiences that the children might have had incidentally or which the teacher might have provided for them. They then dictated sentences about this experience, which the teacher wrote on the chalkboard or on tag board. The children then read the sentences that they had composed. For many years, the first reading material provided to beginners had been a textbook or, in some cases, a commercially prepared chart. Having pupils use stories of their own composition based on firsthand experiences as beginning reading material was, indeed, a radical departure. This practice was not widely accepted until later, but progress had been made in evolving the idea.

VII. Individual Instruction Is Introduced

With the administration of the newly developed tests, a very great fundamental truth became apparent with a violent impact—

the realization that there were wide individual differences in the reading achievement of children, in the same grade, and in the same classroom. This discovery spurred school people to experiment with a variety of adjustments in classroom organization and instruction designed to cope with this newly revealed variation in the learning rate of children.

There were reports of adjustments made in classrooms that maintained the regular organization, such as ability grouping, flexible promotions, and differentiated assignments. But the pulsating new idea was that of breaking up class organization entirely to permit individual progression. This plan of organization received much attention at this time. Speeches, articles, and yearbooks dealt with the subject. In fact, the Twenty-Fourth Yearbook of the National Society for the Study of Education, Part II (86), was entirely devoted to the subject "Adapting the Schools to Individual Differences." In this yearbook, San Francisco; Los Angeles; Detroit; Winnetka, Illinois; Madison, Wisconsin, and other school systems reported results obtained by individual instruction. The states of Connecticut and Illinois reported experiments in individualizing instruction in rural schools. The various plans, on the whole, were patterned after the Winnetka (122) or the Dalton (123) ideas, in both of which individual progression in reading and other subjects was made possible by means of assignments in which the child worked at his own rate through material that increased in small increments of difficulty. The important point to note is that attention to individual differences in reading received its first great impetus during this decade of remarkable progress.

VIII. Teacher Improvement Is a Growing Concern

The day of specialization in the field of reading did not arrive during this period. There was, however, a growing concern toward better preparation of teachers and for the need of supervision. Both of these topics were frequently discussed in the literature of the period, particularly from 1918 to 1924. As interest in remedial reading increased, these concerns were occasionally directed toward special needs in the field of reading. The following quotations express these needs. In 1916, Uhl recommended,

> As a measure of economy of school pupils if not of money, unassigned teachers should be available for every superintendent's use in giving individual attention to pupils who are or will soon be in the retarded group. (118: 275)

In connection with his summary of investigations ended in June 1924, Gray (75) wrote, "There is urgent need for teachers who are trained to engage in diagnostic and remedial work more effectually."

CHAPTER SEVEN

The Period of Intensive Research and Application

In tracing the historical developments in preceding chapters, the reader has noted that American reading instruction has been characterized by periodic emphases, each of which has influenced both the methods and the content of reading instruction throughout a term of years. In considering the last two emphases, for example, between the approximate dates of 1880 and 1910, educators considered the supreme function of reading instruction to be that of developing appreciation for and permanent interest in literature. During the years immediately following, 1910–1925, the school public swung over to entirely new emphases embracing silent reading, speed, reading disability, and other innovations. Most of the changes in this latter period came about as the result of research which had issued forth during the initial period of scientific investigation. In the period to be described in this chapter and extending from about 1925 to 1935, continued and intensive applications were made of this earlier research. There also was a greatly expanded number of additional investigations conducted during this new period, and vigorous applications of this research were made.

The Twenty-Fourth Yearbook of the National Society for the Study of Education, Part I, also was influential in shaping reading instruction at this time. This yearbook advocated broader objectives for teaching reading than had heretofore been expressed. The wide acceptance of its recommendations exerted an influence of great magnitude in changing reading practice. There was, however, a division in philosophy in regard to the teaching of reading during this period. One group believed that children should be given practice on sequential skills carefully planned by an adult. The other group was convinced that learning best took place when the child was permitted to carry out his own purposes, meeting and solving attendant problems within the context of his own experiences and needs and through the medium of his own activities. This philosophy had been growing for several years and it became increasingly strong during the period under discussion. The Thirty-Third Yearbook of the National Society for the Study of Education, Part II, devoted its pages wholly to "The Activity Movement." This movement was an expression of the second type of philosophy briefly stated above. Some of the new developments initiated in the preceding period continued into this period. The experience chart came into wide use and has remained with us ever since. The Dalton and Washburne plans of individual instruction continued but with decreasing interest as indicated by articles in periodicals, yearbooks, and reports of research. Of course, some silent reading texts of the previous period continued to be used, but all the newer basal reader programs were built on a foundation of broader objectives.

The two new developments characterizing this period have already been mentioned: the application of broader objectives, and the teaching of reading in activity programs. Other notable developments were expansion and intensive application of reading research, establishment of the readiness concept, extended development in diagnosis, and first appointments of special supervisors of reading. Each development will be discussed in turn in the ensuing sections.

I. Application of Broader Objectives
in Textbook Instruction

During this period, both materials and methods used in connection with textbook teaching of reading may be characterized as expressing broader goals than heretofore had been expressed at any time in the past. In the new instruction, objectives were not strongly directed toward the development of any one or two skills or end points, but rather toward the development of several different abilities needed in the various purposes for which reading was used in well-rounded living. No one type of instruction was given an exaggerated emphasis overshadowing all others, as had been true in preceding periods.

Influences That Brought About Change

Several influences were responsible for this new viewpoint. One strong factor probably was the attitude of teachers of literature, who saw in the utilitarian emphasis a danger of losing sight of what they considered one of the most important services of reading instruction, that of developing literary appreciation. Much discussion and writing by the teachers so concerned called the attention of the school public to the temporary neglect of this phase of reading instruction. Another influence was exerted by those educators who were primarily concerned with general child development and objected to having children in the early grades spend so much time sitting in their seats carrying out prescribed silent reading exercises. These educators contended that an overabundance of this type of work tended to thwart the child's own creative impulses and to crowd out other activities that would be more valuable to him.

Undoubtedly, the various investigations in regard to the reading interests, purposes, and habits of both children and adults were more influential than any other single factor in bringing about an emphasis on a broader reading program. The decade following 1921 was fruitful in investigations of this type. These various studies and their respective influences are too extensive for adequate discussion here. The results of a few, however, will be presented as a means of indicating the general nature of the studies and of pointing out their possibilities as influences contributing to the broadened objectives movement. Gray, Parsons, and others conducted a series of investigations in which conferences were held with more than 900 adults concerning their uses of reading. Some of the more specific purposes of silent reading revealed by this study were as follows:

> To keep informed concerning current events; to secure specific information of value in making plans; to learn more about events or problems of special interest; to secure the opinions of others concerning civic, social, or industrial problems; to keep in touch with business or professional developments; to secure suggestions concerning efficient methods of doing work; to determine the important items in correspondence, messages, and instructions; to follow directions; to advance in one's field of work; to broaden one's range of information; to keep the mind stimulated with important things to think about; to develop a broad outlook on life; to secure pleasure during leisure hours; to satisfy curiosity. (81: 348)

It was found in this investigation that "fewer than 5 percent read aloud on other than very infrequent occasions." Several important purposes of oral reading, however, were mentioned. The three purposes named with the highest frequency were to inform or entertain others in private or public, to increase one's understanding and appreciation of materials read, and to entertain children or interest them in reading. In the investigation of the uses of reading in school activities, a study was made of the variety of purposes that reading serves in children's classroom work. Lists of ways in which pupils use reading in preparing assignments in content subjects were submitted by 250 teachers of fourth, fifth, and sixth grades. As reported in Gray's (1925) *Summary of Investigations Relating to Reading*, 10 uses most frequently mentioned were as follows:

1. Associating ideas read with previous experience.
2. Finding answers to thought-provoking questions.

3. Finding the author's aim or purpose.

4. Finding the most important idea of a paragraph or selection.

5. Selecting important points and supporting details.

6. Drawing valid conclusions from materials read.

7. Selecting facts which relate to a problem under consideration.

8. Judging the validity of statements.

9. Discovering problems for additional study.

10. Remembering and reproducing what is read. (75: 16)

These same teachers' lists were analyzed to find the ways in which reading is used in the different subjects, some of which are listed as follows:

LITERATURE

To get the central point

To determine the sequence of events

To remember and reproduce the plot of a story

To secure pictures from descriptions, expositions, and characterizations

To determine motives of people and to form ideals by reading of the lives of others

GEOGRAPHY

To prepare detailed, well-organized reports for class discussion

To trace causes leading to certain events

To find out the reasons, the why's, the how's

To compare statements and draw conclusions

To verify conclusions reached in class

HISTORY

To distinguish between the important and the unimportant

To distinguish between cause and effect

To compare arguments or reports in different books

To trace the development of historical events

To select facts from several sources concerning problems discussed
in class

ARITHMETIC

To determine the essential conditions of problems

To secure information necessary in understanding problems

To understand and remember definitions and rules (75: 16, 17)

Children's interests in reading had proved to be another favorite topic of investigation. Jordan, Uhl, Mackintosh, Dunn, Chamberlain, Green, Garnett, Washburne, Grant, Terman and Lima, and others had conducted studies for the purpose of obtaining data on this topic. These studies focused on different phases of reading interests, and each was directed towards its own specific purpose. The outstanding result of these investigations may be briefly summed up in the following statement:

> The most striking fact about children's preferences in reading is that they vary widely at each age and grade level. This is contrary to the view which prevailed earlier to the effect that all children in each grade are interested in and should read to a very large extent the same kinds of books. [1]

Not only did investigation show that both children and adults have a wide variety of motives and interests in reading, but it also revealed the fact that different habits are employed when reading for different purposes, as reported in Judd and Buswell's *Silent Reading: A Study of the Various Types* (82).

The cumulative effect of such data in regard to the diversity of purposes for reading, and the different abilities necessary in achieving these purposes, was probably responsible, to a large extent, for calling attention to the need of a more liberal provision of varied materials for children to read, and for the use of methods of instruction designed to develop many different reading habits and abilities. The response type of silent reading exercises, emphasized so universally during the preceding period, definitely developed the abilities needed in using reading for some of the purposes and interests listed above. It became obvious, however, that more diversified reading instruction must be provided if we would best prepare children to meet the varied reading needs of their lives, both present and future.

The culminating influence in developing the new emphasis was the Twenty-Fourth Yearbook of the National Society for the Study of Education, Part I, which was given over entirely to the subject of reading instruction. Evidently, the committee that prepared this section of the yearbook had considered carefully the various influences discussed above and others, and felt the need to advocate a broader program of reading instruction, because the book seems to be directed definitely toward this purpose. In the second chapter devoted to reading objectives, the committee formulated a set of objectives broader and more inclusive than any others that had yet appeared. This set of objectives undoubtedly has been more powerful than any single influence in shaping the reading instruction of our present period. Nearly every course of study and basal textbook in reading published after the Twenty-Fourth Yearbook set up the same objectives as those that its method and materials were designed to achieve. Frequently, these objectives were rephrased, but they always conveyed the same intent.

It is true that there was some little evidence of this broadened concept of reading instruction in a few courses of study and in at least two sets of readers that appeared just previous to the Twenty-Fourth Yearbook. The movement did not become general, however, until sufficient time had elapsed for the preparation and distribution of new courses of study and textbooks that applied the objectives set forth in the yearbook. For this reason, the initial date of this emphasis may be set as 1925. But in this case, as in all others, no specific date can be defended as the exact time at which a change of emphasis took place. Undoubtedly, many schools in the country continued for some years to emphasize the narrower program of instruction, but with the abundant supply of new materials that provided for a broader program, the situation changed rapidly.

Reading Objectives

Because the courses of study and textbooks so largely reflect the objectives of the Twenty-Fourth Yearbook, the aims stated therein are presented here as the most representative of the period. As its first broad aim, the yearbook states,

> The primary purpose of reading in school is to extend the experience of boys and girls, to stimulate their thinking powers, and to elevate their tastes. The ultimate end of instruction in reading is to enable the reader to participate intelligently in the thought life of the world and appreciatively in its recreational activities. (86: 9)

The second objective deals with the development of permanent interest in reading. This aim was an important one in the period of emphasis on reading as a cultural asset. At that time, however, the aim was limited to the development of interest in literature. A glance at the aim that follows will reveal how much more inclusive and far-reaching is the more recent aim in regard to developing interests in reading.

> A second objective of reading instruction is to develop strong motives for, and permanent interests in reading that will inspire the present and future life of the reader and provide for the wholesome use of leisure time. This includes not only permanent interests in reading in a narrow sense of the term, but in addition keen interests in life, in the world and its people, a desire to keep posted concerning current events and social problems, and the habit of reading systematically for recreation and intellectual stimulation. (86:11)

In addition to the aims of rich and varied experience and strong motives and permanent interests in reading, the yearbook also recognized the objective which, up to that time, had been abstractly and almost universally stated as, "mastery of the mechanics of reading." This inclusive and somewhat indefinite aim was now analyzed into its specific elements and expanded until it also took on the broader aspect of the other two objectives. The general statement made was this:

> A third aim of reading instruction, therefore, is to develop the attitudes, habits, and skills that are essential in the various types of reading activities in which children and adults should engage. Unfortunately, a complete classification of these attitudes, habits, and skills has never been made. A sufficient number have been distinguished, however, to enable teachers to recognize numerous teaching problems. They will be listed separately first under appropriate headings in order to emphasize their variety and specific characteristics. This outline will be followed by a discussion which shows that these habits and skills enter into various combinations to form the step or procedures appropriate to given reading situations. (86: 12)

Analysis of this aim resulted in the following list of attitudes, habits, and skills:

1. Important habits common to most reading situations
   a. recognition of sentences as units of thought and the anticipation of the sequence of ideas in different types of sentences
   b. recognition of words and groups of words
   c. recognition and interpretation of typographical devices
   d. such matters as holding the book correctly at the right distance from the eyes, securing proper light, and retaining a good sitting or standing position while reading
2. Habits of intelligent interpretation
3. Effective oral interpretation of selections to others
4. Skillful use of books, libraries, and sources of information
   (86: 12–15)

II. The New Reading Materials

Professional Books

The professional books published during this period present an interesting array of subjects. Curious as it may seem, not one of them use the term "silent reading" in its title. This did not mean that these authors were disregarding silent reading. Practically all of them recognized this phase of reading instruction and pointed out its importance, but the topic had lost its novelty and was now considered in its relation to various other aspects of reading, which were also given due attention.

The wide range of topics treated is indicated in the titles of some of the more prominent books: *Reading Objectives* by Charles J. Anderson and Isobel Davidson, *Children's Reading* by Lewis M. Terman and Margaret Lima, *The Reading Interests and Habits of Adults* by William S. Gray and Ruth Munroe, *Reading and Study* by Gerald A. Yoakam, *Reading and Word Meanings* by Edward W. Dolch, *The Improvement of Reading and New Methods in Primary Reading* by Arthur I. Gates, *Teaching the Child to Read* by Samuel W. Patterson, *Reading Activities in the Primary Grades* by Grace E. Storm and Nila B. Smith, *Applied Psychology of Reading* by F.D. Brooks, and *Reading, Its Psychology and Pedagogy* by J.A. O'Brien. The broader topics of interests, methods, and psychology of reading seem to be the most popular subjects of discussion in these professional books. All the authors, however, refer to and make much use of the various investigations in the field of reading.

Courses of Study

There was a decided increase in the publication of courses of study devoted solely to the subject of reading. Following is a sampling of cities that published courses in elementary reading, 1925 to 1930: Wausau, Wisconsin (1925); Buffalo, New York (1926); Dallas, Texas (1926); Toledo, Ohio (1927); Madison, Wisconsin

(1929); New Castle, Pennsylvania (1929); New York (1930); and Raleigh, North Carolina (1930).

Literature was recognized much more frequently as a distinct subject in courses of study. Sometimes it appears as a separate publication; and sometimes it is placed in the same book with other subjects, particularly reading or spelling. Sample titles indicative of this trend are "Course of Study in Literature" (New York, 1927), "A Tentative Course in Literature and Spelling" (Port Arthur, Texas, 1928), and "Reading and Literature" (Trenton, New Jersey, 1930).

A new and rather strong trend is seen in the separate courses devoted to different phases of reading instruction or to specific reading abilities; for instance, Seattle, Washington, published "A Tentative Course of Study in Audience Reading" (1926), "Reading Problems" (1927), "Illustrations for Using Arithmetic Problems as Silent Reading Exercises" (1928), and "Suggestions for Remedial Reading" (1929). Buffalo, New York, published a general course of study in reading and an additional course on "The Interpretation and Study of Factual Material" (1926). York, Pennsylvania, produced a course of study called "Some Important Reading Abilities" (1927). Minneapolis, Minnesota, published two separate courses, one on "Recreational Reading" (1925–1929), and one on "Work-Type Reading" (1928–1929). The State Department of Indiana had a course called "Vocabulary Development and Reading Seatwork Exercises" (1929). Denver, Colorado, had an innovation in its course of study devoted to "Arithmetic and Reading for the Slow-Learning" (1930).

There were fewer instances in which reading was incorporated in a general course for all the elementary subjects. Some new courses in reading, however, were included in an English or language course covering such subjects as reading, composition, and spelling. Portland, Oregon, for example, had a publication called "Tentative Course of Study in Reading, Spelling, and Language"

(1930). Cleveland, Ohio, included reading in a "Tentative Course of Study in English" (1927).

Teachers' Manuals

The teachers' manual at the opening of this period was rapidly approaching the status of a dignified, attractive, and informative professional book. We have noted that previous to 1925 the teachers' instructions for the use of readers generally appeared in one of two forms: either interleaved with teachers' editions of the readers or in paper-covered pamphlets. An examination of the teachers' manuals [2] of 10 prominent sets of readers published since 1925 show that only one is interleaved with the primer content, and it also appears as a separate paper-covered book. The other nine are published only in one form, as a book in separate cover from the reader content. Six are bound in cloth and three in paper. The color of the cover is usually dark blue or green. Two sets of teachers' manuals have different and vivid colors for each volume.

In the majority of cases, the instructions for the second and third grades are combined in a single book, as are those for the fourth, fifth, and sixth grades. Four of these series have separate manuals for the primer and the first reader, and six provide one manual for both the primer and the first reader. The first-grade manual, containing instructions for both primer and first reader, is usually a very sizable book: one published in 1926 has 304 pages; three published in 1927 have 254, 219, and 269 pages, respectively; one published in 1929 contains 434 pages; and one published in 1930 contains 406 pages.

Each manual has its own list of topics, its own organization, and its own way of treating the reading method. The variety in subject matter is so great that no one description would cover all their contents. Certain background subjects, however, seem to receive universal recognition: scientific investigations and theories of learning; reading objectives; preprimer methods; procedure by lessons or stages of development; word recognition and phonetics; tests; individual needs and remedial work; suggestions for varied supplemental activities, such as the use of reading in connection with class enterprises or units of work, seat work, and silent reading exercises; and lists of reference books. In general, the instructions are much less dogmatic than those in many manuals of earlier years. Frequently, the teacher is given choices as to optional procedures, and such a wide range of supplemental activities is suggested that she has considerable latitude in using her own initiative and originality.

Supplemental Materials

Supplemental books never before had been so abundant, so beautiful, or so varied in content. The quality of writing was sometimes excellent, but often, it was very poor. Perhaps the best way of summarizing the varied subject matter treated in the new supplemental materials is by giving the titles of some of the popular books. There were many realistic stories, such as *Billy Gene and His Friends* by Maude Dutton Lynch (Ginn), and *Shug, the Pup* by F.M. Reynolds (Beckley-Cardy). Several informational books, particularly in science and social science, had appeared; for example, *Science Readers* by William F. Nida and Stella H. Nida (D.C. Heath), and *Busy Carpenters* by James S. Tippett (World Book). Numerous fanciful tales were being written, such as *Timothy Crunchit, the Calico Bunny* by Martha Jane Hall (Laidlaw), *Millions of Cats* by Wanda Gag (Coward-McCann), and *The Magic Boat* by Lula E. Wright (Ginn). However, very little was being done in the way of reviving the old folktales or stories from literature that were popular in preceding periods.

A new trend is seen in the publication of sets of small books, all of the same general nature but each developing a different subject. Examples of this new type of supplemental reader were Social Science Readers (Charles Scribner's Sons, 1928), Little Folk's

Library (Newson, 1928), The Happy Hour Books (Macmillan, 1929), and Little Color Classics (McLoughlin Brothers, 1928).

The effect of the broadened objectives in reading was evident in the book lists recommended for supplemental reading in many of the current courses of study. Both the recreatory and work types of supplemental reading were recognized and provided for, even in the first grade. Evidence of this tendency is seen in the following list from a course of study in reading, spelling, and language for Portland, Oregon (1930):

FIRST GRADE
Recreatory Type

Andersen: *Fairy Tales*
Anderson: *All About the Three Bears*
Barrie: *Peter Pan*
Bryant: *Stories to Tell to Children*
Bryce: *Short Stories for Little Folks*
Carroll: *Alice in Wonderland*
Cox: *Brownies at Home*
Field: *Poems of Childhood*
Kipling: *Just So Stories*
McCullough: *Little Stories for Little People*
O'Shea: *Six Nursery Classics*
Potter: *Tale of Peter Rabbit*
Wiggin: *The Child World*
Wiley: *Rago and Goni*
Suhrie and Gee: *Story-Folk*
Winston: *Primer*
Dopp: *Bobby and Betty at Home*
Clark: *Belle Rine's Friends in Wings and Feathers*

Study Type Readers for Silent Reading
Thought Test Reader, First Grade

First Lessons in Learning to Study
Silent Reading Hour, First Reader
Lippincott: *Silent Reading for Beginners*
LaRue: *In Animal Land*
Kinscella: *Music Appreciation Readers, Book I*
Davidson and Anderson: *Lincoln Readers, Primer*
Social Science Readers, Book I
Child-Story Readers, Primer, Book I

The supplemental materials furnished with the basal series of readers ranged from none at all to lists of 20 or 25 articles. The one new piece of material that practically every basal series provided during this period was a workpad, consisting of directions and pictures for silent reading exercises that children might carry out by themselves during seat work periods. Such pads were usually provided for each of the first three grades.

Another new type of supplemental equipment was the chart card holder, used as a receptacle for sentences, phrases, and words that the teacher placed in the holder for reading exercises. Other supplemental materials were similar to those described in the preceding chapter and consisted of items such as phonetic cards, word and phrase cards for recognition games, and silent reading cards. The elaborate sets of perception cards, which followed close on the heels of the investigations of eye movements in the preceding period, were quite neglected in the new publications.

The Chief Characteristics of Readers

The data presented in this section were drawn from an analysis of 16 sets of basal readers published since 1925. Some of the popular readers published previous to that date have been revised in light of recent theories and practices in regard to the teaching of reading and are deserving of inclusion in the books listed under this period of emphasis. For the purpose of making a study of trends, however, it seemed advisable to limit the readers examined only to those that have appeared for the first time since 1925, or that have been drastically revised since that time. The series used for this study of trends were

True Story Series by Clara. B. Baker and Edna D. Baker (Bobbs-Merrill).

Newson Readers by Catherine T. Bryce and Rose L. Hardy (Newson).

The Pathway to Reading by Bessie B. Coleman, Willis L. Uhl, and James F. Hosic (Silver Burdett).

Child-Story Readers by Frank N. Freeman, Grace E. Storm, Eleanor M. Johnson, and W.C. French (Lyons & Carnahan).

The Work-Play Books by Arthur I. Gates and Miriam Blanton Huber (Macmillan).

Story and Study Readers by Mathilde C. Gecks, Charles E. Skinner, and John W. Withers (Johnson).

The Curriculum Foundation Series by William S. Gray et al. (Scott Foresman).

The Child's Own Way Series by Marjorie Hardy (Wheeler).

Horton-Carey Readers by Edith Horton and Annie Carey (D.C. Heath).

The Happy Childhood Readers by Albert C. Lisson, Evelyn V. Thonet, and Emma G. Meader (F.A. Owen).

Real Life Readers by Cora M. Martin and Patty S. Hill (Charles Scribner's Sons).

Moore-Wilson Readers by Maude Moore and Harry B. Wilson (D.C. Heath).

The Children's Own Readers by Mary E. Pennell and Alice M. Cusack (Ginn).

The Smedley and Olsen Series by Eva A. Smedley and Martha C. Olsen (Hall & McCreary).

Fact and Story Readers by Henry Suzzallo, George E. Freeland, Katherine L. Mclaughlin, and Ada M. Skinner (American Book).

The Study Readers by Alberta Walker, Ethel Summy, and Mary R. Papkman (Charles E. Merrill).

Do and Learn Readers by Margaret L. White and Alice Hanthorn (American Book).

The number of basic readers in a series by grades seemed to be on the decrease. In the preceding period of emphasis, it was customary to publish a reader for each of the eight grades, and in most cases, a primer also was included in the series. The examination of 17 new series of basal readers showed that only one provided readers for the entire eight grades and seven for the first six grades. There were eight series that covered only the first three grades; some of these authors planned to extend their series through the sixth grade, but several indicated their intention not to prepare additional readers for the intermediate grades.

The preprimer was an innovation of this period. Authors of primers have been ever distraught between their desire to provide interesting and well-written primer stories, which necessarily require a large number of new words, and the limited recognition ability of the children who are learning to read. The preprimer came into existence as a means of meeting this problem. Some of the preprimers were planned as specific preparation for a series of readers that they accompany, and others were designed for use independently of any one series.

Interesting trends were evident in regard to binding color and cover designs. In 1922, Bamberger published the results of a study in which she drew the conclusion that "the color of the cover exerts an influence. Brightness is a pleasing factor to children. Blue, red, and yellow are the favorite colors for covers" (155). This study probably had an effect upon readers published in the immediately ensuing years.

At that time, the majority of readers were bound in tan or gray covers. After Bamberger's study had had time to receive some attention, readers began to appear in blue covers. Eleven out of 16 series of basal readers published after 1925 had blue covers, and most of them are bright in shade. Several series originally published previous to this time reappeared in revised form in bright blue covers. Such an abundance of blue books, of course, changed the situation existing at the time of the study in which the children preferred blue. Evidently, some publishers sensed the disadvantage of too many blue books. Four series (The Children's Own Readers, Do and Learn Readers, Fact and Story Readers, and Real Life Readers) employed a variety of colors—red, green, blue, yellow, tan—a different color for each reader.

The mechanical make-up of readers had reached a high degree of excellence. Their most striking feature was the beautiful, bright-colored pictures that are so generously distributed throughout the pages. Primers and first readers often devoted 40 percent of their space to full- or half-page pictures, excellently drawn, truly portraying their accompanying content, and often appearing in vivid three-color combinations. There was a strong note of realism in all the pictures of the new readers. Even the characters in fanciful stories were usually portrayed as real people and real animals, without artificial dress or action. The readers for grades above first now contained more pictures. The illustrations in the new second and third readers were colored, but less brilliantly than in the primers and first readers. The pictures in the fourth, fifth, and sixth readers were generally in black and white, although some of the series have used color in the illustrations of their intermediate readers.

The placement of pictures in primers and first readers was usually across the upper part of the page. In advanced readers more variation was evident in placement, but in no case were pictures permitted to cut into the text at the side of the pages. The paper was universally dull in finish, light cream in color, and sufficiently opaque so that type or pictures did not show through from the reverse side. The type was bolder in primary books and much larger in second and third readers than in the preceding period. One frequently finds wider spacing between lines. In most primers and first readers, the sentences requiring more than one line were carefully divided between phrases, although this practice was not always followed in first readers.

The authors of readers were, in the majority of cases, women holding public school positions. These authors frequently collaborated with men or women in professional positions in universities. The authors generally held a degree, ranging from bachelor to doctor. There were exceptions, of course, to these generalizations;

for example, two men professors who were foremost reading authorities (William S. Gray and Arthur I. Gates) took leadership in developing basal reading series.

One prominent characteristic of the readers of this period was the use of standard word lists as a basis for selecting the vocabulary. Writers of textbooks took meticulous care to have the vocabulary in their primers and first readers consist almost wholly of words having the highest frequency in the vocabulary lists from publications such as Thorndike's *The Teacher's Word Book* (156), Gates's *A Reading Vocabulary for the Primary Grades* (157), and Kircher's *Analysis of the Vocabulary of Thirty-Seven Primers and First Readers* (158). All the teachers' manuals state in terms of percentages the agreement of their vocabularies with these lists.

A significant trend was seen in the reduction of primer vocabularies. In a study by E. Sleek and G.A. Selke the numbers of different words were counted in each of 12 primers in 1922 (159). Six years later (1928), M.M. Beck counted the number of new words in 12 different primers (160). The figures from these two studies [3] may be compared with the vocabulary count, made by the writer, of the new words in 7 primers published between 1928 and 1931.

1922	630,	579,	546,	436,	427,	427	Average 406
	396,	383,	377,	308,	208,	157	
1928	682,	453,	446,	436,	429,	370	Average 378
	362,	322,	319,	303,	280,	134	
1931	333,	323,	306,	207,			Average 289
	300,	277,	274				

(Primers from the following series were included in this study: Real Life Readers, The Happy Childhood Readers, Fact and Story Readers, Story and Study Readers, Smedley and Olsen Series, The Work-Play Books, and The Children's Own Readers.)

After 1928, primer vocabularies decreased in size by almost one fourth. Furthermore, several methods provided a preprimer in which many of the words in the primer vocabulary were taught previous to the use of the primer itself. Repetition was provided by nearly all authors in their primers and first readers, and in some cases, in the second and third readers. The average number of repetitions per word in readers was usually stated in teachers' manuals. Additional repetition was provided in the workpads that accompanied most of the basic primary readers. The trend toward a higher percent of repetitions in first readers is well shown in a study reported by Edward W. Dolch (161):

REPETITION OF WORDS IN FIRST READERS

Percentages of different words in five first readers (published in years stated) used with the frequencies specied. (Inflected forms combined.)

| | FIRST READERS | | | | |
| | A | B | C | D | E |
FREQUENCY	1913	1918	1921	1925	1929
1 or 2 times	43	43	33	21	18
3 to 5 times	18	20	24	25	27
6 to 10 times	13	15	14	22	22
11 or more times	26	22	29	32	33

The first two books are strikingly similar, though by different authors and publishers, and represent the practice of the earlier time when no attention was paid to word repetition. Note that in these two books 43 words out of every hundred were used only once or twice, giving little chance indeed for the children to get so familiar with their appearance as to recognize them at "half a glance." The third book in the table, published about ten years ago, shows fewer words used once or twice only, and a great number used over 10 times. The fourth book progresses in the same direction, and the fifth continues the change. A first reader now in preparation has no word in it used less than five times, and a great percentage used over ten times. This means in 10 years an enormous advance in the endeavor to give in school readers the practice that becomes automatic.

The content of readers published from 1925 to 1931 is so varied, and at the same time of so much interest, that it seems advisable to present two tables containing the data resulting from an analysis of several of these readers (see tables, pages 206 and 207). Primers and fourth readers were selected for this study as being fairly representative samplings of the series. Ten widely used primers and six fourth readers have been analyzed. Because many of the series had not included readers for the intermediate grades, the number of fourth readers in the list is necessarily limited.

It is difficult, of course, to draw any hard and fast subject matter lines in an analysis of this sort. In order to secure some check of opinion in this particular case, the author asked another investigator to make an independent analysis of the same readers. The two analyses were then checked one against the other and the results tabulated.

The most striking fact revealed by the table on primer content is the strong preponderance of realistic stories over all other types of material. Every primer in the list contains a large number of pages devoted to this kind of subject matter. A total of 84 percent of all pages is made up of realistic narratives. Silent reading exercises come next in order of frequency. Eight out of the 10 primers contain such material, but it is used rather sparingly as the total amounts only to 7 percent.

The old folktales have not entirely disappeared in modern primers; only three of the primers, however, contain such stories, and the total percentage is but 3.77. Modern fanciful tales seem to constitute a strong rival for the old tales; four of the primers contain such material, and the total percentage is about the same as that for folktales. Poetry is decidedly on the wane in primers. Only four of the new primers contain poetry, and in such small

ANALYSIS OF THE CONTENT OF PRIMERS

Primers	Realistic Narratives	Old Tales	Modern Fanciful Tales	Informational Selections	Poetry	Fables	Silent Reading Exercises
The Children's Own Readers (1929)	113		16				9
Children's Story Readers (1927)	44	15					6
The Work-Play Books (1930)	112						8
The Child's Own Way Series (1926)	120						
New Wide Awake Readers (1929)	103						2
Story and Study Readers (1928)	81		6		3		21
Smedley and Olsen Series (1926)	66	9	12		10		21
Newson Readers (1927)	69	22	11		2		14
True Story Series (1928)	135				9		8
The New Path to Reading (1929)	172						
Total number of pages	1015	46	45		24		89
Total percent of pages	83.26	3.77	3.69		1.97		7.30

ANALYSIS OF THE CONTENT OF FOURTH READERS

The figures indicate the number of pages devoted to each type of subject matter.

Fourth Readers	Realistic Narratives	Informational Selections[1]	History Stories	Civics Stories	Silent Reading and Study Exercises	Old Folktales	Modern Fanciful Tales	Myths	Fables	Poetry
Story and Study Readers	74	71	18	6	60		77	2		25
Child-Story Readers	47	88	37	46	92	25				12
Children's Own Readers	52	63	48	38	13		11	25		15
The Pathway to Reading	61	48	23	2	27	46	59		3	19
Newson Readers	72	46	39		16		108			40
Study Readers	54	92	31	3	81	15	23	8		8
Total number of pages	360	408	196	95	289	86	278	35	3	119
Total percent of pages	19.26	21.83	10.49	5.08	15.46	4.60	14.87	1.87	.16	6.37

[1] *This includes geography, nature, industry, and science.*

amounts that it is only 1.97 percent of the space in the 10 primers. Fables, which once were considered to be ideal "little stories" for primer content, have been generally abandoned.

One important generalization that may be gleaned from the table on page 207 is that the recent fourth readers represent a wide variety of subject matter. Two of the books contain nine different types of content; two contain eight types, and the other books six or seven different types. Informative material seems to be the most popular subject matter in fourth readers because it leads all others with a percentage of 21–83. In many cases this informational content is given in the form of a realistic narrative with the evident intention of conveying information. Realistic narratives written just for entertainment rank next, with a percentage of 19.26. History stories occupy 10–49 percent of the pages, and stories of civic content take up 5.08 percent of the total space. All together, these four factual types of subject matter make up 56.66 percent or more than half the total contents of these fourth readers. Silent reading exercises and directed study materials occupy 15.46 percent of total space, showing that such content has a prominent place in recent readers but does not overshadow other types of content.

In examining the fanciful materials, we find that the modern fanciful tale (14.87 percent of total pages) is used much more frequently than the old folktale (4.6 percent). Myths (1.87 percent) and fables (16 percent) are still represented, but sparingly. Three books do not contain any myths, and five contain no fables. Poetry appears more frequently than the old folktales, civics stories, myths, or fables, occupying a total of 6–37 percent of the total reader content.

Some Representative Basal Reading Series

Throughout this book, descriptions of a few representative readers have been given as an illustration of types of reading material provided for children at the time that a particular emphasis is in effect. This practice will be continued in this chapter also, but because it is necessary to devote so much space to other aspects of reading instruction, the descriptions of readers will be limited.

During this period, two "giants" in the field of reading instruction turned their great funds of knowledge to practical application in developing basal reader programs. These giants, in so far as reading goes, were Arthur I. Gates and William S. Gray, both of whom, during the immediately preceding years, had conducted research of great magnitude and produced writings in great volume concerning the teaching of reading.

The Work-Play Books. This series was produced by Arthur I. Gates and collaborators and consisted of a primer, six readers, and a workbook to go with each reader. The first four readers were prepared by Gates and Miriam Blanton Huber, and the last three by Gates and Jean Y. Ayer. The work-play idea is that of dividing the program into two parts, one being that of definite hard work in acquiring the skills, and the other being the play or enjoyment in natural reading of every kind of literature. Some "Unit Readers" were also published in connection with the series to supply "easy stepping stones."

The books are bound in bright blue and decorated with orange and black pictures on both front and back covers. This is the first set of readers to have a design on the back covers. The pictures in the primer are vivid and full of child interest, and are printed in three primary colors together with black. They are of various sizes, but most frequently they occupy a third of a page. The illustrations cover approximately 36 percent of the total pages in the book. The content of the primer is made up entirely of realistic stories representative of child experiences:

> Peter and Peggy and Baby sit
> with Mother by the fire.

The fire is warm and red.
Mother has a story
in a big book.
Mother reads the story
to the children. [4]

The third reader of the Work-Play Books is characterized by many colored pictures and content of several different varieties. There are 70 illustrations ranging from a half page to a full page in size. The remaining pictures occupy one third or one fourth of a page. The total picture space is about 18 percent of the book, which is an unusually large amount of picture space in a third reader.

An analysis of the third reader shows a preponderance of realistic narratives: 71 pages devoted to such stories; old tales occupy 53 pages; informational selections, 33 pages; silent reading exercises, 31 pages; modern fanciful tales, 27 pages; poetry, 12 pages; and fables, 3 pages. Following is an excerpt from "Wahb, the Grizzly," [4] one of the realistic stories in the early part of the third reader.

Wahb was born away up in the wildest part of the wild West.

His mother was a silvertip grizzly who lived the quiet life that all bears like. She looked after her family and only asked to be let alone.

It was July when she took her remarkable family down the mountain side, and showed them what strawberries were, and where to find them.

Hers was a remarkable family, because there were four of her cubs. It is not often a grizzly mother has more than two.

The distinctive features in method embodied in this series will be pointed out in the section on "Methods," pages 215–227.

The Scott Foresman Reading Program. In 1930, William S. Gray, a coauthor of the Elson-Gray Readers (see chapter six) and reader director of The Curriculum Foundation Series, together with several collaborators, revised the original Elson-Gray series and added a large number of new books. The series was then combined with The Curriculum Foundation Series and became known by that name and has been carried throughout the years and was in use at the time that this book was published.

The basic series embraces two preprimers, a primer, a first reader, and a reader for each of the grades two through six. Workbooks for the readers and the junior dictionary were also introduced in the early 1930s. In addition to the basic readers, there is a series of supplemental readers, The Literature and Life Series, which provide one book each for the first four grades. The most spectacular feature of the new program, however, is the provision of books in different curricular fields correlated with the basic readers. During this period, two books are developed in social studies, four in "numbers," three in health, three in art, and four in science. Additional books are planned for these series.

The Child's Own Way Series. This series by Marjorie Hardy is a set of five books: a preprimer, a primer, and a reader for each of the first three grades (Wheeler Publishing). These readers are the first to make use of a separate title for each book, as *Wag and Puff* for the primer, *Surprise Stories* for the first reader, and so on—a plan to be widely adopted in other readers of the future.

The books are bound in dark blue cloth decorated with a picture in bright yellow, combined with blue and black. The primer and first reader are profusely illustrated with many full-page, three-quarter page, and half-page pictures, all well drawn and brightly colored. The second and third readers also are well illustrated with colored pictures. Approximately 45 percent of the primer and 12 percent of the third reader is devoted to pictures that are predominantly a half page in size.

211

The content of the books is drawn largely from the social study fields and deals with such subjects as farm life, city life, travel and transportation, and industry. The stories are nearly all realistic. Those in the first and second grades are based on mostly child experiences, and those in the third grade are largely informational in nature, with a few legends included. There are no poems in any of the books except the third reader, which contains 11 poems. An example of the primer content and a selection from the third reader follows.

> Billy's father went to the farm every week.
> He went to see the farmer.
> Billy's mother went to get milk and eggs.
> Billy went to see the animals. (133: 34)

RAISING SHEEP FOR WOOL

When Christopher Columbus, who discovered this great America of ours, made his second voyage across the Atlantic Ocean, he brought a few sheep to this new continent. Other explorers, too, brought these useful animals to this country. Families coming to settle in America usually brought two or three sheep with them, for they found that they could use the sheep in many ways; they could use its wool for clothing, its flesh for food, and its hide for leather. These sheep were the beginning of the great flocks that are now found in many parts of our country. (136: 183)

The Child-Story Readers. This series provides a primer and a reader for each of the first six grades. The first four readers were prepared by Frank N. Freeman and Grace E. Storm, University of Chicago; Eleanor M. Johnson, supervisor at York, Pennsylvania; and W.C. French, Superintendent of Schools, Drumright, Oklahoma. The fourth, fifth, and sixth readers were prepared by Johnson and Freeman.

The books are bound in dark green cloth, with the covers decorated with large, attractive pictures, in red, yellow, and black for the primary grades, and in red and black for the upper grades. The illustrations are artistically drawn; in the primer they make use of several colors—red, blue, green, yellow, and brown in vivid shades. Pictures, two thirds of a page in size, predominate in the primer. Approximately 53 percent of the space in the primer is occupied by pictures. The illustrations in the readers for the intermediate grades are printed in combinations of red, brown, and black. The predominating size in the fourth reader is a quarter of a page. Approximately 5 percent of the book is devoted to illustrations. The primer contains both literary and factual material: 15 pages of old tales, 44 pages of realistic stories based on child life, and 6 pages of silent reading exercises. Following are samples from the primer and the fourth reader:

> Jack and Jane met the paper boy.
> They met the milkman.
> They met the iceman.
> They met the postman.
> They met them on the way to school. [5]

NEW PLANTS FOR OLD
You will like to read about Luther Burbank. When he was a young man he was planting vegetables for his father. He saw a queer seed ball growing on a potato plant. No one had ever seen such a seed ball. The farmers always planted the eyes of the potatoes. New potatoes grew from the eyes. These were just like the old potatoes. Burbank wondered what would grow if he planted the potato seeds. [5]

The Children's Own Readers. This series consists of preprimers, a primer, and six readers, prepared by Mary E. Pennell, formerly Assistant Superintendent of Schools, Kansas City, Missouri, and Alice M. Cusack, Director of Kindergarten and Primary Grades in the same city.

The readers are attractively bound in blue, red, yellow, green, and tan, a different color for each book. The covers are decorated with large, interesting pictures in contrasting colors. The primer is illustrated with vivid and artistic pictures full of action and interest. The colors of red, yellow, blue, green, brown, and orange are all represented in these pictures. The space occupied by illustrations approximates 30 percent of the total space in the book. The illustrations in the readers for the upper grades are well drawn and uncolored. In the fourth reader the majority of the pictures are a half page in size, although there are is full-page illustrations. Approximately 9 percent of this book is devoted to pictures.

The most distinctive feature of this series is that the content was selected as the result of an extensive investigation of children's interests and teachers' judgment, which is described in the teachers' manual for the first grade. Here is a sample of the primer content:

> Nan looked in the yard.
> She looked and looked.
> She did not find her pet.
>
> Then Nan called.
> She called, "Blackie! Blackie!
> Where are you hiding!"
>
> Blackie did not come.
> She did not come to Nan. [6]

The following excerpt from "Dangers of the Desert" is presented as a sample of the fourth reader content:

> There were seven thousand camels gathered together at the edge of the great Sahara Desert of Africa. A thousand men were getting ready for a journey.
> "I haven't seen you for a whole year," said one man to another. "Are you going with the salt caravan this year?"
> "Yes," replied the other man. "I dread the hard trip across the desert, but I want to get a supply of salt from the salt pits of Bilma. Many of our people will not buy the salt brought to Africa from other countries. They do not think it is so good as the salt at Bilma." [7]

III. Methods of Teaching Reading

Possibilities of Integration

An outstanding characteristic of the methods described in the teachers' manuals of this period was the general tendency to teach reading in connection with various activities and interests throughout the school day and not to confine it to periods devoted solely to reading instruction. This was done rather generally during the preprimer stage, to a less extent throughout the primary grades, and very slightly in the upper grades. The suggestions for reading activities not connected with the readers usually embraced the following kinds of work: making and reading charts and booklets based on the children's experiences; reading notices on a bulletin board and making "newspapers" of their own; listening to stories and poems read by the teacher; reading books on the "library table" in the room or books drawn from the school library; and making use of reading in connection with units of work.

The reader itself was in some cases organized into reading units based on topics of similar subject matter. Such an arrangement made it possible to bring about a closer relationship between reading and other activities that might be connected with these reading units.

Daily and systematic study of the basal reader, however, constituted the main feature of reading instruction, and aside from the preprimer period, the use of additional reading activities largely took the form of concentration or correlation rather than integration, in so far as general method is concerned. Perhaps it is advisable at this point to define these terms as they are here used in describing reading method. *Concentration* is used to denote that type of method in which the subject of reading is considered as the central core, and all other activities, such as those mentioned above, are organized around the reading core and made subordinate to it. The term *correlation* is used to designate the method in which reading is not thought of as the central core around which all these

215

other activities should revolve, but rather as having a correlation or equal relation to other subjects and activities. For example, if the children are reading a unit in their readers based on the Japanese, then in geography they study Japan, in arithmetic they work concrete problems about Japan, in spelling they spell words taken from their reading about Japan, and in art they draw Japanese pictures. The various subjects and activities are drawn upon equally and are related by the fact that the textbook or teacher prescribes a unit of work in which it is desired to make use of the several different subjects. In such cases, the connections between reading and other subjects and activities are often forced and unnatural.

Now to define the term *integration* as used in this description of reading method. In the fully integrated method, reading is not taught as a separate subject ending in itself, nor are the other subjects correlated with it on the basis of having the several different subjects deal with one topic at the same time. Instead, reading is used as a tool in furthering the interests and activities of children, and both reading and the other subjects are drawn upon as they are needed and as they enter naturally into the children's in-school and out-of-school activities. The teacher, of course, guides the reading activities to ensure opportunity to use reading in the various ways that will contribute to a well-rounded development of the different reading skills, but these skills are largely acquired as used in connection with activities organized around some central purpose or interest of the children. Thus reading becomes an integral part of the pupil's total experiences. The procedures advocated in teachers' manuals show that textbook writers were reaching toward integration, but thus far correlation was the principle most generally applied in basal reading methods.

Methods of Approach

The methods of approach used in teaching beginning reading had never been more varied. An analysis was made of the methods

216

of approach recommended in the manuals for the following readers series: The Child's Own Way, The Work-Play Books, The New Path to Reading, Child-Story Readers, Newson Readers, The Children's Own Readers, The Pathway to Reading, and The Child's World. The analysis revealed these procedures:

Reading charts composed by the children about their *experiences*	2 (+ 1 optional)
Reading Mother Goose rhymes, plus stories composed by the children about their *experiences*	1
Reading and performing action sentences, plus reading stories composed by the children about *pictures*	1
Reading and performing action sentences, plus reading rhymes (not Mother Goose)	1
Dramatizing the pictures and phrases and sentences concerning them	1
Telling the first book story, then dramatizing and reproducing it	1
Reading from prepared charts containing the early primer vocabulary	1

The specific activities are mentioned in these eight reading series with the frequency indicated:

Reading stories composed by the children	3
Reading and carrying out direction sentences	2
Dramatizing stories	2
Learning and reading rhymes	2
Reading from a prepared chart	1

The unit of approach advocated by the different methods also shows variation. There is no case in which such small units as letters or words are used in introducing the child to reading. A complete story; a small thought unit; and a combination of sentences, phrases, and words are the three types of introductory units most frequently employed. The following tabulation is based on the reading methods mentioned on page 216 and gives an indication of the frequency with which these different units of approach are used in recent methods.

A complete story   1

A few sentences expressing a complete unit of thought   2

A combination of sentences, phrases, and words   5

Phonics

There was an impression among some teachers that phonics was in disgrace, that this phase of reading instruction was of no value and was generally being abandoned. Although some of the textbook writers were less certain than writers of former times on this subject, nothing indicates that any of them took the extreme attitude of dispensing with phonics entirely. Every manual that appeared in connection with a basal series of readers during this period recognized phonics. Various states of confidence in the value of phonics were expressed by the authors, but they all discussed this phase of reading and outlined procedures for teaching it. Gates's "Intrinsic" method was outstandingly different. As described by Harris in *The Reading Teacher* (November, 1964), the method is as follows:

> The "intrinsic" method of teaching word analysis skills devised by Arthur I. Gates of Teachers College fitted naturally into the progressive point of view. Gates was against phonic drills in isolation and in favor of practice exercises in which children had to discriminate carefully among word forms in meaningful settings. Since Gates favored systematic, sequential instruction and was the author of a popular set of basal readers, his views on many aspects of reading instruction did not agree with those of most Progressives. On the phonics issue, however, his attack on the older methods of teaching phonics was greatly appreciated by progressive educators and his intrinsic method provided an alternative which was generally compatible with a progressive philosophy. (p. 133)

More specifically, the phonic procedure advocated in the Work-Play series may be described as one in which practice in the recognition of similarities and differences in word elements is given through comprehension exercises requiring choices from various words or phrases that look much alike. In the *Third Grade Manual*, the authors say, "The exercises are so constructed...as simultaneously, without detracting from other purposes, to test tendencies to confuse words, to attract attention to common elements in words, and to lead to habits of utilizing both context clues and word-form clues in the working out of perception, pronunciation, and meaning of words." In this way the teaching of phonics becomes an intrinsic part of silent reading exercises; hence its name "the intrinsic method." However, in The Work-Play Books, Gates tried to apply intrinsic learning to all phases of the program including the development of a strong intrinsic drive to read all kinds of materials in all sorts of situations.

The word-attack program of The Curriculum Foundation Series is geared toward teaching children to associate sound and meaning with the printed form of words already in their speaking vocabulary. Children are taught to sound out words for themselves—but "always when they have sounded out a word we want them to associate meaning with it and to check its meaning with the sentence in which they encountered it." [8]

Pennell and Cusack say,

Many authorities on the subject of reading feel that the study of phonetics, wisely taught, is justified for most children, provided it develops "independence in the recognition of words by means of word study and phonetic analysis introduced in special drill periods after the pupil has acquired a basic vocabulary through content reading." For these reasons *The Children's Own Readers* suggest that a moderate amount of phonetic training be given. [9]

The usual procedure in teaching phonics consisted of ear training and eye training in the recognition of similarities and differences of sound elements, and practice in blending these elements into various combinations. Some manuals advocated the method of using the initial blend, as *f-at*; some advocated teaching the final blend, as *fa-t*; others offered the choice of using either method, as the teacher preferred.

Several changes have manifested themselves in phonic procedures in general. Some new techniques, gleaned from various sources, will be summed up briefly. When the sound of a new element is taught, the sound is usually generalized from several known words containing that element, rather than being taught in isolation. In solving a new word, children are taught to think the sounds of separate elements rather than to say them orally before pronouncing the word as a whole. Children are frequently given training in finding out words through context clues as well as attacking them phonetically.

In general, phonics also was taught much more moderately than formerly and was subordinated to other phases of reading instruction. It was not taught to all children, but only to those who needed it. In many cases, the class was divided into groups of those who needed specific types of practice, and those who needed no phonics at all, and instruction was given accordingly. Such training came in a separate period and not as a part of the reading lesson.

There was a decided tendency to delay the teaching of phonics much longer than had previously been the case. The criterion most frequently used in determining the time to start phonics work was that of observing when the children themselves began to notice similarities and differences in words. Some authors, however, gave more definite advice in regard to the time of introducing phonics. Miss Hardy in The Child's Own Way series says, "If phonics is taught, it should not be begun before the tenth week and preferably later." Gates and Huber in their *First Grade Manual* say, "Extensive phonetic drill is not recommended for the first half year. The reason for this is that several studies have shown that extensive drill in teaching particular phonograms by conventional methods at this time does relatively little good." There were a few educators who would postpone the work in phonics for a year or a year and a half. The phonetic elements to be taught were often selected on the basis of lists resulting from scientific investigations conducted for the purpose of determining the number and frequency of phonetic elements.

Developing Different Reading Abilities

Emphasis on the broadened objectives in reading was marked by clear recognition of the different types of reading ability, and by definite provision of procedures and materials to use in developing these different abilities. Teachers' manuals were unanimous in making a distinction between work-type and recreatory reading, and in providing for the development of ability in both of these types. Thus, they extended their methods to cover the outstanding points of emphasis in each of the two preceding periods: emphasis on appreciative, leisurely reading, and emphasis on the utilitarian use of reading in the practical affairs of life. Furthermore, some authors made provision for, or at least called attention to, some of the more specific reading abilities needed in furthering both types of reading. To illustrate this tendency, we may summarize from a chart that accompanies the Scott Foresman program.

General skills in the Scott Foresman program were to be developed in connection with the Elson-Gray Basic Readers. These skills were organized broadly into the following categories: comprehension, retention, interpretation and appreciation, organization, and research. Several different activities were provided under each heading for use in developing the major skill named in the heading. Specialized skills in this program were to be developed in the Curriculum Foundation Series: understanding the meaning and use of technical vocabulary, and special meanings of common words; knowing how to read problems and how to record and report observations and experiments; and others that do not apply to general reading activities, but to a particular field of study.

In The Work-Play Books, skill development was planned in terms of two specific areas of growth, reading enjoyment and practical uses, which are illustrated as follows:

> By the provision of stories, rhymes, and other compositions, the pupil is introduced to reading as a means of securing enjoyment. His free reading is thus relieved of the difficulties which commonly made it laborious, halting, and incomplete in the beginning stages. Consequently, he is enabled to realize the maximum satisfaction in the story itself as he does when stories are read to him.
>
> Abundant materials are also included, particularly in the workbook, to encourage various interesting and important types of practical reading.... Reading, then, is not confined to story-reading, but is developed in its many important types so that a pupil can apply his skill and extend it by the opportunities provided in every classroom, street, and home. (Personal communication from Arthur I. Gates, December 8, 1964)

Following is a quotation from The Children's Own Readers:

> No complete classification of reading habits and skills has been made, but the following outline, which is in accordance with that given in the Twenty-Fourth Yearbook, gives the essential habits and skills that must be developed:
>
> 1. General habits common to most reading situations.
>
> 2. Habits of recognition in oral and silent reading.
>
> 3. Habits of intelligent interpretation.
>
> 4. Effective oral interpretation.
>
> 5. Skillful use of books, libraries, and other sources of information. [10]

Following the above quotation, the authors state the specific habits and abilities that fall under each heading. The authors' treatment of "Habits of Intelligent Interpretation" illustrates the more detailed analysis which manuals contain.

> Interpretation is a form of clear, vigorous thinking. To assure that interpretation or thinking shall take place, there must be keen interest in the material to be read and a strong motive for reading. The following attitudes and habits are involved in such thinking: (1) concentrating attention on what is being read, (2) associating meanings with symbols, (3) anticipating the sequence of ideas, (4) associating meanings, (5) bringing past experiences to bear on new material, (6) selecting important meanings or elements of meaning, (7) associating and organizing meanings, (8) evaluating meanings, and (9) retaining meanings. [10]

Authors of teachers' manuals no longer found it necessary to advance lengthy arguments concerning the advantages of silent reading over oral reading. The place of each in the reading program was generally recognized and was disposed of in a paragraph or so, which usually gave an explanation such as this one from The Pathway to Reading:

> In the primary grades, before many basal words have been learned, and when recognition of words and phrases is slow, oral reading has especial value. This value resides in the fact that at this stage of reading development the pronunciation of words does not impede the rate of reading; also, oral reading at this stage provides a simple check upon the pupil's accuracy of visual perception and enunciation. By the time the fourth grade is reached, however, the process of recognizing many basal words has been fairly well mastered and has become more rapid than the process of pronunciation. At that stage of reading, therefore, oral reading impedes the rate of reading, and silent reading must be relied upon for rapid reading. While recognizing the value of oral reading in the drill work of the primary grades, the teacher should not overlook the value of silent reading for the same grades. In general, silent study should precede oral reading. Furthermore, the prime importance of silent reading in later school and adult activities commends it to teachers as an essential process for all grades. (141: 7)

Adjustment to Individual Needs

In the preceding chapter we noted that a beginning had been made in the recommendation of ability grouping in reading, the use of diagnostic tests, and remedial work—all as a means of meeting individual differences. The number of teachers' manuals and courses of study, however, which made such recommendations prior to 1925, was exceedingly limited. Since that date, practically every publication of either type has devoted considerable space to a discussion of these topics, some of them giving an entire chapter to the subject of individual needs.

Grouping according to individual needs was the solution most frequently proposed at this time. The following quotation from the Child-Story Readers is typical:

> The first problem that confronts the third grade teacher on the opening day of school is that of ascertaining the varying abilities of her pupils and of dividing them into homogeneous groups. The pupils in any third grade should be divided into about three groups according to their reading abilities and each group should be permitted to progress as rapidly as its ability will allow. In this way the teacher's instruction can be adapted to meet the needs of the accelerated or fast group who learn with little or no difficulty; of the middle group who will proceed at a slightly slower rate than the fast group; and of the slow group who cannot proceed at the same rate as the other two groups. [11]

In both The Work-Play Books and Curriculum Foundation Basic Reading Series, flexibility in grouping was suggested and responsibility placed on the teacher to make individual adjustments. To quote Dr. Gates:

> I have always believed that if one accepts the theory that the basal reading program must be used it should be adjusted to individual needs and that each child should be encouraged to move on into wider and more advanced material as rapidly as possible. The basal program in theory should include nothing that would be inadvisable

for the superior pupil. It might include less than enough, but the assumption is that the teacher would have sense enough to supply additional materials for each child. (Personal communication, December 8, 1964)

The philosophy expressed in The Curriculum Foundation Series was as follows:

> According to generally accepted practices, children are divided into groups for reading instruction. Most teachers find that three groups serve best in the primary grades. More groups force children to sit too long unattended; they do not allow time for adequate teacher preparation or for directing the reading of each group. Fewer groups do not sufficiently recognize differences in the rate of growth.
>
> The key to the success of any grouping plan, teachers find, is to keep the groups *flexible*. By using materials from the *CF Basic Reading Series* with *all* groups, your teacher follows a consistent plan of vocabulary development and method. This makes it possible for her to shift a pupil from one group to another as his achievement level and needs vary. [12]

An advance also is seen in a more scientific attitude toward the factors to be considered in classifying children into groups for reading instruction. Formerly, intelligence was frequently used as the sole basis of selection. In this 10-year period, teachers' manuals were almost unanimous in recommending a consideration, not only of intelligence, but also of many other factors, such as reading abilities or disabilities as revealed by reading tests, special reading interests, social background, physical condition, and emotional maturity.

As evidence of this broader concept in regard to the consideration of causes in individual differences and the combined use of different bases of selection in forming ability groups, we may note a page from the manual of The Study Readers for the intermediate grades. Miss Walker and Miss Parkman give these directions for grouping pupils and for developing their abilities in reading and study:

Groups for Study

1. Students who need little or no training in study habits. They should be given the opportunity to go ahead by themselves. *The Study Readers* have some difficult material on which such a group would be stimulated to work. At the end of the *Fourth Year Book* is a project designed especially for a group of superior readers.

2. Students who are slow but accurate. Such individuals should be given speed tests frequently. They doubtless can read faster. Improvement in rate takes place very rapidly so that such a group can easily be aroused to interest through watching the sudden rise of their scores.

3. Students who are quick but inaccurate. It is not necessary to say "more slowly," but a definite check on comprehension should be emphasized. Giving a certain number of things to be done and then requiring a check-up is an effective way of making a group careful.

   Such challenges as the following put the student upon his mettle, and he soon learns to play detective in the right way.

   Find 5 reasons. (Teacher will not accept any other number.)
   You have been asked to follow 20 directions. How many did you get right? Try to improve upon that record tomorrow.
   Something has been left out in this paragraph. Find out what it is.

4. Students who are slow and inaccurate. Such a group should be given again the tools of reading. No matter what the grade, they must have eye training in grasping groups of words. Flash cards like those used in primary grades are essential. The subject matter, however, should suit the age of the children being taught. These pupils will only be discouraged if forced to compete with superior readers.

5. The normal group of readers. These are probably the majority in the grade and can be taught by following closely the lessons as presented in *The Study Readers*. (144: 28)

Attention was given to diagnosis and remediation in connection with most basal reading series. The influence of Gates's background in research and writing is apparent in a quotation from a letter from Gates to the author:

> My diagnostic program was first formulated in late 1919, and various publications including several monographs came out prior to the appearance of the more rounded account in my *Improvement of Reading* (165). All of these embodied the basic idea that the teacher should become a genuine expert in diagnosing a child's limitations and aptitudes relating to reading and that her teaching should be guided accordingly, nicely adjusted to individual differences. This I believe is basal to good instruction in reading whether with poor, average or superior readers. (Personal communication, December 8, 1964)

Although more space in teachers' manuals was devoted to suggestions for meeting the needs of homogeneous groups, practically all manuals recognized these special cases and suggested many practical exercises for use in overcoming their individual difficulties.

IV. Teaching Reading in the Activity Program

Many schools during this period were teaching reading largely as it entered into or flowed out of children's interests, problems and activities. This type of reading instruction had its origin in "The Activity Movement" that had been growing in influence during the last few years. The protagonists of this movement were actuated by a philosophy that they believed to be a combination and a culmination of the soundest principles advocated by the great educational philosophers of the past and present, especially Rousseau, Froebel, Pestalozzi, Dewey, and Kilpatrick.

John Dewey and Francis W. Parker used the activity method of teaching reading to a certain extent in their experimental schools in Chicago—the laboratory school founded by Dewey at the University of Chicago in 1896, and the Francis W. Parker School of Chicago, opened by Parker in 1901. Some elements of the reading procedure were evident also in the laboratory school founded in 1904 by J.L. Meriam at the University of Missouri. No doubt there are other schools that have used some phases of this method of teaching reading during preceding decades.

Part I of the Nineteenth Yearbook of the National Society for the Study of Education (1920) devoted 10 pages to a description of materials prepared cooperatively by teacher and children. Many schools in various parts of the country have for some time been using such materials as a method of approach to prepare children for their first book reading. It was not until about 1930, however, that several schools dared to dispense with a basal reader throughout the grades, and to organize their reading instruction entirely around the needs and activities of the children.

In the Thirty-Third Yearbook of the National Society for the Study of Education, Part II, the entire volume was devoted to a discussion of "The Activity Movement." One of the definitions of *activity curriculum* contained in this book is as follows:

> An activity curriculum is a network of experiencing. It begins with something which an individual or group has already experienced; and, through the desire of the individual or group to further interpret the experience, difficulties arise and through the effort of the individual or group to overcome these difficulties, new interests are created and new problems appear, and so on. It is a never-ending process. In brief, these individuals are experiencing and each experience leads on to further experiencing, thus forming an intricate network, which involves investigating, questioning, planning, performing, evaluating, appreciating, achieving, and enjoying. (87: 62)

The yearbook also shows the following table that indicates the constituent elements of the activity movement as revealed in an analysis of definitions, curricula, and books (see table, page 229).

The significant implication to be gleaned from this table is that any one or perhaps a combination of two of these terms could be used to characterize a classroom program representing the activity movement, and that was exactly what happened. Several different terms were employed in identifying this program, however, "activity program" appeared to have been used more frequently than any of the others.

Many difficulties stood in the way of effecting such a program. Materials caused a problem. It was difficult to obtain enough books relating to one subject, particularly books representing a sufficient number of levels of difficulty to accommodate an entire class. Furthermore, there was need for the development of new types of materials in order to make adequate provision for well-rounded development of the various reading skills.

There were also administrative difficulties that hindered the use of the method. In addition, there were some teachers who, unacquainted with the philosophy behind the method, "taught it in name only and not in the spirit." Confusion resulted under such

Features of the Activity Movement as Expressed in the Definitions of Experts in Curricula and in Books.

I. Varying Constituent Elements of the Curriculum	Definitions	Curricula	Books
1. Activities	33	19	15
2. Experiences	20	4	10
3. Units	10	13	12
4. Projects	7	2	8
5. Problems	8	3	3
6. Enterprises	2	0	5
7. Centers of interest	2	4	6
8. Central theme	1	2	3
			(87: 47)

instruction. In spite of these obstacles, however, this method of teaching reading rapidly gained a foothold throughout the country and was used in many schools, although the majority of schools continued to use basal readers.

Educational literature does not contain a complete description of this method. There are several accounts of the use of reading materials based on children's experiences and activities as a method of approaching reading. Accounts are lacking, however, of the procedure employed in schools using the activity program throughout the elementary grades. Possibly this lack of descriptive material is due partly to the fact that the method does not lend itself to any set procedure; it is bound to vary with every group of children and every teacher who uses it. To illustrate the general nature of the method, it seems desirable to present at least one concrete example drawn from a classroom in which the procedure was used effectively.

An Illustration of Reading Activities in the Third Grade

The methods and materials described in this illustration were used by Martha Greenawald, third-grade teacher and observed firsthand by the author through visitation at the Berkeley Institute of Brooklyn, New York, in 1934. It is typical of what was being done in many schools in the country at that time.

In the classroom, the teacher said that her specific aims of reading instruction varied with each child, that they were dependent upon each child's individual reading problems, but that certain general aims were constant for all individuals and all groups. She wished to make reading an adventure to her pupils, resulting in discovery and growth: discovery of the joy and satisfaction to be found in reading; intellectual growth that comes from the knowledge achieved through reading; and social growth that comes from the direct sharing of reading experiences in the classroom and from appreciating vicariously the experiences of people both in the

United States and in foreign lands. More specifically, the teacher desired to achieve the following broad aims:

1. To cultivate interest in both recreatory and informative reading materials.
2. To enrich experience through the reading of poetry and literary selections as well as historical, geographical, and biographical materials, and records of current events.

In order to equip her pupils with the tools necessary in realizing these aims, she was also attentive to the following objectives:

1. To develop an understanding and an appreciation of what the public library contains, and control of the mechanics of taking out and returning books.
2. To develop comprehension in silent reading, so that the children may become able to Interpret increasingly difficult passages, to select important facts and central ideas, to find answers to questions, to organize their findings into summaries, to raise intelligent questions on reading content, and to follow directions.
3. To develop such fluency in oral reading as will enable the children to read intelligently and entertainingly the selections needed in the group activities.
4. To give control over the mechanics of reading: speed; accurate recognition; wide eye span and rhythmical eye movements; and the skillful use of the various features of books, such as page numbers, table of contents, indexes, and footnotes.

In discussing method, the teacher classified her reading activities under three main headings: (1) reading for pleasure, (2) reading to further group and individual interests, and (3) reading for practice and remedial purposes. In the phase of the work concerned with reading for pleasure, each child selected a book he wished to read, sometimes with the help and suggestion of the teacher. He then proceeded to read this book silently during odd times at school and at home. If he encountered words that he could not find out for himself, he asked for help from the teacher, from other children, or his parents. No check was required that might detract from the child's enjoyment of this type of reading. Once a week, however, a period called "Story Hour" was devoted to a discussion of the stories read. At this time, the children shared with one another the most interesting parts of the stories they had read since the last meeting. Some children read snatches from their story to others; some told parts of the story; or if two or three were reading the same book, they sometimes dramatized an episode for the enjoyment of the group. At the end of each Story Hour, the child who gave the most interesting report and showed that he had read his book well was chosen to act as chairman at the next meeting. It was the duty of this chairman to find out who was ready to report, to arrange the program, and to preside at the meeting for which he was appointed.

The type of reading activities involved in furthering group interest is evident in the following description of a unit of work on Indians. Early in the fall, the teacher and the children discussed plans for the things they wished to do during the year. A boy who had spent the summer in the West told about some Indians he had seen, and said that he wished they could find out more about Indians during the year. The third-grade class of the preceding year had also studied Indians. The combined influences caused these children to agree unanimously on the Indian interest. The next step was to list the particular information they wished to find. Their questions were printed on a chart and hung up in the classroom, to be checked off one by one as the answers were found. Here are some of the questions:

> What do Indians look like?
> What kind of houses did they have?

What kind of food did they eat?
What kind of tools did they use?
How did they take care of their babies?
Why did they fight so many wars?
Why don't Indians have beards?
Are there any real Indians living today? Where?

A visit was paid to a museum to see Indian utensils, tools, weapons, and art work. Each child jotted down in a notebook sketches and notes on things he had seen and further questions he wished to ask. Following the visit, several books on Indian life were collected from the school, home, and city libraries. Among these books were *How the Indians Lived* by Dearborn, *Indian Folk Tales* by Nixon-Roulet, *The Indian Twins* by Perkins, *The Little Indian Weaver* by Brandeis, *Indian Tales for Little Folks* by W. S. Phillips, *The Runaway Papoose* by Moon, *Loldmi, the Little Cliff-Dweller* by Bayliss, and *Red Feather* by Morcomb.

The books were read with avidity for the purpose of finding answers to the questions the class had proposed, and also to find new questions that would be interesting to follow up. Some reading was done silently during study or reading periods, each child reading along whatever lines of inquiry he chose to pursue; and some reading was done in general class work, when all the children read and discussed the same content. The latter procedure was used especially with books in which the vocabulary was difficult for third-grade pupils.

As the children became more and more interested in Indians, various other activities were suggested, all requiring their due proportion of reading. One activity consisted of preparing a large Indian picture that covered almost entirely one of the side walls of the room. As the picture finally evolved, it represented the various occupations and customs of one tribe of Indian people. There were tepees; there was a stream with a canoe and with wild rice growing on its banks; there was an Indian woman weaving a rug, a woman cooking with stones, a man hoeing in the garden with a big shell, and a buffalo hunt was shown in the distance. It required wide reading to discover what phases of Indian life would be suitable for illustration, and also to find descriptions in books so vivid and interesting as to constitute the basis for a good picture.

An Indian book was made by each member of the class. This entailed the reading of literary materials for the purpose of getting ideas that would help in writing Indian stories and poems, as well as informative materials from which facts were obtained for use in writing accounts of different phases of Indian life. Occasionally, a child found a bit of literature that appealed to him so much that he wished to copy it in his book. Each composition was illustrated with crayons, and the cover of the book was generally decorated with an attractive Indian design. The books bore such titles as "My Indian Book," "My Book of Indian Stories," and "Stories About Indians." The children eagerly read each other's books while they were making the books and after they were completed.

A sample of the stories and informative paragraphs written for the Indian book is given below:

HOW TWO CHILDREN WERE SAVED
BY THE INDIANS

Once two children, Mary and Joseph, were left in their house alone. Their house was the only one in that place. Their mother and father were at a fair. Now it happened that a tribe of Indians were coming through that part of the country and seeing the house they thought they would get something. They thought nobody was home. They had heard about the fair, too. Just as they were looking around in the kitchen the children made a noise. They were playing circus, when all at once they saw the Indian men. They knew that the Indians were from a strange tribe. They quickly went out the back door. Now there was a friendly tribe of Indians near the house. The children went to the friendly camp and told them about the other Indian tribe coming in their house. The friendly tribe got their weapons and started to go the house. Mary and Joseph stayed at the camp. After the Indians came back the children went to their house again. Their home was saved because the friendly Indians had gone to help Mary and Joseph.

A PEACE PIPE
You know that Indians fight a lot. When the fight is over, to show that they will be friends they use a big peace pipe which is made of clay and feathers of eagles. The two chiefs and two men smoke it. And that shows that they will be friends.

After reading poetry about the Indians, the children became imbued with so much poetic spirit and inspiration that they created bits of verse themselves. Another group interest led to the making of a class poetry book. This interest was narrower in scope than the Indian unit but lasted longer. It was sustained throughout the year and stimulated much reading of poetry in books, as well as the reading of one another's writings. A few examples of these children's poems are noted:

THE FLOCK OF WILD GEESE
Like painted arrows in the sky,
See the flocks of wild geese going by,
Flying north to their nest
Where their young ones soon will rest;
Like painted arrows in the sky
Are the wild geese on high.

THE SHIP
Once a ship with sails of white
Went skimming over the sea.
The sea was calm, the wind was light,
As light as light could be.

THE DREAM MAN
The Dream Man
Every night
Comes through the street

With a little light
And opens the door.
He lays some dreams
Upon the floor.
Then as light dawns
He yawns
And takes the sand
Back to fairyland.

TIDES

The tides come in, the tides go out,
They don't know what they're playing about.
The tides go out, the tides come in,
They lap upon the shore.
They don't know what they're playing for.

Whales constituted the subject of another group interest that proved rich in reading possibilities. A visit to a museum resulted in a discussion of deep-sea life, which finally focused on whales. The children read widely to obtain more information about whales. This interest not only carried them to books in their homes and in the city library, but it also extended to magazines and newspapers. Many interesting clippings and pictures were brought to the classroom. One particularly stimulating clipping described a journey around Antarctica for the purpose of taking a census of the whales in that region. During this journey, it was discovered that two or three small islands represented on the map did not exist. The article was accompanied by a map showing the route of the journey and the islands in question. The article led not only to increased interest in following up additional news items on this topic, but also to interest in map making and geographical information.

The children also were encouraged and helped in reading along the lines of their individual interests. One child became interested in astronomy as a result of things her father had told her about the stars; another child had read a book about silk and cotton and wished to know more about these subjects; another made a book of "Things I Have Found Out" and wished to read anything that would provide new facts to put in her book. The teacher helped each one to get additional reading material pertaining to his particular interest. When a child had read the books suggested and came to her to ask for new material, the teacher discussed with him the reference he had just read, for the double purpose of checking his comprehension of the content, and determining whether his interest was growing or standing still.

With this third-grade class, no one reader was used for consecutive practice. The teacher used different books as the interests and needs of her pupils varied, but there was no regular reading from basal readers as a class exercise. During the intervals of several weeks while children were working on a group interest, such as Indian life, no periods at all were devoted to reading with the class as a whole.

Readers were not excluded from the books available, but when readers were used for general class activities, the work might take any one of several forms. The children might select an interesting story, read it to the class, and discuss it, asking and answering their own questions. They might read orally a fairy tale or myth that they had previously read silently and enjoyed so much that they wished to read it aloud as a group activity. They might dramatize a story they had found in a reader and would like to act out; they might read aloud, discuss, and compare the poems found in readers on some topic of interest. They might be given an informal speed test on a section of the reader to see how fast they could read; they might be given an informal comprehension test to see how well they could answer questions, check true-false statements, and fill in completion exercises.

Some reading workpads were available, but generally the children were not required to spend a definite period each day with a workpad. Each child might pick up a workpad and use it as his time and interest dictated.

This general description should make clear the chief characteristics of this particular reading program: it was varied, it was broad enough to cover many different types of reading ability, no set procedure was followed, and any use that was made of readers was incidental and subordinated to the other reading activities described in this report. More definitely prescribed procedures were used as remedial measures with children who were not making satisfactory reading progress. These children were provided with easy materials and were given progressive practice in reading with the teacher's help. In the first few weeks of the term, all poor readers were placed in one group for special practice during a daily reading period. Later, some children were able to dispense with this extra help entirely, and the others were divided into smaller groups made up of children who needed a special type of assistance such as with phonics, eye-movement practice, comprehension exercises, or speed drills. Three periods a week were then devoted to this kind of work, and an extra after-school period was frequently used for this purpose.

The reading activities described in this illustration of a reading program are representative of the type of instruction directed largely by children's purposes, needs and activities, rather than by a detailed, predetermined, and fixed procedure. This method of teaching reading met a response on the part of many progressive teachers and continued to gain footholds in the public schools throughout the period now under discussion.

V. Expansion and Intensive Application of Reading Research [13]

This period was remarkable in productivity of reading research, both in quantity and scope. From July 1, 1924, to June

30, 1935, a total of 654 published studies were reported, which included problems related to an unusually wide variety of topics. The quality of the research showed a marked improvement. The topics were more basic and more sharply restricted, experimental techniques were improved, and interpretation became more discriminating. There still was much to be desired, however, in the way of improved techniques, information, and concerns, which might lead to still better research.

Those topics occurring with the highest frequency throughout the period were reading interests, reading disability, and readiness for beginning reading. Other topics of high interest were: vocabulary load in reading materials, evaluation of reading tests and scales, factors involved in reading achievement, and phonics. Investigations in the hygiene of reading continued throughout the period, with reports of from six to eight studies per year. During the early part of the period, many studies reported on the subject of silent reading, but by the latter part, investigators showed little interest in this subject. Studies concerned with reversals and dominance seem to have reached their respective peaks during this period, then receded. Word blindness was rarely mentioned. Individual instruction in reading seemed no longer to be a favored topic of investigation. Eye-movement studies were greatly limited in number during the latter part of the period.

On the other hand, there were topics that began with very modest mention but increased in substantial numbers as the period progressed. Among the most conspicuous of these was that of reading in different curriculum areas. The number of studies on this topic rose steadily throughout this period. Interest in high school, college, and adult reading increased during the period. More studies were reported on college reading than on either high school or adult reading. Studies in speed occurred in larger numbers than previously, but the output was still modest.

Thirty-five doctoral dissertations came to the attention of the writer as having been completed during this period. These investigations followed the same general trends in topics as did the published reports discussed above. Studies in the area of reading disabilities led in number. Reading readiness and phonics were favored choices, and studies of reading achievement were next in order. There were several academic studies at high school and college levels, and, as was the case in published research, the studies concerned with college reading outnumbered those conducted with high school students.

VI. Extended Developments in Remedial Reading

The diagnosis and remediation of children with reading disabilities underwent major development through these years. As indicated in the preceding section of this chapter, remedial reading was the chief subject of study during this period. In his summary of studies having to do with deficient readers, Miles Tinker reported that 180 studies had been conducted up to that time (*The Elementary School Journal*, April 1934).

The causes of reading disability most widely discussed during this period were inadequate mental ability, heredity, conditions related to cerebral balance, abnormal emotional tendencies, visual and auditory deficiencies, and faulty reading habits. Although the word-blindness theory diminished in acceptance, a new theory attracted a great deal of attention—the theory of cerebral dominance advocated by Samuel T. Orton, a physician. According to this theory, Orton associated causes of reading deficiency with left or mixed laterality—handedness, eyedness, and footedness. Orton (166) also added a new word to the remedial reading vocabulary—*strephosymbolia*, meaning twisted symbols.

A remedial technique that received some attention during this period was the kinesthetic method introduced by Grace M.

Fernald. As mentioned in chapter six, Fernald was doing her initial experimentation with this method at that time. She continued to experiment during the years of 1925 to 1935. Interest in her method grew as a result of information dispersed in periodical literature and through personal visitation to her laboratory. Some clinical psychologists began using the method; however, wide use of the method was not made until the following period. The chief characteristic of the kinesthetic method was that the child traced a word that had been written for him, using one or two fingers. As he traced, he said the word in parts, which continued until the child could reproduce the word without looking at the copy. He then used it in writing a label or story.

The terms *reading disability* and *reading deficiency* continued to be used, especially in psychological studies. *Remedial reading*, however, came into more general use in connection with reading improvement in schools. *Clinical work* and *clinics* were mentioned occasionally in the literature of this period. The clinics mentioned, however, appear to have been psychological clinics for diagnosis only and not for remedial instruction, although there were probably some exceptions. Early in 1935 Gray wrote,

> Because the needs of many poor readers cannot be determined readily through classroom diagnosis, institutions and school systems in increasing numbers are establishing educational clinics. These clinics are rendering very valuable service as shown by the work of Baker and Leland in Detroit, Betts in Shaker Heights, Ohio, and Witty at Northwestern University. (167: 410)

VII. The Reading Readiness Concept Gains Recognition

The reading readiness concept had been evolving for nearly two centuries preceding 1925. During this long period of evolution, the protagonists of child study had been intuitively groping toward the convictions that eventually moved the American school public to accept and apply the idea. This did not take place, however, until the period under consideration. As a matter of background, the reader may be interested in some brief information concerning the unfolding events that led up to this acceptance.

Rousseau (168) etched faint outlines of the readiness concept in his plan for teaching, *Emile*, published in 1762. According to this plan, he would reject the formal teaching of the schools and educate Emile according to nature. Throughout his discussion, one catches glimpses of crude beginnings of the readiness concept. Pestalozzi scrawled bolder and more complete outlines of the readiness concept into educational thinking. For example, in *How Gertrude Teaches Her Children* (169), Pestalozzi said,

> Not till after the foundation of human knowledge has been fairly laid and secure would I begin the dull, abstract work of studying from books.

Froebel (170) and Herbart (171) each contributed additional ideas that strengthened the outline of the readiness concept and that straightened out some of the asymmetrical features in the contour of its design.

Then, finally, in the midst of our educational lethargy, there arose our own great philosopher, John Dewey. It was during the first quarter of the 20th century that Dewey began to publish his important books (172, 173), and that the significance of his teachings had its initial effect. In so far as readiness implications are concerned, Dewey crystallized this concept and stated it repeatedly in such vigorous terms that educators could not fail to feel the impact of his convictions. Dewey even went so far as to recommend that children should not be taught to read until they were eight years old.

Thus it was that the concept of reading readiness had been evolving and growing in momentum for many years. It finally received initial recognition in American school practice early in the period under discussion. The medium that facilitated this recognition was the Twenty-Fourth Yearbook of the National Society for the Study of Education (86) published in 1925. The authors of Part I of this yearbook recognized the "preparatory period" as one period of growth in total reading development, and devoted an entire chapter to this period, including in their discussion suggested procedures to use in preparing children for reading. This book was widely distributed, and it undoubtedly exerted a very strong influence in initiating the practice of providing preparatory work preceding first-grade reading.

In 1926, the International Kindergarten Union in cooperation with the United States Bureau of Education conducted an investigation on *Pupils' Readiness for Reading Instruction Upon Entrance to First Grade* (174). This was a questionnaire study in which teachers in all parts of the country were asked to give their opinions in regard to their pupils' readiness for first-grade reading. This study brought reading readiness problems sharply to the attention of teachers in widespread areas. Its published results strongly focused attention on needs at the initial stage of reading, and probably served as a vigorous influence in bringing about immediate action.

It was in 1927 that Reed's investigation (175) revealed startling data to the effect that one in every six children failed at the end of the first semester in first grade, and that one in every eight failed at the end of the second semester in first grade.

By this time educators everywhere began to awaken to the needs for attention to readiness at the beginning level. Some administrators and teachers in various parts of the country initiated experimentation in their attempts to meet these needs. The fire once kindled soon became a conflagration that finally enveloped the vast majority of public schools in the country. The period of conquest for the application of the readiness concept at the beginning reading stage was comparatively short, historically speaking. This crusade seems to have begun early in the second quarter of the century, to have reached its zenith in the years 1938 to 1940.

An examination of Gray's summaries of investigations covering published studies in the field of reading reveals interesting trends. In his first summary that appeared in 1925 (75), no mention was made of any readiness investigations, nor was any mention made of such studies in the summaries reported in 1926 and 1927 (107). In the summary published in 1928, however, three studies on initial reading readiness were reported. From that time on, the number of such studies gradually increased, reaching its climax in the next period to be discussed. The first doctoral dissertation on reading readiness was reported in 1927 (175).

The first articles on reading readiness were published in *Childhood Education*, January 1927 (176). Two articles on the topic that included the term "reading readiness" appeared in this issue, and additional articles appeared later. Thus it was that the reading readiness concept at last gained recognition in American schools.

VIII. Interest Continues in Supervision and in Teacher Preparation

The first supervisors in the public schools were those who had charge of special fields: music, drawing, physical education, manual training, domestic science, and handwriting. The employment of such supervisors had been growing rapidly since 1880. Statistics, for example, in regard to the percentage of city school systems that had handwriting supervisors at various dates is as follows: 14 percent in 1885, 22 percent in 1908, and 65 percent in 1923.

During the years 1915–1925, there was considerable discussion concerning the supervision of the basic subjects in the elementary curriculum. Although much of this attention was directed toward the need for principals to supervise instruction, some supervisors having general supervision of elementary school subjects were appointed.

In 1920 H.W. Nutt's *Supervision of Instruction* appeared, and in 1922, William H. Burton's *Supervision and the Improvement of Instruction* was published. Although these books had to do with supervision in general and were published during the preceding period, two new books appeared that dealt specifically with the supervision of reading: *The Teaching and Supervision of Reading* (177) by Arthur S. Gist and William A. King, published in 1927; and *Supervising and Teaching Reading* (178) by Julia M. Harris, H.L. Donovan, and Thomas Alexander, published in 1927. The book by Gist and King was directed largely toward the responsibility of principals. The authors said,

> A large element of success in the teaching of reading will be attained through adequate and efficient supervision, much of which will be the responsibility of the building principal. (177: 7)

Harris et al. directed their publication to supervisors and teachers as indicated in this quotation from their book:

> Despite the vast amount of scientific investigation of the teaching of reading, there is no field in which teachers and supervisors are in greater need of help than this one. (178: 1)

The practice of appointing general elementary supervisors grew so rapidly that by 1928 the Department of Supervisors and Directors of Instruction had formed in the National Education Association. The organization's first yearbook appeared in 1928 and, appropriately, the first chapter dealt with "The Rise of Supervision."

In 1930, Gist wrote that there were general supervisors found in cities of more than 25,000 in population and that, "The number of general supervisors seems to be increasing." By 1930, however, in addition to the rising trend to have general supervisors,

Detroit and a few other large cities had taken another step. They had replaced their general supervisors with special supervisors in the basic school subjects, one each for arithmetic, language, spelling, and reading. It was at this point that the special supervisor of reading entered the scene in American schools.

As concerns for better teacher preparation deepened, offerings in colleges increased encouragingly and more teachers attended college. Walton (179) found that although 132 graduate courses in education were offered in 12 universities in 1900, the number had multiplied to 1,636 in 1930. An increase of 500 percent in summer school attendance took place between 1900 and 1930. Along with the development of interest in higher standards for teacher preparation in general and more offerings in colleges, special courses in the teaching of reading were introduced. Gist and King said,

> But a few years ago...few schools of education had special courses in reading, and when they were introduced they often were offered first as special summer-session courses. Now comprehensive and varied courses on instruction in reading are common in all progressive teacher training institutions. (177: 7)

CHAPTER EIGHT

The Period of International Conflict

Events resulting from progress in science overshadowed all other indications of progress during the period 1935 to 1950. The "birthday of the atomic age," was officially set as December 2, 1942, when Dr. Enrico Fermi turned on the first successful nuclear energy machine in Chicago. On August 6, 1945, the first atomic bomb destroyed Hiroshima, Japan. On the face of things, this terrifying scientific discovery, with its possibilities for good and evil, reduced to comparative insignificance the scientific achievements in reading. Yet, could this discovery have been possible without reading? Can we cope adequately with its future destructive and beneficial effects, as the case may be, without more efficient reading skill and a wider reading citizenry?

The atomic age and reading immediately become interactive, but it was not realized at the time. We were too close to this earth-shaking event to sense its import for reading instruction. The full impact did not become apparent until the period to be discussed in the next chapter. However, because of its grave future significance, the initial release of nuclear energy is mentioned at this point. Although the explosion of the atomic bomb had a delayed effect on reading, international problems and World War II had immediate effects. A brief review of events that brought about these changes will be presented.

During the years following World War I, the United States and other nations had lived through a period of peace. In the early 1930s, however, increasing dissatisfaction was heard concerning treaties and pacts, and in 1933 Hitler began to reveal his aggressive tendencies and continued to do so in the immediate years ahead. So the earliest years of the period 1935 to 1950 were marked with international strife and stress. This unrest continued and eventuated in the beginning of World War II in 1939. The United States soon became involved indirectly, but it did not declare war until the Japanese attack on Pearl Harbor on December 7, 1941. Several trying, war-torn years followed, during which time the United States had developed the atomic bomb. On August 6 and August 8, 1945, atomic bombs were dropped on the cities of Hiroshima and Nagasaki. A peace treaty followed on September 2 of that year.

Although the war ended in 1945, many problems still plagued the United States in the way of labor disputes; shortages in food, clothing and shelter; and the Russian aggression in building up communist governments in other countries, and in extending its party activities in the United States. It is apparent then that the entire period 1935 to 1950 was marked with national and international unrest. Through it all, the schools carried on. During the war years, reduction in teaching personnel often had been responsible for crowded classrooms, and the employment of poorly trained or untrained substitute teachers meant teaching was not always of a high quality. These temporary disadvantages, however, were soon overcome after the war, and schools recovered their normal functions remarkably well during the last years of the period. With this brief review of national and international conditions in mind, we shall now examine resultant effects on American reading instruction.

Probably the most obvious effect of this period was a reduction in output of research and instructional materials. The number of reports of published research from July 1943 to June 1944 dropped to a low of 54, almost half the number reported per year from 1930 to 1940, which was 110. After the war, the number per year gradually increased, totaling 98 for the school year 1949 to 1950. The writer found only one reading dissertation, completed in 1941, the first year of the war, whereas in 1940 there had been 114. Dissertation production was somewhat erratic during the rest of the period, but it ended with 12 in 1947, 17 in 1948, and 9 in 1949. The number of new series of basal readers published during this period was drastically reduced. There had been 16 new basal series listed in the preceding period. During this period, four series were published before the war, and publication begun on the primary programs of an additional two during the last 2 years of the period.

A second effect of the worldwide tension and strife was that a few fore thinkers began to state a fresh viewpoint in regard to the contribution that reading might make to the American democracy. For half a century we had been concentrating in succession on literary appreciation, silent reading, and a broader program of skills, but with no mention of nationalism. During this new period, the aim of living effectually in our democracy began to crop up, with emphasis on the complexities of modern life. This viewpoint was not mentioned frequently, but its occasional mention foreshadowed a more pronounced trend in this direction that developed during the next period. Here is an example of this viewpoint as expressed in the introduction of a Los Angeles County course of study:

> The man or woman who desires to live fully and competently in the world of the nineteen-forties needs to be able to read with both speed and understanding. As in no earlier period, the citizen of today must be able to think his way through a perplexing labyrinth of communication. He must be able to recognize validity, to detect speciousness, to deal sagaciously with propaganda. His civic life calls upon him to read involved and confusing propositions on his ballot, to interpret legal documents and intricate statements of governmental policy and procedure. He must be able to solve problems. He uses reading to gather, verify, organize, interpret, and evaluate information. Through these processes of interaction, cooperation, critical thinking, and problem solving, children in a democracy are

helped to develop common understandings, common meanings, and common skills. (180: 1)

A perusal of topics treated under the heading of "Reading" in the *Educational Index* (208) from 1935 to 1950 indicates that several articles were published during the latter part of this period such as "Functional Reading in a Democracy," "Education for Democracy," and "Reading and Democracy."

A third effect of unsettled national and international conditions was a new emphasis on the social values of reading. In Gray's "Summary of Reading Investigations" (182) for the year July 9, 1939, to June 30, 1940, the heading "Social Uses and Effects" appeared for the first time over a group of studies relating to this topic. In later summaries, the title "Sociology of Reading," used to embrace studies relating to social uses and values of reading, persisted all through the 1940s, indicating an increasing interest in this topic. In discussing studies dealing with social effects, which appeared in Gray's summary of 1946–1947, he states,

> Thirty or more have been published during the last two decades. A summary of such studies shows that reading does affect accuracy of information as well as morale, beliefs, judgments, and actions.

(Parenthetically, it might be added that the vast majority of these studies were reported during the period under discussion.) In his summary of 1949–1950, Gray states, "There is an increasing interest in the social relationships and implications of reading."

The Thirty-Sixth Yearbook of the National Society for the Study of Education, Part 1, emphasizes reading in contemporary life:

> During the decade since 1925, social changes have occurred with unusual rapidity. New issues and problems have presented themselves on every hand. The need for clear understanding and discriminating insight has never been greater. Young people and adults have drawn heavily upon every available source of information—the forum, the

press, the radio—in facing emergencies as well as in meeting the normal demands made upon them. Furthermore, individuals, agencies, and 'pressure groups' have used these means in developing attitudes and sentiments. As a result, the social significance of reading, as well as that of other means of informing or influencing the public, has greatly increased during recent years. (88: 10)

Another major effect of the war was the shocking rediscovery that, in this day and age, thousands of young men in the military service could not read well enough to follow the simple printed instructions for camp life. Coupled with this discovery was the revelation that reading could be taught to these young men in army camps in an amazingly short time. Concurrently, several new investigations disclosed reading deficiencies in large numbers of high school and college students. These influences combined to produce a spurt in attention to reading at these higher levels. Immediately following the war, a great deal of professional literature on reading emerged, and among these publications, several bulletins and one yearbook appeared dealing with high school and college reading. Chief among these publications was a bulletin of the National Education Association titled *Reading Instruction in Secondary Schools* (181), and *Reading in High School and College* (Forty-Eighth Yearbook of the National Society for the Study of Reading, Part II) (90). The actual teaching of reading at these levels had not progressed far at this time, but the idea was vigorously expanding.

Coincidently, with the discovery that so many of our youth could not read, together with results of research, we find a general tightening up of informal procedures for teaching reading and a renewed emphasis on systematic reading instruction. An examination of article titles in the *Education Index* (208) indicates that, in the last years of this period, there was a sharp decrease and finally an omission of articles having to do with reading taught only in connection with projects, units of work, and the activity program. Furthermore, an examination of all 1948–1949 courses of study in reading, which were available to the writer, advocated systematic instruction with the use of basal readers. In the Thirty-Sixth Yearbook of the National Society for the Study of Education, Part I, there are several statements in regard to the systematic teaching of reading, three of which are quoted:

> The basic instruction given should be organized so as to provide more widely than in the past for continuous, successful progress from one stage of development to another. (88: 14)

> The advantage of carefully planned procedures in attaining specific types of progress in reading has been demonstrated. For example, investigators [1] have found that a systematic method of teaching beginning reading is more effective in promoting the development of basic reading habits than incidental or opportunistic methods. Carefully planned guidance [2] relating to other phases of reading has proved equally valuable in promoting rapid progress. Such findings have wide implications in efforts to improve instruction in the future. (88: 15)

> Until further evidence develops, the Yearbook Committee recommends the use of specific periods for carefully planned guidance in reading throughout the elementary-school, secondary-school, and college periods. (88: 19)

Reading suffered its first strong threat from mass communication in this period. During the years 1938–1950, the radio replaced the lamp for reading on the living room table of practically all homes in America. The comics and movies also were becoming increasingly popular. Television did not attract much attention until the next decade, but during this period wide dissemination of entertainment through the other mass agencies aroused worry on the part of school people and parents. They feared that interest in listening to radio, looking at comics, and viewing movies would reduce interest in reading and thus decrease the amount of reading done. Numerous popular articles bemoaned the situation and pointed out its dangers. Several studies were conducted directed toward the exploration of students' interests in this area and finding out how much time they devoted to offerings of these types. Thus initial steps were taken in obtaining information to combat what was thought to be the first menace to reading.

I. Specific Reading Objectives

Practically all statements of objectives for a decade after the Twenty-Fourth Yearbook appeared either stated or restated in slightly different phraseology the objectives set forth in that yearbook. In reading the following quotations from two yearbooks that were published during this period, the reader will note that the objectives at this time were much broader, and that they embraced several new considerations not mentioned in the Twenty-Fourth Yearbook. Aims stated in the Thirty-Sixth Yearbook, Part I, are as follows:

> The broad objectives of reading; namely, to enrich experience, to broaden interests, to develop appreciations, and to cultivate ideal and appropriate attitudes have changed but little during recent years. However, many of the specific aims of reading assume a new significance in the light of contemporary social and educational developments. Examples of such aims are to broaden the vision of readers, to make their lives richer and more meaningful, and to enable them to meet the practical needs of life more effectively; to develop social understanding and the ability to use reading in the intelligent search for truth; to promote a broad common culture and a growing appreciation of the finer elements in contemporary life; and to stimulate wholesome interests in reading. (88: 18)

In the Forty-Eighth Yearbook, Part II, the committee who prepared the yearbook lists eight major criteria of a sound reading program. According to the committee, a good reading program in an elementary school

1. Is consciously directed toward specific valid ends which have been agreed upon by the entire school staff;

2. Coordinates reading activities with other aids to child development;

3. Recognizes that the child's development in reading is closely associated with his development in other language arts;

4. At any given level, is part of a well-worked-out larger reading program extending through all the elementary and secondary school grades;

5. Provides varied instruction and flexible requirements as a means of making adequate adjustments to the widely different reading needs of the pupils;

6. Affords, at each level of advancement, adequate guidance of reading in all the various aspects of a broad program of instruction: basic instruction in reading, reading in the content fields, literature, and recreational or free reading;

7. Makes special provisions for supplying the reading needs of cases of extreme reading disability, in other words, the small proportion of pupils whose needs cannot be satisfied through a strong developmental program;

8. Provides for frequent evaluation of the outcomes of a program and for such revisions as will strengthen the weaknesses discovered. (90: 11)

II. The New Reading Materials

Professional Books

Several professional books on reading were published during this period. A new feature in regard to these books was that several dealt solely with a specific aspect of reading. Among the new books treating reading in general were Emmett A. Betts's *Foundations in Reading Instruction*; Albert J. Harris's *How to Increase Reading Ability*; Gertrude Hildreth's *Learning the Three R's*; Guy Bond and Eva Bond's *Teaching the Child to Read*; Donald Durrell's *Improvement of Basic Reading Abilities*; E.W. Dolch's

Problems in Reading, Clarence Stone's *Better Primary Reading*, and Luella Cole's *The Improvement of Reading*.

The first two books devoted to reading at the secondary level published during this period were Guy Bond and Eva Bond's *Developmental Reading in the High School*, and Ruth Strang, Constance McCullough, and Arthur Traxler's *Problems in the Improvement of Reading*. Books dealing with specific aspects of reading were Douglas Waple's *What Reading Does to People*, Lillian Lamoreaux and Doris Lee's *Learning to Read through Experience*, Lucile Harrison's *Reading Readiness*, and Matthew Luckiesh and Frank K. Moss's *Reading as a Visual Task*. Several books treating various aspects of reading disabilities are mentioned in section VI, page 280.

Courses of Study

The courses of study published during the early part of this period followed closely in format and content to the courses of the preceding period. Generally, they were still influenced by the Twenty-Fourth Yearbook, by stating the objectives found in the yearbook, listing skills designed to obtain these objectives, discussing grouping and individual differences, and by the supplemental reading.

The writer was unable to find any courses of study produced during the war years or immediately after. Several new courses were published in 1948. With the exception of two courses that contained all subjects of the elementary grades and two that named "reading and literature" in their titles, all others were confined solely to the subject of reading. Some of the new courses listed broad objectives similar to those stated in the preceding period, and then added one or two new objectives, which pointed toward the use of reading in the current complex society. The following example presents a new aim added to the usual "broadened objectives" aims in a Wyoming *Course of Study for Elementary Schools*:

The public school should proceed in such a way that it is possible for each boy and girl to acquire an understanding of the present social order with all its complexities and problems, and to achieve the maximum of his potential ability, to contribute and live in a complex society. To do this it is imperative that each individual acquire adequate skill with the necessary fundamentals. The purpose of reading is to meet these fundamental needs. (183: 1)

Several new courses did not list objectives or aims. Instead they stated "principles," as in a Denver, Colorado, course:

1. Intelligent reading is important to the democratic way of life.
2. Reading is a life-long process.
3. Individuals vary in ability.
4. Definite objectives should be set up.
5. Reading is important in all subjects.
6. There are many good methods.
7. Types of material differ for various purposes.
8. Learning to read is a process of growth.
9. Purposeful reading is important.
10. Many factors affect reading growth and development. (184: 1)

Teachers' Manuals

During this period, the number of teachers' manuals for a series of readers increased. There was a strong trend toward having more manuals at the first-grade level. Two of the new series to be described had separate manuals for the readiness period, three had separate manuals for the preprimer books, three had separate manuals for the primer and also for the first reader. Thus it was quite common to have four manuals for the first grade, alone. There was an addition also in the number of manuals for second and third grades in series that published two readers for each of these grades. In such cases, a manual was provided for each reader. All series had at least one manual for grades 2 to 6. One series had a "General Manual" for grades 1 to 6, in addition to the separate teachers' manuals.

Some manuals were bound in paper, others had hard covers. Usually the cover of the book matched the color of the reader that it accompanied. New names appeared for teachers' manuals during this period, also, such as "Teachers' Guide" or "The Teachers' Guide Book." The size of the teachers' manual usually corresponded with that of the readers, which has become standardized to 6 by 8 inches. In one case, however, the manuals were 8 ½ by 11 inches.

On the whole the teachers' manuals for grades 2 to 6 contained more pages than before, some having more than 500 pages. Those for the various stages in the first grade usually had 500 pages or more when all the separate manuals were combined. Some manuals showed a new trend in art work, containing diagrams, sketches, and drawings. They usually were printed in easy-to-read typeface, and typographical arrangements were conducive to a ready grasp of the organizational structure. Skill charts were included in most of the manuals, which helped to give an overall view of the scope and sequence of the skill development program.

In one series of readers, there was an abrupt change in the style of writing. A narrative was told about "Miss Davis" as she guides a group of children through the readiness book and the two preprimers. The pictures, the conversations, and the descriptive sections of the story convey to the teacher procedures to use while working with the beginning materials of the series. In general, such topics as these were treated in the teachers' manuals: a balanced reading program, word recognition, comprehension, study activities, relationships to other subjects, evaluation and testing, and enrichment activities. In addition the teachers' manuals, of course, gave suggestions of procedures to use in teaching children to read specific pages in their readers.

The Chief Characteristics of Basal Readers

As indicated at the beginning of this chapter, the number of new series published during this period was small compared to the number published during each of the two preceding periods. Some new series did come out, however, between 1940 and 1950, which were selected for analysis of trends. The six series analyzed were

Emmett Betts and Carolyn Welch's Betts Basic Readers (American Book)
Gertrude Hildreth and others' Easy Growth In Reading (John C. Winston)
Mabel O'Donnell's The Alice and Jerry Basic Readers (Row, Peterson)
David Russell and others' The Ginn Basic Readers (Ginn)
Nila Banton Smith's Learning To Read (Silver Burdett)
Paul Witty and others' Reading for Interest (D.C. Heath)

Several changes took place in basal reader series during this period. One change was that the wide acceptance of the reading readiness concept revolutionized beginning programs. Authors now considered the development of reading readiness to be so important that they provided material for and instructions to the teacher for use during a readiness period.

Reading readiness books for first-grade children were introduced. Usually there were two readiness books, one that the teacher used with groups of children and one that the children used individually. The material in the readiness books provided for activities that would give children language experiences and practice in matching pictures, geometric figures, and sometimes letters and words; selecting an appropriate item from several other items; following sequence in pictured stories; and acquainting pupils with the characters they would meet in reading the first preprimer. As previously stated, an entire teachers' guide usually was provided for the teachers' use in developing readiness.

In addition to new readiness materials, there was a spurt also in providing more preprimers. In the preceding period, one preprimer for a series was an innovation. Authors now provided two, three, or even four preprimers in their respective programs. Having two books per grade beyond first grade was a new development. Nearly all of the new series provided a first- and second-semester book for each grade beyond first. The content of the new readers drew upon literature to a greater extent than in the past. It still was predominantly realistic, but many old tales from literature were used and poetry was returning. The quality of writing in the realistic stories was improving.

The art work occupied still more space than previously. The colors on the whole were more vivid. The beginning readers were really beautiful picture books, and colors were used much more freely in fourth-, fifth-, and sixth-grade readers. Full-page illustrations were not uncommon now in upper grade readers.

Picture placement and arrangement showed beginnings of new trends. Instead of placing pictures straight across the tops of pages in primary books, they appeared in various places, perhaps top and/or bottom on the same page with the text in between. Sometimes the same picture extended down the side of a page giving an illusion of a full-page picture. This was usually a tree shown extending from bottom to top of the page, the trunk bounding the text, but not cutting into it or distracting from it.

One important change in regard to the mechanical features of readers published during this period was the complete disappearance of the hanging indention in first-grade readers. In the past, beginning readers universally had an indented run-over line in a sentence that had to be divided because of length, as follows:

> Janet and Susan sat down to eat
> the popcorn.

Authors during this period changed to regular paragraph style when it was necessary to carry a part of a sentence to the next line, as shown in the following example:

Janet and Susan sat down to eat
the popcorn.

This change in indention probably was due partly to the results of eye-movement studies, which revealed children's difficulties in fixating on the return sweep from the end of one line to the beginning of another. Another influence that might have helped to bring about this change was that of the newer philosophies that urged all school situations be kept as close to life situations as possible.

The number of authors per series showed marked differences ranging from one or two to eight. In all cases in which several people authored a series, there was a balance between authors having public school experience and others giving courses in teacher education institutions. All participating authors held academic degrees ranging from the bachelor's degree to the doctorate. In most situations, the leading author was serving in a college or university position and possessed a doctoral degree.

Vocabularies of beginning readers continued to show reduction. It will be recalled that in Selke's study (159) presented in the preceding chapter, primers in 1931 had an average of 289 new words per primer. The writer's study of primers launched during this period shows that the primer vocabulary in six new primers ranged from 62 to 127 with an average of 122. The reduction in primer vocabularies was due partly, but certainly not wholly, to the publication of more preprimers. The number of new words introduced in preprimer programs ranged from 44 to 79. The average number of total preprimer words per series was 52. Adding this average to the average number of primer words, we find the total to be only 174 as compared with an average of 289 words in primers during the preceding periods. So when both preprimers and primers are considered together, we still see a drastic reduction in the number of new words presented to children before the first reader period.

Authors continued to check their early reader vocabularies with scientifically determined vocabulary lists such as those prepared by Thorndike, Gates, and the International Kindergarten Union, and they made sure that the majority of words in their early readers occurred with high frequency in these lists.

Repetition of new words in primary readers beyond first grade was much better controlled. All words appearing in the preprimers and the primer of each series were repeated in the first reader, and repetition was continued with a high percentage of these words reappearing in all primary readers. The authors also took careful account of the number of times each word was repeated, and higher numbers of repetitions of single words was another earmark of the present period.

Some Representative Readers

Four of the reading programs developed during this period will be described. Because of the many new developments between 1935 and 1950, these descriptions must be brief.

The Reading for Interest Series. This entire series, prepared under the consultantship of Paul Witty and several other reading specialists and story writers, was published during the 1940s. The program consists of a readiness book, four preprimers, two primers, a first reader and one reader each for grades two through six. There is a practice book for the first three preprimers, one for the fourth preprimer, one for the primer, and one for each of the readers. Sentence, phrase, and word cards are also provided for use in the initial program. The most distinctive feature emphasized by authors is the interest factor, which they consider to be of first importance in learning to read.

The books appear in various colors with a picture on the front and back covers surrounded with a pleasing all-over design in black. The pictures in the early books are done in the three primary colors along with brown, yellow, and black. In the primer, the predominating size of the pictures is half page, and pictures appear on nearly all pages. In the upper-grade readers, the pictures are not so large and numerous, and some appear in black and white. The primers contain realistic stories. Beginning with second grade, the readers contain realistic stories, fanciful stories, and poems. Following are samples from the second primer and the fourth reader:

> "Meow!"
> Around the house came a kitten.
> Around the house came Sandy.
> Around the house came Blinker.
> "Meow!" said the kitten.
> "Meow!" (197: 4)

Mark loved the busy East River. Almost every day he would run down to the docks after school to watch the boats loading and unloading. His favorite dock was the one where the banana boats were tied up, for often the sailors would show him monkeys or bright-colored parrots that they had brought back from South America. They had many stories of adventure to tell the small boy, and Mark's round brown eyes almost popped out of his face as he listened. (199: 17)

The Learning to Read Program. This program, prepared by Dr. Nila Banton Smith, appeared between 1940 and 1945. The stories were written by well-known authors of children's literature. The series as originally published consists of two readiness books, two preprimers, a primer, a first reader, and one reader each for the second and third grades. In a short time after publication, however, the demand arose to have both a first-semester and a second-semester book at second- and third-grade levels. In order to meet this demand, the original second- and third-grade books were simplified and reduced to make a first-semester book in each case and two additional new books for second-semester use. The original full-year editions continued to be supplied to those who wished to have only one book each at second- and third-grade levels. There is a practice pad for the readiness book, the preprimers, primer, first reader, and each reader for grades two through three. Teachers' guides accompany all the books. Word and phrase cards are provided for beginning levels.

One distinctive feature of the series was that it was first to provide social studies and science content designed to accompany curricular topics in these areas. Each section in the fourth-, fifth- and sixth-grade readers contains material organized around a social studies or science topic appropriate for the grade represented by the reader. Another distinctive feature at the time was the extensiveness, specificity, and careful organization of the skill development program.

The art work in these books is unusually attractive for readers of the 1940s. Pictures were used more profusely and they appear in greater numbers and in larger sizes than in readers preceding this period. The pictures in the primary books are printed in red, green, blue, yellow, and black, and are unusually attractive. In the primer, the average size of the pictures is one-half page. There are three double-page picture spreads and one full-page picture. The upper-grade books contain many pictures that make use of all the colors, although a few pictures are done in gray or in one secondary color. In the fourth reader, there are five full-page pictures, seven double-page spreads, five pictures that are three-quarter page, and the remaining are predominantly half page.

The content of the primary readers is largely realistic although some fanciful tales appear. The primer content is mostly realistic with the exception of one fanciful tale that appears at the end of the book. The upper-grade books are devoted almost entirely to realistic stories and informative selections, with settings in the social studies or science areas of curriculum. A poem begins each group of selections and a fanciful tale or an old tale ends each group in the books. Samples of the primer content and fourth reader follow:

> Bill played with the airplane.
> He made the airplane go.
> It did not go over the tree.
> It did not go over the house.
> It did not come down. (193: 45)

Leif and his men sailed into the Atlantic Ocean and headed for home. Strong winds and ocean currents carried them much farther south than they wanted to go. They were far off their course, but at first they did not know this. They sailed and sailed for many days until at last they saw land ahead. (195: 283)

The Ginn Basic Readers. This series was launched in 1948 and 1949. The primary readers were published at the same time, and the middle-grade readers were published early in the 1950s. The extension of the Ginn program to levels above third grade will be discussed in chapter nine. The authors were Dr. David H. Russell and several other reading specialists.

The primary series consists of two reading readiness books, three preprimers, a primer, a first reader, two second readers, and two third readers. A Big Book, which was a reproduction of *PrePrimer 1*, is provided, as well as picture cards, and word, phrase, and sentence cards. Seven workbooks are provided, one for the three preprimers, one for the primer, and one for each of the five readers. Teachers' manuals are provided for all levels. A testing program of separately published tests is also included in the program.

The book covers are done in various colors of green, orange, and blue with an attractive picture on the front cover of each book. The pictures in the primer are interesting and full of action, and make use of the primary colors plus brown, yellow, and black. The majority of the pictures are of half-page size, although there is a two-page spread at the beginning of the book and a full-page illustration preceding each remaining group of stories.

In the *Third Reader 2*, the same colors are used as in the primer. The average size of the pictures are a quarter page. Each section of stories is preceded by a full-page illustration. One of the distinctive features of the Ginn Basic Readers is what the authors term *a vertical arrangement*. According to this plan the program is planned not only horizontally in grade levels but also vertically across grade lines to ensure continuity in skill development. The program also provides for language and speech activities to be integrated with the reading activities.

Most of the stories in the beginning books deal with every day lives of children, but classical stories and fanciful tales, as well as realistic stories, appear in all the books. The authors' intention was to introduce children to the best in children's literature, and as a part of this plan, they included poems. The following are examples of the realistic and informative content of the primer:

> The children looked at the kittens.
> "I like this kitten," said Betty.
> "She looks like my Frisky."
>
> Susan said, "I like this kitten.
> I will take this black kitten.
> Come here, little kitten." (185: 11)

Sam's helpers have been spreading the cement over the dirt. It must be good and thick to make a strong floor. Some of the men are smoothing it off with a long board. Sam is pleased with their work. (187: 76)

The Betts Basic Readers. This program was prepared by Dr. Emmett A. Betts and Carolyn M. Welch. The first edition for all six grades of the series was published during the last years of this period and consisted of a readiness book, three preprimers, a primer, a first reader, and seven additional readers for grades two to six. There was a preprimer study book (workpad), a primer study book, and a study book for each reader. A teachers' guide book is provided for the readiness material, the preprimer books, the primer, and one for each reader. Word cards are provided for use with the preprimers and primer. Tests also are provided. (For recent revisions see chapter nine, page 317.)

The pictures in the primer are in vivid primary and secondary colors. Predominantly, these pictures are a half page in size, and there are six full-page illustrations. The pictures in the later books are colorful also. In the fourth reader, most of the pictures are a quarter page in size. A two-page spread precedes the first group of stories, and a full-page picture precedes each of the additional groups of stories.

Most of the stories in the primer are realistic although some of them are fanciful stories in which animals and toys are personified. Primer content appears in paragraph form. This is the first time in which primer content has been paragraphed in many years. In the fourth reader, several groups of stories have their settings in neighboring lands such as Canada, Mexico, and South America. Following is an example of the primer content followed by a paragraph from the fourth reader:

Jack rides up the hill.
He stops at a little house.
He stops at a big house.
Kim sees Jack come up the hill.
He wants to help.
Kim likes to go with jack. (189: 30)

North of the United States lies Canada, the land of the maple leaf. In the wilds of Canada is the mining town where Polly Daniels lives. Her house stands next to the field where her father, head of the Daniels Flying Service, keeps his airplane. (191: 112)

One distinctive feature of this program as stressed by the authors was the integration of reading study skills and techniques in curricular settings. A second distinctive feature was the built-in-program providing for utilizing interrelationships with the other language arts. In fact, the Betts Basic Readers program was one part of a larger program under the general caption "Language Arts Series."

Revisions and Extensions

Many of the basal readers of the preceding period continued to be used during this period and some underwent slight revisions. One basal program, however, was not only revised but was extended in substantial ways as indicated here.

The Curriculum Foundation Series. In 1937, the authors of this series added their first prereading book. During the 1940s, they added three preprimers, provided two books per grade for the second and third grades, added Independence Readers to their basic program, introduced the Beginning Dictionary, and completed their primary programs in social studies, arithmetic, health, art, and science. Furthermore, they renamed their workpads "Think and Do Books," and in their teachers' guides they were first in this period to use the term *structural analysis* to identify the skills belonging to this word-recognition technique.

III. Methods of Teaching as Advocated in Basal Reading Series

Interrelationships in Various Curriculum Areas

A new concept developed during this period in regard to the relationship of reading to other facets of the language arts constellation. The new concept is expressed in the following quotation that represents the philosophy of the authors of The Ginn Basic Readers:

> Today reading is an important part but only one part of the group of children's activities known as the language or communication arts. The language arts are all concerned with the communication of ideas. In reading silently the child is obtaining ideas from others, in reading orally he is sharing ideas with others. Thus reading is closely allied to such language arts as listening and speaking.
>
> All children need to communicate and all need different language abilities to express and receive ideas and to aid their other school learnings. To develop mature reading abilities the child must develop speaking, writing, and other language abilities as fully as possible.

In their teachers' guides, most authors listed language skills that could be developed in connection with specific reading lessons, and offered suggestions of procedures for use in teaching these other skills. Another indication of authors' provisions for extending reading skills and their functions to applications in other curricular areas is seen in the content of two new reading series. As indicated previously in these two series, the stories and informative articles have settings in social studies areas that correspond to the topics to be taught at specific grade levels. One series also includes groups of stories with science applications. The following quotation from Smith illustrates this viewpoint:

> Children's interests and activities in the elementary school are centered primarily upon people—how and where they live, what they do, and what they have; and upon the natural and physical world about them. Therefore the practical application of the new viewpoint of reading as a continuing process of growth means that for much reading content we must turn increasingly to social studies and science, which form the basis of children's activities and interests.
>
> With these considerations in mind, the materials in DISTANT DOORWAYS were written about topics drawn from the field of social studies and from the field of science. In order that these topics

might coincide with the social studies and science topics which most frequently form the core of the curriculum in the fourth grade, extensive research was conducted. (196: 2)

The teachers' guides accompanying those basal readers, which contained social studies or science content, offered many suggestions for integrating reading with these subject areas.

Methods of Approach

The rapid and wide acceptance of the reading readiness concept ushered in a new approach to reading. As indicated previously, reading readiness books were provided to children, and teachers' guides gave instructions for the use of these books. The teachers' guides, however, contained much more than instructions for using the basal materials. There was a trend toward recognizing general child development in the teaching of reading. Dr. Russell and his authors say, "This series views the teaching of reading in the broad perspective of each child's mental, physical, emotional, and social development."

Another new viewpoint was the need for recognizing reading readiness at all levels. Several authors make this point in their teachers' guides. Before closing this discussion on methods of approach, it should be added that most authors recommend the use of experience charts composed by the children as a supplement to the basal materials.

Word Recognition Techniques

The use of context clues and structural analysis appeared for the first time as techniques that should be taught to children as aids in working out the pronunciation of unrecognized words. Authors of all new series include context clues, and authors of three series include the study of word structure. Phonics is included in all basal reading programs, but in most cases only a limited amount of instruction is recommended at first-grade level. Dr. Witty sums up the situation in his *General Manual* when he states,

> Experimentation in the teaching of phonics has led to contradictory claims and some confusion over the value of phonic principles in "unlocking" new words. Nor is there agreement concerning the nature or number of the specific units to be taught, nor the levels at which the various units should be introduced. In general, the practice followed in modern schools is to delay phonic analysis of words until children have a start in reading for meaning and a stock of sight words. (201: 106)

Visual discrimination and *auditory discrimination* were new terms that first came into the teacher's vocabulary in connection with phonics during the 1940s. *Visual discrimination* was the term used to designate children's ability to see likenesses and differences in words and letters, and *auditory discrimination* was used to indicate the ability to sense likenesses and differences in sound through hearing. In most reader programs, visual and auditory discrimination of the consonants was taught during first grade, and phonic analysis was delayed until second grade. Phonics was taught with greater emphasis in this grade and in the third grade. Practically all phonic elements were covered by the end of the third grade. In the middle grades, phonics was applied to dictionary usage.

Skill Development in Elementary Grades

Skill development programs expanded greatly during this period and they included new classifications. During the preceding period skills were generally classified under the headings of "Recreational Reading" and "Work-Type Reading" with subheadings such as phonics; silent reading; oral reading; comprehension; skillful use of books, and libraries and other sources of information.

In this period, authors provided long, carefully organized skill charts to indicate the many different skills to be developed. "Word Recognition" is now used as a general heading to include context clues, structural analysis, and phonics. "Work-Type Reading" now is designated as "Work Study Skills," or in some cases, "Study Skills." Under such headings are new terms: locating information, evaluation, organization, and retention. The skills indicated by these terms began to receive special attention shortly after the publication of the Thirty-Sixth Yearbook of the National Society for the Study of Education, Part I. This yearbook stressed the need for teaching reading in other curricular areas, and the skills named above were pointed to as desirable ones to use for this purpose. The following quotation represents this viewpoint.

> Although much has been written about the importance of reading in the various curricular fields, the degree to which reading limits learning does not in practice seem to be fully recognized. Under present conditions, and perhaps under ideal conditions, pupils must obtain from books a large part of their knowledge and much of their stimulation to thinking. Reading is therefore an essential tool in the study of most parts of the curriculum. Closely related to reading is the ability to locate books and articles that deal with problems met in and out of school; to select, understand, and appraise pertinent problems; to organize the data, often secured from a variety of references, so that the information will aid in the solution of their problems; and to provide for the retention, the improvement, and the use of what has been learned. Shortcomings in any of these types of abilities are quickly reflected in the quality of the pupils' work in all subjects studied from books. (88: 134)

There was a beginning attempt to break down the general term *comprehension*, and attention was called to different kinds of meaning-getting processes. Durrell's analysis of comprehension skills included "simple comprehension," "higher mental processes," and "critical thinking." It was during this period that we first encountered the term *critical reading*, which Betts defined as "evaluating relevancy and adequacy." "Speed of reading" and "skimming" now appeared in skill development categories. Three examples will be given of the major headings appearing in the skill charts that accompanied new basal reading programs of this period. In all cases, specific subskills were listed under each major skill heading, but in the interest of space will not be presented here.

In the Learning to Read series, skills are listed under the following headings: I. Skills Needed in Using an Expanded Vocabulary, II. Skills Needed in Locating Information, III. Skills Needed in Comprehension and Interpretation, IV. Skills Needed in Selecting and Evaluating Materials, V. Skills Needed in Organizing Material, VI. Skills Needed in Retention, VII. Abilities and Appreciations Needed in Reading Literature, and VIII. Skills Needed in Developing Speed of Comprehension (196: 179–87).

Major skill headings appearing in the program for the Ginn Basic Readers are Vocabulary Building, Literary Appreciation, Skills in Locating, Skills in Evaluating, Skills in Comprehending, Skills in Organizing, and Skills in Remembering.

Some of the major skill headings listed for the Betts Basic Reader program are Word Recognition, Semantic Analysis, Dictionary Usage, Language Structure, Location of Information, Skimming, Rapid Reading, Study Type Reading, Assimilative Reading, Critical Reading, Interpretation of Punctuation and Typographical Cues, Organization, and Versatility (192: 5–7).

Adjustment to Individual Needs

Authors of professional books, yearbooks, and basal reading programs were alike in their sensitivity to individual differences and to the need for adjusting reading instruction to meet these differences. Grouping was still the most frequently used medium in adjusting to individual needs. Advances are evident, however, in suggestions for making other adjustments in addition to grouping. Gray et al., and Betts also, introduced the idea of *flexibility*. Gray and collaborators made this suggestion in connection with their basal reading program:

> The key to the success of any grouping plan, teachers find, is to keep the groups *flexible*.... For example, take Judy, in the top or middle group, who has been absent for a few days. Sitting in on some extra sessions with the immature group helps her pick up the new skills she may have missed. Or Jim who has made a sudden spurt, can be shifted to a higher group with only a minimum of individual help to bridge the gap. (204: 11)

After discussing the three-group plan, Betts continued with a discussion of flexibility:

> These groups are always flexible and tentative. Changes from one group to another are made throughout the year. Moreover, the pupils may work in one group for reading and in another group for art or music. Such flexible and tentative grouping of the pupils makes for better-rounded social and academic adjustments....
>
> When a child begins to outrun other members of his group, he should be considered for another group. The change is made after a careful appraisal of his level of achievement and of his needs. If he can meet the challenge of another group, he is transferred.
>
> When a child falls behind his group, he should be considered for transfer. An informal analysis is made of his level of reading achievement and of his needs, and a change is made before the pupil has formed poor reading habits. (192: 64–65)

Durrell pointed out that grouping doesn't solve the problem:

> The classroom teacher must bear most of the responsibility for providing for individual differences. While various types of ability grouping tend to make classes more homogeneous, particularly in general achievement levels, a wide variety of differences is always present....

Ability grouping will generally decrease the range of reading levels in classrooms, but it leaves unsolved the major problems of providing for individual differences. (88: 325–326)

Durrell followed the statement with several suggestions other than grouping for adjusting to individual needs such as providing suitable materials; individual conferences; extensive individual silent reading; long-range assignments; workbooks, standard test lessons, and other self-administering materials; and small groupings of five to six pupils.

Russell and Wulfing suggested grouping, the use of diversified materials, and several other procedures. For example, the following were among the additional suggestions for meeting individual needs in the intermediate grades:

1. The use of supplementary books of related materials in the classroom or school library.
2. Individual coaching.
3. Diagnosis and clinical study.
4. Tests based on specific selections in the reader.
5. Individual word lists.
6. Reference materials for work done in other parts of the school program.
7. Jokes, poems, etc. brought by pupils for reading to the class.
8. Records of free reading.
9. Variation in assignments and reports.
10. Book reviews.
11. Workbook and how-to-study activities. (188: 27)

IV. The Teaching of Reading in Secondary Schools and Colleges

In the last two years of this period, there was a strong upswing of interest in the teaching of reading at the higher levels and a new concept emerged—that of teaching developmental reading in high school. The primary influence that brought about this interest probably arose from the large number of research reports that had to do directly with reading at secondary and college levels. Specific reasons for interest in reading at these levels are enumerated in *Reading in the High School and College* (Forty-Seventh Yearbook of the National Society for the Study of Education, Part II). These reasons reflect research findings.

> A heightened appreciation in the importance of reading, a growing recognition of the nature of the reading problems faced by students, wider and more varied use of reading required by recent curriculum changes, greater ability needed to interpret critically, the unsatisfactory character of the personal reading of many students, wide recognition and concern for the poor reader, and competence in reading acquired through continuous development. (89: 1–4)

Up until 1948, the year in which the Forty-Seventh Yearbook was published, any reading instruction that had been done at the higher levels was remedial in nature. Now Gray urges for much more than remedial reading:

> A vigorous attack on reading problems at the more advanced levels is a responsibility of all high schools and colleges. The effort made during recent years to correct the deficiencies of poor readers is only one important aspect of the problem. A basic need today is to develop a sound reading program in high schools and colleges which recognizes (1) that growth in reading is continuous, (2) that the function of guidance in reading is to start with the student at his present level of reading ability, and (3) that it should carry him forward to higher levels of competence in harmony with his capacity and the increasing demands made upon him when reading. Until notable progress has been made in providing students with appropriate stimulation and guidance, general education cannot make its largest contribution to the personal and social development of youth. (89: 42)

In the previous quotation, Dr. Gray is suggesting a sound reading program for high schools and colleges in addition to remedial instruction. Dr. Bond makes further distinctions between these two types of programs:

> The reading program in the high school may be divided into two rather distinct divisions. The first of these embraces the students who have the ability to continue their growth in each of the five areas through the developmental program; the second, those relatively few students who have markedly failed to make adequate progress in any or all of the five areas of the reading program. The latter group of students, in addition to continuing the developmental program, should be given remedial instruction designed to meet their individual needs. (205: 46)

In so far as the writer's research revealed, the term *developmental reading* was first used by Dr. Bond in distinguishing between a remedial reading program and a program planned for all high school students in terms of their development. Dr. Bond explains the nature of developmental reading in high school as follows:

> The secondary school developmental reading program is concerned fundamentally with the continued refinement and development of the more mature aspects of the self-same types of abilities that were being refined and developed in the elementary school. This refinement and development likewise continue as long as the individual continues to learn. The newer demands made on reading by the secondary school curriculum make it unreasonable to expect the elementary school to complete the developmental process. (205: 54)

Concerns about reading in the special content fields at the high school level were expressed, and attempts were made to meet these concerns. Harris states,

> In recent conferences and meetings, teachers have shown increasing concern over the ineffective way in which many students read ma-

terials in the content fields. Two distinct groups of problems appear to be involved. One group relates to the special reading skills and abilities necessary for effective reading in particular content fields. The other group relates to those basic conditions of learning through reading with which all teachers of all subjects are necessarily concerned. (89: 116)

The authors of the two new professional books on reading in the secondary school, as well as the authors of the Forty-Seventh Yearbook, Part II, devote considerable space to the teaching of reading in the content fields. Suggestions are given for the teaching of reading in connection with each of the following subjects: social studies, literature, science, and mathematics.

V. Reading Research Has a Setback[3]

The period of years extending from 1935 to 1940 were highly productive in reading research; however, the number of studies reported between 1940 and 1950 showed a sharp decrease. During the 15 years from 1935 to 1950, Gray reported summaries of published research yearly beginning with July 1 of one year and extending to June 30 of the succeeding year. The number of studies published annually beginning in 1935–1936 and continuing until 1941–1942 were as follows: 100, 98, 126, 126, 119, 114, 114, 110. The last three numbers represent the years 1940 to 1942, and it will be noted that the number of studies per year began to decrease in 1940. In the war years, 1943–1944, only 54 were reported. During the next three years, 89, 80, and 89 were reported, respectively. In 1949–1950, the number had risen to 98, but even that was below the yearly number in the pre-war years.

There was also a drop in the number of doctoral dissertations completed during the war years (see page 248). The decrease in published studies, as well as in dissertations, was due of course to the involvement in war efforts of those who otherwise might have been conducting research.

High interest topics of the period were diagnosis and remedial work with emphasis on causes and visual defects; reading interests; vocabulary load and meaningful vocabulary; phonics, particularly its limitations and values; evaluation of reading tests; effective reading and study habits; reading in content subjects; and the hygiene of reading. Interest in reading in the content subjects became strong in the early 1940s, 19 such studies having been reported in the 1940–1941 period and 18 in the 1941–1942 period. Studies on this topic continued at the rate of from 6 to 8 per year up until 1950. As previously indicated, the results of this research were strongly reflected in the new professional books and basal reader programs, both of which devoted much space to reading in the content subjects.

The topic of reading readiness reached its zenith as a research interest in 1940 when 22 studies relating to this subject were reported in one year. From this time on, accounts of published research on this topic decreased rapidly in number. As for unpublished research, this period of interest in readiness was the heyday of aspiring masters and doctors in finding problems for research. The number of master and doctoral studies on readiness increased steadily from 1927, reaching its peak in the years 1937 to 1940. The writer found 14 such studies that were completed in 1937, 15 in 1938, 14 in 1939, and 12 in 1940. Following this last date, only from one to three studies on readiness were completed per year up until 1950.

Studies having to do with the sociology of reading became so numerous during this period that Gray provided a special heading for this classification. (See page 375 for more specific evidence of the growing research interest in this topic.) Likewise, studies having to do with the physiology and psychology of reading took a spurt in numbers, and for that reason studies of these types were for the first time given a special heading in the Gray summaries.

The topic of readability emerged as a new research interest. The Yoakam, Lorge, and Flesch readability formulas were published during the early 1940s, and these formulas undoubtedly stimulated research related to this topic. Several mechanical aids to reading appeared on the market, and these new instruments received their share of investigation. Concern about radio, comics, and moving pictures called forth some studies in hitherto unexplored areas. A study having to do with radio appeared for the first time in Gray's summaries of 1940–1941. From that time on, additional studies having to do with mass communication agencies were reported.

During the latter part of the period several published studies had to do with the relationships between reading and other language arts. The effects were immediately seen in professional books and basal reader programs. Authors of reading materials now definitely recognized reading as one strand in the language arts constellation and suggested ways of capitalizing on language arts relationships in teaching reading.

All academic levels and ages were included in the studies of this period from kindergarten to adults. The number of studies at the elementary level decreased somewhat and studies at secondary, college, and adult levels increased, with many more at college level than at the secondary or adult level.

Doctoral dissertations completed during this period dealt with the same general topics of study as those reported in published research. Like published research, the highest number of studies in dissertation topics had to do with reading disability, in which studies at the college level far outstripped studies with students in other school levels. It should be stated, however, that the doctoral candidates showed special interest in reading in the content

279

areas and in the new topics of readability, language arts interrelationships, and mechanical aids.

Laboratory studies continued during this period, and important investigations came from the Psycho-Educational Clinic under Dearborn at Harvard University; Betts's Clinic at Oswego, later at Pennsylvania State College; Buswell's laboratory at the University of Chicago; Gates's at Columbia; Eames's at Boston University and Dartmouth; and Tinker's at the University of Minnesota.

Increasing numbers of studies were also conducted in classrooms and in reading centers. Frequent complaints were made about the quality of some of these studies as concerned with design and statistical techniques.

VI. Interest in Reading Disability Increases

Evidence of the increased interest in reading disability during the 15 years from 1935 to 1950 is found in three sources: summaries of investigations, articles in educational journals, and new professional books dealing exclusively with this subject (see discussion on research, page 277). The *Educational Index* (208), from 1935 to 1950, shows numerous articles and new professional books relating to this subject (Source: 1965 edition).

The professional books treating diagnosis and remedial reading are: *Remedial and Corrective Instruction in Reading* by James Maurice McCallister; *Children Who Cannot Read* by Marion Monroe; *The Improvement of Reading* by Arthur Gates; *Prevention and Correction of Reading Difficulties* by Emmett Betts; *Why Pupils Fail in Reading* by Helen Robinson; *Diagnostic and Remedial Teaching in Secondary Schools* by Glenn M. Blair; *Reading and the Educative Process* by Paul Witty and David Kopel; and *Prediction and Prevention of Reading Difficulties* by Margaret Stanger and

Ellen Donahue. Never before had there been such a fresh array of books on a specialized aspect of reading!

The use of informal diagnosis with basal readers was an innovation. Betts was first to describe this technique in his discussion of "The Informal Inventory" appearing in the first edition of *Foundations of Reading Instruction* (207: 443–481).

Perhaps the most important contribution of this period was the development of the multiple-causation theory of reading disability. Studies probed much more deeply into causes, and new insights were gained particularly in the fields of physiology and psychology. Not only were numerous studies made in these fields, but periodical literature frequently carried titles of articles with topics such as personality factors in reading, reading and the emotions, play therapy, psychiatric insights into reading difficulties, and psychological treatment for reading disability.

Two studies described in books published during this period deserve special mention because of the contributions that they made in broadening perspective in regard to causation of reading disability. Marion Monroe's *Children Who Cannot Read* (209) contained evidence to the effect that reading disability might be due to any of several different causes:

> [L]imited learning capacity, congenital or acquired neurological defects, conflicting cerebral tendencies, poor perceptual habits, ill health, improper glandular functioning, poor vision or hearing, abnormal emotional reactions, poor environment, inappropriate teaching, etc. (209: vi)

Helen Robinson's *Why Pupils Fail in Reading* (210) describes a 5-year study in which the following specialists cooperated:

> [A] social worker, a psychiatrist, a pediatrician, a neurologist, three ophthalmologists, a speech-correction specialist, an otolaryngologist, an endocrinologist, a reading specialist, and the investigator who acted as psychologist and reading technician. (210: 3)

This group of specialists diagnosed and treated 30 remedial cases. One of the conclusions drawn was

> This study indicates that the pooled opinions of several experts in varied fields is more reliable than opinion of a reading examiner alone.

A second conclusion was

> This study shows clearly that a large proportion of children who are considered "unreachable" may learn to read when adequate diagnostic and remedial steps are taken. The findings give promise of definite help for a much larger proportion of seriously retarded readers than has been achieved in the past. (210: 237)

This new and broader concept of disability causation was a profound contribution of this period.

Two spectacular diagnostic innovations appeared in the provision of mechanical aids to reading difficulties. Betts launched his telebinocular, designed to indicate defects in vision, and American Optical Company produced the opthalmagraph, used in making photographic reproductions of eye-movements.

Several other instruments were invented and other materials were prepared for use in mechanical devices. All were designed primarily to increase speed. Among these instruments and materials were the metronoscope, the tachistoscope, and the Harvard Films. The principle was the same in all the devices: words, phrases, or sections of content were flashed for recognition under controlled time allotments that could be decreased as the student gained in ability to grasp them more quickly. Grace M. Fernald's (1943) *Remedial Techniques in Basic School Subjects* described in detail her kinesthetic method, which caused quite a stir in some quarters, and several clinicians and teachers began using the method in teaching pupils retarded in reading. The term *remedial reading* was defined by Gray, as used in this period, and in 1940 he stated,

> The term *remedial reading* has been used increasingly during recent years to refer to the corrective work undertaken by schools with groups of individuals who are retarded in reading. (107)

The term *clinic* was still used loosely to cover many situations, psychological and educational. However, having reading clinics in the public schools evidently was the beginning of a trend in this period. The Thirty-Sixth Yearbook, Part I (1937), provides a glimpse of the status of reading clinics:

> The tendency to establish reading clinics for intensive study of serious cases of reading disability is one of the newer developments associated with improved supervision of reading. In one city at least three reading clinics have been established. In another city remedial classes under cadet teachers have been organized in junior high schools and senior high schools; furthermore, reading clinics for elementary schools and junior high schools have been established and provisions have been made for training teachers in remedial reading. The practices in these cities illustrate the tendency to make the best possible use of clinical methods of diagnosis in the discovery of causes of reading disabilities. (88: 431)

It is interesting to note that by 1942 the term *reading clinics* had become so prevalent and so many articles were being written about this subject that the term became a classification of articles under the general heading of "Reading" in the *Educational Index*.

VII. Special Supervision in Reading Becomes Established

As indicated in the preceding chapter, interest in the supervision of the basic school subjects had been growing rapidly during the past decade. Interest in having a special supervisor in reading was given fresh impetus in the Thirty-Sixth Yearbook of the

National Society for the Study of Education, Part I, in which an entire chapter was devoted to "The Reorganization and Improvement of Instruction in Reading Through Adequate Supervision." This chapter outlined the supervisory program in reading and expressed the need for having supervisory services at all school levels.

> In reading, the supervisory program should be as comprehensive as possible. It should be constructive as well as remedial. It should be definite and positive. It should provide for unity and continuity in the educational experiences of pupils and for steady growth on the part of teachers. A broad supervisory program is necessary in reading especially because of the large importance of reading in school subjects and activities. Because increasing demands are made on the child for intelligent reading at successive levels of advancement, adequate supervision and guidance should be provided from the kindergarten to college. (88: 420)

Dr. Gerald Yoakam, author of the chapter, gathered reading problems for discussion from supervisors in several cities and states. From this fact, it might be assumed that supervisors having charge of reading were already employed in quite a number of places. However, there is no indication as to how many supervisors were special reading supervisors. Some educators were beginning to suggest additional training for the reading specialist. The following quotation from the Forty-Seventh Yearbook, Part II, is indicative of a beginning trend.

> In addition to the treatment of reading in general professional courses and in special methods courses, specialized courses in reading should be provided for those who will render special services. (89: 290)

Finally, the following statement by Betts gives some indication of the status of reading supervision in 1949:

In most states, general supervisors help teachers to discover individual needs and to provide the necessary differentiated instruction in reading. At the time of this writing, departments of public instruction for three states provide special supervisors or consultants in reading.

A number of county, district, and local school systems have supervisors of reading instruction. Occasionally, however, the supervisor is given the responsibility for all the language arts. The activities of special supervisors are under the administration of the director of elementary education.

Supervisory service is rendered through consultations, demonstrations, workshops, child study groups, institutes, and course-of-study committees. This service is most effective when attention is given to reading needs in all curriculum areas. (90: 283)

The terms most frequently used during this period to designate the reading specialist in a public school system were "reading supervisor," "reading coordinator," "special supervisor in reading." The first time that the writer encountered the term "consultants in reading" was in the previous quotation by Betts.

The need that teachers were feeling for better training in reading is indicated in the following quotation that appeared in the Forty-Seventh Yearbook, Part II.

Of great significance is the fact that teachers and school officers in increasing numbers realize the need for better preparation to meet their responsibilities in this area. Evidence to this effect is found in the growing feeling of incompetence on their part to organize and direct reading activities, in the increasing enrolments in courses in reading in summer sessions and extension divisions, in the popularity of reading conferences and workshops, and in the demand for professional literature on reading. School-wide cooperative efforts to improve reading programs also point to the urgent need for better training. (89: 277)

The yearbook places responsibility directly at the door of colleges and universities:

The need is urgent at present for increased service on the part of colleges and universities to teachers in the field. This need arises out of the lack of adequate preparation in reading at the preservice level and out of a growing recognition of the importance of a broader understanding of reading problems. These needs can be met in large part through courses in reading during summer sessions, extension and homestudy courses, workshops, reading conferences, and consultant services. (89: 291)

CHAPTER NINE

The Period of Expanding Knowledge and Technological Revolution

Two influences that shaped reading instruction during the period 1950 to 1965 were expanding knowledge and technological revolution. Underscoring both and adding motive and impetus was of deep concern for the survival of democracy. During this period, U.S. citizens became increasingly aware of the need for vigorous effort in maintaining leadership as a nation, and in preserving a cherished way of life. These combined influences plunged the United States into the most serious problems in the history of mankind, and unexpectedly, these problems present many new challenges to those engaged in the teaching of reading. In fact, because of these problems, reading has suddenly leapt into a new magnitude.

The key solution most frequently proposed for solving the problems that are currently plaguing humanity is education, and reading is basic to education. Education cannot proceed without reading, hence a compelling new objective is to increase literacy. This new objective is lifting the horizon of reading far above its established bounds, and revealing vast new frontiers—frontiers of creativity, responsibility, and of obligation and privilege. The door to an exciting new epoch in the history of reading would seem to be not only ajar, but swinging wide open. Let us consider the more direct effects that these influences are having on the teaching of reading. First is the accumulation of knowledge. We are living in the midst of an explosion of knowledge: social, scientific, ideological, economic, and political. This vast expansion of knowledge is changing continuously and, undoubtedly, will continue to change at ever accelerating rates. We realize now that what a child is learning in school today or what an adult learned in school yesterday may be of little or no use to him tomorrow, metaphorically speaking. Therefore, if children in school and adults in present day life are to keep step with our ever-changing age, they must be able to read well and with discriminating understanding in all fields of endeavor. So it is that these expanding and changing accumulations of knowledge are placing heavy new responsibilities on those who teach reading at all levels.

The technological revolution is affecting reading instruction, also. Technology is rapidly replacing manpower with machines. Thousands of unskilled laborers and high school drop-outs find themselves without jobs. This trend will increase at an alarming rate unless the jobless are trained for newer and higher types of skills. Education will be necessary to hold the jobs of the future, and education cannot proceed without reading competency. Furthermore, the entire population will be consumers of products of this ever-advancing technology, and as such, they must read to make decisions about whether to buy products, how to use those products, and how to live effectually with those not within their control. This situation in technological developments opens up an entirely new frontier in the field of reading.

As for the nationalistic concern, all through the late 1940s, differences between the Western Powers and Russia continued to divide the world, and Russia's intention to expand Communism was plainly evident in the fact that it had taken over seven small countries. In 1950, shortly after communists had attacked the Republic of Korea, President Truman declared a national emergency as a means of strengthening the United States against Communism. This meant enlarging the armed forces and producing large quantities of weapons. The feeling for nationalism now became strong, and its effect was immediately felt in education. The following quotation from Gwinn represents the thinking of educators in 1951:

> The task of public education in this age is to develop the knowledge, appreciations, skills and attitudes necessary for living in a changing world, to develop faith in the values of democracy, to develop the understandings and ideals necessary to the achievement of a free world, and to develop the ability to defend democracy against the threat of totalitarianism. (218: 263)

This concern for national preservation caused changes to be made in materials that children had to read in school such as trade books and weekly magazines. Teaching reading in the content fields became more important, and interest in the subject of improving reading as a national asset advanced quickly.

Accompanying nationalistic worries, sociological concerns also had their effects on reading. Interest in the social effects and values of reading increased steadily during the beginning years of the period 1950 to 1965 and accelerated in later years. In the 1965 summaries of reading research (255, 256), the number of studies dealing with sociological topics reached an all-time high. Since 1950, these studies frequently had to do with attitudes, beliefs, opinions, and persuasive effects resulting from reading. Articles in newspapers and magazines were used to conduct most of these studies, which indicated concern about effects of national and international news items on those who read them. Investigators and teachers alike evinced great interest in reading habits and the use of libraries—both of which were considered important in the lives of those living in a defensive United States.

The three influences of expanding knowledge, technological revolution, and national concern continued to affect reading instruction throughout the period. Other events, however, brought about more intensive emphases and more specialized effects of these influences as the period proceeded. Two of the most important of these events and their consequences are discussed.

Pressures Following the Flight of Sputnik

It was not until 1957 that extraordinary concern about the teaching of reading began to manifest itself. This was undoubtedly due to an event of grave international significance—the launching of Sputnik, the first Russian satellite. Up until this time, the United States had possessed the most deadly weapon of warfare and had already sent a rocket 250 miles into space. These achievements assured its supremacy as a nation able to defend itself against aggression. But now the Russians were developing atom bombs, and on October 4, 1957, they startled the world by sending Sputnik 560 miles into space where it began its orbit around the earth. The supremacy of the United States was now challenged by the technological achievements of another nation, which avowedly was determined to establish world Communism. Education felt this challenge in all of its branches. As William Carr (1960)[1] said, "The first Sputnik was followed by a thundering public demand for education" (p. 7). As a part of this general demand, reading instruction now became a subject charged with unprecedented activity.

Educators and laymen alike awakened to the sharp realization that more vigorous effort must be put forth if we were to preserve and improve the American way of life. In all aspects of national endeavor, pressures were felt to produce more and more and to do it faster and faster. In reading, pressure to produce higher competency in a shorter time immediately became apparent. This trend reflected the larger motive and tempo, which, up to the time in which this chapter was being written, was to control increased production in all other aspects of American life. Investigators, authors, and publishers worked feverishly in seeking new methods and in preparing new materials that they hoped would produce faster and better results in learning to read.

As a minor influence beginning in the years immediately following Sputnik, certain criticisms were leveled against reading instruction. During this period, for the first time in history, reading instruction in U.S. schools underwent harsh and severe criticism by laymen and by some instructors in subject fields other than reading. Teachers of reading and reading specialists maintained that the criticisms were unfair and rose to defend their methods through articles, speeches, discussions, and investigations. Several comparative studies of "then and now" were made, which included comparative studies of different methods, and "status of reading" studies conducted in some states and cities, and in the United States as a whole. These studies, generally speaking, were reassuring.

Insofar as progress is concerned, the criticism by laymen probably had three good effects: it caused educators to examine their present methods more carefully; it stimulated the interest of parents and other laymen in reading instruction; it offered motives and opportunities for educators to explain the research, psychology, and philosophy on which the present methods were based. So in this situation as is often the case in others, criticism caused reading to move forward.

The Impetus of Governmental Support

The culminating influence of this period, and the one that more than any other gave a fresh and hitherto unrecognized status to competency in reading, was governmental concern for and support of education for the masses. President John F. Kennedy took an unprecedented interest in education and asked Congress to approve larger amounts of money to promote education than had previously been requested by other presidents. In 1963, President Lyndon B. Johnson announced his intention to make war on joblessness and poverty, and to provide "civil rights" for all citizens. The basic medium advocated for furthering all three objectives was education, and, as previously stated, reading is commonly recognized as the foundation on which education is built.

The United States government and many communities stimulated by governmental interest recognized the immediacy of the threat of unemployment and made appropriations and arrangements for retraining both adults and youth. Job training centers were set up, and a mass movement was undertaken to educate out-of-school individuals.

This strong interest in teaching youth and adults not attending school extended reading instruction far beyond its established bounds. Throughout history, the United States provided reading instruction to children in primary grades. It was then extended through elementary school to high school and college and, in a limited way, to adults outside of college. Now it suddenly became mandatory to teach millions of adults and youths out of school to read better so that they might hold jobs and lead productive lives. To teach these people, new materials must be prepared, new methods must be devised, and new skills discovered and taught.

The war on poverty had similar implications for the teaching of reading. There is a definite relationship between the defeat of poverty and victory of education, and if education is to be victorious, poverty-stricken people must be taught to read. The U.S. government realized this need, and education for those in poverty was one of its strong objectives.

During this period, one fifth of the U.S. population was living in poverty. Some of these people could read a little, others were functional illiterates, and others could not read at all. With one fifth of the population to be taught to read or to read better, heavy new demands were placed on instructional resources— teachers, methods, and materials.

In addition to the problems of joblessness and poverty was the special problem of integration in the United States, the solution of which was one of the goals of the incumbent government administration. Joblessness among Negroes was high, and many of them were living in intense poverty. Measures had to be taken to teach new skills, often including reading, to individuals so afflicted, and adjustments had to be made for children from poorer homes and unfavorable environments to enter schools located in more favorable home and environmental settings.

Thus, in order to improve the social and economic lives of people, education was the basic first step. The Johnson administration fully recognized the need for this basic step and provided for it. In his message to Congress on January 13, 1965, President Johnson proposed an expanded aid-to-education program and asked for the unprecedented sum of $1.3 billion. The bill was signed April 11, 1965. During the course of his message, President Johnson said,

In the past, Congress has supported an increasing commitment to education in America. Last year, I signed historic measures passed by the 88th Congress to provide:

Facilities much needed by universities, colleges and community colleges;

Major new resources for vocational training;

More loans and fellowships for students enrolled in higher education;

Enlarged and improved training for physicians, dentists, and nurses.

I propose that the 89th Congress join me in extending the commitment still further. I propose that we declare a national goal of full educational opportunity.

Every child must be encouraged to get as much education as he has the ability to take.

We want this not only for his sake—but for the nation's sake.

Nothing matters more to the future of our country: not our military preparedness—for armed might is worthless if we lack the brain power to build a world of peace; not our productive economy—for we cannot sustain growth without trained manpower; not our democratic system of government—for freedom is fragile if citizens are ignorant. (211: I: 20)

Among his specific suggestions related to reading, the President recommended legislation for grants to states for use in purchasing books for school libraries and for student use. He deplored the fact that almost 70 percent of elementary schools had no libraries. As for textbooks, he said, "The explosion of knowledge and the rapid revision of curricula in the schools has created new demands for school textbooks. The obsolete text can suffocate the learning process." The President asked for money to correct both these situations. In discussing the need to extend research and development in education, he mentioned reading and the need for extension to all levels. In regard to remedial reading, the President stated, "Remedial reading courses open up new vistas for slow learners."

So it was that the President of the United States, in the interest of our national freedom and welfare, was advocating policies that required education for solution of current problems. Furthermore, he recognized that education is basic to the achievement of these goals and recommended liberal financial aid to improve education and to extend educational opportunities. And withal, it is evident that he recognized reading as the stepping stone to educational progress.

In addition to the high interest paid by the President and Congress to Federal aid to education, the Office of Education and other government agencies, as well as private philanthropic foundations, made liberal grants to support research, and large numbers of these grant-supported studies dealt with reading. Financial aid was also given for the improvement of teacher education in reading. Furthermore, in towns and cities throughout the country, public schools, welfare and church groups, and social and service clubs organized groups of youth and adults for free reading instruction. Never in the history of our country had reading been the subject of such high interest. Never had opportunities to learn to read been extended to so many individuals at all age levels, in school and out. Truly, reading instruction had grown to entirely new dimensions in the enlarged and important role that it was to play in achieving national goals.

Perhaps it would be well to conclude this section as President Johnson closed his Congressional message on education. If the reader is engaged in some aspect of reading instruction, he may wish to apply to his own field of specialization the more general implications of the President's message:

> We are now embarked on another venture to put the American dream to work in meeting the new demands for a new day. Once again we must start where men who would improve their society have always known they must begin—with an educational system restudied, reinforced, and revitalized. (211: I: 20)

I. Reading Objectives and Courses of Study

One of the best statements of reading objectives in this period was made by Dr. William S. Gray in 1961 in an article in which he discusses the goals of the future and the broad goal of education in terms of the needs of a changing society: "The goal is increased capacity on the part of children to engage independently at a reflective, creative level in pursuit of knowledge and in the solution of difficult problems." Referring specifically to reading he says, "As far as can be foreseen at this time the changes needed are not so much in the general scope and design of the reading program as upgrading the program in harmony with changing needs" (212: 26–28).

Dr. Gray continues with several suggestions for future developments in reading:

Considering possible changes in basic reading instruction.... Of primary importance is far wider provision for developmental training in reading throughout the upper grades, high school and junior college.

For several reasons, the future basic reading period and the selections used may well assume even greater importance than in the past. First, during an era of special pressure for subject-matter learning, safeguards are needed against neglecting the personal development of pupils. Careful selection and use of reading material may give pupils additional help in gaining an understanding of themselves and others and including capacity to identify the nature of their own problems and to solve them rationally.

Second, a surprisingly large number are culturally deprived to a serious extent. It follows that a highly important function of the reading period in the future will help to overcome this deficiency and to expand the cultural background of all the children.

Third, the number of juvenile delinquents is rapidly increasing. This is due largely, it is maintained, to attitudes, values and behavior patterns acquired from unfavorable home and neighborhood environments. The need for cultivation of wholesome societal attitudes, moral sensitivity, and study of conditions that will guide both thinking and behavior is important. Promoting growth in these directions through reading provides unlimited opportunities for research and experimentation in the future.

I wish to refer to the urgent need for reading in the content fields. Herein lies one of the great possibilities for developing mature, competent readers in the future.

Curriculum efforts to adjust to individual differences will also be greatly extended.

In efforts to provide maximum progress both in and through reading, early training will be given in other language arts—listening, speaking, writing—and will be continued with increasing intensity at all school levels.

We can expect increasing and effective use of audio-visual aids such as filmstrips, films, recordings and other devices.

We can't tell how much men's ingenuity and technology may modify traditional practices in teaching the basic skills of reading. If the experimental use of new procedures shows that the teacher's time can be saved and more rapid and effective learning achieved, we should adopt them wholeheartedly. More energy will then be released for promoting growth in higher and more mature forms of interpretation.

The goal sought is a closely coordinated, sequential program of reading improvement in all curriculum fields and for all levels of schooling. The ultimate success depends on the continuous blending of old blood and new—on holding fast to that which has proved its worth, while marking out new trails and conquering new frontiers. (212: 26–28)

The long and detailed lists of "objectives" that appeared previously in courses of study seem to have outlived their usefulness. It is extremely rare, indeed, that we find the term above a detailed list of skills in courses published between 1950 and 1965. In these courses, we are much more apt to find such headings as "Point of View," "Viewpoint," "Philosophy," "Guiding Principles," and "Goals." A large number of courses emphasize reading needs in the changing society of our democracy. A Columbia, Missouri course of study states,

Reading in modern society has become an essential tool to the "masses" instead of a "few." Its multiple function makes it a tool needed in all educational processes: therefore, it places a great responsibility upon us as teachers, to teach each child to become as efficient as his abilities allow so that reading can be *used* to fulfill his particular needs in life. (213: 3)

A New York City course of study presents this viewpoint:

Children today are growing up in a very complex and rapidly changing world. The fact that many influences are bearing upon their lives and many media of communication are demanding their attention makes it imperative that children be helped to develop well-integrated personalities and strong inner resources. To maintain this integrity, children must be informed concerning the past and alert to the present. They must be able to think creatively as well as critically, to deal with things of the spirit as well as of the mind, to seek social progress as well as personal fulfillment.

Reading is still the "open sesame" to the treasures of the past and the accomplishments of the present. No other medium offers the enduring and complete record of man's thoughts and deeds that is to be found in books. It is more vital than ever, therefore, in an era of competing media of communication, that children's experiences with books be of such a nature that they will turn increasingly to reading for various purposes and grow steadily in their ability to read independently a great variety of materials. (214: 1)

Flexibility in terms of change is stressed in some of the courses. For example, we find the following statements under "Points of View" in a Detroit, Michigan, course of study.

In a city system as large as ours, there can be no one method nor one set of reading material that will begin to meet the widely differing individual needs represented in our schools.

Further, it must be understood that what we do here anyhow in the way of streamlining may have to be done all over again in our schools six months or a year from now. (215: 13)

Those who write the recent courses appear to be fully conversant with research findings in reading as well as with present societal needs, and these findings are used as bases for several of their general statements. A Baltimore, Maryland, course of study, for example, makes the following statements under the heading "Guiding Principles Basic to a Reading Program":

Personal needs and the demands of society determine the planned instruction in reading.

A strong desire to read promotes effective reading instruction.

Home, school and community combine to insure success in reading.

A reading program capitalizes on the maturing and expanding interests of children.

A program should provide for the systematic development of all reading skills in sequential order.

The purposes, experiences and types of material determine the skills the reader uses and the rate at which he reads. (216: 4–6)

Practically all the courses take the position of advocating reading as one of the language arts and stress the desirability of reinforcing reading with the other language art skills. Representative of this position is the following statement from a course of study prepared by the city schools of San Diego, California:

> Reading is one of the four communication skills. The other three are writing, spelling, listening. Communication is always a two-way process with a sender and a receiver of a message.... Speaking, listening, and writing activities are essential to an efficient program in reading.... Children clarify their ideas and concepts gained from reading by engaging in a variety of listening, spelling, and writing activities. (217: 1)

In general, courses of study in reading show several new publishing trends. Some contain more pages and appear in one thick book while others appear in separate books for different grade levels or for special groups such as slow learners. In the latter cases, the total number of pages in these combined books is more than in the former one-book courses. Many reading courses are incorporated in a general course of study for all the language arts. Nearly all the separate courses of study devoted to reading include literature, as well as skill development in the teaching of reading. All courses provide many more practical suggestions for developing reading skills than they did previously. Many list bibliographies of books and materials available for use by the teacher and children.

II. Professional Books on Reading

This period was unusually productive in bringing forth new professional books on the teaching of reading. Many books dealt with reading at the elementary level, but several were published at the secondary level, and a new frontier was opened with the publication of books for college and adult levels. The appearance of books for parents in regard to children's reading also was an innovation.

Among the new professional books published at the elementary level were William H. Burton's *Reading in Child Development* (Bobbs-Merrill); Albert J. Harris's *Effective Teaching of Reading* (McKay); Gertrude Hildreth's *Teaching Reading* (Holt); Homer L. J. Carter and Dorothy J. McGinnis's *Learning to Read* (McGraw); Mildred A. Dawson and Henry A. Bamman's *Fundamentals of Basic Reading Instruction* (Longmans); John J. DeBoer and Martha Dallmann's *The Teaching of Reading* (Holt); Lillian Gray and Dora Reese's *Teaching Children to Read* (Ronald); Arthur W. Heilman's *Principles and Practices of Teaching Reading* (Charles E. Merrill); Margaret McKim's *Guiding Growth in Reading* (Macmillan); Miles A. Tinker and Constance McCullough's *Teaching Elementary Reading* (Appleton); David H. Russell's *Children Learn to Read* (Ginn); Nila Banton Smith's *Reading Instruction for Today's Children* (Prentice-Hall); George D. Spache's *Toward Better Reading* (Garrard), which also contains two excellent chapters on diagnosis and remediation, and *Children, Books and Reading* (International Reading Association).

Professional books for the secondary school were Henry A. Bamman, Ursula Hogan, and Charles E. Greene's *Reading Instruction in the Secondary School* (Longmans); Robert Karlin's *Teaching Reading in High School* (Bobbs-Merrill); Ruth Strang and Dorothy K. Bracken's *Making Better Readers* (Heath); and *Reading in Secondary Schools* written by a group of specialists for publication by the International Reading Association.

The publication of a large number of books for college students and adults to use in improving their reading ability was an innovation in this period. Many new soft-cover workbooks containing reading exercises were published as were several hard-cover books in which a large portion of content was devoted to discussion of reading theory and explanation of skills, as well as containing selections for practice purposes: Homer L.J. Carter and Dorothy J. McGinnis's *Effective Reading for College Students* (Dryden); Horace

Judson's *The Techniques of Reading* (Harcourt); Paul D. Leedy's *Reading Instruction for Adults*, and *Read with Speed and Precision* (McGraw); Nila Banton Smith's *Read Faster and Get More from Your Reading* (Prentice-Hall); and Paul Witty's *How to Become a Better Reader* (Science Research Associates). Two soft-covered professional books devoted entirely to the theory and practice of teaching reading at the higher levels are the International Reading Association's *College-Adult Reading Instruction*, and *New Developments in Programs and Procedures for College-Adult Reading* (Twelfth Yearbook of the National Reading Conference).

As a part of the trend toward working more closely with parents in helping them to guide their children's reading interests and activities, new books on reading began to appear for the use of this group such as Nancy Larrick's *A Parent's Guide to Children's Reading* (Trident), and *A Parent's Guide to Children's Education* (Doubleday); and Ruth Strang's *Helping Your Child Improve His Reading* (Dutton).

Collections of articles from periodicals formed the content of some new books, such as Albert J. Harris's *Readings on Reading Instruction* (McKay); and Walter B. Barbe's *Teaching Reading: Selected Materials* (Oxford). Two books on the psychology of reading were Irving H. Anderson and Walter F. Dearborn's *The Psychology of Teaching Reading* (Ronald); and Emerald V. Dechant's *Improving the Teaching of Reading* (Prentice-Hall). Books on reading concerned with the special fields of linguistics and of reading disabilities are mentioned in section VIII, page 356, and section XI, page 372, of this chapter.

III. Materials Provided in Basal Reading Programs

Teachers' Manuals

Today the trend is toward having even more teachers' manuals than in preceding years. The number of first-grade manuals remains about the same as previously: one for the readiness material, one each for the collection of preprimers, the primer, and the first reader. In some series, however, there are separate manuals for the practice pads. This innovation doubles the number of manuals that were provided only to accompany the textbooks.

Another new feature to appear is annotated and keyed editions of manuals. These editions contain the children's book and the regular teacher's manual, which is a departure from the usual teachers' editions, in that notes to the teacher are placed directly on the pages of the children's book for easy access to them while the children are reading. Among these notes are keys giving references to page numbers in the regular teachers' guide or in supplemental materials used by the pupils. These numbers indicate references helpful to the teacher in working with particular pages. Most reading programs provide a teachers' edition that contains both the children's book and the teachers' manual, and include a separate teachers' manual without the children's book. Most often the teachers' edition is titled "Teachers' Edition" and appears on the cover of the children's book, the pages of which are included in this edition; therefore, the teachers' edition usually is a hardbound book. The separate manual, usually titled "Teachers' Manual," is a soft-bound book. "The Teachers' Guide" also continues to be used as a title. In annotated editions, we find titles such as "Teachers' Edition: Annotated and Keyed" (Betts Basic Readers), and "Teachers' Annotated Edition and Guide" (Macmillan Reading Program).

Changes in the conventional 6 by 8 size of both manuals and readers is an innovation of this period. There are also departures in matching manual size to reader size. In one new series, the manuals measure 8 $\frac{1}{2}$ by 11 inches, matching the size of the workbooks; and in another series, the manuals measure 6 $\frac{1}{2}$ by 8$\frac{1}{4}$, matching the size of the accompanying readers. Manuals now have many new typographical features designed to facilitate their use by teachers. The suggestions given are for the most part clear, comprehensive in their coverage of reading skills, and practical in application. Procedures for teaching each story usually fall into three categories: teacher directed activities, independent work, and extended activities.

Characteristics of Basal Readers

Several new basal reader series were published from 1950 to 1965, while some authors who had published only primary programs before 1950, revised and completed their series during this period. Two other programs launched before 1950 have been drastically revised and widely expanded. The reading programs indicated in these classifications were selected for analysis of trends:

Guy L. Bond et al., The Developmental Reading Program (Lyons and Carnahan).
Albert J. Harris, Mae Knight Clark, et al., The Macmillan Reading Program (Macmillan).
Glenn McCracken and Charles Walcutt. Basic Reading (Lippincott).
William D. Sheldon, Mary C. Austin, Queenie Mills, and Robert A. McCracken, The Sheldon Basic Reading Series (Allyn & Bacon).
Russell G. Stauffer, Alvina Burrows, et al., Winston Basic Readers (Holt, Rinehart & Winston).

Reading programs partially published in the preceding period but revised and completed during this period:

Emmett A. Betts and Carolyn Welch, Betts Basic Readers (American Book).
David Russell et al., The Ginn Basic Readers (Ginn).

Reading programs in which the complete series was published in preceding years but were revised and extended during this period:

William S. Gray et al., The Curriculum Foundation Series (Scott Foresman).
Paul McKee, Lucile Harrison, et al., Reading for Meaning (Houghton Mifflin).
Paul Witty et al., Reading for Interest (D.C. Heath).

The most obvious new development in reading programs during this period was the provision for multiple texts. In addition to the basal readers, authors provided additional texts such as enrichment readers; supplementary reading series; associated readers; simplified versions of the basal texts for slow readers; a supplemental reader in addition to two basal readers for each of the grades from two through six; an additional sets of readers for the unusually good readers and the unusually slow readers; and a set of "free" paperbacks, in addition to each reader. These additional books indicate that authors and publishers were putting forth outstanding efforts to provide for individual differences, which could not be accomplished with only one or two basal readers per grade.

Another innovation is the departure from the standard-reader size of 6 by 8 to $6\frac{1}{2}$ by $8\frac{3}{8}$, $6\frac{5}{8}$ by $8\frac{3}{4}$, $6\frac{1}{2}$ by $9\frac{3}{8}$, $6\frac{1}{2}$ by $8\frac{5}{8}$, or $7\frac{1}{8}$ by $9\frac{1}{4}$. The size of a book no longer stamps it as a reader, and this variation in size is a welcome change.

Some programs now extend through seventh and eighth grades, whereas in the past, sixth grade was the generally accepted stopping point. This reflects the trend towards teaching developmental reading at higher levels.

The nature of the content of readers did not change much during this period except that the stories may have been a bit more interesting, intriguing, and higher in literary quality. The larger number of themes and informative articles may have had to do with topics of current interest. The content of primers and first readers, however, still consisted wholly of realistic stories. The largest proportion of content in the second and third readers also is realistic, but some fanciful tales and informative selections are included. At the higher levels, a considerable number of informative selections appeared, and poems and stories from literature seemed to be more popular as reader content than they had been for several years.

Art work became more colorful and profuse at the early levels. In later programs, however, an advance was seen in the use of softer colors, resulting in more pleasing illustrations. Beginning with the third grade, many series introduced black and white illustrations, and pictures of this type increased in numbers in the upper-grade readers. Full-page illustrations and double-page spreads seemed not to be used as generously as in the preceding period.

The authorship of the new reading programs usually consisted of several people. The leading author usually was a college professor, held a doctoral degree, and had received national recognition as a reading authority before preparing a reading program. The number of collaborators varied from four to six, and the authors often were affiliated with public school systems and had degrees ranging from the bachelor's to the doctorate.

In considering vocabulary of series published during this period, the average number of words in preprimers was 59, and the average number of new words in primers was 89. These figures indicated a decrease over the preceding period. Repetitions were carefully controlled, and all authors, except those of one series, checked their vocabularies with scientific word lists. The authors of the excepted series stated that they did not check with such lists because they say that such a practice had many fallacies.

New Basal Reading Programs

In keeping with preceding chapters, some of the basal reading programs published between 1950 and 1965 are described as representative of this period. Due to the many new developments in reading that must be recognized in this chapter, the writer regrets that it is necessary to restrict the number of reading programs to be discussed, and to give brief and limited descriptions of those that are included.

The Sheldon Basic Reading Series. This series, prepared by William D. Sheldon, Mary Austin, Queenie Mills, and Robert McCracken, was first launched in 1957 and revised in 1963. The

1963 edition, which is described, provides the following books for the first-grade level: two readiness books, three preprimers and a senior preprimer, a primer, and a first reader. For the second-grade level, there is a readiness second reader, a second reader, and a supplemental second reader. This pattern of three readers per grade is followed for the third-grade level. Next is a "Transition Reader, 3-4," followed by a fourth reader and a supplemental fourth reader. A regular reader and a supplemental reader are provided for the fifth- and sixth-grade levels. A separate reader is provided for the seventh- and eighth-grade levels. This reading series is one of the few basal reading programs that extends its texts to include levels beyond the sixth grade. A new feature is a transition reader for use between third and fourth grades. Book-length novels are provided for the middle grades. Boys' interests are especially emphasized in these materials.

Throughout the first six grades beginning with the preprimers, the readers at each level are accompanied with an Activity Book and an Independent Activities Pad. This is the first series of readers to provide activity books for the readers at the various levels. Furthermore, there is a teachers' edition for each activity book and a teachers' manual for each independent activities pad. This is an innovation because teachers' editions or manuals previously have not been provided for the commonly called "practice pads" that accompany readers in a basal reading program.

Another feature included in the manuals and activity books are the Sheldon Diagnostic Tests. These tests are designed to serve the teacher in three ways: to indicate each pupil's readiness for reading on a new level by comparing his achievement on materials from preceding levels; to identify a pupil's particular reading abilities and weaknesses; and to make it possible to group pupils for effective instruction. Achievement tests are also available. Teaching equipment for the series includes word cards; boxed sets of word, ending, and punctuation cards; picture cards; a pocket chart; and a Big Book.

This is a series that departed from the conventional reader size of 6 by 8. The texts for the first six grades are 6 1/4 by 8 1/2, and those for the seventh and eighth grades are 7 by 9 1/2. The skill program of the series is very carefully built and is reinforced at each successive level to ensure continuity of skill growth from grade one through grade eight.

The selections in the readers are well written and have strong interest appeal. In the early books, the content is realistic and based on experiences common to most children. As the books progress through the grades, they contain a great variety of stories, informative selections, poems, and plays. The authors stress moral and spiritual values in the reader content. Selections are classified under three headings in which such values may be developed: Group and Family Living, Respecting Rights of Others, and Understanding and Accepting One's Self.

The artwork is colorful and attractive and variously placed at the tops and bottoms of pages. As in reader programs in general, several black and white illustrations appear in the upper-grade readers, but these are done very effectively. Full-page pictures and double-page spreads are not used; however, one very attractive feature is the section divider that appears before each new section of content throughout the reading texts. The divider is printed on solid color paper (varying with each section) and contains an illustration appropriate for the theme of the selections that follow. Following is an example of the primer content, and an example of the third readers.

It was the pet show day.
Big pets came to school.
Little pets came to school.
Mothers came and children came.
Rags and Midnight came to be in the show.
Ricky and Mother came to see the show. (219: 55)

It was no longer quiet after Waggles came. He ran after the ducks and chased the chickens. He barked at the cattle, the horses, the pigs, the sheep, and the lambs. He even put his nose through the spider's new web in the barn and chased a field mouse back to his hole. (220: 148)

The Winston Basic Readers, Communication Program. The series was prepared by Russell G. Stauffer and Alvina Treut Burrows with the assistance of several collaborators. The entire program for the elementary grades was published between 1960 and 1962. Dr. Stauffer writes,

> At the heart of this program is the authors' firm belief that children can and do think, and that reading is importantly concerned with the thinking process. Deliberately selected stories in each of the readers focus on problem-solving situations. From first through sixth grade, the Directed Reading-Thinking Activity invites children to value and to improve their skill in critical thinking.

The primary purpose of the authors in preparing this program was to capitalize on the interrelationships of the language arts skills by providing experiences in reading, writing, speaking, and listening, as each one augments the other. In order to facilitate such a program, two different sets of books were prepared: American English Books, and Winston Basic Readers. The American English Books is a program that develops reading, writing, spelling, and speaking skills, as well as literary appreciation. The Winston Basic Readers is a part of the total communication program with which this description is particularly concerned.

In addition to the aim of taking strong advantage of the language arts skills in a reading program, the authors of the basic readers have another primary and unique objective in mind. They advocate "a modified approach" that makes use of teaching reading by the individualized plan as well as by the group-oriented arrangement. Suggestions are given in the teachers' editions for using each of these approaches.

The texts provided in the basic reading program are as follows: two readiness books; three preprimers; one primer; one first reader; two readers each for second, third, and fourth grades; one fifth reader; and one sixth reader. There is a study book to accompany the three preprimers, and one to accompany each of the other books. Thirteen teachers' editions are provided, each of which contains the basic text, instructions to the teacher, and the accompanying study book.

The supplemental materials include a set of "Big Pictures" to extend the readiness program; a set of word cards for the teacher and sets of small word cards for the children; a set of cardboard-cutout materials for visual extension of the interrelated communications program; a cohere-o-graph, a felt board on which children can portray scenes and stories for visual extension of the communications program; a vis-o-graph, a transparent, acetate cover that is placed on top of the Big Pictures and others so that children may trace lines or mark on a picture without marking the original.

The readers are exceptionally well written and excellent in literary quality. The text in the early books is based on interesting child experiences. Both the primer and the first reader contain fanciful tales. One unique feature in the first reader is a fanciful tale done in a comic-strip format. Poems are introduced in the third grade and appear in all successive books. Also included in the third reader, as well as the middle-grade readers, are realistic stories that have considerable substance. There is also a good balance of classical stories and modern tales. Drama offers children opportunities to read this form of literature.

The artwork is pleasing. Colors are soft but vivid. Illustrations usually are placed at the tops and bottoms of pages, but in some special selections they are placed in various arrangements. Color is used more generously than usual in the upper-grade readers. A unique feature is the use of several actual photographs. Following is sample content from the first reader:

> It was a hot, hot day, but Nancy worked faster and faster.
> She did many things for Grandmother.
> Soon the garden was clean,
> and the two went to the store. (221: 57)

Following is a sample paragraph from the first third reader:

> The first boy up hit a high fly and was an easy out. The next boy went down swinging. Then the third boy was a strike out, and the side was out. (222: 188)

The Macmillan Reading Program. This series is the latest to be developed in this period. The senior authors are Albert J. Harris and Mae Knight Clark, assisted by several collaborators. The primary materials for this program were published in 1965, and the readers for grades six through eight are to be launched in 1966. In discussing their program, the authors say,

> The space race and automation, concern about America's place in today's world, concern about the place of the individual in today's America, and the "knowledge explosion" now doubling the sum of man's knowledge every ten years are the factors which have heightened concern about the school's ability to keep up. They have led to curriculum revision in math and science. And they are the factors behind the revisions achieved in the Macmillan Reading Program.

This statement expresses a worthy ambition and one that certainly is in keeping with the conditions in our changing civilization.

The first-grade program of the series embraces a readiness book, three preprimers, a primer, and a first reader. Grades two and three have two books each, and grades four, five, and six have one book each. There is a Teachers Annotated Edition and Guide for the readiness level, preprimer level, and for each of the readers.

Work books for skill practice, Discovery Books, are designed around the role of discovery in learning and are characterized by pupil involvement and self-help features. Exercise sheets on master stencils, an alternate accessory, also apply the learning-by-discovery principle. First-grade story cards for the teachers is a new feature. Stories for "free" reading are provided in 25 paperbacks for grades one through three and are written by authors of popular juveniles.

Self-help dictionaries are a feature of grade-one materials. A self-help dictionary is bound in the back of each of the three preprimers. A separate reference aid, My Self-Help Dictionary, contains all words introduced in first grade. These self-help materials are not picture dictionaries or are they primarily dictionaries of word meanings, but they employ initial letters and a context of words and pictures to help pupils identify and discover the meanings of words found earlier in a teacher-directed situation. A magnetic display stand, the first of its kind, has been developed for use in grade one. This accessory is designed for convenient display of the program's story cards and word- and sentence-building cards.

In the upper-grades, a skill development program is included in the readers that includes (a) brief introductions that provide background and suggest purposes for reading; (b) brief selections that give pupils information about how to read efficiently; (c) one or more comprehension exercises after each selection; (d) a planned sequence of skills, with one or more skill-building sections after nearly every selection; and (e) in the fourth-grade book, a phonics handbook appears as an Appendix, to be used as needed for individual or small-group practice.

The content of the readers is totally realistic at beginning stages. The text in the intermediate- and upper-grade books provides a balance of fiction and nonfiction. Nonfiction includes biography, encyclopedia selections, and map reading. Fiction includes both classical and contemporary authors.

A new feature of the series integrates the teaching of word recognition skills with the introduction of new vocabulary. Much of the instruction in the use of context, phonics, structural analysis, and dictionary is in the preparatory part of the lesson plans. The following is what the authors say in regard to content:

> The articles acquaint the pupil with his historical heritage, and with some of the latest scientific developments in today's world; they introduce him to great men and women whose lives inspire emulation; through poetry and prose, they demonstrate the power of the printed word to move the reader to tenderness, to laughter, to triumph over fear. (226: 10)

The artwork in the readers is beautiful with colors that are rich and deep but soft, often having the appearance of paintings. Instead of being placed in boxes at the tops and bottoms of pages, they are placed randomly throughout. Usually placed on the upper part of the page, they extend to the edges of the pages and often have some feature of the picture bleeding downward in an artistic manner. There are many full-page or nearly full-page pictures in the primary readers. Following is a sample of content from the preprimer:

> Jeff said, "Mike is a cowboy.
> Mike can play."
> Mary said, "Not Mike!
> Mike can't ride a bike."
> Mike said, "I can ride.
> I want to play with Jeff." (224: 39)

Following is a sample from the fifth-grade basal reader:

> In writing her biography of me, Suzy is a frank historian. She doesn't cover up one's faults, but gives them an equal showing with one's handsome qualities. It is clear that several times, at breakfast and

dinner, in those long-past days, I was posing for the biography and I also remember that Suzy recognized it. (225)

The Developmental Reading Program. This series, prepared by Guy L. Bond and Leo Fay, with the assistance of several collaborators, was launched between 1950 and 1958, revised and extended in 1962, and is described here.

A distinctive feature of this reading program is that each basal reader, beginning with the primer and through the eighth grade, is published in a simplified edition, bound in the same cover as the regular edition, and contains the same stories and illustrations. The only difference between the regular and simplified edition is that the latter contains fewer new words, perhaps 20 percent or less. The simplified edition for each first-grade book is called the "Companion Primer" or "Companion First Reader." For readers beyond the first grade, the simplified edition is called the "Class Book Edition."

The regular series provides "Stories In Pictures" and "Pictures to Read" for the reading readiness period. It contains four preprimers and one primer. There is one reader for the first grade, two each for the second grade and the third grade, and one each for grades four through eight. The "Classmate Editions" add another nine readers to the program. Skill Development Workbooks are provided for the entire program—one for the readiness period, one for the four preprimers, and one for each of the readers. There are manuals and teachers' editions available for the reading materials at all levels.

Equipment for the series includes a Big Book, pictures, word cards, and cardholder. The pictures in the beginning books are unusually vivid, with much color used throughout all the books. In the more advanced readers, there are both one-color and black and white illustrations. A full- or double-page illustration is rarely used. The covers of the books are unusually attractive, depicting full-page outdoor scenes in pleasing colors.

The content of the first-grade readers is largely realistic, although a few fanciful tales are introduced. Many of the realistic stories relate amusing experiences that children have with animals. The humor in these beginning books is unique and refreshing.

The authors believe that children should be taught to read materials of many different types. For this reason, from the first grade throughout the series, factual materials of science, history, geography, and other areas are included. Stories both realistic and imaginative are included, as well as biographies and poetry. Here is a sample from the primer:

> Billy saw a clown.
> He said, "Look at the funny man.
> He is a clown.
> Look at his funny mouth.
> He has funny feet, too." (227: 90)

The following sample is representative of text in the fourth reader, regular edition.

> A stranger on horseback rode into San Antonio, a city in Mexico. His bright, blue eyes looked at the stone and adobe buildings that stood along the dust-covered streets. From behind adobe walls, the soft music of guitars could be heard. (228: 297)

Basic Reading. This is the general title of a program prepared by Glenn McCracken, Charles C. Walcutt, and others, which was published from 1963 to 1965. The first-grade books consist of a preprimer, a primer, and two first readers. There are readers for grades two through six. Workbooks and teachers editions are provided for books throughout the series, and filmstrips accompany the primary books.

The series' chief characteristic that differentiates it from the others described is that it represents a highly specialized phonic approach that begins as soon as a child enters first grade. On the first page in the preprimer, three apples are pictured and the letter *a* appears in lower-case and in capitalized forms as *a A*. In the first lesson, children are taught to recognize the two forms of the letter *a* and to recognize the sound of short *a*. The text continues in this pattern introducing the sounds of short *e, i, o,* and *u*. It also introduces sounds of several single consonants *st, nd,* and *mp* as endings, and of *gr, dr,* and *sp* as beginnings. One page always introduces the new phonic element or elements. This is followed by brief text in which the child is given practice reading words containing the newly introduced phonic element or elements. In the primer, the sounds taught are *ar, er, ir, or, ed, ow, l, b, j, s, k, le, ck, nk,* long *a, e, o,* and the digraphs *ea, ai, ie, oa, oe.* Many additional phonic elements are introduced in the first reader; several are introduced in the second and third readers; and at each level, provision is made for continued maintenance of elements previously taught.

Another characteristic of this series is that no reading readiness materials are provided. Children are supposed to start immediately with the preprimer as described above. However, the teachers' edition for the preprimer contains suggestions for readiness activities "for those who need it." These readiness activities are designed to teach readiness skills "at the same time that the child is learning the names, shapes, and sounds of the letters."

The covers of the readers have solid, intense colors, and each has a simple and appropriate design. All the books, including the preprimer, are large in page size, measuring approximately 6 ½ by 9 inches. The artwork is vivid, uncluttered with detail, and used generously. There are full-page pictures, and in the second and third readers, each chapter is preceded with a full-page illustration and chapter title for the next group of stories.

The content varies. In the first-grade books, many pages list phonic elements. Much of the narrative material could have happened within the experiences of the children reading them. There are many fanciful stories, however, in which animals talk, and occasionally there is a story in which a character is a camel, an Arab, a king, or a queen. Old tales and an occasional fable are introduced in the first reader. Beginning with the primer, poems are included that involve many of the phonics elements taught. The narrative selections are contrived to contain words that will give practice on certain phonic elements. They are well reinforced by the pictures, however, and most have a plot.

The teachers' guides place heavy emphasis on phonics, but they also contain suggestions for enrichment reading, activities that make use of other language arts skills and various related activities. The workbooks, as well as the teachers' guides, place strong emphasis on phonics by devoting several pages to practicing phonic elements. In addition, however, there are pages containing true-false, multiple-choice, sequential, classification, and other types of exercises designed to check meanings.

In the second- and third-grade readers, some stories are realistic, some fanciful, and some informative; the scenes take place in current times and in olden times. Poems appear in all the books. There are a few phonic pages in the first-semester second reader but none in the succeeding readers. Beginning with the second-semester second reader, a "Phonic Guide" is placed at the end of each book that lists the sounds of the phonics elements previously taught together with words, which are to serve as examples of the sounds.

Because it would be meaningless to present a page from the primer with the narrative text without accompanying it with the preceding phonics page, a sample of each is presented as follows:

ar

arm	darn	tar	dart	tart	cart
art	card	mar	hard	harm	part
are	star	car	farm	far	scarf (229: 1)

Tom is a farm hand.
Tom has a farm cart.
A card is on the cart.
Tom puts eggs in his cart. (229: 2)

The following paragraph appears in the first-semester third reader of the series:

Maggie Muggins ran as fast as she could to the cucumber patch to see Mr. McGarrity. Maggie had something on her mind, and that something was worrying her. Mr. McGarrity could see that, and he said to her, "Well, Maggie Muggins, what is troubling you this fine day?" (230: 62)

Revisions and Extensions of Basal Reading Programs

Two newly revised and extended programs deserve review because of their wide use and the contributions they are making at the time this is being written.

Betts Basic Readers, Third Edition. The first edition of this program (fully described on pages 266–267) was revised in 1958–1959, and the third revision of the entire series, published in 1963, will be discussed here.

The beginning program includes a language readiness book, a reading readiness book, Big Book stories, three preprimers, a primer, and a first reader. There are two readers each for grades two and three, and one reader each for grades four, five, and six. Teacher's editions and study books are available for all levels. A special sight saving edition and a Braille edition have been published.

317

In the third edition, the readers have new covers with colorful backgrounds on which attractively shaped pictures are superimposed. There is new art work and new stories and articles to replace the preceding ones.

Although the authors wish to retain the high interest value of the reader content, another important aim is to provide a wide variety of selections in order to develop the many different skills needed for reading different forms of writing and subject matter. Specifically, the goal is to develop ability to read selections varying in literary form (fiction, articles, poetry, plays, essays), and selections varying in content (social studies, science, history, geography, arithmetic, art, music). In order to facilitate this skill-development objective, authors broke sharply from previous reader patterns and placed skill-building material in the readers. Since the exaggerated emphasis on silent reading in the 1920s, exercises have seldom appeared in basal readers. Authors say they have changed their readers into textbooks, which is possibly the beginning of a new trend. More recently revised or published programs also include exercises in the readers.

The study materials in the textbooks consist of end-of-book phonic and thinking pages, starting with the preprimers; end-of-unit study pages, starting with the primer; and end-of-story thinking exercises, starting with the first reader.

The most outstanding innovation of this series is the "Annotated and Keyed Teachers' Edition" in which the pupils' book appears along with the regular manual. This new feature allows for overlaying the pages of the pupils' book with notes to the teacher, which are reprinted in red ink at the tops or bottoms of pages or in the margins. Included are questions to ask, skills to be developed in connection with the content on the page, phonics aids, and references to reinforcement materials. All these aids are in front of the teacher while the students read.

A supply of testing materials is another unusual provision. There are "Phonics Inventories," "Thinking Inventories to Estimate Instructional Levels," and achievement tests that accompany the series from reading readiness through the sixth reader. In addition to word cards, several interesting supplementary items are provided: a set of Individual Phonics and Thinking Activities; Pathways to Phonic Skills (three albums of 12-inch records); the ABC Phonic Charts; and full-color films, "Beginning Dictionary Skills," and "Extending Strips on Dictionary Skills."

The Ginn Basic Reading Program. The first edition of the primary program of this series was published in 1948–1949 (discussed on pages 264–266). The series has been extended to seventh and eighth grades, and ninth-grade materials are in preparation. The program for grades one through six has undergone several revisions and expanded extensively. The 1964 edition of the elementary books will be included in this account, and the program as a whole will be described briefly as it exists at this time.

The program provides the following first-grade materials: a readiness book, three preprimers, a primer, and a first reader. There are two readers each for grades two through six, and one each for grades seven, eight, and nine. Teachers' editions and workbooks are provided at all levels. In the 1964 editions, four pages of exercises appear at the end of each reader.

In revised formats, the covers of the books have attractive pictures superimposed on plain, colorful backgrounds. The effective illustrations are in soft colors, and even in the middle-grade readers, all illustrations are in color. In keeping with recent trends, the overall page size in the elementary readers has changed from a conventional size to a generous 6 ½ by 9 inches.

The content of the readers is of high literary quality, much of it written by well-known contemporary authors, although past well-known authors are included as well. All types of literature are included, along with outstanding poems, and subjects and subject areas, both old and new. Sequential skill development is carefully provided for in the workbooks and in the suggestions and exercises in the teachers' editions.

A significant feature of the total Ginn program is the provision of "Enrichment Readers," which accompany the preprimers as a group, the primer, and each of the readers from first to sixth grade. The selections in these books are outstanding. The middle grade books, particularly, contain excellent selections from children's literature and the classics. "Book-Length Stories" are provided for the middle grades, and the Ginn Story-Time Series for the primary grades is now in preparation.

Among other supplementary materials are the "By Myself" booklets for reinforcing skills at the primary level, a programmed word-study review for the middle-grade level, and self-help activities pads. Other aids to teaching include four card sets; Our Big Red Story Book; Word-Study Charts; "Let's Listen," an album of records to develop auditory training and speech development during the readiness period; song records to use in connection with the early readers; and Sounds We Use, full-color film strips for teaching phonics. Evaluation is provided for in the Ginn Basic Reading Tests with readiness and achievement tests for grades one through six. Word-analysis tests are also available.

The teachers' manuals are large books, usually containing 500 or more pages. In addition to procedures to use in reading a story, the manuals offer suggestions for skill development of all kinds, highlighting word analysis. A considerable amount of enrichment material is included with many suggestions for wide, independent reading.

Three programs launched as a whole previous to 1950 will be reviewed briefly because of their extensive revision and expansion during this period, and because of the wide use of their revised editions at the present time.

The Curriculum Foundation Series. This program, commonly called "The Scott Foresman Readers," has undergone heavy revision and extensive additions. The total program will be described in terms of its development in 1965. The basal readers enumerated previously have been widely revised. In the latest edition, the readers have new covers, enlarged page sizes, improved typeface, and new art work. A very large proportion of the content is also new. Other new developments are two new prereading books, two books for each of the middle grades, the graded dictionary program, and more refined structural and phonetic skills in the guidebooks.

A new basic reading program has been prepared for the middle grades, with new content and a variety of selections, all accompanied by unusually attractive illustrations. Each book is accompanied with a teachers' guide and a Think-and-Do Book.

The New Basic Reading Program for the Sixties. This series is highlighted by two editions of the Basic Reader: the Established and the Multi-ethnic. The Multi-ethnic edition reflects in its selections, illustrations and teaching procedures for 30 cultural and ethnic groups (see page 356 for additional discussion of this edition).

Wide Horizons. This is a special series of readers designed for children who not only meet but exceed the expectations of their grade, and it is intended to serve as an extension of the basal readers. Think-and-Do books and teachers' guides do not accompany these readers because they are self-directing.

The Open Highways Program. This is another special program developed to meet the needs of children who do not come up to the expectations of their grade. The readers contain fresh new content designed to reawaken interest in reading. Teachers' guides and Think-and-Do books accompany the readers. The entire program is planned to reintroduce, reteach, review, and reinforce the reading skills.

Reading for Interest. This series, totally new in design, appears with considerably larger page size and bound in colorful covers. Some show pictures superimposed on plain colors, others show a mosaic of characters and scenes representative of stories in the books. The teachers' guides and the Do and Learn books also have new covers, and the guides have been expanded and revised in ways that reflect recent research and emphases (see pages 261–262 for a description of this series).

Reading Caravan. This is a distinctive and unusually attractive new series of readers developed by D.C. Heath and published in 1964. These books, as well as the basal program, were prepared by Dr. Paul Witty with other coauthors. There are seven books in this series: a primer, a first reader, and a reader for each of the grades two through six. These books are large in page size (approximately 7 by 9 inches), and a complete scene keyed to the title of the book appears on the cover of each. The illustrations in the books are bright, attractive, and variously placed. A full-page illustration precedes each chapter.

The content features literature and is high in interest appeal. Many selections are useful in teaching skills needed in reading in the content fields, and suggestions are given in the books and guides for furthering this purpose. Beginning with the second reader, an introduction is provided, and exercises follow each selection in the book. The exercises are designed to foster appreciation, to develop skills, and to extend reading interest. In the Teachers' editions, a guide is bound in the back of each of the pupils' books, which contain procedures for teaching each story and list references to film strips, recordings, and other books to use for extending reading interests.

Reading for Meaning. This program, by Paul McKee and coauthors, underwent two revisions during this period. The 1963 revision will be reviewed. The series now consists of a Pre-Reading Program, three preprimers, a primer, a first reader, two readers for each of grades two and three, and a single reader for each of grades four through six. These books appear in attractive covers. The illustrations within the books are vivid in color, and several are full-page or near full-page in size. The page size of the middle-grade readers has been enlarged to approximately $7\frac{1}{4}$ by 9 inches.

The content of the readers consists of stories, old and new, poems, and plays. Several informative articles are included. For example, in the fifth reader, we find selections on such topics as "Using the Context" and "You Can Make a Puppet."

The teachers' editions provide reduced facsimiles of the pages in the pupils' books, and, at early levels, the book itself is included. Procedures are given for preparing for reading a selection; reading and discussing; developing reading skills; providing for individual differences and related activities; and broadening reading interests.

A workbook accompanies each text, except at the preprimer stage where one workbook accompanies all three preprimers. Additional supplemental materials are word cards, punctuation cards, picture and key cards; a Big Book and duplicating masters for each unit, appearing in the teachers' editions or available in a separate package; and "Word Introduction Books" provided for each of the three different first-grade levels and for each of the second- and third-grade texts.

A testing program is provided. For each book in the series, there is a nationally normed Basic Reading Test; and the following additional tests are also available for use with this reading program: The Primary Reading Profiles, Levels I and II, by Stroud, Hieronymous, and McKee; and the McKee Inventory of Phonetic Skills, Tests One to Three.

The chief characteristics of this series are emphasis on meanings, with special attention given to the use of context clues; and the teaching of letter and sound associations during the early stages in reading, beginning in the reading readiness period.

IV. Methods of Teaching as Advocated in Basal Reading Programs

Status of Reading

During this period, two national surveys of the status of reading were conducted. Because schools involved in these surveys used basal reading programs, it seems appropriate to present results of these studies in this section.

In the *Columbia-Carnegie Study of Reading Research and Its Communication*, Barton and Wilder mailed questionnaires to a random sample of more than 300 schools throughout the United States and received returns from about half of them. An analysis of these returns revealed many interesting facts; however, only those directly pertinent to the topic of reading method will be reported here. Following are direct quotations (232: 172–174), the first having to do with reading materials, the topic of which, of course, is related to method.

Reading instruction in almost all schools starts from a similar basis: basic readers from a graded series are used by 90% of first-grade teachers and by 92 to 84% of second- and third-grade teachers on "all or most days in the year." In addition to this base, however, somewhat different kinds of supplementary materials are used. About a third of the primary grades use "children's story books which are not part of a reading series" on all or most days. About a third use special books for slow readers on all or most days. A quarter of the first grades use experience charts based on the children's activities or interests on all or most days. Library work in school or public library is used on many days in 40% of the first grades, increasing to 65% in sixth grade. Field trips are used more than just once or twice a year in 35% of first grades, falling to 23% of sixth grades. Films or filmstrips for reading instruction, television for reading instruction, reading machines for improving speed or training eye movements, and kits of graded individual exercises ("reading laboratory") are used on all or most days in less than 4% of the grades 1 through 6. These devices are as rare as basic readers are universal.

Almost all classes have a classroom library, but only 10% of first grades and 30% of higher grades have 75 or more books in it.

The teachers' opinions place great emphasis on the desirability of three things: a basal reading series, a classroom library of many varied children's books, and high-interest reading material for retarded readers.

In regard to phonics, the investigators report the following findings:

Some sort of phonics is universal—and so is some sort of whole-word method. In the first grade, 90% of the classes "learn new words as wholes" on half or more of the days; and 82% of the classes "learn to sound out words from letters and letter-combinations" on half or more of the days. A variety of word recognition practices are used.

Teachers' opinions as they affect method were reported as follows:

One conflict of a generation ago was whether there was a fixed age for beginning reading instruction, or whether individual differences in development made different ages desirable. Almost all teachers now hold the latter viewpoint: 89% believe it desirable for some children to start actual reading instruction before age 6, and 87% believe that some children should not start actual reading instruction until age 7.

A general question on the type of phonetic training found one-fourth of first-grade teachers and one-third of teachers from second grade on favoring "a systematic program to teach the rules for sounding letters and letter-combinations using special class periods and exercises." Almost all remaining teachers favored "a program of teaching the sounds of letters and letter-combinations mainly as they appear in words in the children's reading, but arranged to cover all the major rules of sounding." Only 3% want to limit phonetics to "teaching the sounds of letters and letter combinations to some children who need it, when occasions make it necessary," and no one favored "as little teaching of phonetics as possible."

On the question of when phonetic training should begin, it is possible to make an interesting comparison between teacher opinions and those found in the educational literature. We were somewhat surprised to find how many first-grade teachers believed that "most children should start to be taught the sounds of letters and letter-combinations" without waiting for the acquisition of a sight vocabulary of 50 to 100 words learned as wholes:

11% "before they start learning actual words"
40% "at the same time as they learn their first words"
41% "after they have learned to recognize 50–100 words as wholes"
4% "after they have learned to recognize several hundred words as wholes"
0% "not at all during the primary grades"
4% were undecided or made no answer.

Furthermore, the advocacy of starting phonics without first developing a sight vocabulary was higher among the more recently trained teachers.

There does not seem to be any trend in the textbook literature which matches the trend among teachers; the books in all periods but the earliest are overwhelmingly in favor of developing an initial sight vocabulary (about half specifying 50 or more words, the rest vague things like "an adequate number"). Perhaps the teachers are responding to influences outside the regular teachers-college texts— phonics is "in the air." (232: 172–174)

A second survey was conducted by Austin and Morrison, and the results of this survey are given in "The Harvard Report on Reading in the Elementary Schools" in *The First R*. In conducting the study, investigators sent questionnaires to a sampling of schools in different parts of the United States. Seven hundred ninety-five school systems returned the questionnaires. Supplementing the questionnaires were the opinions of 407 educators. Additional information was gathered by the investigators through direct visitation to schools. The findings and recommendations of the investigators are significant. Only a small number of the total findings are reported here. The reader would find it profitable to examine the book as a whole. A few quotations reporting the results of the study follow.

1. In all the furor over deciding which method of teaching children to read is the most valuable, certain facts have been lost sight of: that children can and do learn to read in a variety of ways; that what is beneficial instruction for one child may not do for another; and that there are many different kinds of experiences which will aid in the attainment of good reading habits, skills, and interests.... Therefore it is recommended

> that no single method of instruction in beginning reading be advocated but that a variety of approaches be utilized and that these be adjusted to the competencies and needs of the individual children, and that research studies be initiated to determine the interrelationship of personality, socioeconomic backgrounds, ability, and the various approaches to teaching reading, particularly at the initial stages of reading instruction.

2. The past decade has brought forth innumerable phonics materials devised to supplement or supplant beginning reading instruction. Bombarded by these materials and prodded by some critics who charge that children are failing to learn to read by present-day methods, school systems have attempted to revise the teaching of word recognition skills, in some instances by over-emphasizing phonics to the neglect of other techniques.... Therefore, it is recommended

> that continued emphasis be placed on helping children develop proficiency in word recognition through the use of meaning clues, visual analysis of word forms, sounding approaches, and the dictionary.

3. Administrators and teachers alike indicate that the teaching of comprehension skills is one of their most persistent problems. In addition, these groups feel that more emphasis should be given to

the development of comprehension and critical thinking in both the primary and intermediate grades.... Therefore, it is recommended

that the emphasis in the beginning and continuing reading programs be placed on the concept that understanding the meaning of the printed passage and not mere word-calling constitutes reading.

4. One deficiency in the teaching of reading today is the absence of a sequentially organized program of reading skills development. While ample time is devoted in most schools to the identification of new words and to the beginning comprehension skills, higher level reading abilities are often neglected or treated only superficially in the intermediate grade curricula.... Therefore, it is recommended

that a definite program be initiated in which all children are taught critical and creative reading skills at levels appropriate for their development, and that teachers find ways to stimulate thinking beyond the literal meaning of passages read.

5. Even where great attention is given to the development of a program of reading skills, those which are essential for growth in the content areas are frequently overlooked. Reading skills which are applicable for social studies, science, and arithmetic differ not only from each other but more specifically from those necessary for reading in basal readers and library books.... Therefore, it is recommended

that a carefully planned reading program be undertaken in the content areas which would include the teaching of specific reading and study skills unique to each area.

6. During the course of the field study, it became obvious that basal readers were often misused. Many teachers apparently were unaware of the real purposes of the basal texts and frequently relied on these books as the sole tool of instruction. Furthermore, although the manuals for most basal series contain specific instructions regarding the use of a wide variety of other materials, few children are exposed to these supplementary materials on anything approaching a regularly sustained basis. The omission of such materials can have serious consequences in limiting the children's education.... Therefore, it is recommended

that teachers be instructed in the appropriate use of basal readers as one instructional tool and that basal readers be used in conjunction with other reading materials, such as trade books, reference books, newspapers, magazines, and audio-visual aids. (233: 220–223)

Methods of Approach

All basal programs described, except one, provide materials for use during a reading readiness period. These materials vary somewhat, but universally, they place heavy emphasis on language ability as a prerequisite to reading. To facilitate this concern, some programs provide sets of pictures that are used for language activities before a readiness book is introduced. One series provides a language readiness book. The use of such materials for developing language facility prior to having the children work with a reading readiness book itself is an innovation of this period.

In addition to pictures or a language book for beginning instruction, most publishers provide either one or two reading readiness books. The exercises in these books involve visual and auditory discrimination, selection of pertinent items, experiences in following sequence, additional opportunities for language development, and often kinesthetic exercises. The teachers' guides of the present time have advanced a long way in making better use of readiness materials in laying the foundation for skills that involve, or are close to, those actually used in reading. Much more substance is put into the readiness work with the re-reading books than previously.

This section on reading readiness, however, would be historically incomplete if the writer failed to mention that criticisms concerning the use and value of reading readiness materials are growing in number. Those who have strong convictions in regard to the philosophy that reading readiness is a function of total child growth express doubt that reading readiness materials can contribute in any substantial way to readiness for undertaking reading. Consequently, they question the effectiveness of such materials as an aid to success in beginning reading. Closely related to this criticism is another to the effect that many teachers place their confidence in the readiness materials and thus tend to disregard other important growth factors. Still another criticism has to do with teachers' disregard for individual differences in using readiness materials. Some children are able to read immediately upon entering first grade. Some educators protest that teachers in general hold all children to a period of using readiness materials, and that this is a waste of time for those who already are reading. The Sixtieth Yearbook of the National Society for the Study of Education [2] states the situation in this way:

> There is general agreement that readiness should be studied and assessed, but the idea that one can "build" readiness has been attacked and the point of view advanced that "drills and exercises cannot do the job that only growth and maturation and living can do." Research seems to indicate, however, that children who have had kindergarten experience have an advantage in the first-grade program over those with no kindergarten experience, and that certain types of specific training designed to enhance readiness for reading are beneficial. (pp. 21–22)

This whole area of reading readiness will probably undergo controversy and discussion during the ensuing period. It is hoped, especially, that considerable research may be conducted for the purpose of shedding more light on effective ways of developing growth skills and abilities, particularly as these measures are within the province of schools.

The trend toward providing language experiences and first-hand experiences of many other varieties for preschool children in culturally deprived areas would seem to have considerable promise. Even this measure, however, remains to be tested under experimental conditions in order to establish definitely its effectiveness as a contribution to success in beginning reading.

Word Recognition Techniques

Phonics has been a subject of high controversy during the present period. Perhaps the best short summary of the conflicting viewpoints can be given through the context of the following two quotations. Both viewpoints are in the Sixtieth Yearbook of the National Society for the Study of Education, the first by Robert C. Pooley,[2] and the second quoted by him in Gerald A. Yoakam's article in the *Pittsburgh Report of the Eleventh Annual Conference on Reading*.[3]

> In recent years, two major complaints have been hurled at teachers of reading: (a) They have abandoned the teaching of phonics to the detriment of the children's progress in reading and writing skills, and (b) they no longer teach any sounds of English, leaving the child helpless to sound out new words as he encounters them. There is some truth in both of these assertions, but it is not significant truth. Phonics of the old-fashioned type has given way to new phonetic systems that teach sounds but not "phonics"; of the second claim, it may be said that for some years past, the emphasis on rapid silent reading did tend to subordinate the teaching of sounds, and, no doubt, some enthusiastic practitioners abandoned the teaching of sounds entirely. But no basic system of reading instruction ever eliminated the teaching of the sounds of words. The situation today may be summed up thus: (p. 42)
>
> Not a reputable system of teaching reading exists today that does not give extensive attention to phonetic training throughout the entire primary and middle grades. The same thing can be said of the modern spelling programs in which phonetic training is a part of the program from the second grade on through the eighth. The writer who accuses the school of doing nothing about phonetics is simply saying things that are not true. (p. 11)

Laymen, who see only children's readers and who are not acquainted with the phonic instruction provided for in the teachers' guides of basal reader programs, are quick to accept the critics' statements that phonics is no longer taught in the public schools of the United States. Parents in many places have insisted that school boards and school administrators initiate phonic programs or place more emphasis on phonics instruction. Publishers of textbooks are urged by both teachers and organized groups to do more about phonics. As a result of these pressures, phonics has been given a strong new emphasis.

All reading programs that have readiness books give practice in auditory and visual discrimination of letters during the reading readiness period. Most of them begin actual phonic work with initial consonants, final consonants, blends, speech sounds, and vowels during the preprimer stage. The Macmillan Readers "begin teaching phonics with the second word," that is, the children compare the second word with the first word to find significant likenesses and differences. In the Basic Reading program, the children learn the name and sound of *a* in connection with the first page of the preprimer, and they continue to place first emphasis on the sounds of letters and blends throughout the preprimer book, itself.

Teachers' guides are increasing the emphasis on phonics. Providing extensive phonic charts for the teacher to examine in connection with basal reading series indicates another emphasis on phonic skills. The charts in each case show the phonic elements taught and maintained throughout the entire range of grades that the series is to serve. Providing supplemental aids for use with the pupils is further evidence of phonic interest at this time. Publishers are providing phonic charts, albums of phonic records, and phonic filmstrips to accompany their basal reading programs. A new note in regard to phonics is sounded by those interested in linguistics, who believe that children should be taught word patterns instead of letter sounds (see The Linguistics Approach, page 356).

The authors of the Betts Basic Readers have attempted to use at least one element of linguistic theory in teaching word recognition. They have set up the three phonic rules that linguists now call "three spelling patterns," and that in their word recognition program spelling pattern is emphasized as the element that triggers perception.

Techniques of word recognition other than phonics are receiving increased impetus. Provisions for teaching the use of picture clues, context clues, and structural analysis are being widely expanded and highly refined. The use of dictionaries is being given more attention, and they now have status in the primary grades. Several programs provide picture dictionaries for these grades, which are either bound separately or included as separate pages in a reader. The practice is also extended to the middle grades in some cases. Teachers' guides, workbooks, supplemental materials, and sometimes exercises in readers themselves all bear evidence of increased emphasis on word recognition skills.

Skill Development in Basal Reading Programs

The following quotation characterizes the skill situation as reading authorities see it at this time in our history:

> The reading process is extremely complex. How very simple it would be to teach reading if there were nothing more to it than spelling and pronunciation, which was the concept of reading instruction for several centuries. In this age we see reading as a many-sided process with innumerable facets which work together in continuously changing combinations. Each reading act is a composite of skills interwoven, interlaced, intertwined. New knowledge comes to us daily about this amazing process. (234: 165)

It is quite evident that the authors of basal reading programs recognize the complexity of the reading act and are taking advantage of information that is currently being revealed concerning reading skills. These authors provide immense skill charts in which the skills in their respective programs are listed under general headings. Usually, specific reader pages are indicated as each skill is developed, and separate skills are also labeled and explained in the teachers' guides and sometimes labeled in the pupils' books.

Some real advances have been made recently in regard to reading skills in the area of comprehension. In this area we find heavy emphasis on the higher thinking skills and on critical reading— not just listed as terms, but as detailed and explicit subskills. Teaching specific word meanings is considered to be an integral part of the comprehension block of reading skills at this time. In addition to advances in comprehension, appreciation attitudes and skills are being strongly emphasized.

Perhaps the most important improvement to be noted is in the increased amount of attention given to study skills or those skills needed in reading in other subject fields. A brief sampling of comprehension and study skills lists will be presented. In regard to comprehension and study skills, the authors of the Sheldon Basic Readers make the following statement in the guide to their fifth reader, and follow it with a list of skills to be developed in connection with this reader.[4] The list includes many of the higher comprehension skills, as well as study skills.

The pupil's ability to demonstrate comprehension of what he sees, hears, and reads is developed through activities, beginning in the readiness books, which involve interpretation, classification, and generalization. These basic comprehension skills are amplified and applied throughout the reading program and form the foundation for learning to perform such higher-level comprehension and reading-study skills as the following:

1. locating main ideas in paragraphs and stories (or other types of material)
2. recalling the sequence of story development
3. making inferences and predicting events on the basis of what has been read

4. noting and recalling significant details

5. classifying ideas

6. generalizing or reaching conclusions on the basis of what has been read

7. reacting critically to ideas that have been met in reading

8. understanding subtle changes of mood and expression, visualizing the setting, and interpreting the feelings and behavior of the characters in a story

9. learning to withhold judgments until more information has been gained

10. following directions

11. skimming, outlining, and summarizing what has been read

12. the use of such reference aids as the index, table of contents, and the glossary and dictionary

13. the use of charts, graphs, tables, maps, and diagrams

14. the ability to use encyclopedias, atlases, and library card catalogues (p. 7)

Authors of the Macmillan Readers list their skills under three headings: word recognition skills, comprehension skills, and organization skills. Many of their organization skills represent the type of skills often called study skills. Following are samples of the comprehension skills and organization skills for their fifth reader:

COMPREHENSION SKILLS

Using context clues
Getting the general significance
Recalling significant details
Identifying characters
Studying plot and action
Judging mood and feeling
Predicting outcomes, drawing
    conclusions, and interpreting
    relationships
Thinking beyond the given material

ORGANIZATION SKILLS

Dramatizing
Summarizing
Classifying
Locating information
    Using table of contents
    Using dictionary
    Using encyclopedia
    Reading a diagram
    Reading a map
Skimming

Reading for enjoyment	Recalling a sequence of events,
Enjoying poetry	taking notes
Using synonyms	Outlining
Using antonyms	
Interpreting colorful speech	
Choosing appropriate meanings	
Checking reading speed	
Checking comprehension	

The various language arts skills are increasingly emphasized in connection with reading instruction. Studies, articles, and books published during this period have enhanced the concept of inter-relating the language arts. *The English Language Arts* (NCTE, 1952)[5] was especially influential in this respect. Following is a quotation from this publication:

> [T]he four facets of language communication are speaking, listen-ing, reading, and writing" (p. 196). These divisions are for analysis only; actually the areas are integrated and merged. "Mastery of the arts of communication occurs in situations in which several or all of the phases of language are present" (p. 196). Curriculums and class-room methods recognize this unity in function of the language arts. "Activities in which children make normal use of all of the elements of the language arts in attacking problems related to their daily life to-gether are increasingly common in American schools" (p. 326).

In keeping with the general movement toward a closer inte-gration of language arts skills, authors of basal reading series are giving increasing consideration to ways and means of providing for practice in listening, speaking, and writing as related to read-ing activities. Following is an example from the Sheldon Fifth-Reader Teacher's Guide of the conviction of reader authors in regard to coordinating reading with the other language arts.

> Reading, inseparable from other language processes, is best taught as part of the whole area of language development. The interrela-

tionships are such that each aspect of language is dependent upon every other.

Two reading series constitute only one part of a total language arts program in which reading is correlated with other language arts books in the total program: the Winston Readers, which forms one part of the Winston Communication Program; and the Betts Basic Readers, included as one section of the Language Arts Series.

Some basal reading programs include supplemental materials for teaching language arts other than reading. The Curriculum Foundation Series provides books titled *Learn to Listen, Speak, and Write*. Each book is accompanied with a practice pad. In its manuals, the Ginn Basic Reading program incorporates in lesson plans an unusually large number of suggestions for oral and written expression, speech work, and listening activities; and it publishes an album titled "Let's Listen" as a supplementary aid.

Adjustments of Basal Reading Programs to Individual Needs

Basal reading programs have made significant advances during this period in their provisions for meeting individual needs. Multiple published texts and procedures offered in teachers' guides provide for much higher degrees of flexibility. The Winston program is unique in that it describes two approaches in all its guides: "The Basic Reader Approach" and the "Modified Basic Reader Approach," the latter being the recommended approach. In the "Modified Basic Reader Approach," children are to use basal readers part of the time, and to read individually from books of their own selection during the other part of the time. The authors state

When a basic reader approach is modified by the self-selection approach...it is recommended that the time be divided equally...between the two approaches. For example, two weeks may be devoted entirely to self-selection and the next two weeks to basic reader instruction; a start may be made by devoting one full week to individualized instruction.... Then the time...can be extended. (223: 233)

Unusual growth is seen in the provision of books in addition to basal readers for the purpose of meeting individual needs. A few of the different types of provisions will be mentioned. The Macmillan Readers include supplemental books and preparatory material that are used in various ways, according to whether children are immature, average, or advanced. In addition to their enrichment books, the Sheldon Basic Reading Program offers the "Independence Pad" and the "Activities Book" at each level, a "Transition Reader" for use with advanced third graders or "limping" fourth graders, and novels for the better readers in the middle grades. The Ginn Reading Program includes enrichment readers and, in addition, "By-Myself" booklets, "Programmed Word Study Skills," and "Self-Help Activity Pads." The Betts Basic Readers feature a set of "Individualized Phonic and Thinking Activities." The Developmental Reading Series provides a simplified edition of each reader for use with slow-learning pupils. The Scott Foresman program includes Wide Horizons, books for more able readers, and the Open Highways Program, for children below expectancy.

The tests provided with many of the basal reading programs are designed for use in diagnosing individual weaknesses and in grouping pupils in terms of their reading competency and needs. These tests should be considered as tools that the authors provide for assessing and meeting individual differences.

V. Reading Instruction at High School, College, and Adult Levels

Reading Instruction in High School

During the preceding period, secondary schools in many places began to offer remedial reading to students deficient in this skill.

Near the end of the period, the concept of teaching developmental reading to all students evolved; however, schools did not immediately put this idea into effect. It was not until between 1960 and 1965 that developmental reading programs underwent rapid expansion. The following quotation from Strang in 1962 accurately describes the situation in regard to developmental reading:

> In a most important advance, some school systems have moved from small remedial groups to developmental classes in reading, for all students, which are concerned with the sequential development of the reading abilities that are appropriate to the high school and college years. These courses are usually included in the junior high school program; sometimes they are offered in the last year of senior high school to college preparatory students. The State of Pennsylvania passed a law requiring all students to take a developmental or remedial course in reading during the seventh or eighth grade. (235: 171)

Data are not available in regard to the total number of high schools in the country that have reading programs. Many reports, however, have come from different localities, four of which are as follows: *The Claremont Reading Conference*[6] reported in 1961 that all but 6 of 52 schools surveyed in Southern California had reading programs. In 1958, Jordan[7] reported that 54% of secondary schools in Florida had reading programs. In 1961, Baughman[8] stated that 65% of high schools in Illinois had reading programs in 1959. In 1963, Smith[9] surveyed high schools in Illinois in regard to programs established prior to 1962. He found that out of 113 programs studied, 68 included seventh and eighth grades, and out of 102 reports that described their programs, 72 stated that developmental instruction was being given. Undoubtedly, surveys made during the next 5 years will reveal a sharp increase in the number of secondary schools that have established both remedial and developmental programs.

Several influences have contributed to the rapidly growing interest in teaching reading at the secondary level. One factor is evidence in regard to the numbers of poor readers in high schools as revealed by reports of surveys that have been conducted continuously all through the decade 1950 to 1960. Two examples of findings typical of those in similar surveys will be given. Penty[10] found that of 2,384 students entering the 10th grade in Battle Creek, Michigan, the lower quarter ranged in reading ability from grade 4.3 to grade 6.9. Donovan[11] reported that 53.2% of students entering academic high schools in New York were below grade norms ranging from 1 year to 5.1 years. Many other studies have revealed large numbers of students who are deficient in reading, both in junior and senior high schools.

The large number of high school dropouts is causing much concern during this period, and investigations reveal that many of these dropouts cannot read well enough to pursue high school studies. Keppel[12] reports the results of a study in one state that he says gives "a picture of the dropout." In this report he states that 45% of these dropouts are reading at the sixth-grade level or lower.

The dropout problem is of considerable importance because of the deep interest that the U.S. government is taking in educating existing and potential dropouts. This interest springs from the drastic decrease in needs for unskilled labor and hence the necessity for educating these individuals in order that they may qualify to hold jobs in the future. As a consequence of this solicitude, high schools are urged to provide more effective reading instruction for those students who are deficient in reading skills, and to continue providing reading instruction to them for a longer time, including junior college years if necessary.

Another stimulus to the teaching of high school reading springs from reports of colleges and universities that state that large numbers of college freshmen cannot read well enough to pursue their studies. These colleges and universities describe programs that they are using in teaching reading to these students. They indicate in most cases that these students are not suffering from serious reading disabilities, but need only to be taken from the point they have reached in reading development and guided to higher levels. Reported successes of teaching efforts with such students yield further evidence for the need to teach developmental reading in high school. In regard to methods of teaching Strang says,

> Many different kinds of reading procedures are to be found in high schools. At one extreme is systematic group instruction in each reading skill; at the other extreme we find reading instruction individualized by means of programmed, self-pacing, or multiple-track materials. In fact, variety is more evident in these procedures than anything that seems progress.
>
> One direction in which we should move is toward a more intensive analysis of the reading processes that are actually used by students with varying backgrounds and degrees of ability when they read different kinds of materials for different purposes. Instruction in reading has been much too general. (235: 173)

The most urgent need seems to be that of better teacher training, which in turn should help to solve another problem, that of enlisting participation in the reading program of the teachers in the various subject fields. An expression of this viewpoint is given by Artley:

> Of all the deceptively easy solutions, the one to guard against is that of turning the responsibility over to the English teachers under the assumption that since reading is one of the communications areas, "George English can do it and the rest of us won't need to get involved...." It would be relatively difficult to find a teacher-training institution including in its curriculum a course in secondary reading procedures as part of the program for English majors. Where it is offered, it is quite likely to be an elective, and academically oriented advisers are more inclined to place the student in

courses in the modern novel, eighteenth-century literature, or specialized courses in Byron, Shelley, and Keats than in one that deals with such mundane topics as word perception, critical reaction, or reading to ascertain idea relationships.

The above is not meant to be critical of English teachers. Traditionally the English program on the secondary level has been concerned with grammar, literature, and composition. Reading has not been considered a part of the English curriculum, under the assumption that this area had been thoroughly covered on the elementary level. (236: 7)

As a result of a survey of practices in three upper-midwestern U.S. states, Simmons says,

A large number of the administrators can be classified as having no formal training in the teaching of reading. Some had fragmentary training, gained as part of a methods course, but there were few reading specialists and only one secondary reading teacher employed in the schools responding to this survey. In most cases, I would speculate, the reading specialist was responsible for the entire school system and was probably spending most of his time with problems in the elementary schools of the community. The study points up further the utter (almost) lack of reading instructors whose chief concern is instruction at the high school level. (237: 235)

In regard to the preparation of teachers in the content fields, Burton (1961)[13] places the blame squarely on the colleges. He says that the reluctance of high school teachers in content areas to teach reading in their courses is "directly chargeable to the academic departments in the colleges and universities which train teachers."

All evidence indicates that the movement to teach reading in high schools is one that is rapidly sweeping the entire country. Because of lack of experience in developing reading programs at the secondary level, lack of training in reading for high school teachers and, in many cases, lack of guidance from a reading specialist, the programs are sometimes growing in lop-sided and irregular ways. But there are, however, many excellent programs and the others *are* growing, and that is significant.

As Early[14] says, "Reading in the secondary school is a still unexplored territory. Guide posts of research are about nonexistent and the secondary school faculty that breaks ground in the field of reading is indeed pioneering." With better teacher training in reading, and with new insights revealed through research, substantial progress should be made during the next decade in the teaching of reading in secondary schools.

It may be appropriate to close this discussion with a quotation from the Sixtieth Yearbook of the National Society for the Study of Education, Part I, in which the authors point out the next steps in research needed to improve reading programs in the secondary school:

> The high school is finding a new and important role in the development of reading among its students. There is much to be done in studying the most useful ways of undertaking the task. Research is needed on many aspects of the high school reading program. The ways that the reading materials and methods may best be related to the needs of the students and how to adjust instruction to individual differences warrant investigation. A further evaluation of the capabilities of the mature reader should be made. Balances between these reading goals deserve careful study. How much of the effort should be focused on increasing speed of comprehension as compared with critical evaluation and reflective reading is an example of the type of study needed. Studies should be made to appraise the effectiveness of various ways of organizing all-school reading programs. The amount of gain made by students when the developmental reading instruction is given as part of the language-arts program by English teachers should be compared with the gains made by students trained in special reading classes. The effectiveness of a developmental reading program in which groups meet twice a week for a year should be compared with that of a program of classes meeting daily for half a year. The ways in which teachers of the content fields may best give instruction in reading specialized

materials warrant investigation. Finally, the growth of students through reading experiences of various kinds presented in various ways should be experimentally studied. By means of the findings of experimental research, the senior high school will be enabled to contribute to the development of independent, mature readers and to promote the greatest gains for students in and through reading. (92: 334–335)

Reading Instruction in College

The practice of teaching reading to college students has burst forth into new dimensions during this period. The growing interest is shown in the increasing numbers of articles on college reading instruction appearing in educational periodicals and numbers of books published on this subject by professional reading organizations and by individuals interested in this area, and by the unusually large number of studies dealing with reading at the college level.

An examination of summaries of published research during this period indicates that many more studies were concerned with the teaching of reading to college students than to students at the secondary level. The topic of college reading also has been popular with doctoral candidates. During the years 1950 to 1965, the number of dissertations dealing with college students far exceeds the number involving students at the secondary level. In Summer's 1962 summary of research, he has this to say about the results of recent investigations in this area:

> As one might suspect, the largest number of studies relate to evaluating programs of college and adult reading. A number of summaries of such studies in the past allow us to make the following generalizations: (a) the great majority of programs reported are conducted for college groups; (b) reported programs represent wide variation in method, materials and mechanical devices used, testing procedures, and length of training; (c) roughly 50% of the programs use some type of evaluation, but few evaluations are done

with control groups, and tests of the significance of the results in terms of probability statements are rare; (d) practically all reports indicate that improvement or gain was achieved for those participating; and (e) the major gains reported are in speed rather than comprehension. (239: 5)

At this point it should be noted that considerable criticism is being voiced in regard to the quality of much of the research conducted at the college level. Smith stated the following example in the 1962 Conference Proceedings of the International Reading Association:

> Our research of college reading is direly in need of improvement. The design of most of the studies reported is one in which nothing more is done than to give parallel forms of a test at the beginning and end of a course. Rarely is a control group used.
>
> Furthermore, the factors measured by research in college reading have been limited. Studies have dealt predominantly with initial and final measures of speed, comprehension, and eye movements as affected by different teaching procedures, instruments, and materials. This research should be extended to include studies of flexibility of speed, transfer to various subject areas and retention of improved skills. (240: 183)

It is true, however, that the quality of research in this area has improved considerably during the last 2 or 3 years of this period and that it will continue to improve in the years ahead.

Two surveys have yielded results that afford glimpses into the status of college instruction in reading. In 1956, Causey[15] conducted a questionnaire study involving 418 colleges and universities. Almost 75% of these institutions reported that they had reading programs for their students. This same study revealed a high increase in the number of students served ranging from 33,341 students in 1955 to 57,052 in 1956. In 1959, Miller[16] also did a questionnaire study, receiving returns from 372 colleges. These returns revealed that during the last 5 years the number of programs in these colleges had more than doubled; 67 stated that they had experienced moderate increases; 34 said they had not had any increase; 20 reported that they could not grow because of administrative policy, and 2 indicated that they did not have information that would enable them to assess growth.

Teaching Reading to Adults

During the 1950s, adults began coming to reading centers for individual or group instruction. These people usually were neither remedial cases nor illiterates; they already could read fairly well but because of being bogged down in their jobs with vast amounts of materials to be read, they wanted to learn how to cover the printed page faster and how to grasp meanings more accurately. Reading improvement courses to meet the needs of these adults became popular.

Very early in the movement to improve the reading ability of adults, the Armed Services became interested in reading improvement. They frequently called on one of their members to teach reading in one of their schools, and they reported successful gains as a result of the training they offered.

Simultaneously with these other developments, executives and personnel directors in business and industrial firms became interested. They were quick to sense how increased reading ability might be an efficiency measure for employees who had to read extensively in connection with their jobs. So these establishments began inviting reading specialists to give courses for their personnel. One survey reported by Patterson [17] in 1957 indicates the status of business and industrial courses in reading at that time. This investigator surveyed a sample of the 500 largest U.S. industrial corporations and found that 59% of those responding either had reading programs in operation or had had such programs during the past 5 years. During the latter part of this period, however, there has been a dwindling of interest in reading courses for

346

personnel in business and industry. The practice is continuing, however, and probably on a more substantial basis.

Up until 1964, adult reading as we have noted was concerned with improving the reading ability of a comparatively small clientele: those who came to reading centers of their own accord, those who were taught in the U.S. Armed Services, and those who were taught in business or industry. Recently, however, an entirely new and extensive theater of action has been opened to those who are interested in adult reading instruction. The need for teaching illiterates or functional illiterates is urgent in order that they may be able to hold jobs in a country in which automation is rapidly reducing job opportunities for unskilled workers. New materials need to be developed, new methods discovered, and additional teachers must be found and trained to meet the reading needs of these men and women. Adult reading instruction is now faced with its greatest challenge!

VI. The Individualized Approach

Beginning in mid-1950 to 1960, much excitement was evident concerning individualized instruction in reading. Numerous articles dealing with this subject appeared in educational journals; conventions of educational organizations featured speeches on this topic; some books (see list) were published that devoted their entire contents to this subject; and other books dealing with general aspects of reading included a chapter or two on the individualized plan. Considerable research was conducted in regard to individualized reading instruction, both published and unpublished. Many doctoral candidates chose this subject as a dissertation topic.

BOOKS ON THE INDIVIDUALIZED APPROACH

Darrow, Helen Fisher, & Howes, Virgil M. (1960). *An approach to individualized reading*. New York: Appleton-Century-Crofts.

Miel, Alice (Ed.). (1958). *Individualizing reading practices*. New York: Bureau of Publications, Teachers College at Columbia University.

Stauffer, Russell G. (Ed.). (1957). *Individualizing reading instruction*. Proceedings of the 39th Annual Education Conference, University of Delaware, Newark.

Veatch, Jeannette. (1959). *Individualizing your reading program*. New York: G.P. Putnam Sons.

Interest in individualized instruction in reading was at its height in the late 1950s and early 1960s. In recent years, excitement concerning this procedure has subsided somewhat, although the topic still appears on educational convention programs and an occasional article is published or study conducted on this topic. Although the novelty of the idea is waning, many teachers throughout the country are using the procedure and, on the whole, are enthusiastic about the plan.

Historically, it may be of interest to consider some past developments as they relate to the present topic of individualized instruction. When reading instruction was first provided for children, it was conducted exclusively on an individual basis. The child was taught as an individual by a scribe, a priest, a tutor, or family member. Even in the early "Dame Schools" in America, each child was taught individually and progressed at his own rate. A small group of children would gather in the Dame's kitchen, and each one would "recite" to her from his own place in the primer or Bible as the Dame busied herself with her household duties. There was no particular philosophy or psychology that guided Dame School practice. The pupils who came to the Dame were at different stages of development and small in number, and there was no particular need to mold them into one achievement level for mass production purposes.

As indicated in chapter six, standardized reading tests evolved between 1910 and 1920. Surveys of reading achievement were made as soon as reading tests were available, and the results of these surveys revealed wide individual differences. Educators became deeply concerned, and between 1920 and 1930, new materials were developed and new procedures were devised that permitted children to progress at their own individual rates while learning to read. Breaking up traditional class organization entirely to permit "individual progression" was a pulsating new idea at that time. This plan of organization received as much attention during the 1920s as individualized reading instruction received during the present period. Speeches, articles, and yearbooks dealt with the subject, and many school systems reported the results obtained from using the individual instruction plan.

The various plans, on the whole, were patterned after the Winnetka plan or the Dalton system. The Winnetka plan was perhaps the plan of individual instruction most widely used in this country. In teaching at first-grade level by the Winnetka plan, self-help materials were provided to enable children to read independently. The material consisted of a picture dictionary and rhymes that a child had memorized to which he could turn to find an unrecognized sight word. From the second grade on, the reading method was as follows: the grade level of each child was determined through administration of a standardized test; each child was given books at his particular grade level to read silently; after completing a book, each child was given a brief test on content; then each child went on to another book.

According to the Dalton system, reading assignments were prepared in steps of increasing difficulty, and the child could proceed from one step to another as fast as he chose or was able to do so. Both the Winnetka plan and Dalton system, which once were procedures of extremely high national interest, have now faded in educational memory as have many other innovations in reading that enjoyed wide popularity for a brief period and were replaced by new interests. It seems, however, that these passing innovations lie dormant for a time and then spring up again in revised and better forms, and such has been the case with the evolving procedures by which children could progress at their own rate in learning to read.

The concept of individualized instruction in reading as it evolved during the present period extends far beyond the earlier plans of permitting children to progress at their own rates. The concept is primarily concerned with reading as it meshes with and promotes child development in many different aspects—physical, mental, social, emotional, linguistic, and experiential. It is interested not only in a child's reading achievement, but also in his interest in reading, his attitude toward reading, and his personal self-esteem and satisfaction in being able to read.

The growing interest in dynamic psychology has called attention to the importance of motivation and levels of aspiration in learning activities. Willard Olson (1962) [18] made several studies of growth, behavior, and development of children. He then synthesized the results of his studies and thinking into three terse terms: "seeking, self-selection, and pacing." It is this crystallization of Olson's psychology that has provided the basis for most individualized teaching of reading in recent years.

It should be noted that as the concept changed so did the terminology. *Individual progression in reading* was the term used in the 1920s, whereas *individualized instruction in reading* is the term most commonly used in connection with the new concept. Some people, however, speak of the plan as *self-selection reading*, also known as *personalized reading*. Still other terms are used, but all apply to the same concept.

Briefly, the procedure used in individualized classrooms can be summarized as follows: Each child selects a book that he wants to read. During the individual conference period, the teacher sits in a particular place in the room as each child comes to her and reads. As each child reads, the teacher notes individual needs, gives appropriate help, and records on a card what the child is reading, his needs, and his strengths. Then another individual conference is held, and so on. If several children need help on the same skills, they may be called together in a group for such help.

Research on individualized instruction is not conclusive. Most studies have evolved from the desire to compare the relative effectiveness of the individualized plan and the group basal reading plan. An overall perusal of research on this topic indicates that as yet there is not enough definitive data from which to draw generalizations. Additional studies are needed in which the various factors are more tightly controlled and in which the two different types of programs are more clearly defined. The studies that have been conducted up to this time, however, result in two general conclusions: (1) that children and teachers using the individualized plan work with higher interest than do those in groups with which they are compared, and (2) that these children read many more books than do those in the control groups.

VII. Reading Programs That Include Different Ethnic Groups

With the emphasis on integration, with the strengthened concept of internationalism, and with problems of teaching reading to increasing numbers of bilingual and culturally disadvantaged children in large cities, a break-through was bound to come in the way of reading programs that reflect these trends. The resulting programs will be described.

The City Schools Reading Program was prepared by the Writers' Committee of the Great Cities School Improvement Program of the Detroit Schools. The chairman of this committee was Gertrude Whipple. The viewpoint of the authors who prepared these books is clearly stated in the teachers' manual that accompanies them.

The major metropolitan areas of the United States have a unique educational problem, which is becoming increasingly urgent: that of educating children of widely different cultures. Each year brings new thousands of immigrants to the great cities, mostly from the rural South, the Southwest [United States], Puerto Rico, and Mexico. In general, these immigrants left their previous homes in order to attain a better life for themselves and for their children. Some quickly adapt their ways of living to the new and complex conditions existing in the city. Others find it difficult to adapt to urban life because of the inadequacy of their cultural background and their lack of training for shifted jobs.

The children of these families enter the public schools, and many are immediately at a disadvantage. They come from environments that are generally rural, and are thrown into an educational system that is urban and far beyond them in its standards and expectations. They are taught by middle-class teachers with textbooks and materials featuring a single culture—suburban, white, middle-class. In no field is this more true than in reading. A glance at the typical reading textbook in the early grades proves this point beyond the shadow of a doubt. (241: 1)

With the above viewpoint in mind, Detroit educators set themselves the task of preparing readers that would narrate interesting situations common to multicultural backgrounds of children in a big city, and that would contain illustrations depicting characters of different races. The books of the series published at the time this chapter is being written include five preprimers, a primer, a workbook for the first three preprimers, and a teacher's manual to accompany the preprimers. Other books are under preparation, and it is planned to extend the series through the third grade. The supplemental materials consist of picture cards, word and phrase cards, and phonic pictures.

The teacher's manual contains clear-cut lesson plans that make use of modern theories of teaching reading. Tests of word recognition, oral reading, and comprehension are provided, as well as suggestions for additional language experiences and for reading enrichment. As a preliminary to the preparation of these books, an extensive study (Thomas, 1961) [19] was made to ascertain the language patterns of children in low socioeconomic areas, and the results were utilized in preparing the books.

The selections in the books are carefully controlled in vocabulary and sentence patterns. At the same time, however, they include interesting out-of-school incidents that could happen in the home or backyard of any child regardless of race or socioeconomic background. Every incident has a climax that usually involves a surprise or a humorous ending to the story. The early preprimer books are bound in soft covers, and the later books have hard covers. The illustrations show children of different races playing together. The first three preprimers introduce pictures of a Negro family and a boy representing a Caucasian family. In the successive readers, people of various races and nationalities are represented.

Results of research conducted in Detroit in regard to the effectiveness of this reading program indicate high-interest value of the books to children. They also reveal gains in word recognition, oral reading, and verbal competence. The study included not only a comparison of test scores but also the preference of the City School Series over a standard series. One conclusion that resulted from the preference study was very wholesome: When asked which readers they preferred, all groups favored the readers of City Schools Reading Program because they preferred Negro characters, chiefly because they appeared in exciting stories (see page 355).

The Bank Street Readers were prepared by professional writers of children's books, who worked in close collaboration with reading specialists and teachers in the Bank Street College, along with the advisement of sociologists, psychologists, and anthropologists who were teaching at this institution. The authors state that the program was prepared in order to provide readers that might reflect the multicultural, multiracial, and multiarchitectural needs of a big city.

The material for the first grade consists of two preprimers, a primer, and a first reader. There are two readers each for the second and third grades. There is a teacher's guide for the readiness period and preprimers, and a teacher's edition for each of the readers. A workbook is provided for the two preprimers, and one for each of the other readers. All the materials have a 1965 copyright.

The content of the readers is one of the unique features of this program. The selections are designed to present an authentic cross-section of life in urban America; consequently, most of the settings are in an urban environment. The characters involve Mexicans, Orientals, Negroes, and Puerto Ricans, as well as Caucasians, all of whom reside in large cities (see page 355).

In short, the selections reflect the homogeneity of city people and carry with them broad social, cultural, and racial implications. The stories are of excellent literary quality, and although most are realistic, some poems, fairy tales, folktales, and selections from classical literature are included.

The art work is distinctive in style and it is colorful. Double-page spreads and many full-page pictures are used freely in the early readers. The illustrations strongly reinforce the content of the books and the intent of the authors in that they depict typical city scenes and involve characters representing different races.

In method, the authors place strong emphasis on phonics and structural analysis with some, but a lesser consideration for context clues. They make use of meaningful words in the children's spoken vocabularies, and if these words do not lend themselves to the usual word recognition techniques, the teacher is advised to tell the children what they are. Experience charts are used more freely in this program than usual. First emphasis is placed on meanings throughout the series.

Linda said, "Here is a big red box.
Is it the box you lost, Larry?"

Larry said, "The box I lost is not red.
It is yellow and green.
And it is little.
Can you help me look for it?"

This is page 22 from the City Schools Reading Program: Primer. *Note the different nationalities represented.*

The New Basic Reading Program of The Curriculum Foundation Series, with the Multi-Ethnic and Established Editions, has been revised by adding many new stories and a large number of new pictures for the purpose of introducing characters of different ethnic groups as they mingle, play, and work together in the American setting. More than 30 different ethnic groups are given prominence in these readers. The Multi-Ethnic and Established Edition are the same in basic organization, characteristics of content, vocabulary controls, types of content, and gradation of content. Changes in the content and pictures, however, plainly mark this series as one that will acquaint children with multiethnic groups and values.

VIII. The Linguistics Approach

Linguistic science is a very old and very complex discipline that has undergone a great deal of research. Interest in this subject has been growing vigorously during recent years, and at the time that this chapter is being written, the entire field of linguistics is very much alive and receiving increased attention. No attempt will be made in this chapter, however, to discuss linguistic theory in general. This discussion will be concerned only with sequential developments in applying linguistic theory to the teaching of reading.

In case the reader is not familiar with the subject of linguistics, it may be advisable to give some brief explanations that will aid in a more accurate interpretation of the examples of materials that follow. Quotations will be given from two authentic sources. Strickland (1964) makes a clear distinction between the linguist's concept of reading and the concept held by those teaching or supervising reading:

> The linguist's concept of reading is not the concept commonly held by the classroom teacher and the reading specialist—that reading

is getting meaning from the print on a page. The linguist conceives the reading act as that of turning the stimulus of the graphic shapes on a surface back into speech. The shapes represent speech; meaning is not found in the marks but in the speech which the marks represent. In the eyes of the linguist, a child can read when he can recognize symbol-sound correspondence to the point that he can respond to the marks with appropriate speech. The linguist recognizes that the school cannot stop here. The rest of what the school calls teaching reading is actually teaching *thinking* with and in response to what is found on the page.

Speech sounds are represented in writing by arbitrary graphic shapes. An alphabet is a set of graphic shapes which represent speech sounds in a fair and nearly one-to-one relationship. The sounds of English are represented in writing by the 26 letters of the Roman alphabet, though the language actually utilizes more than 26 sounds. A *grapheme* is a significant unit of graphic shape and a *phoneme* is a significant unit of speech sound. Mastery of the correspondence between the phonemes (sound symbols) of the language and the graphemes (graphic symbols) used to represent them is essential to the carrying on of the reading process. The task of learning to read, therefore, is the task of developing recognition responses to sets of patterns of graphic shapes. (243: 10)

Fries has clarified the difference between the meaning of the term *phonics* as it is commonly understood by teachers of reading and the term *phonemics* as used by the linguists.

Phonics has been and continues to be a way of teaching beginning reading. It consists primarily in attempting to match the individual letters by which a word is spelled with the specific "sounds" which these letters "say." Phonics is issued by some teachers as one of the methods of helping pupils, who have acquired a "sight-vocabulary" of approximately 200 words, to solve the problems presented by "new" words by "sounding" the letters.

Phonemics is a set of techniques by which to identify and to describe, especially in terms of distribution, the bundles of sound contrasts that constitute the structural units that mark the word-patterns. It is the *phonemes* of the language that alphabetic writing represents. (244: 156)

With these brief explanations in mind, we shall now proceed with a sequence of developments that have taken place in working out applications of linguistics to the teaching of reading.

The first discussion of linguistics, as applied to reading, which this writer discovered was in *Linguistics in Education* (O'Shea, 1927).[20] An entire chapter is devoted to the topic "Acquiring of Word-Ideas in Reading," in which O'Shea places much emphasis on "language unities in teaching reading" and "learning the function of literal symbols."

Perhaps next, mention might be made of an article that described what might be done in applying linguistics the teaching of reading (Bloomfield, 1942).[21] And, during the 1950s, much was heard and read about the Summer Institute of Linguistics in connection with primers developed and used in teaching children of many different languages. In 1956, Henry Lee Smith, Jr.,[22] began producing a film series titled "Language and Linguistics," two of which had direct implications for the teaching of reading: "The Alphabet and Linguistic Science" and "The Teaching of Reading."

Early in the 1960s, numerous articles on linguistics and reading began to appear in American journals, and frequently, speakers on this topic were scheduled on educational convention programs. These two trends are increasing with marked emphases at the time this chapter is being written. Also in the early 1960s, two professional books appeared dealing specifically with linguistics as applied to reading instruction: *Linguistics and Reading* by Charles C. Fries, and *Linguistics and the Teaching of Reading* by Carl A. LeFevre. A 44-page bulletin titled "The Contribution of Structural Linguistics to the Teaching of Reading, Writing and

Grammar in the Elementary School" was published by Ruth Strickland at Indiana University in 1964.

Reading Series Developed on Linguistic Principles

Paralleling the professional publications dealing with linguistics and reading, several sets of material have been published to be placed in the hands of children.

Let's Read. This publication by Leonard Bloomfield and Clarence L. Barnhart (1961) was the first for use by children. In the first publication format, the book contained both reading material for the child and instructions for the person who was to teach the child. Later, nine small readers with workbooks were developed, all based on the original volume, which is described here.

The section for the parent or teacher consists mostly of explanations of the method employed in this book and a discussion of other contemporary methods. Directions and pictures are provided for use in developing reading readiness, and suggestions are given for teaching the various reading lessons and for testing and reviewing.

The book contains 245 lessons. First, children learn the alphabet. Then they practice learning lists of words with similar patterns, followed in each case with sentences containing these words. The emphasis is on symbol-sound correspondences. All reading is done orally, and at this stage of development, the authors believe that the emphasis should be on recognition of words, with little or no attention to meanings.

The content from an early page in *Let's Read* is presented below. In examining this page, the reader must bear in mind that the authors are not teaching *age* as a "family" element in phonics to which various consonants may be added for blending, but rather word patterns.

bag	gag	lag	nag	rag	sag	tag	wag
fag	hag	jag					

a bag   a rag   a rag bag
Tad had a bag.
Nan had a rag bag.

Can Pat tag Nan?
Pat can tag Nan.
Can Nan tag Dad?
Nan can tag Dad.

A cat can tag a rat.

Nan can nag Dad.

A rat ran.   A cat ran.   Wag sat.
Can Wag tag a cat?

gag	hag	lag	nag	rag	sag	tag	
gap	Hap	lap	nap	rap	sap	tap	(245: 5)

Further in the book are longer selections written in paragraph form. Approximately 5,000 words are introduced in the book as a whole.

A Basic Reading Series Developed Upon Linguistic Principles. This program by Charles C. Fries, Agnes C. Fries, Rosemary G. Wilson, and Mildred K. Rudolph has the distinction of being the first graded series of basal readers prepared for the express purpose of applying linguistic theory. The program consists of seven books, each accompanied by a practice book. The professional book, *Linguistics and Reading* by Fries, is considered basic for teachers' use in understanding the materials in the program. However, the book is supplemented by a brief teacher's manual that contains additional explanations of the contents of the children's books and offers suggestions for teaching procedures. The books are bound in soft covers with attractive colors. The type-face is bold and clear.

Beginning reading instruction in this program starts with language activities plus learning the letters of the alphabet in capitalized, then lower-case forms. The children then proceed to learn certain word patterns that in turn are placed in carefully organized sentence sequences. The authors of these readers emphasize meaning as well as word recognition. A set of general principles appearing in the teacher's manual should be enlightening in regard to method used in teaching with this program.

1. Learning to read must begin with and build on the language control already achieved by the pupils.

2. The periods of school time devoted to learning to read should use only the language already controlled by the pupils.

3. Many nonreaders are not aware that the "talk" they have learned is made up of separate units called "words."

4. The most important first step in preparing to learn to read is the learning of the alphabet.

5. From the very beginning, reading is developed as a means of acquiring meanings—not only the meanings of the separate "words," but these meaningful "words" always in "sentences," and therefore, with the grammatical meanings that attach to whole sentences; and, in addition, these sentences in sequences of small units of three to eight sentences with the cumulative meanings of connected discourse.

6. Reading with "expression" depends on the grasp of the cumulative meaning of sentences in sequence.

7. All the significant matters of language are matters of contrast. Contrast, therefore, and especially minimum contrast,

constitutes the fundamental principle of this teaching method from the very beginning.

8. The spelling-pattern approach differs fundamentally from the commonly used practices of "word-method," of "word-families," and of "phonics."

9. Wherever pictures are used, as they are in the Practice Books, the pupil does not proceed from the pictures as clues to the "words" of the text to be read, but rather from the words and sentences that must be read to the pictures he must mark to demonstrate the correctness of his reading.

The materials in this program have been used experimentally with children in regular classrooms and with remedial cases, and excellent results have been reported. The authors indicate that the program is helpful in teaching the disadvantaged as well as the average and bright. The content of two sample pages from *My First Reader* follows, with the first sample indicating the word pattern that is being emphasized, and the second showing some of the sentences in which this word pattern is to be read in context.

cat
fat
Nat

(a)   (is)   (246: 1)

A Fat Cat

Nat is a cat
Is Nat fat?
Nat is fat.
Nat is a fat cat. (246: 4)

Lists of word patterns appear on separate pages throughout the reader, but less frequently in the later books. In each case, the list is followed with sentences in which pupils have an opportunity to read the pattern words in context.

Beginning with *My Second Reader*, the selections begin to assume plots, and this continues in the successive readers. The stories are mostly realistic, but there are some fanciful tales and poems. Following is an example of a poem from *My Seventh Reader*, and the page preceding the poem lists all the words in the poem ending with *le : beetle, needle, steeple, people, bugle, title, idle, maple.*

In Bed

Things that I hear from my bed at night
Are things nearby or far from sight.
I hear beetles clicking in a maple tree
But not Mother's needle as she patches the three
              Rips in my jeans.

I can hear bells chime in a far away steeple
And cars zoom past with hundreds of people.
They rush to places at the end of the day
Places to visit but not to stay
              All night.

It's dark but I can't turn on my lamp;
I can't read the titles of books on the shelf;
I can't be idle or speak to myself;
              So I'll sleep. (247: 85)

IX. Reading Programs Using the Pitman Augmented Roman Alphabet

Designed by Sir James Pitman, the Pitman Augmented Roman Alphabet or Initial Teaching Alphabet, more commonly known as i.t.a., is a modified form of the Roman Alphabet. It contains 43 characters instead of 26 that are in the traditional alphabet. It is planned, however, to make reading easier because of the provision for presenting fewer whole-word representations and phonic symbols. Experimental work with this alphabet began in London in 1960 and is now continuing in a number of schools in the United States. This is a sample paragraph [23] printed in this alphabet:

> wuns upon a tiem ſhær wer
> ſhree bærſ. ſhær woſ a faſher bær,
> hœ had a big gruff vois,
> a muſher bær,
> hœ had a kiend soft vois,
> and a bæby bær,
> hœ had a very skweeky vois.
> ſhæ livd in a hous
> in ſhe wœdſ.   (249 : 1)

A History of Modified and Augmented Alphabets

Before embarking on a description of i.t.a., it may be of historical interest to review briefly other past developments in which alphabets have been modified or expanded. Fries (1963) gives this account of early alphabets:

In English, the invention and use of special phonetic alphabets goes back at least as far as the work of John Hart, who in 1570 published and used such an alphabet in the teaching of reading. He had already used the "newe maner of writing" in his *Orthographie* of 1569 and discussed it in his manuscript *The Opening of the Unreasonable Writing of Our English Toung* in 1551....

Others, like Sir Thomas Smith, William Bullokar, and Edmund Coote in the sixteenth century, Alexander Gill, Charles Butler, and John Wilkins in the seventeenth century, and Benjamin Franklin in the eighteenth century advocated and used phonetic alphabets for English. A.J. Ellis and Isaac Pitman struggled with their Phonotype through the middle of the 19th century. But it was the International Phonetic Association (founded in 1886), that took up Otto Jespersen's suggestion and established in 1888 an alphabet designed to be really international and applicable to all languages. (244: 55, 56)

In the United States between 1852 and 1860, the "Fonotype," devised by Sir Isaac Pitman and A.J. Ellis, was used to teach beginning reading in 10 schools in Waltham, Massachusetts. This experiment was followed with a transition to the traditional alphabet.[24] Schools in St. Louis, Missouri, used a modified alphabet from 1866 to 1886. Results indicated that children saved 1 to $2\frac{1}{2}$ years in learning to read.[24]

Between 1870 and 1920, several Americans developed expanded alphabets, prepared reading books, and experimented in having reading taught with the use of books printed in their respective alphabets. The Leigh, Shearer, Funk and Wagnall, and Ward systems all made use of augmented alphabets during this period. (See page 120 for an illustration of a page from a primer using the Funk and Wagnall alphabet.) In 1925, W.H. Winch published a monograph based on more than 20 years of work with his expanded alphabet called "Phonoscript." In a letter (Personal communication, December 8, 1964), Gates writes,

> Winch practically admitted to me that he got as good results as he reported in his monograph only by virtue of very different efforts of devoted teachers. They may have and probably did put in more time and energy to make the system work than they realized. He stated that although he thought that as good results as he secured would not be obtained in typical normal teaching situations, he gave the more optimistic view in his monograph mainly because he somehow felt that the system was sound and with only a little more

ingenuity than he had been able to develop would at some future time prove its value. I may say that few other people who knew his work agreed.

Specific Reading Programs

During the years following 1925, interest in using augmented alphabets as mediums for teaching reading receded and little was heard about them in the United States for many years. However, interest was revived in the 1960s when reports were heard concerning experimentation in Great Britain with the use of Pitman's Initial Teaching Alphabet. At the time that this chapter is being written, many Americans are showing interest in i.t.a., and one series of readers that makes use of this alphabet has been published in the United States.

The Downing Readers. Although they are not American readers, mention should be made of the Downing Readers, a series prepared by John Downing and collaborators and published in London in the early 1960s. These books, first used in England, are available to schools in the United States, but have been used in this country for experimental purposes only. This set of readers embraces eight basic books and is accompanied by a review book and four additional books for vocabulary extension. The usual supplemental materials are provided. All the books are attractively illustrated in four colors and are bound in soft covers. These books were the forerunners of the American series which is described.

I/T/A Early-to-Read Series. This series was prepared by Albert J. Mazurkiewicz and Harold J. Tanyzer (1963, 1964). The program includes the following: *Ready for Reading Workbook*, a 1A story book, a 1B story book, and six readers of increasing difficulty. Teachers' manuals and workbooks are provided for the different levels. The following supplemental materials are available: *My Alphabet Book*, *Handbook for Writing and Spelling*, sound-symbol cards, vocabulary cards, number book, and an i.t.a binder for the teachers' manuals and handbooks.

The illustrations are stylistic, ranging from cartoon-type to sensitive line drawings. Most appear in bold outline without a background of details. They are done in one color with black in some books; in others, two or three colors are used. The books are bound in soft covers. All books are printed fully in i.t.a except Book 7, which is used in making the transition from i.t.a to the traditional alphabet; hence, the latter two thirds of the book is printed entirely in the traditional alphabet.

A departure is made in the content of these books. The 1A book, for example, is devoted wholly to the story of a dinosaur instead of to customary stories of the home experiences of beginning readers (see below). The content of the series as a whole is designed to extend the child outward from his immediate surroundings—"as far as outer space." There are many fanciful stories and old tales, as well as realistic narratives.

"a tent is the best
for dienosaur ben."

the dienosaur and
his dienosaur den.

In method, this series utilizes a language arts approach. From the beginning, children participate in activities involving reading; handwriting; and creative writing, spelling, and thinking. Sound symbols are introduced gradually and are reinforced in the workbooks. Reports of i.t.a. experiments conducted in Great Britain and the United States show promising results. We await further longitudinal research in regard to this approach.

X. Programmed Learning in Reading

The concept of programmed instruction, which came from psychologists, reflects principles derived from experimental studies in learning. There are three basic principles that must be in effect in programmed learning (Lumsdaine & Glaser, 1960):

> First, continuous active student response is required, providing explicit practice and testing of each step of what is to be earned.
>
> Second, a basis is provided for informing the student with minimal delay whether each response he makes is correct, leading him directly or indirectly to correction of his errors.
>
> Third, the student proceeds on an individual basis at his own rate—faster students romping through an instructional sequence very rapidly, slower students being tutored as slowly as necessary, with indefinite patience to meet their special needs. (252: 6)

Programmed learning is achieved through the use of materials that break subject matter or skills into small learning units. Responses are called for with each unit, and answers are provided to which student may refer immediately after making each response. Originally, programmed learning was associated with "teaching machines," a device that presents the individual student with a program of questions and answers, exercises to be performed, or problems to be solved, together with a feed-back of answers, so that the student may be immediately informed of the success of a response at each step and thus be given an opportunity to correct errors as they are made. In using the teaching machine, the student sits at the machine and responds to a preprogrammed set of questions or exercises that are presented. After making each response, the answer is flashed automatically, or the student may pull a knob, turn a crank, push a lever or button, or slide a panel to reveal the answer.

In December 1924, Sidney L. Pressey aroused much interest in teaching machines through a presentation he gave at a meeting of the American Psychological Association in Washington, D.C. At the meeting, he exhibited a device that he had prepared and described its use. Pressey continued to experiment with teaching machines, and in the ensuing years, several other investigators joined him in this interest.

During the 1950s, there was increased interest in programmed learning as many psychologists, manufacturers, and teachers participated in the movement by preparing programmed materials, inventing teaching machines, and reporting results of experimentation. Special mention should be made of an article on "Teaching Machines" by B.F. Skinner (1958),[25] which is considered a classic because it contributed much in showing the place of programmed learning in schools, and in emphasizing that the success of "a machine depends on the material used in it."

Between 1960 and 1965, many programmed materials have been published that do not require the use of teaching machines. Others use machines or films. Some recent publications in reading will be mentioned.

The Teachall Reading Course[26] is planned for use with the Teachall teaching machine. The programmed material consists of 180 cards to be used in teaching 48 nouns. *First Steps in Reading*[27] is a programmed primer that can be used in a machine and is intended for the use of parents. *Dialogue I*[28] is designed for the teaching of aural-oral phonics. This programmed book is accompanied with tape recordings.

Programmed reading materials have been prepared for use at higher levels also. Steps to Better Reading[29] consists of three books for grades seven, eight, and nine. This series is programmed basically; however, other techniques are introduced. *Lessons for Self-Instruction*[30, 31] include booklets for use in junior high school on "Reading Interpretations" and on "Reference Skills." Coronet Instructional Films offers a programmed booklet for junior high school level titled *How to Improve Your Reading and Vocabulary Growth*.[32]

The Basal Progressive Choice Reading Program [33] is a set of programmed material being used in a study with mentally retarded children. This material places much emphasis on reading readiness. There are two sets of programmed materials in reading, each of which contains a graded series of books, and neither of which requires a teaching machine. These two series will be described in some detail.

The Michigan Successive Discrimination Reading Program is part of a general language arts program that includes discrimination in writing, listening, and language, as well as in reading. The books in the series were prepared by Donald E.P. Smith and collaborators. The purpose, according to the authors, is to teach reading, writing, and listening to all English speaking children or adults.

For the purpose of teaching visual and auditory components, four books are available: Books 1 and 2 for teaching the visual component, and Books 1 and 2 for the auditory component. Books 3 to 8 complete the basal program, covering a vocabulary of 349 words and providing a complete course in phonemic analysis. Books 9, 10, and 11 are designed to prepare the child for independent, analytic reading. Teachers' manuals are provided. Simple line drawings illustrate the books, which are bound in soft covers.

In Book 8, the child is given practice in finding the sentence "He took those pennies." Preceding this page, there is practice in finding this same sentence within another group of sentences, and in finding the word *those* in lists of words. Following this page, the child completes sentences by writing *those* in appropriate places.

He took those pennies

1. He took these peonies He took
    those pennies He takes those panties

370

2. He tickle pinches He took those
   pennies He took the open panes He
3. took all those pennies He took those
   pennies (253: 8–203)

Programmed Reading Books is a series prepared by Cynthia Dee Buchanan, a program director, and Sullivan Associates, and it consists of a "Programmed Pre-Reading Book," a "Programmed Primer," and 21 additional books of increasing difficulty. Teachers' guides accompany the series.

The illustrations for the most part are simple drawings with very little color in the beginning books, but more color used in later books. All books are soft-bound and have colorful pictures on their covers.

Materials provided for the programmed prereading period are a teachers' guide on "Programmed Prereading," the "Programmed Primer," a "Reading-Readiness Test," and alphabet and sound-symbol cards. During this prereading period, the teacher works with chalkboard and card presentations of the letters of the alphabet, which the children learn in their lower-case and capitalized forms. They then learn the sounds of the letters and some words that are made by combining sounds. Much of the sound work is redolent of linguistic theory, which is to be expected since the authors incorporate the findings of structural linguistics in their program. Following the prereading period, children begin to work in the primer and progress to the other books in succession and to the accompanying hardcover readers.

The text in all the books presents small bits of learning units. In many cases, the sentence-picture combination is used, and in all cases, the child is presented with a problem to solve. In order to respond, the child must actually read the sentence, and if there is a picture, he must understand its meaning in relation to the sentence. Provision is made for the child to check his own answers.

The answers are given in a gray strip on the left side of each page. The child is provided with a "slider" with which he covers these answers. When he has written his response, he reveals the answer by pulling the slider down to the black line at the bottom of the section containing the answer (see figure below). The answer strip on the left of the page appears in gray, which contrasts with the white page.

day	The sun rises in the morning and shines all day. When the sun sets at the end of the d y, the sky turns red. After sunset, darkness falls.
	rises.
sets	It gets dark after the sun
	sets.

(254 : 104)

XI. Reading Research Grows in Quantity and Quality [34]

The excellent summaries of reading investigations published in 1965 by Helen M. Robinson in the *The Reading Teacher* (256), and by Theodore L. Harris in *The Journal of Educational Research* (255) enable us to write this section on American Reading Instruction with a note of optimism in so far as research in reading is concerned.

In the introduction to the 1965 summary, Dr. Robinson says, "The number of items in the summary reached an all time high this year, even though a number of action studies are omitted." Although it is true that the number of published investigations reported per year had a set-back in the 1940s, a good recovery was made in the 1950s, and by 1965 the number had increased to over

200 items per year. This was double the number in the 1950s, which averaged about 100 per year. As for variety in topics, Dr. Harris says in the concluding statement of the 1965 Summary,

> The current summary reflects vigorous research activity, especially in the teaching, psychology and sociology of reading. In the teaching of reading, studies in testing, predicting, and diagnosing reading performance are prominent, in addition to national and international surveys. Psychological correlates of reading and learning processes and functions continue to receive strong emphasis in the psychology of reading, while in the sociology of reading the research emphasis is rather evenly divided among the characteristics of materials, reading habits and preferences, and psychosocial effects of reading. Experimental studies employing analysis of variance techniques figure rather prominently in the research as investigators seek to study more precisely the effects of manipulated variables in both laboratory and field settings. (255: 272)

This quotation reflects progress in regard to statistical techniques, as well as indicating wide range in the topics studied.

In reviewing research conducted throughout the period as a whole, one senses continuous and vigorous effort to improve investigations in significance of topics, design of experiments, and use of statistical techniques. It is interesting to take a backward look for a moment and trace the growth in quality of reading research from 1940 to 1965.

In a critical review of research in reading that had taken place between 1940 and 1950, Scott (1954) characterized this research as "voluminous," "fragmentary and unrelated," "varied as to underlying concepts," "practical rather than theoretical," "oriented toward content methods and mechanics," "varied in quality" and "in importance," and "inconclusive and limited." He added that the "most tantalizing and stimulating characteristic of reading research findings is their inconclusiveness."

As for the future, Scott also said that "with proper tending, pruning, and thinning, the contributions of research in reading can be greatly enhanced." In spite of his criticisms, Scott stated finally that research in reading "has contributed much to the welfare of readers and to the skill of those who teach them" (257: 69–81).

In discussing Scott's report in *The Journal of Educational Research*, *48*, Gray (182: 402) said that he heartily agreed with Scott's criticisms and that those who do research in reading should make every effort to avoid mistakes of the past. He went on to say, however, that each decade during the last half century had shown improvement, that increasing proportions of studies are sound, and that in cases where they are not, they merit sympathetic, pointed, and constructive criticisms. These viewpoints give some indication of the status of quality in reading research that emerged between 1940 and 1950. Evidently, long strides toward improvement were taken during the years that followed. Harris (1962) stated,

> Research related to reading in the previous year shows several promising trends. A number of investigations revealed great care in experimental design to control significant variables. Thorough and scholarly analyses of related research accompanied others. A willingness to examine intensively the significant learning processes in reading was likewise evident, as was co-operative endeavor among workers representing several disciplines of study. As such efforts are continued they should advance the understanding of reading processes, effects, and conditions to the more effective utilization of reading in daily life. (255: 210)

In 1964, Holmes and Singer made these statements in regard to reading research:

> A review of research during the past three years makes it clear that the profession is searching not only for ways of ordering the meanings behind objective data collected and relationships calculated in

the past but also for more fundamental data and deeper meanings underlying first interpretations.

Recognition of the need to search for "undermeanings" is evident in concerted efforts (a) to construct new models that will more faithfully than previous models represent the processes at work in the subsystems or casual chains of events that come to focus in the reading act, and (b) to probe deeper with studies that aim to explain reading phenomena in smaller and smaller units.

And finally, the same authors stated:

> The present analysis reveals that, during the period September 1960 through September 1963, at least three new and exciting trends are clearly discernable: (a) a concerted effort at theory building, (b) a greater concern for designs that are experimentally and statistically sophisticated, and (c) a host of new instruments and techniques.
>
> A field of study is generally headed for a spurt of creative productivity when theory construction and experimental research become closely interdependent and mutually directed. (258: 127)

In the light of these evaluations and others made by well-qualified, professional people, it would appear that this has been a period of marked progress in improving the quality of reading research.

Another characteristic of this period is the steadily increasing number of studies that relate to the sociology of reading. The 1965 summaries show the highest number ever reported in this category. These studies reflect concerns about social and cultural influences; the content of what adults and children read; the effects of different types of reading content; mass media in its relationship to reading; use of libraries; reading as related to juvenile delinquents; and the teaching of reading to atypical children such as the mentally retarded, the gifted, the blind, and the deaf. Pressure to improve reading instruction in order better to meet national needs probably is responsible for many pedagogical studies and for several new emphases in regard to reading instruction. For one thing, research in reading readiness, which had been at a low ebb for several years, became strong again as indicated by several studies having to do with reading at preschool, kindergarten, and beginning first-grade levels. Status studies of reading instruction were conducted in some states and cities and in the United States as a whole. Numerous comparative studies of different methods of teaching reading were made. Experiments to find more effective forms of grouping for reading flared up in the latter part of the period, and individualized reading instruction, which had received little research attention since the 1920s, now again became a popular topic for study. Several studies for the first time focused on the efficiency of teachers—their personality, pretraining, inservice education, and role in supervision. There was a burgeoning of new methods and materials by those seeking to find better ways of teaching reading. Hence, near the end of the period, we find some studies dealing with linguistics as applied to reading, use of Pitman's Augmented Roman Alphabet, programmed instruction in reading, and reading for the culturally deprived.

Perhaps the critical attacks on reading instruction were responsible for a resurgence of studies having to do with phonics. To these were added studies of other word-attack skills such as context clues, and the study of word structure. Criticism also may have stimulated "Then and Now" studies in which reading achievement of several years ago in a certain town or city was compared with reading achievement in the same place at a later date.

Psychological studies contributed much to the field of reading during this period. Among the new topics psychological in nature were studies having to do with such topics as personality factors, emotions, self-concept, concept-formation, transfer, reinforcement—all as they were related to reading.

Certain topics investigated previously to some extent, now were given a great deal of attention and probed to greater depths than in the past. Among such studies were intelligence, now especially concerned with psychological factors involved in or related to reading; perception, now dealing with development and functions; interest, now often directed toward needs, differences in locale, and different social groups; vocabulary, now frequently concerned with experience and meanings; and interpretation, now exploring determinants, factors, processes and relationships.

Studies of continuing interest in the area of psychology were concerned with testing and prediction, interrelationships among reading and other subjects, particularly in the field of language arts; visual and auditory discrimination; reading preferences; and personality variables. Reading disability continued to be a popular subject for several years, but studies concerned with this topic dwindled in number during the latter part of this period. Investigations having to do with the hygiene of reading held up well in numbers for several years, but they, too, decreased sharply toward the end of the period.

The physiology of reading is an area in which relatively few studies were made. A new field of exploration was opened up, however, in studying the relationships between total physical growth and reading or specific factors of physical growth and reading. Brain damage as a possible cause of reading retardation was also a relatively new area of investigation. (This should not be confused with the theory of congenital alexia widely advocated by physicians in preceding periods.) Some new studies making use of medication in remedial reading were reported. Relatively few studies were conducted in regard to visual dysfunction, eye movements, and cerebral dominance.

Doctoral studies in reading continued in substantial numbers throughout this period, ranging from 30 to 50 dissertations per year (109, 206). According to the *Phi Delta Kappan* report (109), 35 were completed in 1961, 44 in 1962, and 50 in 1963. (The reports for 1964 and 1965 were not available at the time this chapter was written.) The topics of these recent doctoral studies are, in general, timely, have a great deal of vitality, and carry significant implications.

XII. Interest in Reading Disability Continues and Expands

Interest in reading disability persisted during the years 1950 to 1965. Published articles on this topic increased in numbers throughout this period. In the later issues of the *Educational Index*, the amount of space devoted to the listing of titles pertaining to diagnosis and remedial reading was exceptionably expansive. Reading disability also continued to be a field of exploration frequently chosen by investigators of reading problems. However, the number of researches relating to disability as reported per year in publications and in source references of doctoral dissertations has not been as great during the last 10 years of this period as previously. This may be due to several factors: first, much of the basic research in this area had already been done; second, work with reading disability cases is no longer looked on as a novelty; and third, there is a great multiplicity of new interests in the field of reading to challenge investigators.

Professional books on reading disability published during this period fall into three categories. First, there are those concerned rather generally with the subject as a whole. In addition, two new types have emerged: those that treat one specialized aspect of reading disability, and those that deal with one particular theory of causation. Among the books treating reading disability generally are Guy L. Bond and Miles B. Tinker's *Reading Difficulties, Their Diagnosis and Correction* (Appleton); Florence Roswell and Gladys Natchez's *Reading Disability: Diagnosis and Treatment* (Basic Books); and Maurice D. Wolf and Jeanne A. Woolf's *Remedial Reading* (McGraw-Hill).

Three books that deal with more specialized aspects of disability are Beulah Kantor Ephron's *Reading and the Emotions* (Julian); Clifford J. Kolson and George Kaluger's *Clinical Aspects of Remedial Reading* (Thomas); and Ruth Strang's *Diagnostic Teaching of Reading* (McGraw-Hill). Books about particular theories of causation are Carl H. Delacato's *The Treatment and Prevention of Reading Problems* (Thomas); John Money's *Reading Disability: Progress and Research Needs in Dyslexia* (Hopkins); and Donald E.P. Smith and Patricia M. Carrigan's *The Nature of Reading Disability* (Harcourt).

One characteristic of this period was an increased effort to obtain information related to reading disability by many investigators specializing in disciplines other than teaching. Large numbers of researches were conducted by sociologists, psychologists, and physiologists, and some studies were made in regard to medical treatment for reading deficiencies.

Investigations in the area of sociology revealed information about television viewing in relation to reading. Studies of the reading habits of youth and adults indicated deficiencies that those working with remedial cases at all levels should attempt to overcome. Sociological studies having to do with relationships among the home and environment and reading achievement offer valuable information to those diagnosing and treating reading disability. Studies in this area have disclosed a hostile and intolerant attitude on the part of many parents toward a child who is having difficulty in learning to read and, this of course, points toward the need for more careful counseling between reading teachers and parents.

In the area of psychology, studies have concentrated heavily on personality difficulties as related to reading disability. Emotional disturbance in connection with reading difficulties has been a topic of much research. Other new topics investigated during this period that are of significance to teachers of remedial reading are retention in reading content, transfer of practice in reading, and teaching reading to bilinguals. The unusually large number of studies which revealed high incidence of emotional difficulties in remedial reading cases called forth a variety of psychotherapeutic approaches that were used in treating reading disability cases. These approaches include directive therapy, nondirective therapy, play therapy, individual therapy, and group therapy. Bibliotherapy also received attention during this period as a treatment for reading deficiencies.

Those interested in the physiological aspects of reading disability concerned themselves with such topics as total growth, birth weights, and brain damage as related to reading. They also conducted several studies during this period with physically handicapped individuals such as aphasics and sensory deprived children.

A strong new trend of this period was the proposal of several theories concerning the diagnosis and remediation of reading disability cases. Medication was involved in some of these theories. Smith and Carrigan,[35] for example, hypothesized that certain fundamental difficulties in reading are caused by imbalance in hormonal control of the transmission of neural impulses. In their first studies, they administered multiple vitamins and hormonal treatment. In a later study, they compared the results of giving tranquilizers to some pupils and stimulants to others. Burks[36] measured the effects of medication on brain-damaged pupils and found that this treatment increased their physical activity and socioemotional behavior. Staiger[37] gave a psychic energizer to groups of students at all levels and a harmless placebo to other groups with whom the experimental groups were matched. Improvement resulted in clerical speed and accuracy.

Results from these investigations did not indicate that reading ability was improved by medication in any of the studies described. Additional experimentation, however, might have promise. Holmes[38] advanced the "substrata factor theory" as being useful in teaching remedial reading. After assembling reading skills named in an extensive survey of educational literature, Holmes conducted a series of factor analyses to determine their interrelationships and relative importance. He suggested that the information thus obtained would form a useful approach to remedial reading.

Singer[39] presented a theoretical design for teaching reading in accordance with the substrata factor theory. Another theory was advocated by Delacato.[40] His hypothesis is based on incomplete neurological development in establishing lateral dominance. He places emphasis on incorrect sleep patterns of posturalization, loss of oxygen at or before birth, and contralateral position of the controlled eye to the preferred hand. His treatment includes teaching correct sleeping posture, providing for increased intake of carbon dioxide for hyperactive children, avoidance of use of nondominant limbs in as many activities as possible, and suppression of tonal activities in reading.

Surprisingly, the congenital alexia or word blindness theory that had practically disappeared from educational literature for many years was renewed again in a previously mentioned book published in 1962, *Reading Disability: Progress and Research Needs in Dyslexia.* In this book, the term *dyslexia* is used to mean "a defect in reading." The contents of the book consists of a collection of lectures given at a Johns Hopkins University Conference under the auspices of the Departments of Pediatrics Psychiatry and Ophthalmology. Obviously, the book represents the thinking of men—in the medical profession. These men, however, have broadened their concept of causation. Although they no longer consider a congenital brain defect as the only cause of reading disability as was the case in earlier studies conducted by the medical profession, they still do consider this to be one cause.

The following quotation from the book is pertinent at this point.

Dyslexia has no single cause. Poor hearing and seeing may be implicated, or low intelligence. Early brain damage may hinder the learning of reading, and brain injury in adults may cause even complete loss of reading skill. Dyslexia may also be due to a congenital, perhaps familial, specific disability which is sometimes given the name of word blindness. (259: 1)

None of the theories mentioned on pages 380–382 are accepted generally, and several are under criticism. The vast majority of clinicians and reading specialists subscribe to the multiple-causation theory of reading disability utilizing a variety of educational tests, materials, and methods in terms of individual needs, and often calling for aid from other disciplines such as psychology, neurology, psychiatry, pediatrics, ophthalmology, optometry, audiology, endocrinology, and sociology.

There were few new developments in regard to the teaching of reading to individuals with a disability. Additional training in perception, more attention to vocabulary, and better parental guidance are among the newer emphases. The term *reading improvement* entered the reading nomenclature during this period. This term is most often applied to instruction given to college students or adults who are not disabled, but who wish to raise their reading skills to higher levels of achievement. As for reading clinics, the quotation below sums up the situation very well:

The term Reading Clinic is used broadly at the present time to represent a wide range of organizational structures and services. It is more likely to refer to a short-term corrective or remedial program with a small group of children or one child than to a specifically organized, ongoing, comprehensive service for the diagnosis and treatment of remedial problems. (260: 1)

During this period, hundreds of centers have sprung up for the purpose of improving reading ability. These organizations specializing in reading services are given various names such as "reading clinics," "reading laboratories," "reading institutes," and "reading centers." Specialists in reading are concerned that some centers are not staffed with qualified personnel and do not have adequate equipment and supplies. However, the vast majority of universities and many of the colleges in the United States do have clinics that meet standards approved by authorities in the field of remedial reading. Many public school systems also have clinics thoroughly qualified to conduct diagnoses and to give instruction in remedial and developmental reading.

XIII. The Outlook for Reading Specialization and Teacher Preparation Is Optimistic

Many advances were made during this period in regard to the preparation of reading specialists and teachers of reading. Perhaps the most distinguished mark of progress was the yielding of this important aspect of reading instruction to the scrutiny of research. Prior to 1950, investigations in regard to different positions in the field of reading and the qualifications of reading specialists and of teachers of reading were practically nonexistent. Along with the strong interest of the nation, the schools, and the community in the improvement of reading, research finally took hold at the very source of reading instruction and began probing for facts. The facts thus revealed formed bases for discussion, recommendation, and action; and, in these functions, this research has been extremely valuable. Some school systems had reading supervisors at the beginning of this period, but the demand for reading specialists did not become great until the first half of the 1950 decade. During these years, large numbers of school administrators felt the need for having additional staff to assist in reading improvement activities. Consequently, many new reading positions became available. The time was ripe for an investigation on positions in the field of reading, and such a study was conducted by Dever and published in 1956.

At the time of her study, Dever classified the positions in reading under four headings: Special Teachers of Reading, Supervisory Reading Specialists, Reading Specialists in Higher Education (in colleges and universities), and Specialists in Reading Clinical Work. As for the duties of reading specialists she states that

> These reading specialists devoted the greater amount of their time to teaching reading, supervision, testing and diagnosis, and counseling; their lesser functions were administrative and clerical work, research, public relations, and community activities.

Dever's study disclosed these findings in regard to the locations where reading specialists worked, and the duties of reading specialists in colleges and clinics.

> For the most part, special teachers of reading, as their name implies, were located in one school where their principal concern was to teach pupils retarded in reading. The supervisory reading specialists served several schools and worked more directly with teachers and less directly with pupils. The reading specialists in colleges and universities often had the dual responsibility of helping the college students to develop better reading and study habits and of preparing those interested in education to be competent teachers of reading. From the more limited data received from clinicians, counselors, and psychologists, it was evident that their two main functions were diagnosis and remediation. (261: 146)

As for qualifications, Dever found that the general professional status of the reading specialist was high. The majority had a master's or higher degree. Of the latter she stated one-fourth were at the doctoral level. However, only 60 of the 272 specialists had majored in reading. In regard to the status of the field of reading specialization in 1956, the following quotation is enlightening:

It is a relatively new field. Approximately one fifth of these special-ists were the pioneers; they were first to develop reading programs in their schools or school system; they had no precedents to follow. It seems possible that the number of pioneer positions may have been larger than one-fifth, although this information was not specifically requested.

It is a rapidly growing field. Positions have been created hurried-ly. There is need for adequately prepared specialists. When these are not available, classroom teachers and teachers of English have been asked to assume the responsibility. In many instances, teachers have entered new reading positions without sufficient preparation and have tried to develop the necessary skills on the job. (261: 148)

Another important study in regard to reading specialization was completed by Helen Robinson in 1957 titled "An Occu-pational Survey of Reading Specialists in Junior and Senior High School." This investigator found that reading specialists worked under a great variety of titles, but the two most commonly used were "remedial reading teacher" and "reading teacher." Of those responding to the questionnaire 21 percent were male and 79 per-cent were female. As for qualifications Robinson says,

The majority possessed bachelor's or master's degrees accompanied by a considerable amount of classroom experience. They had far more course work in English and psychology than in any other area. Most felt they should have more intensive training in reading, itself. (262: 62)

It will be noted that both of the investigators in these pioneer studies found that many reading specialists were not adequately prepared in the field of reading. Strong efforts have been made during recent years to raise the requirements for reading special-ists. In the Sixtieth Yearbook of the National Society for the Study of Education, Gray recommended qualifications for reme-dial reading teachers and clinicians. He quoted the following summary by Helen M. Robinson with the cooperation of 109 teachers of remedial reading:

1. A broad background in educational psychology, mental hygiene, the nature of reading deficiencies and related causal factors, remedial and therapeutic measures, pertinent tests and diagnostic instruments, and case study technique.

2. Wide participation and guided practice in selecting and using tests and other diagnostic instruments, in interpreting the data secured, in the use of various remedial and therapeutic measures, and in preparing and interpreting to others reports of diagnosis and remedial treatment.

3. Broad familiarity with the literature of the field and the results of relevant research; capacity to read critically and evaluate published studies and to apply the findings in appraising and using diagnosis and remedial procedures. (92: 158–159)

As for the preparation of "Supervising Reading Specialists," Gray suggested a still broader program of study:

To render the various types of service required today, a supervisor or consultant needs much broader preparation. The current trend is for prospective specialists in this field to engage in one or two years of graduate study leading to a master's degree or a certificate of qualification. Areas of intensive study are suggested by the following course titles: the psychology of reading, basic principles underlying a sound coordinated reading program in elementary and secondary schools, review of research relating to causes and remediation of reading disabilities, essentials in dynamic leadership, testing and evaluation, and supervised practice.

Additional courses are also recommended which are elected in harmony with individual needs: literature for children and youth; mental testing; emotional factors in learning; principles and procedures in guidance. A second year is devoted to an internship which provides participation in supervisory activities in elementary schools, high schools, and junior colleges, and in reading clinics, accompanied by weekly seminars. Thus, the preparation of supervising specialists is becoming broader and more thorough. (92: 160)

At the time that this chapter is being written, a number of universities and colleges are offering broad programs of courses to prepare individuals in reading specialization. There also is a trend toward certification of reading specialists by state departments of education, which is a very significant indication of progress. In a survey conducted in 1960 by the Standards Committee of the International Reading Association, it was found that the following states had such certification: Connecticut, Delaware, Indiana, Massachusetts, Oregon, Pennsylvania, and Wisconsin. In a survey conducted in 1964 under the same sponsorship, 14 additional states "indicated that reading as a specialty was recognized in some form or another in their requirements for teacher certification." [41]

The university or college programs for reading specialization vary from one college to another, and certification requirements differ somewhat among the states having reading certification. The significant consideration, however, is that many institutions of higher learning are offering broader programs in reading specialization, and that many states are recognizing the need for special preparation in this field through certification requirements. Both these trends are new in the period under discussion, and both are expanding as this chapter is being written. During the latter years of this period, there was a heavy demand for qualified reading specialists that was considerably greater than the supply. Perhaps the lag will be caught up during the next decade. Until such time, the fact that demand is greater than supply is a wholesome indication in itself.

Now we shall turn attention to the preservice and inservice preparation of classroom teachers who teach reading. In 1961, *The Torch Lighters* (Austin, Morrison, et al.) was published. This book encompassed the results of a nationwide survey of samplings of schools "to learn how the colleges and universities in the United States are now preparing tomorrow's teachers of reading and to suggest recommendations for improving that preparation." The findings of this study revealed that nearly all colleges and universities require one course in reading. This course, however, is taught as an integrated course of language arts or other subjects about as frequently as it is taught as a separate course. In the former case, the time given to reading may be as little as 12 hours. Therefore the investigators of this study recommended "that the class time devoted to reading instruction, whether taught as a separate course or integrated with the language arts, be equivalent to at least three semester hours' credit" (263: 144). Furthermore, the findings of this study revealed that much more emphasis is placed upon primary reading skills in college courses than on intermediate grade reading skills. So the investigators recommended "that the basic reading instruction offered to prospective elementary teachers be broadened to include content and instructional techniques appropriate for the intermediate and upper grades" (263: 145). In addition, because of the strong trend to teach reading in junior and senior high school, the investigators made this recommendation: "that a course in basic reading instruction be required of all prospective secondary school teachers" (263: 147).

As a result of this study, it was also suggested that many elementary school administrators and supervisors should take a course in reading so that they would be better prepared to assist their teachers. This specific recommendation was phrased as follows: "that colleges offer a course, or inservice training, in reading instruction specifically designed for principals, supervisors, and cooperating teachers" (263: 147). Many other recommendations for the improvement of college reading courses were made as a result of this study. These recommendations as a whole have not been fully realized at this writing. However, the study undoubtedly has been influential in raising standards in regard to reading preparation in many universities and colleges.

The inservice education of teachers of reading is another aspect of teacher preparation that has been the subject of much discussion, experimentation, and research. Inservice programs in general were provided widely in the country during the early 1950s. A nationwide study in 1952 revealed that inservice education programs were in operation in public school systems in all 48 states.[42] In 1951, the National Education Association studied inservice education practices in 1,615 urban school systems: 1,488 of these school systems reported special opportunities for inservice education and professional growth of teachers.[43] In 1952, the Research Department of the Hartford Public Schools in Connecticut conducted a study of the inservice education programs of 218 cities over 25,000 in population: 90 percent of the 218 cities reported that "planned" professional growth programs were being conducted in their school systems.[44] In a study conducted in 1954, the California Teachers Association found that 155 school systems in California had organized programs of new-teacher orientation.[45] Many other studies indicate widespread interest in inservice growth activities.

As for inservice activities in the specific field of reading, information is available as the result of another survey by Austin and Morrison (1963) that culminated in *The First R*. In sampling representative schools in the United States, these investigators found schools using inservice activities in reading in the following order of frequency: workshops, preschool orientation meetings or institutes, demonstrations, visits to other classrooms, faculty meetings, grade level meetings, and area meetings. The authors summarize their findings in regard to inservice programs in reading with an optimistic outlook for the future.

> Inservice programs, which might well be thought the *sine qua non* for the improvement of existing and future reading programs, commonly evidence weaknesses. Approximately one-third of all the school systems sampled offered no such services, and those that did

provided programs so sporadic as to cast doubt on their over-all effectiveness. Nevertheless, many school systems are now making determined efforts to effect more viable, comprehensive, and challenging programs. The active participation of teachers in planning the content and conduct of such projects is becoming more widespread. Similarly, the involvement of teachers in experimental projects is an encouraging sign that inservice programs will be more helpful to teachers in the future than they have been in the past. (233: 180)

One additional point that should be emphasized before concluding this section is that investigations began to probe two other aspects of efficiency in reading instruction hitherto unexplored through research techniques: assessing the needs and attitudes of teachers themselves, as related to the successful teaching of reading; and measuring preservice and inservice courses to ascertain their effectiveness in improving classroom instruction.

The teacher is the source and conductor of reading instruction. Aiding her in developing and improving her competence is a matter of basic importance. The facts and trends discussed in this section seem to be leading strongly toward this goal. Therefore, it would appear that the road ahead in teacher improvement is one of real promise.

IN RETROSPECT

Between the covers of this book, the pageant of American reading instruction has passed in review—interesting, colorful, ever-changing. For over three and a half centuries this pageant has been moving forward, and during all this time children in the United States have been learning to read.

Many turning points have marked this ever-continuing story. For a period of years, reading methods and materials are quite similar, so similar in fact that an uninformed examiner might arrive at the conclusion that all had been turned out of the same matrix, with just a slightly different crimp here and there in the contour of the mold. Then rather suddenly, this pattern is abandoned and readers representing it march out of classrooms passively, silently, noiselessly to repose in the dusty attics of homes or the unused storage rooms of schools. Then a new plan becomes popular and we teach reading according to this plan until another turning point arrives. Thus, epoch after epoch of reading instruction passes through the chronicles of time.

As we review these epochs, we have a right to feel assured and gratified. Progress has been taking place all through the centuries. Periods of change, however, have become more frequent and shorter in duration as the years have passed. This of course indicates that progress is proceeding at a more rapid tempo.

Change during the 20th century has been most exciting. For one thing, interest in reading instruction became practically universal during this era. There was a time when primary teachers were the only people interested in the teaching of reading. Now teachers of all subjects and at all levels are teaching reading and seeking information about reading. Parents are asking questions and pursuing books and articles on reading. Students at high school and college levels and adults beyond college are flocking to reading centers. Slick magazines and laymen are discussing reading freely. Perhaps most important of all, governmental agencies are deeply concerned with reading improvement both in school and out. Not only is the government encouraging the improvement of reading instruction and wide-spread teaching of reading, but it is offering financial assistance in furthering both of these objectives. A great conflagration of interest has been ignited amongst teachers and students, the lay public, and the government. This is a most auspicious occurrence.

Also with a growing awareness of the complexity of the reading process, there has been a spurt of activity in the increase and improvement of reading courses in the curriculums of teacher-training institutions and in the inservice offerings for teachers. Concurrently with this interest, standards are being raised in regard to the qualifications of teachers of reading and of reading specialists. This movement toward better preparation of teachers in reading is a big step forward.

Perhaps the supreme achievement for which this century always will be distinguished is that it brought to us the gift of scientific investigation. With instruments of measurement and diagnosis, we no longer need to depend solely upon judgment in assessing the needs of those whom we instruct or the effectiveness of theories, methods, and materials that we use. We can now obtain objective data in regard to many aspects of reading. This is an accomplishment of great magnitude.

In looking back, we might wonder if ever there could be another 65 years so productive as those that have elapsed since 1900. In consideration of the newly developed tools of investigation, the intensity of our motives to learn, and the multitude of studies conducted, we might reason that almost all facets of reading instruction have been explored and, thus, another era could never be so great as this.

If we come to this conclusion, we probably are wrong. We pioneered during this period in unexplored territory. Metaphorically speaking, we chopped down and cleared away the large virgin trees, but perhaps some of the humble shrubs or creeping vines or fragile mosses may hold even more significance for us than the strikingly obvious, first-sight timbers. These more obscure constituents will not yield their significance with the use of heavy saws and axes. We shall need fresh, piercing insights in choosing which of these to select for study, and then we shall need unique, delicate tools to pry them loose from their tangled settings and to test the potency of their effect; and withal, great ingenuity will be required in shaping reading methods and materials in the image of our findings.

Although our accomplishments have been very great, indeed, it may be that we have only penetrated the first layer, the troposphere, so to speak. Undoubtedly, brilliant new insights will be revealed, ingenious new techniques of experimentation will be evolved, and more effective methods and materials will be devised. Possibilities of such developments portend opportunities for unlimited achievement in the future.

ENDNOTES

Chapter Two

1. From Johnson, Clifton. (1904). *Old-time schools and school-books* (p. 25). New York: Macmillan. By permission of the Macmillan Company.

Chapter Five

1. References used in obtaining facts for this section are listed as 75–78 in the Selected Bibliography.

Chapter Six

1. From Wheat, Harry Grove. (1923). *The teaching of reading* (p. 6). Boston: Ginn. By permission of Ginn and Company.
2. From Watkins, Emma. (1925). *Silent reading for beginners* (p. 98). Chicago: Lippincott. By permission of J.B. Lippincott Company.
3. From Watkins, Emma. (1922). *How to teach silent reading to beginners* (p. 31).
   . Chicago: Lippincott. By permission of J.B. Lippincott Company.
4. References used in obtaining facts for this section are listed as 75, 77, 78, 108, and 109 in the Selected Bibliography.

Chapter Seven

1. From Gray, William S., & Munroe, Ruth. (1929). *The reading interests and habits of adults* (p. 105). New York: Macmillan. By permission of the Macmillan Company.
2. The ten series used in this study of manuals were the Children's Own Readers, the Work-Play Books, the Child's Own Way Series, Child-Story Readers, Pathway to Reading, Newson Readers, the Study Readers, the Smedley and Olsen Series, Story and Study Readers, and New Path to Reading. (See p. 200 and Selected Bibliography.)
3. Primers of the following series were included in this study: Real Life Readers, the Happy Childhood Readers, Fact and Story Readers, Story and Study Readers, the Smedley and Olsen Series, the Work-Play Books, and the Children's Own Readers.
4. From Gates, Arthur I., & Huber, Miriam Blanton. (1930). *The Work-Play Books, Primer* (p. 20) and *Third reader* (p. 23). New York: Macmillan. By permission of the Macmillan Company.

5. From Freeman, F.N., Storm, G.E., Johnson, E.M., and French, W.C. (1927). *Child-Story Readers, Primer* (p. 59); *Fourth reader* (p. 270). Chicago: Lyons and Carnahan. By permission of Lyons and Carnahan.
6. From Pennell, Mary E., & Cusack, Alice M. (1929). *The Children's Own Readers, Primer* (p. 15). Boston: Ginn. By permission of Ginn and Company.
7. From Pennell, Mary E., & Cusack, Alice M. (1929). *The Children's Own Readers, Book four* (p. 206). Boston: Ginn. By permission of Ginn and Company.
8. *The administration handbook* (p. 16). (no date). Chicago: Scott Foresman.
9. From Pennell, Mary E., & Cusack, Alice M. (1929). *The Children's Own Readers: Teachers' annual, first grade* (p. 280). Boston, Ginn. By permission of Ginn and Company.
10. From Pennell, Mary E., & Cusack, Alice M. (1929). *The Children's Own Readers: Teachers' manual, Books four, five, and six* (pp. 20–21). Boston: Ginn. By permission of Ginn and Company.
11. From Johnson, Eleanor M. *Child-story readers: Third reader manual.* (p. 8). Chicago: Lyons & Carnahan. By permission of Lyons & Carnahan.
12. *The administrators handbook on reading* (p. 11) (Curriculum Foundation Basic Reading Series). Chicago: Scott Foresman.
13. References used in obtaining facts for this section are listed as 107, 108, 109, 110, and 182 in the Selected Bibliography.

Chapter Eight

1. Gates, Arthur I., Batchelder, Mildred I., & Betzner, Jean. (1926). A modern, systematic versus an opportunistic method of teaching: An experimental study. *Teachers College Record, 27*, 679–700.
2. Hilliard, George H. (1932). Extensive library reading versus special drill as an aid in improving certain reading abilities. *Educational News Bulletin, 2*, 6–12. (Western State Teachers College, Kalamazoo, Michigan)
3. References used in obtaining facts for this section are listed as 107, 108, 109, 110, and 206 in the Selected Bibliography.

Chapter Nine

1. Carr, William G. (1960, January). Action—Not talk. *National Education Association Journal, 7.*
2. National Society of the Study of Education. (1961). *Development in and through reading* (Sixtieth Yearbook of the National Society of the Study of Education, pp. 21–22). Chicago: Author.
3. Yoakam, Gerald A. (1955). *Report of the eleventh annual conference on reading* (p. 11). Pittsburgh, PA: University of Pittsburgh.

4. Sheldon, William D., & Esther Glass. (1963). *Finding the Way: Teachers' manual* (p. 7). Boston: Allyn & Bacon.

5. National Council of Teachers of English. (1952). *The English language arts.* New York: Appleton-Century-Crofts.

6. From *The Claremont Reading Conference.* (1961). Claremont, CA.

7. Jordan, James W. (1958, September). A survey of certain policies and practices in Florida junior high schools. *Bulletin of the National Association of Secondary School Principals, 42,* 71–77.

8. Baughman, Millard Dale. (1960, November). Special reading instruction in Illinois junior high schools. *Bulletin of the National Association of Secondary School Principals, 44,* 90–95.

9. Smith, Kenneth. (1963). *A Survey of seventh and eighth grade reading programs in selected AAA schools of Missouri.* Unpublished doctoral dissertation, University of Missouri, Columbia.

10. Penty, Ruth C. (1956). *Reading ability and high school dropouts* (p. 19). New York: Bureau of Publications, Columbia University Teachers College.

11. Donovan, Bernard E. (1955). *Survey of reading abilities of pupils entering the academic high schools in September 1955* (p. 3). New York: Board of Education.

12. Keppel, Francis. (1964, October). Research: Education's neglected hope. *Journal of Reading, 8*(1), 3–10.

13. Burton, D.L. (1961). Some trends and emphases in high school reading and literature. In J.A. Figurel (Ed.), *Changing concepts of reading instruction* (International Reading Association Conference Proceedings, Vol. 6, pp. 265–269). Newark, DE: International Reading Association.

14. Early, Margaret J. (April, 1960). A high school faculty considers reading. *The Reading Teacher, 13,* 286.

15. Causey, Oscar S., & Eller, William. (April 1959). Starting and improving college reading programs. In the *Eighth Yearbook of the National Reading Conference* (pp. 179–282). Fort Worth, TX: Texas Christian University Press.

16. Miller, Lyle L. (April 1959). Current use of workbooks and mechanical aids. In the *Eighth Yearbook of the National Reading Conference* (p. 67). Fort Worth, TX: Texas Christian University Press.

17. Patterson, Harry O. (1957). A survey of reading improvement programs in industry, techniques and procedures in college and adult reading programs. In O.S. Causey (Ed.), *Sixth Yearbook of the Southwest Reading Conference for Colleges and Universities* (pp. 121–133). Fort Worth, TX: Texas Christian University Press.

18. Olson, Willard. (1962, Spring). *Seeking, self-selection and pacing in the use of books by children, the packet* (pp. 3–10). Boston: D.C. Heath.

19. Thomas, Dominic R. (1961). *Oral language sentence structure and vocabulary of kindergarten children living in low socio-economic areas.* Unpublished doctoral thesis, Wayne State University, Detroit, Michigan.

20. O'Shea, M.V. (1927). *Linguistics in education.* New York: Macmillan.

21. Bloomfield, Leonard. (1942, April/May) Linguistics and reading. *Elementary English Review, 19,* 125–130, 183–186.

22. Smith, Henry Lee, Jr. (Producer). *Language and linguistics* [Film series]. New York: University of Buffalo and the National Educational Television and Radio Center.

23. Downing, John, & Graham, Faith. (1964). *A walk in the woods* (p. 1) (The Downing Readers). London: Initial Teaching Publishing.

24. Downing, John A. (1961, July 21). The Augmented Roman Alphabet: Experiment in systematized spelling. *The Times Educational Supplement* (London), p. 81.

25. Skinner, B.F. (1958, October 24). Teaching machines. *Science, 128.*

26. Publishers Company. (1962). *Teachall reading course.* Washington, DC: Author.

27. Teaching Materials Corporation (Distributor). (1962). *First steps in reading* (Teaching Machines Inc.). New York: Grolier.

28. Brogan, Andrews, & Hotchkiss, Emily. (1963). *Dialogue I* (An Aural-Oral Course in Phonics). Chester, CT: Chester Electronic Laboratories.

29. Schramm, Wilbur, Potell, Herbert, & Spache, George D. (1963). *Steps to Better Reading: Books 1, 2, and 3.* New York: Harcourt, Brace & World.

30. Bostwick, Gracecarol. (1963). *Lessons for self-instruction: Reading interpretations I,* and *Reading interpretations II* (Basic Skills Series). Monterey, CA: California Test Bureau.

31. Bostwick, Gracecarol, & Midloch, Miles. (1963). *Lessons for self-instruction: Reference skills—The dictionary.* (Basic Skills Series). Monterey, CA: California Test Bureau.

32. Abraham,Willard. (1963). *How to improve your reading and vocabulary growth* [Learning Incorporated booklet]. Chicago: Coronet Instructional Films.

33. Woolman, Myron. (1962). *The basal progressive choice reading program.* Washington, DC: Institute for Education Research.

34. References used in obtaining facts for this section are listed as 109, 182, 206, 255, and 256 in the Selected Bibliography.

35. Smith, Donald E.P., & Carrigan, Patricia M. (1959). *The nature of reading disability.* New York: Harcourt Brace.

36. Burks, Harold F. (1957, December). The effect of brain pathology on learning. *Journal of Exceptional Children, 24,* 169–172.

37. Staiger, Ralph C., et al. (1960, February). *The usefulness of a psychic energizer in treating reading retardation*. Paper presented at the American Educational Research Association Convention, Atlantic City, NJ.

38. Holmes, Jack A., & Singer, Harry. (1961). *The substrata-factor theory: Substrata factor differences underlying reading ability in known groups*. Washington, DC: U.S. Office of Education.

39. Singer, Harry. (1962). Substrata-factor theory of reading: Theoretical design for teaching reading. In *Challenge and Experiment in Reading* (Conference Proceedings of the International Reading Association, Vol. 7, pp. 226–232).

40. Delacato, Carl H. (1959). *The treatment and prevention of reading problems*. Springfield, IL: C.C. Thomas.

41. Dietrich, Dorothy. (1965, January 22). *Standards Committee Report to the Board of Directors of the International Reading Association*. Newark, DE: International Reading Association.

42. Federal Security Agency. (1952). Schools at work in forty-eight states. *Office of Education Bulletin, No. 13*, 133–134. Washington, DC: Government Printing Office.

43. National Education Association. (1954, February). *In-service education of teachers* [Mimeograph] (p. 15). Washington, DC: Author.

44. Hartford Public Schools. (1953, March 25). *Professional growth programs in 218 cities* (pp. 1–2). Hartford, CT: Author.

45. California Teachers Association. (1954, November). Teacher orientation in California elementary schools. *California Teachers Association Research Bulletin* (No. 7, p. 25) San Francisco: Author.

SELECTED BIBLIOGRAPHY

Apreproximately 2,500 pieces of material were examined in collecting information for this book. This Selected Bibliography includes references to the publications that are quoted directly or specifically described in this volume.

At the time this book was first published, authorities in historical research advised that the references be listed in the order of the successive periods discussed rather than in alphabetical order according to the first letter of the author's surname. In updating the book, fresh material was added for chapters six through nine, inclusive, hence many new references were needed. The reference pattern established in the first edition of the book has been continued in arranging references for the new material in this revised edition.

PERIOD 1607–1776

1. Tyler, Edward B. (1896). *Early history of mankind.* New York: Henry Holt.
2. Clodd, Edward. (1900). *The story of the alphabet.* New York: D. Appleton.
3. Tuer, Andrew W. (1896). *History of the Horn Book* (Vols. 1 and 2). London: Leadenhall Press.
4. Ford, Paul Leicester. (1897). *The New-England Primer, A history of it's origin and development.* New York: Dodd, Mead.
5. Green, J.R. (1895). *Short history of the English people.* New York: Harper & Brothers.
6. Watson, Foster. (1908). *English grammar schools in 1660.* Cambridge, UK: Cambridge University Press.
7. Hoole, Charles A. (1660). *New discovery of the old art of teaching school.* London: J.T. Crook. (Reprinted by C.W. Bardeen, Syracuse, NY, 1912).
8. Clews, Elsie W. (1899). *Educational legislation and administration of the colonial governments.* New York: Columbia University Press.
9. ——— (1916). *American Antiquarian Society proceedings.* Worcester, MA.
10. ——— *Massachusetts Historical Society collection* (Series 5, Vol. 5). Boston.
11. ——— (1760). *The New England Psalter.* Philadelphia: W. Dunlop.

12. Heartman, Charles F. (1922). *The New England Primer* [Pamphlet]. Metuchen, NJ.

13. ——— (1727). *The New England Primer*. Boston: S. Kneeland and T. Green.

14. Evans, Charles. (1903). *American bibliography of printing*. (Vol. 1). Chicago: Blakely Press.

15. Fox, George. (1760). *Instructions for right spelling*. Newport, RI: S. Southwich.

16. Dilworth, Thomas. (1770). *A new guide to the English tongue*. Philadelphia: Thomas and William Bradford.

17. ——— (1750). *The child's new plaything*. Boston: Jessup Draper.

18. Johnson, Clifton. (1904). *Old-time schools and school-books*. New York: Macmillan.

PERIOD 1776–1840

19. Cobb, Lyman. (1835). *The North American reader*. New York: B. and S. Collins.

20. ——— (1840). *Juvenile reader* (No. 1). New York: W.H. Dean.

21. Webster, Noah. (1798). *The American spelling book*. Boston: Isaiah Thomas and Ebenezer Andrews.

22. ——— (1800). *An American selection of lessons in reading and speaking*. Philadelphia: David Hogan.

23. ——— (1790). *The little reader's assistant*. Hartford, CT: Babcock.

24. ——— (1782). *A grammatical institute of the English language*. Hartford, CT: Hudson and Goodwin.

25. Leavitt, J. (1820). *Easy lessons in reading*. Keene, N.H.: J. and J.W. Prentiss.

26. Bingham, Caleb. (1807). *The Columbian orator*. Hartford, CT: Lincoln and Gleason.

27. ——— (1815). *The American preceptor*. Middlebury, NY: T.C. Strong.

28. ——— (1832, 1833). *The New England magazine*, 2 and 4. Boston: J.T. and E.B. Buckingham.

29. Hillard, George. (1831). *The popular reader*. Greenfield, MA: A. Phelps.

30. ——— (1831). *The Franklin primer*. New York.

31. Murray, Lindley. (1822). *English reader*. Albany, NY: E. and E. Hosford.

32. ——— (1839). *The Christmas school primer*. New York: William W. Allen.

33. Barber, Jonathan. (1825). *Exercises in reading and recitation*. Boston: Miller and Hammonds.

PERIOD 1840–1890

34. Peers, Benjamin O. (1839). *American annals of education*, 9. Boston: Otis, Broaders.

35. ——— (1842, January 1). *The Common School Journal*, 4. Boston: William B. Fowle and N. Capen.

36. Mann, Horace. (1842, January 1). Teaching young children to read. *The Common School Journal, 4*, and (1844, April 1). Method of teaching young children on their first entering school. *The Common School Journal, 6*. Boston: William B. Fowle and N. Capen.

37. —— (1837). *American annals of education, 7*. Boston: Carter and Hendee.

38. Tower, David B. (1871). *Tower's third reader*. Baltimore: Kelly, Piet.

39. —— (1853). *The gradual primer*. Boston: Sanborn, Carter, Bazin.

40. Vail, T.H. (1856, August). Hints on reading, quotation from Alonzo Potter. *American School Journal, 2*(1). Hartford, CT: F.C. Brownell.

41. Blumstead, Josiah F. (1840). *My little primer*. Boston: Perkins and Marwin.

42. —— (1844). *My first school book*. Boston: Perkins and Marwin.

43. —— (1848). *Third reading book*. Boston: Perkins and Marwin.

44. Webb, J. Russell. (1846). *The new word method*. New York: Sheldon, Lamport, and Blakeman.

45. —— (1856). *Webb's normal reader*, No. 3. New York: Sheldon, Lamport, and Blakeman.

46. —— (1856). *Webb's normal reader*, No. 4. New York: Sheldon, Lamport, and Blakeman.

47. Thayer, Gideon. (1857). Letters to a young teacher. *Barnard's Journal of Education, 4*.

48. Town, Salem, & Holbrook, N.M. (1857). *Progressive primer*. Boston: Carter, Bazin.

49. McGuffey, William H. (1866). *McGuffey's new first eclectic reader*. Cincinnati, OH: Van Antwerp, Bragg.

50. —— (1838). *McGuffey's eclectic fourth reader*. Cincinnati, OH: Trumen and Smith.

51. —— (1848). *McGuffey's newly revised eclectic fourth reader*. Cincinnati, OH: Winthrop B. Smith.

52. Russell, William, & Goldsbury, John. (1845). *Introduction to the American common-school reader & the speaker*. Boston: Charles Tappan.

PERIOD 1890–1910

53. Brown, George P. (1880). Books and reading for the young. *State Report*. Indianapolis, IN: Carlon and Hollenbeck.

54. Arnold, Sarah Louise. (1899). *Reading: How to teach it*. Newark, NJ: Silver Burdett.

55. Herbart, J.F. (1895). *Science of education and aesthetic revelation of the world*. Boston: D.C. Heath.

56. Eliot, Charles W. (1898). *Educational reform*. New York: Century.

57. —— (1891, July). Literature in the school. *Educational Review, 2*.

58. Farnham, George L. (1895). *The sentence-method of reading*. Syracuse: C.W. Bardeen.

59. McMurry, Charles A. (1899). *Special method in the reading of complete English classics*. Bloomington, IL: Public School Publishing.

60. Funk, Isaac Kaufman, & Montrose, Mose I. (1902). *Standard Reading Series, First readers* (p. 70). New York: Funk and Wagnall.

61. Shearer, James W. (1894). *Combination speller* (p. 3). St. Louis.

62. Pollard, Rebecca S. (1889). *Pollard's synthetic method, A complete manual*. Chicago: Western Publishing House.

63. Ward, Edward G. (1894). *The Rational Method in Reading, Primer*. Newark: Silver Burdett.

64. ——— (1899). *Third reader*.

65. Fassett, James H., & Norton, Charles H. (1922). *The Beacon Readers: A manual of instructions for teachers*. Boston: Ginn.

66. Fassett, James H. (1912). *The Beacon primer*.

67. Free, Margaret, & Treadwell, Harriett T. (1910–1916). *Reading-Literature Series, Primary manual*.

68. ——— *Primer*.

69. Coe, Ida, & Christie, Alice J. (1913). *Story Hour Readers, Manual*. New York: American Book.

70. Arnold, Sarah Louise, & Gilbert, Charles B. (1897). *Stepping Stones to Literature, First reader*. Newark: Silver Burdett.

71. ——— *Fifth reader*.

72. Spaulding, Frank E., & Bryce, Catherine T. (1906). *The Aldine Readers, Primer*. New York: Newson.

73. Judson, Harry Pratt, & Bender, Ida C. (1899). *Graded Literature Readers, First book*. New York: Charles E. Merrill. (formerly Maynard, Merrill & Company).

74. Elson, William H. (1909–1914). *Elson-Runkel primer, Elson primary school readers*, and *Elson grammar school readers*. Chicago: Scott, Foresman.

75. Gray, William S. (1925). *Summary of investigations relating to reading* (Supplementary Monograph, No. 28). Chicago: University of Chicago.

76. Dearborn, Walter F. (1906, March). The psychology of reading. *Archives of Philosophy, Psychology, and Scientific Methods, 1*(4), 7–132.

77. ——— (1914, April). Professor Cattell's studies of reading and perception. *Archives of Psychology, Psychology, and Scientific Methods , 7*(30), 34–35.

78. Huey, Edmund Burke. (1908). *The psychology and pedagogy of reading*. New York: Macmillan. (Revised 1912, 1915)

PERIOD 1910–1925

79. Parker, Francis W. (1894). *Talks on pedagogics*. Chicago: Kellogg.

80. Starch, Daniel. (1915, January). *Journal of Educational Psychology*.

81. Gray, William S. (1924, January). The importance of intelligent silent reading. *Elementary School Journal, 24*. Quotation from Parson, Rhey Boyd. (1923). *A study of adult reading*. Unpublished master's thesis, University of Chicago, Illinois.

82. Judd, Charles H., & Buswell, Guy T. (1922). *Silent reading: A study of the various types* (Yearbook of the National Society for the Study of Education). Chicago: University of Chicago.

83. Eighteenth Yearbook, Part II.

84. Nineteenth Yearbook, Part I.

85. Twentieth Yearbook, Part I and Part II.

86. Twenty-Fourth Yearbook, Part I and Part II.

87. Thirty-Third Yearbook, Part II.

88. Thirty-Sixth Yearbook, Part I.

89. Forty-Seventh Yearbook, Part II.

90. Forty-Eighth Yearbook, Part II.

91. Fifty-Sixth Yearbook, Part I.

92. Sixtieth Yearbook, Part I.

93. Thiesen, W.W. (1921). *Factors affecting results in primary reading* (Twentieth yearbook of the National Society for the Study of Education, Part II). Bloomington, IL: Public School Publishing.

94. Wheat, Harry Grove. (1923). *The teaching of reading*. Boston: Ginn Company.

95. Craig, Clara E. (1919). *The beginnings of reading and writing*. Providence, RI: Rhode Island Normal School.

96. Lewis, William D., Rowland, Albert L., & Gehres, Ethel H. (1920–1924). *The Silent Readers, First reader manual*. Philadelphia: John C. Winston Co.

97. ——— *First reader*.

98. ——— *Fourth reader*.

99. Buswell, Guy T., & Wheeler, William H. (1923). *The Silent Reading Hour, Teachers' manual for the second reader*. Chicago: Wheeler Publishing.

100. ——— *Second reader*.

101. ——— *Teachers' manual for the third reader*.

102. ——— *Third reader*.

103. Horn, Ernest, & Shields, Grace. (1924). *The Learn to Study Readers, Book one*. Boston: Ginn.

104. Watkins, Emma. (1922). *How to teach silent reading to beginners*. Chicago: J.B. Lippincott.

105. State Department of Education. (1924). Silent reading. *Maryland School Bulletin, 5*(11). Baltimore: Author.

106. Bolenius, Emma M. (1923). *The Boys' and Girls' Readers, First grade manual.* Boston: Houghton Mifflin.

107. Gray, William S. (1925–1932). Summary of investigations relating to reading. *Elementary School Journal.*

108. U.S. Library of Congress, Catalog Division. (1913–1940). *American doctoral dissertations* [Lists]. Washington: Government Printing Office.

109. Good, Carter V. (1923–1953). Doctoral studies completed or under way. *Phi Delta Kappan.* (Additional issues with Lyda, Mary Louise; Jenson, Glenn; Brown, Stanley; Anderson, Harold; 1954–1963).

110. Betts, Emmett Albert, & Betts, Thelma Marshall. (1945). *An index of professional literature on reading and related topics.* New York: American Book.

111. Uhl, Willis L. (1923). *The materials of reading.* Newark, NJ: Silver Burdett.

112. Romanes, George John. (1884). *Mental evolutions in animals.* New York: Appleton.

113. Abell, Adelaide M. (1894). Rapid reading, *Educational Review, 8*, 283–286.

114. Quantz, J.O. (1897). *Problems in the psychology of reading* (Psychological Monograph Review Supplements, Vol. 2, pp. 1–5).

115. Courtis, S.A. (1915). *Standards in rates of reading* (Fourteenth yearbook of the National Society for the Study of Education, Part I). Bloomington, IL: Public School Publishing.

116. Gray, William S. (1915, December). A cooperative study of reading, *Elementary School Journal, 17*, 250–265.

117. Bronner, Augusta F. (1917). *The psychology of special abilities and disabilities.* Boston: Little, Brown.

118. Uhl, W.L. (1916, December). The use of the results of reading tests as bases for planning remedial work. *Elementary School Journal, 17*, 273–280.

119. Anderson, C.J., & Merton, E. (1921, January). Remedial work in reading, *Elementary School Journal, 21*, 336–348.

120. Gray, W.S., et al. (1922). *Remedial cases in reading: Their diagnosis and treatment* (Supplemental Educational Monograph). Chicago: University of Chicago Press.

121. Gray, Clarence Truman. (1922). *Deficiencies in reading ability: Their diagnosis and treatment.* Boston: D.C. Heath.

122. Washburne, C.W. (1918, October 5). Breaking the lockstep in our schools. *School and Society, 8*, 391–402.

123. Dewey, Evelyn. (1922). *The Dalton Laboratory Plan.* New York: E.P. Dutton.

PERIOD 1925–1935

124. Pennell, Mary E., & Cusack, Alice M. (1929). *The Children's Own Readers: Friends, A primer.* Boston: Ginn.

125. —— *First grade teachers' manual.*
126. —— *Book four.*
127. ——*Teacher's manual* for Books Four, Five, and Six.
128. Gates, Arthur I., & Huber, Miriam B. (1930). *The Work-Play Books, Primer.* New York: Macmillan.
129. —— *First grade manual.*
130. —— *Third reader.*
131. —— *Third grade manual.* (Jean Y. Ayer, Coauthor)
132. Gates, Arthur I. (1964, December 8). Personal letter to Nila Banton Smith.
133. Hardy, Marjorie. (1926–1927). *The Child's Own Way Series: Wag and Puff* (A Primer). Chicago: Wheeler Publishing.
134. —— *First grade manual.*
135. —— Second and third grade manuals.
136. —— *Best Stories*, a third reader.
137. Freeman, Frank N., Storm, Grace E., Johnson, Eleanor M., & French, W.C. (1927–1928). *Child-Story Readers, Primer.* Chicago: Lyons & Carnahan.
138. —— *First grade manual.*
139. —— Johnson, Eleanor M. *Third reader manual.*
140. —— *Fourth reader.*
141. Coleman, Bessie B., Uhl, Willis L., & Hosic, James F. (1925–1927). *Pathway to Reading: Teacher's manual, Primer.* Newark, NJ: Silver Burdett.
142. —— *Teacher's Manual*, Fourth, fifth, and sixth readers.
143. Bryce, Catherine T., & Rose L. Hardy. (1927). Newson Readers. New York: Newson.
144. Walker, Alberta, Summy, Ethel, & Parkman, Mary R. (1925). *A manual to accompany the Study Readers* (Fourth, Fifth, and Sixth Years). New York: Charles E. Merrill.
145. Smedley, Eva A., & Olsen, Martha C. (1926–1929). The Smedley and Olsen Series. Chicago: Hall and McCreary.
146. Gecks, Mathilde C., Skinner, Charles E., & Withers, John W. (1928). Story and Study Readers. Richmond, VA: Johnson Publishing.
147. Cordts, Anna D. (1929). The New Path to Reading series. Boston: Ginn.
148. Baker, Clara B., & Baker, Edna D. (1928). True Story Series. Indianapolis, IN: Bobbs- Merrill.
149. Horton, Edith, & Carey, Annie. (1927). Horton-Carey Readers. Boston: D.C. Heath.
150. Lisson, Albert C., Thonet, Evelyn V., & Meader, Emma G. (1930). Happy Childhood Readers. Dansville, NY: F.A. Owen.
151. Martin, Cora M., & Hill, Patty S. (1930). Real Life Readers. New York: Charles Scribner & Sons.

152. Moore, Maude, & Wilson, Harry B. (1927). Moore-Wilson Readers. Boston: D.C. Heath.

153. Suzzallo, Henry, Freeland, George E., McLaughlin, Katherine L., & Skinner, Ada M. (1930). Fact and Story Readers. New York: American Book.

154. White, Margaret L., & Hanthorn, Alice. (1930). Do and Learn Readers. New York: American Book.

155. Bamberger, Florence E. (1922). *The effect of the physical make-up of a book upon children's selection*. Baltimore: Johns Hopkins Press.

156. Thorndike, Edward L. (1921). *The teacher's word book*. New York: Columbia University Teachers College.

157. Gates, Arthur I. (1926). *A reading vocabulary for the primary grades*. New York: Columbia University Teachers College.

158. Kircher, H.W. (1925). *Analysis of the vocabulary of thirty-seven primers and first readers* (Twenty-fourth yearbook of the National Society for the Study of Education, Part I). Bloomington, IL: Public School Publishing.

159. Selke, E., & Selke, G.A. (1922, June). A study of the vocabulary of beginning books in twelve reading methods. *Elementary School Journal, 22*.

160. Beck, M.M. (1928). *An analytical study of the vocabulary of twelve primers*. Unpublished master's thesis, George Peabody College, Nashville, Tennessee.

161. Dolch, Edward W. (1932, April). Value of reading practice. *Elementary English Review, 9*, 249–251.

162. Murray, Clara. (1929). The New Wide Awake Readers. Boston: Little, Brown.

163. Withers, Sarah, Browne, Hetty S., & Tate, W.K. (1917). *The Child's World*. Richmond, VA: Johnson Publishing.

164. National Education Association. (1937). *Fifteenth yearbook of the department of superintendents*. Washington, DC: Author.

165. Gates, Arthur I. (1927). *The improvement of reading*. New York: Macmillan. (Revised 1935, 1947)

166. Orton, Samuel T. (1928, April 7). Special reading disability—Strephosymbolia, *Journal of American Medical Association, 90*, 1095–1099.

167. Gray, William S. (1935, February). *Journal of Educational Research, 28*, 410.

168. Rousseau, Jean Jacques. *Emile*. New York: D. Appleton.

169. Pestalozzi, Johann H. (1898). *How Gertrude teaches her children*. Syracuse, NY: C.W. Bardeen.

170. Froebel, Friedrich. (1887). *The education of man*. New York: D. Appleton.

171. Herbart, John F. (1909). *Outlines of educational doctrine*. New York: Macmillan.

172. Dewey, John. (1913). *Interest and effort in education*. New York: Houghton Mifflin.

173. ———, & Dewey, Evelyn. (1915). *Schools of tomorrow*. New York: E.F. Dutton.

174. United States Department of the Interior. (1926). *Pupils' readiness for reading instruction upon entrance to first grade* (City school leaflet, No. 23). Washington, DC: Bureau of Education.

175. Reed, Mary Maud. (1927). *An investigation of the practice for the admission of children and the promotion of children from first grade*. Doctoral dissertation, Columbia University Teachers College, New York.

176. *Childhood Education*. (1927, January). 215–223.

177. Gist, Arthur S., & King, William A. (1927). *The teaching and supervising of reading*. New York: Charles Scribner & Sons.

178. Harris, Julia M., Donavan, H.L., & Alexander, Thomas. (1927). *Supervision and teaching of reading*. Chicago: Johnson Publishing.

PERIOD 1935–1950

179. Walton, Sidney, as quoted by G.A. Yoakam. (1935, April). The supervision of instruction in reading. *Educational Method*, *15*.

180. Los Angeles County Schools. (1940). *The improvement of reading in the secondary school*. Los Angeles: Author.

181. National Education Association. (no date). *Reading instruction in the secondary schools*. Washington, DC: Author.

182. Gray, William S. (1932–1960). Summary of reading investigations. *Journal of Educational Research*.

183. State of Wyoming Board of Education. (1937). *Course of study for elementary schools* (Bulletin 11). (1937). Cheyenne, WY: Author.

184. Denver Public Schools. (1945). *Toward better reading*. Denver, CO: Author.

185. Russell, David H., Ousley, Odille, Wulfing, Gretchen, & Haynes, Grace B. (1948–1951). *The Ginn Basic Readers, Primer* (p. 11). Boston: Ginn. (Revised 1964)

186. ——— *Primer manual*.

187. ——— *Third reader, No. 2* (pp. 76, 78).

188. ——— *Third reader, Manual II* (p. 27).

189. Betts, Emmett A., & Welch, Carolyn M. (1948–1951). *Betts Basic Readers, Primer* (first edition). New York: American Book. (Revised 1963)

190. ——— *Teacher's guide book, Primer program*.

191. ——— *Fourth Reader* (first edition), 78.

192. ——— *Teacher's guidebook, Fifth reader*, 20.

193. Smith, Nila Banton. (1940–1945). *Learning to Read, Primer* 45. New York: Silver Burdett.

194. ——— *Teacher's guide, Preprimer*, 7–10.

195. ——— *Fourth reader*, 283.
196. ——— *Teacher's guide, Fourth reader*, 179–187.
197. Witty, Paul A., Wright, Lula, Cadwallader, Dorothy K., & Nolan, Barbara. (1942). *Reading for Interest, Primer, Second* (p. 4). Boston: D.C. Heath. (Revised 1946, 1955).
198. ——— *Teacher's guide, Primer* (p. 17).
199. ——— *Fourth reader* (p. 17).
200. ——— *Teacher's guide, Fourth reader*.
201. ——— *General manual* (p. 106).
202. Gray, William, et al. (1927). The Curriculum Foundation Program. Chicago: Scott, Foresman. (Latest revision, 1965)
203. McKee, Paul, et al. (1950). *Reading for meaning*. Boston: Houghton Mifflin. (Revised 1957, 1963)
204. *The administrator's handbook on reading* (The Curriculum Foundation Program). (no date). Chicago: Scott, Foresman.
205. Bond, Guy L., & Bond, Eva. (1941). *Developmental reading in high school*, 54. New York: Macmillan. Reprinted with permission of the publisher.
206. *Dissertation abstracts*. (1938–1963). Ann Arbor, MI: University Microfilms.
207. Betts, Emmett A. (1946). *Foundation of reading instruction* (pp. 438–485). New York: American Book.
208. H.W. Wilson Company. (1930–1964). *Educational index*. New York: Author.
209. Monroe, Marion. (1936). *Children who cannot read*. Chicago: University of Chicago Press.
210. Robinson, Helen M. (1946). *Why pupils fail in reading*. Chicago: University of Chicago Press.

PERIOD 1950–1965

211. Johnson, Lyndon B. (1965, January 11). The President's message to Congress. *The New York Times Company*, *1*, p. 20. Reproduced by permission.
212. Gray, William S. (1961, February 6). Looking ahead in reading. *Educational Digest*, *26*, 26–28.
213. Columbia Public Schools. (1959). *Reading instruction in Columbia elementary schools* (pp. 1–3). Columbia, MO: Author.
214. Public Schools of New York City. (1957). *Reading and literature in language arts* (p. 1). New York: Author.
215. Public Schools of Detroit. (1950). *Curriculum guide in reading* (pp. 13, 14). Detroit: Author.
216. Public Schools of Baltimore. (1959). *Course of study in reading* (pp. 4–6). Baltimore: Author.

217. San Diego City Schools. (1961). *San Diego curriculum guide* (Grade one, p. 1). San Diego, CA: Author.

218. Gwinn, Herbert D., & Brinegar, John B. (1951, July). Educating for Americanism (California State Department of Education). *California Schools, 22*, 263–276.

219. Sheldon, William D., Austin, Mary C., Mills, Queenie, et al. (1957). *Sheldon Basic Readers, Primer* (p. 55). Boston: Allyn & Bacon. (Revised 1963)

220. —— *Third reader* (3^1), (p. 148).

221. Stauffer, Russell G., Burrows, Alvina Treut, et al. (1960–1962). *Winston Basic Readers, Communication Program, First Reader,* (p. 57). Philadelphia: John C. Winston.

222. —— *Third reader,* (3^{10}), p. 71.

223. —— *Teacher's edition, Third grade,* (3^{11}), p. 33.

224. Harris, Albert J., Clark, Mae Knight, et al. (1965). *The Macmillan Reading Program, Preprimer, 1* (p. 39). New York: Macmillan. Reprinted with permission of the publisher.

225. —— *Fifth reader.*

226. —— *Guide, Preprimer* (p. 10).

227. Bond, Guy L., et al. (1950–1958). *The Developmental Reading Series, Primer* (p. 90). Chicago: Lyons & Carnahan. (Revised 1962)

228. —— *Fourth reader* (Regular Edition, p. 297).

229. McCracken, Glenn, & Walcutt, Charles C. (1963). *Basic Reading, Primer* (1–2). Philadelphia: J.B. Lippincott.

230. —— *Third reader,*(3–1), 62.

231. —— *Teachers Edition, Preprimer and Primer,* 1–4.

232. Barton, Allen, & Wilder, David. (1962). *Columbia-Carnegie study of reading research and its communication.* (Quoted from David Wilder's report in Proceedings of the International Reading Association, New York: Scholastic Magazines, pp. 172–174.

233. Austin, Mary C., & Morrison, Coleman. (1963). *The first R* (pp. 220–223). New York: Macmillan. Reprinted with permission of the publisher.

234. Smith, Nila Banton. (1963). *Reading instruction for today's children* (p. 165). Englewood Cliffs: Prentice Hall.

235. Strang, Ruth. (1962, December). Progress in the teaching of reading in high school and college. *The Reading Teacher, 16,* 171.

236. Artley, A. Sterl. (1964). Implementing a developmental reading program on the secondary level. *Reading Instruction in Secondary Schools* (pp. 1–11). Newark, DE: International Reading Association.

237. Simmons, John S. (1963, September). The scope of the reading program for secondary schools. *The Reading Teacher, 17,* 31–35.

238. Bond, Guy L., & Kegler, Stanley B. (1961). Reading instruction in the senior high school. *Development in and through reading* (Sixtieth yearbook of the National Society for the Study of Education pp. 334–335). Chicago: University of Chicago Press.

239. Summers, Edward G. (1962, Autumn). Recent research in college and adult reading. *Journal of Developmental Reading*, No. 1.

240. Smith, Nila Banton. (1962). Challenge and experiment in reading. *Scholastic Magazines* (International Reading Association Conference Proceedings, pp. 179–183).

241. Whipple, Gertrude (Chair). (1964). *City Schools Reading Program: Teachers' manual for the preprimers*, 1. Chicago: Follett.

242. ——— *Primer* (p. 22).

243. Strickland, Ruth G. (1964). The contribution of structural linguistics to the teaching of reading, writing, and grammar in the elementary school. *Bulletin of the School of Education*, *40*(1), 10. Bloomington, IN: Indiana University.

244. Fries, Charles C. (1963). *Linguistics and reading*. New York: Holt, Rinehart & Winston.

245. Bloomfield, Leonard, & Barnhart, Clarence L. (1961). *Let's read* (p. 5). Detroit: Wayne State University Press.

246. Fries, Charles C., Fries, Agnes C., Wilson, Rosemary, & Randolph, Mildred K. (1965). *A Basic Reading Series Based Upon Linguistic Principles: My first reader* (pp. 1, 4). Columbus, OH: Charles E. Merrill.

247. ——— *My seventh reader* (p. 85).

248. ——— *Manual for teachers* (p. 2).

249. Downing, John, & Graham, Faith. (1964). *The Downing Readers: A walk in the woods* (p. 1). London: Initial Teaching.

250. Mazurkiewicz, Albert J., & Tanyzer, Harold J. (1963, 1964). *Early-to-Read i/t/a Program: Book 1A*, 34. New York: i/t/a Publications.

251. ——— *Book 6* (p. 14).

252. Lumsdaine, A.A., & Glaser, Robert. (1960). *Teaching machines and programmed learning: A source book*, 6. Washington, DC: Department of Audiovisual Instruction, National Education Association.

253. Smith, Donald E.P., et al. *Michigan Successive Discrimination Reading Program: Book 8*, 8–203.

254. Buchanan, Cynthia D. (Program Director) & Sullivan Associates. (1963, 1964). *Programmed reading, Book 10* (p. 104). St. Louis, MO: Webster Division, McGraw Hill.

255. Harris, Theodore L. (1962, February; 1965, February). Summary of investigations relating to reading. *The Journal of Educational Research*, *55*, 210; *59*, 280. Madison, WI: Dembar Educational Research Services.

256. Robinson, Helen M. (1965, February). Summary of investigations relating to reading. *The Reading Teacher, 18,* 331.

257. Scott, C. Winfield. (1954, Spring). A 'forest' view of present research in reading. *Educational and Psychological Measurement, 14,* 208–214.

258. Holmes, Jack A., & Singer, Harry. (1964, April). Theoretical models and trends toward more basic research in reading. *Review of Educational Research, 34,* 127–155.

259. Money, John (Ed.). (1962). *Reading disability: Progress and research needs in dyslexia.* Baltimore: Johns Hopkins Press.

260. Kress, Roy A., & Johnson, Marjorie S. (1966). *Providing clinical services in reading: An annotated bibliography.* Newark, DE: International Reading Association.

261. Dever, Kathryn Imogene. (1956). *Positions in the field of reading* (pp. 146–148). New York: Bureau of Publications, Columbia University.

262. Robinson, H. Alan. (1957). *An occupational survey of reading specialists in junior and senior high school* (p. 61). Unpublished doctoral dissertation, New York University, New York.

263. Austin, Mary C., Morrison, Coleman, et al. (1961). *The torch lighters* (pp. 144–145). Cambridge, MA: Harvard Graduate School of Education, Harvard University Press.

EPILOGUE

Norman A. Stahl

Northern Illinois University

I t is with our field's first tentative steps into the 21st century that we find the International Reading Association (IRA) releasing a fourth edition of *American Reading Instruction* by Nila Banton Smith. For any text to go through the issuance of three formal editions across three widely disparate decades of the 20th century demonstrates the importance of *American Reading Instruction* to the profession. Yet with its publication lineage put aside, the logical question that must be asked is whether this text of the 1930s and revised for the 1960s is one for the ages but not for the uncertain world of the United States in the 21st century. Now may be exactly the time we most need to have *American Reading Instruction* released again. In times of uncertainty, both political and pedagogical, the reading profession will find solace and wisdom in touchstones from the past.

So we must ask, Has *American Reading Instruction* stood the test of time? The answer is two-sided—perhaps so, perhaps not. This text more so than many others has gone through what might best be called a bibliographic version of developmental life stages. It is with such an understanding or scholarly lens that we can best judge the staying power of *American Reading Instruction*, and then we may draw from the text appropriate teachings for the 21st century. First, the work must be viewed from the perspective of a dissertation that came forth from Columbia University Teachers College during the midst of the Great Depression. Smith's study was built on the pretechnological era identification and review of over a thousand different primary and secondary sources. It brought together in one source the philosophy, theory, and research on reading; the materials of reading instruction; and the personalities of reading from across the centuries of U.S. history. Today, this endeavor, in and of itself, would lead to the work being seriously considered for an award for dissertation of the year from any of four literacy organizations (i.e., the IRA, the National Reading Conference, the College Reading Association, or the IRA History of Reading Special Interest Group). The legacy of the dissertation can be seen as well in other dissertations such as Paul D. Leedy's seminal work, *A History of the Origin and Development of Instruction in Reading Improvement at the College Level* (1958), for which Nila Banton Smith served on the dissertation committee. In a sense, each time *American Reading Instruction* is read by a doctoral student, the message is put forward that historical questions are most appropriate for dissertation research.

Next, *American Reading Instruction* must be viewed as the most identifiable source available for at least 50 years on the history of the nation's endeavor to bring reading instruction to the masses. As Theodore Clymer noted in the 1965 edition, it was the "only complete and insightful treatise on the history of reading instruction in the United States." Although other excellent sources such as Mitford Mathews's *Teaching to Read: Historically Considered* (1966) became available to the field, Smith's work tended to be the text that introduced several generations of reading professionals to the historical perspective on the field. Perhaps this was due to *American Reading Instruction* being a widely available source, or because of the bully pulpit afforded it through IRA holding publishing rights, or due to its ease of reading given its straightforward chronological presentation so closely akin to the high school history texts of one's youth.

In recent years, the book has been overshadowed in varied circles by works such as Aberto Manguel's *A History of Reading* (1996), Guglielmo Cavallo and Roger Charter's *A History of Reading in the West* (1999), and Adrian Johns's *The Nature of the Book: Print and Knowledge in the Making* (1996), as all have been readily available through large chain bookstores and the Internet. In other ways, Smith's work might appear to be historiographically simple without intensity of coverage or underlying philosophical or sociological perspective. For example, other works have focused on more specific topics, such as *The Roots of Phonics* by Miriam Balmuth (1982), or have approached history from a clear philosophical perspective, such as Patrick Shannon's critical analysis *Broken Promises: Reading Instruction in Twentieth-Century America* (1989). Still, other sources look more directly at the legacy of a particular individual and his or her work, such as Jennifer Monaghan's *A Common Heritage: Noah Webster's Blue-Back Speller* (1983). Deborah Brandt's *Literacy in American Lives* (2001) exemplifies the growing interest in oral history methodology and cross-generation life history narratives in literacy. Although other historians may have practiced a higher level of historiography, the value of Smith's chronicle was that it was readily available, easily accessible, and often the first book read on the topic of literacy history by members of several academic generations. Unfortunately, it was often the only book read on the topic.

Finally, *American Reading Instruction* should be judged for what it has become—a classic text. Indeed, it should be read by each leader in the reading field in the same manner as classics such as Edmund Burke Huey's *The Psychology and Pedagogy of Reading* (1908), Helen M. Robinson's *Why Pupils Fail in Reading* (1946), Jeanne S. Chall's *Learning to Read: The Great Debate* (1967), or Shirley Brice Heath's *Ways With Words: Language, Life and Work in Communities and Classrooms* (1983). Yet to gain an appropriate understanding of the classic status of such works, one must have one foot in the past so as to consider the importance of the work for the era in which it was written; one foot in the present so as to understand how it helps to inform the theory, research, and best practice in our field today; and with an eye to the future so as to predict the coming directions for the field while preventing unproven fads and follies from cropping up again and again.

So now the question becomes, What can we gain by reading *American Reading Instruction* for the first time or even a second or third time? The answer is threefold. First, in critically reading the book, we come to understand that history is our first and best teacher. We learn how our academic forebears either faced or sidestepped the great pedagogical questions of their eras. Then by using our historical understandings along with comparative method to analyze their successes and their failures, we can consider options for the problems facing us in our times. Such a process teaches us that we need to raise questions about theory, research, and policy even though we challenge the status quo. It teaches us that our problems may not be so difficult or so intractable as we might believe when in the midst of dealing with them.

Second, through reading *American Reading Instruction*, we come to understand that the philosophical pendulum has swung repeatedly from theoretical stance to theoretical stance across the past two centuries. Hence, the recent blitzkrieg-like shift in pedagogical perspectives now influencing the field, along with the emergence of new hierarchical status groups, were both ever so predictable. Equally predictable was that established publishing conglomerates would strive to create new and needed markets based on paradigm shifts so as to bolster deflated revenues. Furthermore, it is predictable that a new circle of insiders will feel the exhilaration of a pedagogical and political victory until that point when they too eventually fall sway to the personal and professional decadence that comes with the public attention and the fiscal opportunities that follow pedagogical power. Still, history has demonstrated convincingly that power is fleeting, and as it is at its zenith, the pendulum begins its return motions only to create other philosophies destined to create still new economic markets and to constitute a new pedagogical power hierarchy. And, as for the children, history has mercifully demonstrated that, like the protagonist's survival in the classic tale "The Pit and the Pendulum," the children will survive the swath of the pedagogical pendulum. Perhaps more important, as we learn from *American Reading Instruction*, the children will learn to read.

Third, the implicit message from *American Reading Instruction* is that the reading field truly becomes a profession when its history is valued by its professoriate, its associations (such as IRA), and its current and future generations of reading specialists. It is with the legacy of *American Reading Instruction* that the field must create a historical agenda such as advocated in works by Cranney (1989), Moore, Monaghan, and Hartman (1997), or Stahl and King (2000), as well as through the mission and activities of the IRA History of Reading Special Interest Group. It is with the legacy of *American Reading Instruction* that all doctoral-level graduate programs must begin to offer course work focusing on the history of literacy, and that future editions of national standards will lead all reading specialists to have knowledge of and positive dispositions about the profession's proud lineage of theory, research, and practice.

Lastly, whenever opportunists attack our professionalism and dedication to our literacy mission, it is through the legacy of *American Reading Instruction* and the study of our history that as literacy professionals we can confirm that we have had more successes than failures, and we have risen to meet and overcome the new challenges across the decades. There is no greater calling than to be part of American reading instruction and no greater advocate of that mission than *American Reading Instruction* by Nila Banton Smith.

REFERENCES

Balmuth, M. (1982). *The roots of phonics*. New York: McGraw-Hill.

Brandt, D. (2001). *Literacy in American lives*. Cambridge, UK: Cambridge University Press.

Cavallo, G., & Charter, R. (1999). *A history of reading in the west*. Amherst, MA: University of Massachusetts Press.

Chall, J.S. (1967). *Learning to read: The great debate*. New York: McGraw-Hill.

Cranney, A.G. (1989). Why study the history of reading? *History of Reading News, 12*(4), 5.

Heath, S.B. (1983). *Ways with words: Language, life and work in communities and classrooms*. New York: Cambridge University Press.

Huey, E.B. (1908). The psychology and pedagogy of reading. New York: Macmillan.

Johns, A. (1996). *The nature of the book: Print and knowledge in the making*. Chicago: University of Chicago Press.

Leedy, P.D. (1958). *A history of the origin and development of instruction in reading improvement at the college level*. (Doctoral dissertation, New York University.) (UMI No. 59-01016)

Manguel, A. (1996). *A history of reading*. New York: Viking-Penguin Books.

Mathews, M. (1966). *Teaching to read: Historically considered*. Chicago: University of Chicago Press.

Monaghan, E.J. (1983). *A common heritage: Noah Webster's blue-back speller*. Hamden, CT: Archon.

Moore, D.W., Monaghan, E.J., & Hartman, D.K. (1997). Conversations: Values of literacy history. *Reading Research Quarterly, 32*, 90–103.

Robinson, H.M. (1946). *Why pupils fail in reading: A Study of causes and remedial treatment*. Chicago: University of Chicago Press.

Shannon, P. (1989). *Broken promises: Reading instruction in twentieth-century America*. Granby, MA: Bergin & Garvey.

Stahl, N.A., & King, J.R. (2000). A history of college reading. In R.F. Flippo & D.C. Caverly (Eds.), *Handbook of college reading and study strategy research* (pp. 1–23). Mahwah, NJ: Erlbaum.

P. David Pearson

University of California, Berkeley

This chapter is an account of reading instruction in the last third of the 20th century, from roughly the late 1960s onward.[1] In fact, I take the publication of Jeanne Chall's (1967) *Learning to Read: The Great Debate* as my starting point. It will end, as do most essays written at a century's turn, with predictions about the future. My hope is to provide an account of the past and present of reading instruction that will render predictions about the future transparent. I will end this piece with my speculations about pedagogical journeys that lie ahead in a new century and a new millennium.

Beginning at Mid-Century Setting the Scene: Reading in the 1960s

The period that spans roughly 1935 to 1965 is best viewed as a time in which we engaged in fine-tuning and elaboration of instructional models that were born in the first third of the century. Most important, the look-say approach (start off with a corpus of high-frequency sight words practiced often in highly controlled stories and then teach phonics on the basis of already taught words), which had started its ascendancy at the turn of the century, gained increasing momentum throughout the middle third of the century until, as has been documented in survey research conducted in the 1960s, over 90% of the students in the country were taught to read using one commercial variation of this approach or another.[2] So common was this approach that

Jeanne Chall (1967) felt comfortable describing the then prevailing approach as a set of principles, which can be roughly paraphrased as follows:[3]

- The goals of reading from the beginning of grade 1 should include comprehension, interpretation, and application, as well as word recognition.

- Instruction should begin with meaningful silent reading of stories that are grounded in children's experiences and interests.

- After a corpus of sight words is learned (between 50 and 100), analytic phonics instruction should begin. Phonics should be regarded as one of many cueing systems, including context and picture cues, available to children to unlock new words.

- Phonics instruction should be spread over several years rather than concentrated in the early grades.

- Phonics instruction should be contextualized rather than isolated from real words and texts.

- The words in the early texts (grades 1–3) should be carefully controlled for frequency of use and repeated often to ensure mastery.

- Children should get off to a slow and easy start, probably through a readiness program; those judged as not ready for formal reading instruction should experience an even longer readiness period.

- Children should be instructed in small groups.

Although a few elements in her list are new, such as the early emphasis on comprehension and interpretation and the contextualization of phonics instruction, virtually all the elements introduced in the early part of the century were included in her description of the conventional wisdom of the 1960s. A few things are missing when one compares Chall's list of principles underlying the conventional wisdom with our earlier account of the key developments through 1935. One is the role of skills in commercial reading programs. Although skills did not make it onto Chall's (1967) list of principles, it is clear from several chapters (specifically, chapters 7 and 8) that she was mindful of their importance and curricular ubiquity. By the 1960s, skills lessons in the teachers' manual, accompanied by workbooks allowing students to practice the skills, were much more elaborate than in the 1930s, 40s, or 50s. The other missing piece is the elaborate development of the teachers' manual. Earlier, I implied that the manuals got larger with each succeeding edition of a series. By the middle 1960s, the small teachers' guide section in the back of the children's book of the 1920s and 30s had expanded to the point where the number of pages devoted to the teachers' guide equaled the number of student text pages in the upper grades, and exceeded it in the primary grades.[4]

The materials of the 1960s continued traditions begun early in the century and documented in great detail in Nila Banton Smith's editions of *American Reading Instruction*.[5] Students read stories and practiced skills. Text difficulty was carefully controlled in the basal reading materials published between the 1930s and the 1960s. In the earliest readers (preprimer through first reader, at least), vocabulary was sequenced in order of decreasing frequency of word usage in everyday written and oral language. Because many of the most frequent words are not regularly spelled (*the, of, what, where*, etc.), this frequency principle provided a good fit with the whole-word or look-say emphasis characteristic of the words-to-reading approach so dominant during this period.

Students were still the recipients and teachers still the mediators of the received curriculum. Meaning and silent reading were more important in the 1960s version of reading curriculum than in 1900 or 1935, as evidenced by a steady increase in the amount of time and teachers' manual space devoted to comprehension activities; but it was still not at the core of the look-say approach. When all is said and done, the underlying model of reading in the 1960s was still a pretty straightforward perceptual process; the simple view—that comprehension is the product of decoding and listening comprehension (RC = Dec* LC)—still prevailed. Readers still accomplished the reading task by translating graphic symbols (letters) on a printed page into an oral code (sounds corresponding to those letters), which was then treated by the brain as oral language. In both the look-say approach to learning sight vocabulary and its analytic approach to phonics, whether the unit of focus is a word or a letter, the basic task for the student is to translate from the written to the oral code. This view of reading was quite consistent with the prevailing instructional emphasis on skills. If sight words and phonics knowledge was what children needed to learn in order to perform the translation process, then decomposing phonics into separable bits of knowledge (letter-to-sound, or in the case of spelling, sound-to-letter, correspondences), each of which could be presented, practiced, and tested independently, was the route to helping them acquire that knowledge.

The Legacy of the Scholarship of the 1960s

In beginning reading, the decade of the 1960s was a period of fervent activity. In the early 1960s, in an effort to settle the debate about the best way to teach beginning reading once and for all (this time with the tools of empirical scholarship rather than rhetoric), the Cooperative Research Branch of the United States Office of Education funded an elaborate collection of "First-Grade Studies," loosely coupled forays into the highly charged arena of preferred approaches to beginning reading instruction.[6] Although each of the studies differed from one another in the particular emphasis, most of them involved a comparison of different methods of teaching beginning reading. They were published in a brand new journal, *Reading Research Quarterly*, in 1966. Jeanne Chall completed her magnum opus, *Learning to Read: The Great Debate*, in 1967. It, too, had been funded in order to put the debate behind, but Chall would use different scholarly tools to accomplish her goals. She would employ critical review procedures to examine our empirical research base, the content of our basal readers, and exemplary classroom practices. In 1965, Lyndon Johnson's Elementary and Secondary Education Act, one key plank in his Great Society platform, brought new resources for compensatory education to schools through a program dubbed Title I. And, Commissioner of Education James Allen would, at decade's end, establish the national Right to Read program as a way of guaranteeing that right to each child in the United States. The country was clearly focused on early reading, and many were optimistic that we would find answers to the questions about teaching reading that had vexed us for decades, even centuries.

Chall's book and the First-Grade Studies had an enormous impact on beginning reading instruction and indirectly on reading pedagogy more generally. One message of the First-Grade Studies was that just about any alternative, when compared to the business-as-usual basals (which served as a common control in each of 20+ separate quasi-experimental studies), elicited equal or greater performance on the part of first graders (and, as it turned out, second graders).[7] It did not seem to matter much what the alternative was—language experience, a highly synthetic phonics approach, a linguistic approach (control the text so that young readers are exposed early on only to easily decodable words grouped together in word families, such as the *-an* family, the *-at* family, the *-ig* family, etc.), a special alphabet (i.e., the Initial Teaching Alphabet), or even basals infused with a heavier-than-usual dose of phonics right up front—they were all the equal or the better of the ubiquitous basal. A second message, one that was both sent and received, was that the racehorse mentality of studies that pits one method against another to see which would win had probably run its course. By accepting this message, the reading research community was free to turn its efforts to other, allegedly more fruitful, issues and questions—the importance of the teacher, quite irrespective of method, the significance of site, and the press of other aspects of the curriculum such as comprehension and writing.[8] With the notable exception of the Follow-Through Studies in the 1970s, which are only marginally related to reading, it would take another 25 years for large-scale experiments to return to center stage in reading.[9]

In spite of a host of other important recommendations, most of which had some short-term effect, the ultimate legacy of Chall's book reduces to just one—that early attention to the code in some way, shape, or form must be reinfused into early reading instruction. For the record, Chall recommended five broad changes, each of which will be discussed later:

(1) make a necessary change in method (to an early emphasis on phonics of some sort),

(2) reexamine current ideas about content (focus on the enduring themes in folktales),

(3) reevaluate grade levels (increase the challenge at every grade level),

(4) develop new tests (both single-component tests and absolute measures with scores that are independent of the population taking the test), and

(5) improve reading research (including its accessibility).

The look-say basals that had experienced virtually uninterrupted progress from 1930 to 1965 never quite recovered from the one-two punch delivered by Chall's book and the First-Grade

Studies in 1967. Given the critical sacking they took from Chall and the empirical thrashing they took from the First-Grade Studies, one might have expected one of the pretenders to the early reading throne, documented so carefully in the First-Grade Studies, to assume the mantle of the new conventional wisdom in the years that followed. Ironically, it was the basals themselves, albeit in a radically altered form, that captured the marketplace of the 1970s and 1980s. This feat was accomplished by overhauling basals to adapt to a changing market shaped by these two important scholarly efforts. Basal programs that debuted in the five years after Chall's book appeared were radically different from their predecessors. Most notably, phonics, which had been relegated to a skill to be taught contextually after a hefty bank of sight words had been committed to memory, was back—from day one of grade 1—in the series that hit the market in the late 1960s and early 1970s. Surprisingly, it was not the highly synthetic alphabetic approach of the previous century or the remedial clinics of the 1930s (which one might have expected from reading Chall's book). It is better described as an intensification and repositioning (to grade 1) of the analytic phonics that had been taught in the latter part of grade 1, and in grades 2 to 4 in the look-say basals of the 1960s.[10] Equally significant, there was a change in content, at least in grade 1. Dick and Jane and all their assorted pairs of competing cousins—Tom and Susan, Alice and Jerry, Jack and Janet—were retired from the first-grade curriculum and replaced by a wider array of stories and characters; by the early 1970s, more of the selections were adaptations of children's literature rather than stories written to conform to a vocabulary restriction or a readability formula.

It is difficult to determine how seriously educators and publishers took Chall's other three recommendations. For example, in the basals that came out after Chall, the grade 1 books (the preprimers, primers, and readers) were considerably more challenging than their immediate predecessors, mainly by virtue of a much more challenging grade 1 vocabulary—more words introduced much earlier in the grade 1 program.[11] One series even divided its new vocabulary words into words that ought to be introduced explicitly as sight words, and those words, which they dubbed decodable, which should be recognized by the students by applying the phonics skills they had been taught up to that point in the program.[12] Beyond grade 1, however, changes in difficulty were much less visible, and no appreciable increase in the readability scores of these later levels occurred.

In testing, a major change toward single-component tests did occur, although it is difficult to attribute this change solely to Chall's recommendation. Beginning in the early 1970s and continuing through at least the late 1980s, each successive edition of basal programs brought an increase in the number of single-component tests—tests for each phonics skill (all the beginning, middle, and final consonant sounds; vowel patterns; and syllabication), tests for each comprehension skill (main idea, finding details, drawing conclusions, and determining cause-effect relations) at every grade level, tests for alphabetical order and using the encyclopedia, and just about any other skill that comes to mind.

But, other events and movements of the period also pointed toward single-component tests. For one, owing to the intellectual contributions of Benjamin Bloom and John Carroll, the mastery learning movement[13] was gathering its own momentum during the late 1960s. According to proponents of mastery learning, if a complex domain could be decomposed into manageable subcomponents, each of which could be taught and learned to some predetermined level of mastery, then most, if not all, students should be able to master the knowledge and skills in the domain. Second, criterion-referenced tests were spawned during this same period.[14] The logic of criterion-referenced assessment was that some predetermined level of mastery (say 80% correct), not the average for a group of students in a given grade level, ought to be the reference point for determining how well a student was doing on a test. A third construct from this period, curriculum-embedded assessment,[15] held that students should be held accountable for precisely what was needed for them to march successfully through a particular curriculum—no less, no more. If one could specify the scope and sequence of knowledge and skills in the curriculum and develop assessments for each, then it should be possible to guide all students through the curriculum, even if some needed more practice and support than others. One can imagine a high degree of compatibility among all three of these powerful constructs—mastery learning, criterion-referenced assessment, and curriculum-embedded assessment. All three provide comfortable homes for single-component assessments of the sort Chall was advocating.

With powerful evidence from mastery learning's application to college students,[16] publishers of basal programs and some niche publishers began to create and implement what came to be called skills management systems.[17] In their most meticulous application, these systems became the reading program. Students took a battery of mastery tests, practiced those skills they had not mastered (usually by completing worksheets that looked remarkably like the tests), took tests again, and continued this cycle until they had mastered all the skills assigned to the grade level (or until the year ended). Unsurprisingly, the inclusion of these highly specific skill tests had the effect of increasing the salience of workbooks, worksheets, and other skill materials that students could practice on in anticipation of (and as a consequence of) mastery tests. Thus, the basals of this period were comprised of two parallel systems: (1) the graded series of anthologies filled with stories and short nonfiction pieces for oral and silent reading and discussion, and (2) an embedded skills management system to guide the development of phonics, comprehension, vocabulary, and study skills.

Chall's last recommendation was to improve reading research. Research had been too inaccessible (to the very audience of practitioners who most needed it), too narrow in scope, and too dismissive of its past. All that needed to change, she argued. As I will detail in the next section, reading research changed dramatically, but not necessarily in a direction Chall envisioned.

One other change in basal reading programs in this period worth noting was the technology that placed reduced facsimiles of student text pages onto pages surrounded by teaching suggestions and questions for guided reading. This was hailed as a major advance in the utility of manuals, because teachers did not have to turn back and forth from student text to the teachers' section in order to guide the reading of a story.

This was the scene, then, in the early 1970s, just as the reading field was about to embark on a new curricular trek that continues even today. If the middle third of the century was characterized by a steady, unwavering march toward the ever-increasing prominence of a particular philosophy and set of curricular practices encapsulated in ubiquitous basals that championed a look-say approach,[18] the early 1970s brought major challenges in philosophy and pedagogy—harder texts, more phonics, and a skill development program unlike anything seen before.[19]

But even with some alterations in the materials available and some new pedagogical twists, the pedagogy of the early 1970s revealed little fundamental change in the underlying assumptions about the role of the teacher and learner or the nature of reading and writing. Teachers, armed with their basal manuals, controlled the learning situation as never before, and students continued to play the role of passive recipient of the knowledge and skills mediated by the teacher. Most important, reading was still a fundamentally perceptual process of translating letters into sounds. If anything, the perceptual nature of reading was made more salient in the 1950s and 1960s by the return of phonics to center stage.

Developments in the Last Third of the Century

Reading as the Province of Other Scholarly Traditions[20]

Somewhere during this period (the exact point of departure is hard to fix), we began a journey that would take us through many new twists and turns on the way to different landscapes than we had visited before. Along the way, we confronted fundamental shifts in our views of reading and writing and began to create a variety of serious curricular alternatives to the conventional wisdom of the 1970s. Just beyond the horizon lay even more unfamiliar and rockier territory—the conceptual revolutions in cognition, sociolinguistics, and philosophy—which would have such far-reaching consequences for reading curriculum and pedagogy of the 1980s and 1990s.

Reading became an ecumenical scholarly commodity; it was embraced by scholars from many different fields of inquiry. The first to take reading under their wing were the linguists, who wanted to convince us that reading was a language process closely allied to the language processes of writing, speaking, and listening. Then came the psycholinguists and the cognitive psychologists, followed soon by the sociolinguists, the philosophers, the literary critics, and the critical theorists. It is not altogether clear why reading has attracted such interest from scholars in so many other fields. One explanation is that reading is considered by so many to be a key to success in other endeavors in and out of school; this is often revealed in comments such as, "Well if you don't learn to read, you can't learn other things for yourself." Another is that scholars in these other disciplines thought that the educationists had it all wrong, and it was time for another group to have their say. Whatever the reasons, the influence of these other scholarly traditions on reading pedagogy is significant; in fact, the pedagogy of the 1980s and 1990s cannot be understood without a firm grounding in the changes in world view that these perspectives spawned.

Linguistics. In 1962, Charles Fries wrote a book entitled *Linguistics and Reading*. In it, he outlined what he thought the teaching of reading would look like if it were viewed from the perspective of linguistics. In the same decade, several other important books and articles appeared, each carrying essentially the same message: The perspective of the modern science of linguistics, we were told, would privilege different models and methods of teaching reading. It would tell us, for example, that some things do not need to be taught explicitly because the oral language takes care of them more or less automatically. For example, the three different pronunciations of *-ed*, (as in *nabbed, capped,* and *jaded*), need not be taught as a reading skill because our oral language conventions determine the pronunciation almost perfectly. English in its oral form demands the voiced alternative /d/ after a voiced consonant such as /b/. It demands the unvoiced alternative /t/ after an unvoiced consonant, such as /p/, and it requires the syllabic version /əd/ after either /d/ or /t/. To teach these rules, which are very complex, would likely make things more confusing than simply allowing the oral language to do its work without fanfare.

Another linguistic insight came to us from the transformational generative grammars that replaced conventional structural linguistics as the dominant paradigm within the field during the 1960s and 70s. Noam Chomsky published two revolutionary treatises during this period: *Syntactic Structures* in 1957 and *Aspects of a Theory of Syntax* in 1965. With these books, Chomsky revolutionized the field of linguistics and paved the way, theoretically, for equally dramatic changes in the way that psychologists thought about and studied the processes of language comprehension and language acquisition.

Chomsky also provided the basis for a nativist view about language acquisition—a view that holds that humans come to the world "wired" to acquire the language of the community into which they are born. He and others drew this inference from two basic and contrasting facts about language: (a) language is incredibly complex, and (b) language is acquired quite easily and naturally by children living in an environment in which they are simply exposed to (rather than taught!) the language of their community well before they experience school. Only a view that children are equipped with some special cognitive apparatus for inferring complex rules could explain this remarkable feat.

Because our prevailing views of both reading comprehension and reading acquisition were derived from the same behavioristic assumptions that Chomsky and his peers had attacked, reading scholars began to wonder whether those assumptions would hold up when we applied similar perspectives and criticisms to analyses of written language comprehension and acquisition.[21]

Psycholinguistics. During the decade after the publication of *Syntactic Structures*, a new field of inquiry, psycholinguistics, evolved. In its first several years of existence, the field devoted itself to determining whether the views of linguistic competence and language acquisition that had been set forth by Chomsky and his colleagues could serve as psychological models of language performance. Although the effort to develop a simple mapping from Chomsky to models of language performance waned after a few unsatisfactory attempts, the field of psycholinguistics and the disposition of psychologists to study language with complex theoretical tools had been firmly established.

Particularly influential on our thinking about reading were scholars of language acquisition,[22] who established the rule-

431

governed basis of language learning. In contrast to earlier views, these psycholinguists found that children did not imitate written language; rather, as members of a language community, they were participants in language and invented for themselves rules about how oral language worked. This insight allowed researchers to explain such constructions as "I eated my dinner" and "I gots two foots." Roger Brown and his colleagues showed conclusively that children were active learners who inferred rules and tested them out. Much as Kenneth Goodman would later show with written language, "mistakes," especially overgeneralizations, in oral language could be used to understand the rule systems that children were inventing for themselves.

The analogy with oral language development was too tempting for reading educators to resist. Several adopted something like a nativist framework in studying the acquisition of reading, asking what the teaching of reading and writing would look like if we assumed that children can learn to read and write in much the same way as they learn to talk, that is, naturally. What would happen if we assumed that children were members of a community in which reading and writing are valued activities that serve important communication functions? What if we assumed that the most important factors in learning to read and write were having genuine reasons for communicating in these media and having access to a database in which there was so much print and talk about print that students could discover the patterns and regularities on their own, much as they do when they discover the patterns and regularities of oral language? Although the seminal work involved in putting these assumptions to empirical tests would wait for a couple of decades, the seeds of doubt about our perceptually based views of reading acquisition were firmly planted by the middle 1960s.

Two influential individuals, Kenneth Goodman and Frank Smith, led the reading field in addressing these kinds of questions. In 1965, Goodman demonstrated that the errors children made while reading orally were better viewed as windows into the inner workings of their comprehension processes than as mistakes to be corrected. He found that the mistakes that children made while reading in context revealed that they were trying to make sense of what they read. In another seminal piece, "Reading: A Psycholinguistic Guessing Game," Goodman (1967) laid out the elements of language that he thought readers employed as they constructed meaning for the texts they encountered. In reading, he conjectured, readers use three cue systems to make sense of text: syntactic cues, semantic cues, and graphophonemic cues. By attending to all these cue sources, Goodman contended, readers could reduce their uncertainty about unknown words or meanings, thus rendering both the word identification and comprehension processes more manageable.[23]

Smith's revolutionary ideas were first presented in 1971 in a book entitled, *Understanding Reading*.[24] In this seminal text, Smith argued that reading was not something one was taught, but rather something one learned to do. Smith believed that there were no special prerequisites to learning to read, indeed, that reading was simply making sense of one particular type of information in our environment. As such, reading was what one learned to do as a consequence of belonging to a literate society. One learned to read from reading. The implication, which Smith made explicit, was that the "function of teachers is not so much to teach reading as to help children read" (p. 3). This certainly challenged the notion of the teacher as the individual who meted out knowledge and skills to passively waiting students. For Smith, all knowing and all learning were constructive processes; individuals made sense of what they encountered based on what they already knew.[25] Even perception, he contended, was a decision-making, predictive process based on prior knowledge.

Smith also argued that reading was only incidentally visual. By that, Smith meant that being able to see was necessary but not sufficient to achieve understanding. He identified four sources of information: orthographic, syntactic, semantic, and visual, all of which he claimed were somewhat redundant. He argued that skilled readers made use of the three sources that were part of their prior knowledge (the orthographic, syntactic, and semantic) in order to minimize their reliance on visual information. In fact, the danger in relying too heavily on visual information is that readers might lose sight of meaning.

The psycholinguistic perspective had a number of influences on reading pedagogy. First, it valued literacy experiences that focused on making meaning. This meant that many classroom activities, particularly worksheets and games, which focused on enabling skills such as specific letter-sound correspondences, syllabication activities, structural analysis skills, specific comprehension activities, or study skills, were devalued. Second, it helped us to value texts for beginning readers (see Table 1, example 1) in which authors relied on natural language patterns, thus making it possible for emerging readers to use their knowledge of language to predict words and meanings. This meant that texts that relied on high-frequency words in short, choppy sentences (what we have come to call "basalese"; see Table 1, example 2) or those based on the systematic application of some phonics element (i.e., a decodable text; see Table 1, example 3) were correspondingly devalued.

Third, the psycholinguistic perspective helped us to understand the reading process and to appreciate children's efforts as readers. Errors were no longer things to be corrected; instead, they were windows into the workings of the child's mind, allowing both the teacher and the child to understand more about the reading process and reading strategies. Understanding miscues also helped educators focus on comprehension and appreciate risk-taking.

TABLE 1
Sample Texts for Beginning Reading

1. Red Fox, Red Fox, what do you see?
   I see a blue bird looking at me.
   Blue Bird, Blue Bird, what do you see?
   I see a green frog looking at me.
   Anon, anon.

2. Run, John, run.
   Run to Dad.
   Dad will run.
   Run, Dad.
   Run, John.
   See them run.

3. Nat can bat.
   Nat can bat with the fat bat.
   The cat has the fat bat.
   The rat has the fat bat.
   Nat has the fat bat.
   Bat the bat, Nat.

Fourth, psycholinguists gave us a means (miscue analysis) and a theory (reading as a constructive process) that was remarkably distinct from previous ideas about reading. The perspective made explicit links between oral and written language acquisition and helped us view reading as language rather than simply perception or behavior. In a sense, psycholinguistics continued the changes and traditions begun by the linguistic perspective; however, within the reading field, its influence was deeper and broader than its academic predecessor.

Most important, psycholinguistics affected our views of teaching and learning in a fundamental way. Reading scholars began to rethink ideas about what needed to be taught, as well as the relation between teaching and learning. So, instead of asking, "What can I teach this child so that she will eventually become a reader?" we began to ask, "What can I do to help this child as a reader so she will make the progress she deserves to make?" Some teachers began to welcome all children into what Smith referred to as "The Literacy Club" as an alternative to teaching children so-called prerequisite skills.[26]

Cognitive Psychology. If psycholinguistics enabled psychologists to reexamine their assumptions about language learning and understanding by placing greater emphasis on the active, intentional role of language users, cognitive psychology allowed psychologists to extend constructs such as human purpose, intention, and motivation to a greater range of psychological phenomena, including perception, attention, comprehension, learning, memory, and executive control of all cognitive process. All of these would have important consequences in reading pedagogy.

This was not tinkering around the edges; it was a genuine paradigm shift that occurred within those branches of psychology concerned with human intellectual processes. The previous half-century, from roughly the teens through the fifties, had been dominated by a behaviorist perspective in psychology that shunned speculation about the inner workings of the mind: Show the surface-level outcomes of the processes, as indexed by overt, observable behaviors and leave the speculation to the philosophers. That was the contextual background against which both psycholinguistics and cognitive psychology served as dialectical antagonists when they appeared on the scene in the late 1960s and early 1970s.

The most notable change within psychology was that it became fashionable for psychologists, perhaps for the first time since the early part of the century, to study reading.[27] And, in the decade of the 1970s, works by psychologists flooded the literature on basic processes in reading. One group focused on text comprehension by trying to figure out how it is that readers come to understand the underlying structure of texts. We were offered story grammars—structural accounts of the nature of narratives, complete with predictions about how those structures impede and enhance human story comprehension. Others chose to focus on the expository tradition in text.[28] Like their colleagues interested in story comprehension, they believed that structural accounts of the nature of expository (informational) texts would provide valid and useful models for human text comprehension. And, in a sense, both of these efforts worked. Story grammars did account for story comprehension. Analyses of the structural relations among ideas in an informational piece did account for text comprehension. But, what neither text-analysis tradition really tackled was the relationship between the knowledge of the world that readers bring to text and the comprehension of those texts. In other words, by focusing on structural rather than the ideational, or content, characteristics of texts, they failed to get to the heart of comprehension. That task, as it turned out, fell to one of the most popular and influential movements of the 1970s, schema theory.

Schema theory[29] is a theory about the structure of human knowledge as it is represented in memory. In our memory, schemata are like little containers into which we deposit particular experiences that we have. So, if we see a chair, we store that visual experience in our chair schema. If we go to a restaurant, we store that experience in our restaurant schema, if we attend a party, our party schema, and so on. Clearly schema theory is linked to Piaget's theories of development and his two types of learning: assimilation and accommodation. When we assimilate new information, we store it in an existing schema; when we accommodate new information, we modify the structure of our schemata to fit the new data. The modern iteration of schema theory also owes a debt to Frederic Bartlett, who, in the 1930s, used the construct of schema to explain culturally driven interpretations of stories. For Bartlett, cultural schemata for stories were so strong that they prevented listeners, whether European or native Alaskan in background, from adopting the story schema of the other culture to understand its stories. Bartlett's account predates the current constructivist models of cognition and learning by 60 years; and his view is as inherently constructive as those who have succeeded him. In essence, Bartlett was saying exactly what modern constructivists say, that readers and listeners actively construct meanings for texts they encounter rather than simply "receiving" meaning from the texts.[30]

Schema theory also provides a credible account of reading comprehension, which probably, more than any of its other features, accounted for its popularity within the reading field in the 1970s and 80s.[31] It is not difficult to see why schema theory was so appealing to theoreticians, researchers, and practitioners when it arrived on the scene in the 1970s. First, schema theory provides a rich and detailed theoretical account of the everyday intuition that we understand and learn what is new in terms of what we already know. Second, schema theory accounts for another everyday intuition about why we as humans so often disagree about our interpretation of an event, a story, an article, a movie, or a TV show: We disagree with one another because we approach the phenomenon with very different background experiences and knowledge. Third, schema theory accounts for an everyday intuition that might be called an "it's-all-Greek-to-me" experience: Sometimes we just don't have enough background knowledge to understand a new experience or text.

Although these insights may not sound earthshaking after the fact, for the field of reading, and for education more generally, they were daunting challenges to our conventional wisdom. Examined in light of existing practices in the 1970s, they continued the revolutionary spirit of the linguistic and psycholinguistic perspectives. Schema theory encouraged us to ask:

What is it that my children already know? And, how can I use that to help them deal with these new ideas that I would like them to know? rather than,

What is it that they do not know? And how can I get that into their heads?

More specifically, with respect to reading comprehension, schema theory encouraged us to examine texts from the perspective of the knowledge and cultural backgrounds of our students in order to evaluate the likely connections that they would be able to make between ideas that are in the text and the schema that they would bring to the reading task. Schema theory, like the psycholinguistic perspective, also promoted a constructivist view of comprehension; all readers must, at every moment in the reading process, construct a coherent model of reading for the texts they read. The most important consequence of this constructivist perspective is that there is inherent ambiguity about where meaning resides. Does it reside in the text? In the author's mind as she sets pen to paper? In the mind of each reader as he or she builds a model of meaning unique to his or her experience and reading? In the interaction between reader and text?

Sociolinguistics. Sociolinguistics as a discipline developed in parallel with psycholinguistics. Beginning with the work of William Labov, and Joan Baratz and Roger Shuy, sociolinguists had important lessons for reading scholars.[32] Mainly, these lessons focused on issues of dialect and reading. Sociolinguists were finding that dialects were not ill- or half-formed variations of standard English. Instead, each dialect constituted a well-developed linguistic system in its own right, complete with rules for variations from standard English and a path of language development for its speakers. Speakers of dialects expressed linguistic differences, not linguistic deficits. The goal of schooling was not, and should not be, to eradicate the dialect in the process of making each individual a speaker of standard English. Instead, sociolinguists stressed the need to find ways to accommodate children's use of their dialect while they are learning to read and write. Several proposals for achieving this accommodation were tried and evaluated. The first was to write special readers for dialect speakers. In the early 1960s, several examples of black-dialect readers appeared and, almost as rapidly, disappeared from major urban districts. They failed primarily because African American parents did not want their children learning with "special" materials; they wanted their children to be exposed to mainstream materials used by other children.[33] The second equally unsuccessful strategy was to delay instruction in reading and writing until oral language became more standardized. Teachers who tried this technique soon found out just how resistant and persistent early language learning can be. The third and most successful approach to dialect accommodation involved nothing more than recognizing that a child who translates a standard English text into a dialect is performing a remarkable feat of translation rather than making reading errors. So, an African American child who says /pos/ when he sees *post* is simply applying a rule of black English, which requires a consonant cluster in ending position to be reduced to the sound of the first consonant. Unfortunately for children who speak a dialect, we, as a field, did not take the early lessons of the sociolinguists to heart. We continue to find schools in which children are scolded for using the oral language that they have spent their whole lives learning. We also continue to find children whose dialect translations are treated as if they were oral reading errors.

Prior to the advent of the sociolinguistic perspective, when educators talked about "context" in reading, they typically meant the print that surrounded particular words on a page. In the 1980s, and primarily because of the work of sociolinguists, the meaning of the word *context* expanded to include not only what was on the page, but what Bloome and Green referred to as the instructional, noninstructional, and home and community contexts of literacy.[34] From a sociolinguistic perspective, reading always occurred in a context, one that was shaped by the literacy event at the same time it shaped the event. The sociolinguistic versions of knowledge and language as socially and culturally constructed processes moved the constructivist metaphor to another plane, incorporating not only readers' prior knowledge in the form of schemata, but also the meanings constructed by peers and by one's cultural ancestors.

The most significant legacy of the sociolinguistic perspective was our heightened consciousness about language as a social and, therefore, cultural construction. Suddenly, reading was a part of a bigger and more complex world. Sociolinguists examined the role of language in school settings. For example, they pointed out that often success in reading was not so much an indication of reading "ability" per se, but of the success the individual experienced in learning how to use language appropriately in educational settings. Thus success, according to a sociolinguistic analysis, was more an index of how well children learned to "do school" than how well they could read. They contrasted the functions that language serves in school with the functions it serves outside of school and helped us rethink the role of language within the classroom. By studying the community outside of school, sociolinguists made us conscious of social, political, and cultural differences; as a result, we began to rethink our judgments of language and behavior. We saw that any judgment call we made, rather than reflecting the "right" way, simply reflected "our" way—

the way we as teachers thought, talked, and behaved because of the cultural situation in which we lived, outside as well as inside school. By focusing on the role of community in learning, sociolinguists caused many educators to rethink the competitive atmosphere of classrooms and of school labels and recommended changes within schools so that children could learn from and with each other. With these contributions from sociolinguists, it was becoming more and more apparent that reading was not only not context-free, but that it was embedded in multiple contexts.

Literary Theory Perspective. One cannot understand the pedagogical changes in practice that occurred in the elementary reading curriculum in the 1980s without understanding the impact of literary theory, particularly reader-response theory. In our secondary schools, the various traditions of literary criticism have always had a voice in the curriculum, especially in guiding discussions of classic literary works. Until the middle 1980s, the "new criticism" that had emerged during the post–World War II era had dominated for several decades, and it had sent teachers and students on a search for the one "true" meaning in each text they encountered. With the emergence (some would argue the reemergence) of reader-response theories, all of which gave as much (if not more) authority to the reader than to either the text or the author, the picture, along with our practices, changed dramatically. Although there are many modern versions of reader response available, the work of Louise Rosenblatt has been most influential among elementary teachers and reading educators. In the 1980s, many educators reread (or more likely read for the first time) Rosenblatt's (1938) 1976 edition of *Literature as Exploration*, and *The Reader, the Text, the Poem*, which appeared in 1978. Rosenblatt argues that meaning is something that resides neither in the head of the reader (as some had previously argued) nor on the printed page (as others had argued).[35] Instead, Rosenblatt contends, meaning is created in the transaction between reader and document. This meaning, which she refers to as "the poem," resides above the reader-text interaction. Meaning is, therefore, neither subject nor object nor the interaction of the two. Instead, it is transaction, something new and different from any of its inputs and influences.[36]

The Pedagogical Correlates of New Perspectives

Although the post-Chall basal tradition continued well into the decade of the 1980s, new perspectives and practices began to appear in classrooms, journal articles, and basal lessons in the early 1980s.

Comprehension on Center Stage. Comprehension, especially as a workbook activity and a follow-up to story reading, was not a stranger to the reading classrooms of the 1930s through 1970s. As indicated earlier, it entered the curriculum as a story discussion tool and as a way of assessing reading competence in the first third of the 20th century.[37] Developments during mid-century were highlighted in an earlier National Study of School Evaluation yearbook devoted to reading;[38] by mid-century, the infrastructure of comprehension had been elaborated extensively and infused into the guided reading and workbook task. It was a staple of basal programs when Chall conducted her study of early reading, and had she emphasized reading instruction in the intermediate grades rather than grade 1, it undoubtedly would have been more prominent in her account.

During the late 1970s and through the decade of the 1980s, comprehension found its way to center stage in reading pedagogy. Just as a nationally sponsored set of research activities (i.e., the First-Grade Studies and Chall's book) focused energy on reforms in beginning reading in the late 1960s, it was the federally funded Center for the Study of Reading, initiated in 1976, which focused national attention on comprehension. Although the Center's legacy is undoubtedly bringing schema theory and the knowledge-comprehension relationship into our national conversation, it also supported much research on comprehension instruction,[39] including research that attempted to help students develop a repertoire of strategies for improving their comprehension.[40] This research was not limited to the Center; indeed many other scholars were equally involved in developing instructional strategies and routines during this period, including emphases on monitoring comprehension,[41] transactional strategies instruction,[42] K-W-L graphic organizers,[43] and, more recently, questioning the author.[44] Many of these new strategies found their way into the basals of the 1980s, which demonstrated substantially more emphasis on comprehension at all levels, including grade 1.[45]

Literature-Based Reading. Even though selections from both classical and contemporary children's literature have always been a staple of basal selections dating back to the 19th century (especially after grade 2 when the need for strict vocabulary control diminished), literature virtually exploded into the curriculum in the late 1980s. A short burst in literary content occurred after Chall's critical account of the type of selections and the challenge of basal content; more excerpts from authentic literature appeared, even in the grade 1 readers. But these selections had two characteristics that had always offended those who champion the use of genuine literature: excerpting and adaptation. Rarely were whole books included; instead, whole chapters or important slices were excerpted for inclusion. And, even when a whole chapter was included, it was usually adapted to (a) reduce vocabulary difficulty, (b) reduce the grammatical complexity of sentences, or (c) excise words (e.g., mild profanity) or themes that might offend important segments of the market.

Beyond basals, children's literature played an important supplementary role in the classrooms of teachers who believed that they must engage their students in a strong, parallel independent

reading program. Often this took the form of each child selecting books to be read individually and later discussed with the
teacher in a weekly one-on-one conference. And, even as far back
as the 1960s, there were a few programs that turned this individualized reading component into the main reading program.[46]

But in the late 1980s, literature was dramatically repositioned.
Several factors converged to pave the way for a groundswell in the
role of literature in elementary reading. Surely, the resurgence of
reader response theory as presented by Rosenblatt was important, as was the compatibility of the reader-response theory and
its emphasis on interpretation, with the constructivism that characterized both cognitive and sociolinguistic perspectives. Research
also played a role; in 1985, for example, in the watershed publication of the Center for the Study of Reading, *Becoming a Nation
of Readers*, Richard Anderson and his colleagues documented the
importance of "just plain reading" as a critical component of any
and all elementary reading programs.[47] This period also witnessed
an unprecedented expansion in the number of new children's
books published annually. Finally, a few pieces of scholarship exerted enormous influence on teachers and teacher educators.
Perhaps most influential was Nancie Atwell's (1987) *In the
Middle: Writing, Reading, and Learning With Adolescents*, in which
she told her story of how, as a middle school teacher, she invited
readers, some of whom were quite reluctant, into a world of books
and reading. The credibility of her experience and the power of
her prose were persuasive in convincing thousands of classroom
teachers that they could use existing literature and "reading workshops" to accomplish anything that a basal program could accomplish in skill development while gaining remarkable
advantages in students' literary experience.[48]

In terms of policy and curriculum, the most significant event
in promoting literature-based reading was the 1988 California
Reading Framework. The framework called for reading materials

that contained much more challenging texts at all levels. More important, it mandated the use of genuine literature, not the oversimplified adaptations and excerpts from children's literature that had been the staple of basal programs for decades. Publishers responded to the call of California's framework and produced a remarkably different product in the late 1980s and early 1990s than ever had appeared before on the basal market.[49] Gone were excerpts and adaptations and, with them, almost any traces of vocabulary control. Skills that had been front and center in the basals of the 1970s and 80s were relegated to appendix-like status. Comprehension questions were replaced by more interpretive, impressionistic response to literature activities. All this was done in the name of providing children with authentic literature and authentic activities to accompany it. The logic was that if we could provide students with real literature and real motivations for reading it, much of what is arduous about skill teaching and learning would take care of itself.

Book Clubs and literature circles are the most visible instantiations of the literature-based reading movement.[50] The underlying logic of Book Clubs is the need to engage children in the reading of literature in the same way as adults engage one another in voluntary reading circles. Such voluntary structures are likely to elicit greater participation, motivation, appreciation, and understanding on the part of students. Teachers are encouraged to establish a set of "cultural practices" (ways of interacting and supporting one another) in their classrooms to support students as they make their way into the world of children's literature. These cultural practices offer students both the opportunity to engage in literature and the skills to ensure that they can negotiate and avail themselves of that opportunity.

Process Writing. In the middle 1980s, writing achieved a stronghold in the elementary language arts curriculum that it had never before held. Exactly why and how it achieved that position of prominence is not altogether clear, but certain explanations are plausible. Key understandings from the scholarship of the 1970s and 80s paved the way. Functionality associated with the sociolinguistic perspective, process-writing approaches encouraged teachers to ask students to write for genuine audiences and purposes. The psycholinguistic notion of "error" as a window into children's thinking allowed us to worry less about perfect spelling and grammar and more about the quality of the thinking and problem solving children were producing. The general acceptance of constructivist epistemologies disposed us to embrace writing as the most transparently constructive of all pedagogical activities. All these constructs allowed us as a profession to take a different developmental view on writing, one consistent with the emergent literacy perspective that was gaining strength in early childhood literacy. We came to view all attempts to make sense by setting pen to paper, however deviant from adult models, as legitimate and revealing in their own right if examined through the eyes of the child writer. Led by Donald Graves and Lucy Calkins, we revolutionized our views of early writing development.[51] Finally, we began to see reading and writing as inherently intertwined, each supporting the other.

Integrated Instruction. It is impossible to document the history of reading instruction in the 20th century without mentioning the ways in which we have attempted to integrate reading with other curricular phenomena. Two stances have dominated our thinking about how to integrate reading into other curricula: integration of reading with the other language arts (writing, speaking, and listening) and integration across subject matter boundaries (with mathematics, science, social studies, art, and music). Like literature-based reading, both senses of integration have long been a part of the thinking about elementary reading curriculum.[52] In fact, a look back to the progressivism of Dewey and other scholars in the first part of the century reveals substantial rhetoric about teaching and learning across curricular boundaries.[53] From that early spurt of energy until the late 1980s, however, integrations assumed a minor role in American reading instruction. In basal manuals, for example, integration was portrayed almost as an afterthought until the late 1980s; it appeared in the part of the lesson that follows the guided reading and skills instruction sections, signaling that these are things that a teacher can do "if time permits." Things changed in the late 1980s. For one, integrated curriculum fit the sociolinguistic emphasis on language in use: the idea that language, including reading, is best taught and learned when it is put to work in the service of other purposes, activities, and learning efforts. Similarly, with the increase in importance of writing, especially early writing of the sort discussed by Graves and his colleagues,[54] it was tempting to champion the idea of integrated language arts instruction. In fact, the constructivist metaphor is nowhere played out as vividly and transparently as in writing, leading many scholars to use writing as a model for the sort of constructive approach they wanted to promote in readers. The notion was that we needed to help students learn to "read like a writer."[55] Also influential in supporting the move toward integrated instruction was the work of Donald Holdaway, who, in concert with many teacher colleagues, had been implementing an integrated language arts approach in Australia for a few decades.[56]

Whole Language. Important as they are, comprehension, literature-based reading, process writing, and integrated instruction pale in comparison to the impact of whole language, which is regarded as the most significant movement in reading curriculum in the last 30 years.[57] In fact, one might plausibly argue that whole language co-opted all four of these allied phenomena—comprehension, literature-based reading, integrated instruction, and process writing—by incorporating them, problems along with strengths, into its fundamental set of principles and practices. Whole language is grounded in child-centered pedagogy reminiscent of the progressive education movement (the individual child is the most important curriculum informant).[58] Philosophically, it is biased toward radical constructivist epistemology (all readers must construct their own meanings for the texts they encounter). Curricularly, it is committed to authentic activity (real, not specially constructed, texts and tasks) and integration (both within the language arts and between the language arts and other subject matters). Politically, it is suspicious of all attempts to mandate and control curricular decisions beyond the classroom level; as such, it places great faith and hope in the wisdom of teachers to exercise professional prerogative in making decisions about the children in their care. Whole language owes its essential character and key principles to the insights of linguistics, psycholinguistics, cognitive psychology, sociolinguistics, and literary theory detailed earlier. It owes its remarkable, if brief, appearance in the national limelight of reading instruction to its committed leaders and a veritable army of committed teachers who instantiated it in their classrooms, each with his or her own unique signature.[59]

When whole language emerged as a movement in the 1980s, it challenged the conventional wisdom of basals and questioned the unqualified support for early code emphases that had grown between 1967 and the early 1980s.[60] One of the great ironies of whole language is that its ascendancy into curricular prominence is best documented by its influence on the one curricular tool it has most consistently and most vehemently opposed, the basal reader.[61] As suggested earlier, basals changed dramatically in the early 1990s, largely, I conjecture, in response to the groundswell of support within the teaching profession for whole language and its close curricular allies, literature-based reading and process writing.

Vocabulary control, already weakened during the 1970s in response to Chall's admonitions, was virtually abandoned in the early 1990s in deference to attempts to incorporate more literature, this time in unexpurgated form (i.e., without the practices of adaptation and excerpting that had characterized the basals of the 1970s and 80s) into the grade 1 program.[62] Phonics, along with other skills, was backgrounded, and literature moved to center stage.

Basal programs appropriated or, as some whole language advocates have argued, "basalized" the activities and tools of whole language. Thus, in the basals of the early 1990s, each unit might have a writing process component in which the rhetoric, if not the reality of some version of process writing, was presented to teachers and students. In the 1980s, comprehension questions, probably following a story line, might have sufficed for the guided reading section of the manual (the part that advises teachers on how to read and discuss the story), but in the 1990s, questions and tasks that supported deep probes into students' response to literature became more prevalent. Another concession to literature-based reading was the creation and marketing of classroom libraries—boxed sets of books, usually thematically related to each unit—that teachers could use to extend their lessons and units "horizontally" and enrich children's literary opportunities.

Basals also repositioned their "integrated language arts" and "integrated curriculum" strands. Dating back even to the 1920s and 1930s, basals had provided at least a "token" section in which teachers were encouraged to extend the themes or skills of the basal story into related writing (e.g., rewriting stories), oral language (e.g., transforming a story into a play and dramatizing it), or cross-curricular activities (e.g., conducting community surveys, tallying the results, and reporting them), but these forays were regarded as peripheral rather than core. In the basals of the early 1990s, as skills moved into the background,[63] these integrated language arts activities were featured more prominently as core lesson components.[64]

These changes can, I believe, be traced to the prominent position of whole language as a curricular force during this period.[65]

Publishers of basals accomplished this feat of appropriation not by ridding their programs of the skills of previous eras, but by subtle repositioning—foregrounding one component while backgrounding another—and creating optional components or modules (e.g., an intensive phonics kit or a set of literature books) that could be added to give the program one or another spin. Unsurprisingly, this created bulkier teacher's manuals and more complex programs.

Acceptance of whole language was not universal. To the contrary, there was considerable resistance to whole language and literature-based reading throughout the country.[66] In many places, whole language never really gained a foothold. In others, what was implemented in the name of whole language was not consistent with the philosophical and curricular principles of the movement; California, whole language advocates would argue, is a case in point. Whole language got conflated with whole-class instruction and was interpreted to mean that all kids should get the same literature, even if teachers had to read it to them.[67]

Nor was there a single voice within the whole language movement. Whole language scholars and practitioners differed on a host of issues such as the role of skills, conventions, and strategies within a language arts program. Some said, if we can just be patient, skills will emerge from meaningful communication activities; others spurred things on by taking advantage of spontaneous opportunities for minilessons; still others were willing to spur spontaneity a bit.

Even so, it is fair to conclude that by the early 1990s, whole language had become the conventional wisdom, the standard against which all else was referenced. The rhetoric of professional articles belies this change. As late as the mid-1980s, articles were written with the presumption of a different conventional wisdom—a world filled with skills, contrived readers, and workbooks. By 1991–1992, they were written with the presumption that whole language reforms, while not fully ensconced in U.S. schools, were well on their way to implementation. The arguments in the 1990s were less about first principles of whole language and more about fine-tuning teaching repertoires. The meetings of the Whole Language Umbrella grew to be larger than most large state conventions and regional conferences of the International Reading Association. By 1995, whole language was no longer a series of assaults on skills and basals that characterized it through the mid-1980s. It had become the conventional wisdom in rhetoric, if not in reality.

Returning to the lenses outlined at the beginning of this chapter (range of materials and practices, role of teacher, role of learner, and the processes of reading and learning to read), in whole language, we finally encountered major shifts in emphasis in comparison to what we found at the beginning of the century. In whole language, teachers were facilitators not tellers. Teachers observed what children did, decided what they needed, and arranged conditions to allow students to discover those very insights about reading, writing, and learning for themselves. Because this was truly child-centered pedagogy, learners occupied center stage. As Jerome Harste puts it, the child was the primary curriculum informant. Students were decision makers involved in choices about the books they read and the stories they wrote. The materials of reading instruction were the materials of life and living—the books, magazines, newspapers, and other forms of print that children can encounter in everyday life are the materials they should encounter in the classroom—no less, no more. There was no need for the sort of contrived texts and tasks of the sort found in basal reading programs. Instructional practices focused not on presenting a diet of skills carefully sequenced to achieve mastery, but on creating activities and tasks that supported the learning students needed at a particular point in time. If skills and strategies were taught, they were taught in minilessons, highly focused forays into the infrastructure of a skill or strategy followed up by immediately recontextualizing the skill in a genuine reading or writing situation. In contrast to previous periods, reading was now regarded as a meaning-making, not a perceptual, process. The reader was an active participant in creating, not a passive recipient of, the message in a text. The process of acquiring reading was also markedly different from the "readiness" perspective so dominant in the first 80 years of the century. Emergent literacy, the alternative to traditional reading readiness views, did not specify a "prereading" period in which children are prepared for the task of reading. All readers, at all stages, were meaning makers, even those who can only scribble a message or "pretend" to read.[68] Thus, at century's end, reading pedagogy finally developed some viable alternatives to the conventional views of teacher, learner, and process that had dominated pedagogical practice for the entire century. As it turned out, the new directions were short-lived, or at least they appear to be so from the perspective of developments in the first few years of the 21st century.

The Demise of Whole Language

At century's end, just when it appeared as if whole language, supported by its intellectual cousins (process writing, literature-based reading, and integrated curriculum), was about to assume the position of conventional wisdom for the field, the movement was challenged seriously, and the pendulum of the pedagogical debate began to swing back toward the skills end of the curriculum and instruction continuum. Several factors converged to make the challenge credible, among them (a) unintended curricular casualties of whole language; (b) questionable applications of whole language; (c) growing dissatisfaction with doctrinaire views of any sort; (d) a paradigm swing in the ideology of reading research; (e) increasing politicization of the reading research and policy agenda, and (f) increasing pressure for educators of all types, especially reading educators, to produce measurable results; and (g) a dramatic shift in the prevailing model of professional development.

Unintended Curricular Consequences. In its ascendancy, whole language changed the face of reading instruction and, in the process, left behind some curricular casualties, few of which were intended by those who supported whole language. Those, myself included,[69] who supported practices that were discarded during the rise of whole language had difficulty supporting the whole language movement even though we might have been philosophically and curricularly sympathetic to many of its principles and practices. This lack of enthusiasm from curricular moderates meant that whole language failed to build a base of support that was broad enough to survive even modest curricular opposition, let alone the political onslaught that it would experience at century's turn.

There were four casualties: skills instruction, strategy instruction, emphasis on text structure, and reading in the content areas. Earlier, I suggested that one of the consequences of whole language was the relegation of skills to the "appendices" of instructional programs. In accepting whole language, we tacitly accepted the premise that skills are better "caught" in the act of reading and writing genuine texts for authentic purposes than "taught" directly and explicitly by teachers. The argument is the same for phonics, grammar, text conventions, and structural elements. These entities may be worthy of learning, but they are unworthy of teaching. This position presents us with a serious conundrum as a profession. Admit, for the sake of argument, that the skills instruction of the 1970s and earlier, with decontextualized lessons and practice on "textoids" in workbook pages, deserved the criticism accorded to it by whole language advocates (and scholars from other traditions). But, a retreat from most skills instruction into a world of "authentic opportunity" did not provide a satisfactory answer for teachers and scholars who understood the positive impact that instruction can have. Many young readers do not "catch" the alphabetic principle by sheer immersion in print or by listening to others read aloud. For some it seems to require careful planning and hard work by dedicated teachers who are willing to balance systematic skills instruction with authentic texts and activities.[70]

Strategy instruction was another casualty. This loss has been particularly difficult for scholars who spent the better part of the early 1980s convincing basal publishers and textbook authors that the thoughtful teaching of flexible strategies for making and monitoring meaning was a viable alternative to mindless skills instruction, where skills were taught as though they were only ever to be applied to workbook pages and end-of-unit tests. But the strategy lessons that filled our basals in the middle to late 1980s—direct advice from teachers about how to summarize what one has read, how to use text structure to infer relations among ideas, how to distinguish fact from opinion, how to determine the central thread of a story, how to use context to infer word meanings, and how to make and evaluate the accuracy of predictions—were virtually nonexistent in the basals of the early to middle 1990s. Although there is no inherent bias in whole language or literature-based reading against the learning and use of a whole range of cognitive strategies, there is, as with phonics and grammar, a serious question about whether direct, explicit instruction in how to use them will help. The advice is to let them emerge from attempts to solve real reading problems and puzzles, the kind students meet in genuine encounters with authentic text. There may have been reason for concern about the strategy instruction of the 1980s. But revision rather than rejection of these strategies was not a part of the rhetoric of whole language.[71]

Structural emphasis was also suspect within whole language. This suspicion extended to formal grammars, story grammars, rhetorical structures, and genre features of texts. As with skills and strategies, whole language reformers do not claim that students should not learn and develop control over these structural tools; they simply claim that, like skills, they are best inferred from reading and writing authentic texts in the process of making meaning. So, the advocates are comfortable in adopting Frank Smith's[72] admonition to encourage kids to read like a writer (meaning to read the text with a kind of critical eye toward understanding the tools and tricks of the trade that the author uses to make her points and achieve her effects on readers), but they would likely reject a systematic set of lessons designed to teach and assess children's control of story grammar elements (such as plot, characterization, style, mood, or theme) or some system for dealing with basic patterns of expository text. As with skills and strategies, many of us see a compromise alternative to both the formulaic approach of the early 1980s and the "discovery" approach of the new reforms—dealing with these structural elements as they emanate from stories that a group is currently reading can provide some guidance and useful tools for students and teachers.

Content area reading also suffered during the ascendancy of whole language and literature-based reading. Content area texts—expository texts in general, but especially textbook-like entries—were not privileged in a world of literature-based reading. This is not an implicit criticism of the literature-based reading movement; rather it is a comment about the reallocation of curricular time and energy that occurs when a movement gains momentum. There is a certain irony in this development, for it is expository reading, not narrative reading, that most concerns middle and high school teachers. The cost here has been very dear. To enter middle school and high school classrooms in order to examine the role of expository text is to conclude that it has none. Occasionally, teachers assign expository texts for homework, but when students come to class the next day, clearly having avoided the assignment, teachers provide them with an oral version of what they would have gotten out of the text if they had bothered to read it. Most high school teachers have quite literally given up on the textbook for the communication of any important content. Although understandable, this approach is, of course, ultimately counterproductive. There comes a time in the lives of students—when they either go to college or enter the work world—when others expect them to read and understand informational texts on their own and in printed form rather than through oral or video transformation.[73]

Because whole language did not go out of its way to accommodate any of these curricular practices, those who were sympathetic with whole language but also champions of one or another approach were not available to help whole language respond to the criticism leveled at it in the late 1990s.

Questionable Applications of Whole Language. One dilemma faced by any curricular challenge is sustaining the integrity of the movement without imposing the very sorts of controls it is trying to eliminate. Whole language did not find and still has not found a satisfying way of managing this dilemma, and it has suffered as a consequence. Many schools, teachers, and institutions appropriated the whole language label without honoring its fundamental principles of authenticity, integration, and empowerment. Basal reader publishers made the most obvious and widespread appropriation, some even positioning their basal series as "whole language" programs. Earlier, I noted another misapplication in which whole language was confounded with whole-class instruction. Nowhere was this conflation more extreme than in the implementation of the California literature framework. The logic that prevailed in many classrooms was that it was better to keep the entire class together at all costs. Implicit in this practice are two interesting assumptions: (1) that getting the content of the stories is the most important goal for reading instruction, and (2) that the skills and processes needed to read independently will emerge somehow from this environment in which many students are pulled through texts that far exceed the grasp of their current skills repertoire. Needless to say, whole language had enough on its hands dealing with its own assumptions and practices; these philosophical and curricular misapplications exposed the movement to a whole set of criticisms that derived from practices not of its own making.

One of the primary reasons for misapplication of whole language was, in my estimate, the lack of an explicit plan for professional development. Whole language gives teachers a wide berth for making curricular and instructional decisions, for whole classes and for individual children. It assumes that teachers who are empowered, sincere, and serious about their personal professional development will be able to tailor programs and activities to the needs and interests of individual children. Such an approach makes sense only when we can assume that teacher knowledge is widely and richly distributed in our profession. To offer these prerogatives in the face of narrow and shallow knowledge is to guarantee that misguided practices, perversions of the very intent of the movement, will be widespread. The puzzle, of course, is where to begin the reform: by ensuring that the knowledge precedes the prerogative, or by ceding the prerogative to teachers as a way of leveraging their motivation for greater knowledge.[74]

Growing Dissatisfaction With Extreme Positions. Although it has reached its peak in the last five years, concern about extreme positions, be they extremely child-centered (such as the more radical of whole language approaches) or extremely curriculum-centered (such as highly structured, unswerving phonics programs) is not new. Voices from the middle, extolling balanced approaches or rationalizing the eclectic practices of teachers, began to be heard even in the earliest days of whole language's ascendancy.[75] Scholars and teachers raised a number of concerns about the assumptions and practices of the whole language movement. Most importantly, they expressed concern about the consequences of whole language outlined earlier in this chapter. They questioned the assumption that skills are best "caught" during the pursuit of authentic reading activity rather than "taught" directly and explicitly. They also questioned the insistence on authentic texts and the corollary ban on instructional texts written to permit the application of skills within the curriculum. They questioned the zeal and commitment of the movement *qua* movement, with its strong sense of insularity and exclusivity. Finally, they worried that the press toward the use of authentic literature and literature-based reading would eradicate, albeit unintentionally, what little progress had been made toward the use of informational texts and teaching reading in the content areas.[76]

Ironically, in the past few years, these voices from the middle have found themselves responding not to those who hold a radical whole language position, but to those who hold steadfastly to the phonics first position. Even so, the fact that those with centrist positions were not inclined to defend whole language when the political campaign against it began in the middle 1990s, they undoubtedly hastened the demise of whole language as the pretender to the title of conventional wisdom.

Changing Research Ideology. Prior to the 1980s, qualitative research in any form had little visibility within the reading research community. Among the array of qualitative efforts, only miscue analysis[77] and some early forays into sociolinguistic and anthropological accounts of literacy had achieved much in the way of archival status.[78] But all that changed in the 1980s and early 1990s. Qualitative research more generally, along with more specific lines of inquiry taking a critical perspective on literacy as a social and pedagogical phenomenon, became more widely accepted as part of the mainstream archival literature.[79] Treatises pointing out the shortcomings of traditional forms of quantitative inquiry, especially experimental research, appeared frequently in educational research journals.[80] In terms of curriculum and pedagogy, it is important to remind ourselves that much of the research that undergirds whole language comes from this more qualitative, more interpretive, more critical tradition. Thus the credibility of this type of research increased in concert with the influence of whole language as a curricular movement.

Somewhere in the mid-1990s, the discourse of literacy research began to take a new turn. Stimulated by research supported by the National Institute for Child Health and Human Development, a new brand of experimental work began to appear in the middle 1980s and gathered momentum that has reached a peak in the past year or two.[81] This is experimentalism reborn from the 1950s and 60s, with great emphasis placed on "reliable, replicable research," large samples, random assignment of treatments to teachers and/or schools, and tried and true outcome measures.[82] This work does not build on the qualitative tradition of the 1980s and early 1990s; instead it finds its aegis in the experimental rhetoric of science and medicine and in the laboratory research that has examined reading as a perceptual process.[83] Although not broadly accepted by the reading education community at the turn of the century, this work has found a very sympathetic ear in the public policy arena.[84]

The political positioning of this research is important, but so is its substance. Two themes from this work have been particularly important in shaping a new set of instructional practices: phonemic awareness and phonics instruction.

The absolutely critical role played by phonemic awareness (the ability to segment the speech stream of a spoken word, e.g., /cat/ into component phonemes /cuh + ah + tuh/ and/or to blend separately heard sounds, e.g., /cuh + ah + tuh/ into a normally spoken word /cat/) in the development of the ability to decode and to read for meaning was well documented in research studies spanning the last 25 years of the 20th century.[85] Irrespective of mode of instruction, the overwhelming evidence suggests that phonemic awareness is a necessary but not a sufficient condition for the development of decoding and reading. First, children who possess high degrees of phonemic awareness in kindergarten or early in first grade are very likely to be good readers throughout their elementary school careers.[86] Second, almost no children who are successful readers at the end of grade 1 exhibit a low level of mastery of phonemic awareness. On the other hand, a substantial proportion of unsuccessful end-of-grade-1 readers possess better than average phonemic awareness; this evidence is the critical piece in establishing that phonemic awareness is a necessary but not a sufficient condition for reading success. Although we can be confident of its critical role in learning to read, we are less sure about the optimal way to enhance its development. Many scholars have documented the efficacy of teaching it directly, but they also admit that it is highly likely to develop as a consequence of learning phonics, learning to read, or especially learning to write, especially when teachers encourage students to use invented spellings.[87] Research in whole language classrooms suggests that writing is the medium through which both phonemic awareness and phonics knowledge develop, the former because students have to segment the speech stream of spoken words in order to focus on a phoneme, and the latter because there is substantial transfer value from the focus on sound-symbol information in spelling to symbol-sound knowledge in reading.[88]

The second consistent thread in the new experimentalism of the 1990s is the simple but undeniable emphasis on the code in the early stages of learning to read.[89] Reminiscent of Chall's earlier conclusions, scholars in this tradition tend to advocate phonics—first, fast, and simple.[90] Less well documented, and surely less well agreed upon, is the optimal course of instruction to facilitate phonics development. Even Gough, a classic bottom-up theo-

461

rist, while arguing that what distinguishes the good reader from the poor reader is swift and accurate word identification, suggests that an early insistence on reading for meaning may be the best way to develop such decoding proficiency. Both Philip Gough and Connie Juel are convinced that students can learn how to read when they have "cryptoanalytic intent" (a disposition to decipher the specific letter-to-sound codes), phonemic awareness, an appreciation of the alphabetic principle (i.e., regardless of the numerous exceptions, letters do stand for sounds), and data (some texts to read and someone to assist when the going gets tough).[91]

After reviewing available instructional evidence, two of the most respected scholars in this tradition, Marilyn Adams and Connie Juel, independently concluded that children can and should learn the "cipher" through a combination of explicit instruction in phonemic awareness and letter-sound correspondences, a steady insistence on invented spellings as the route to conventional spellings in writing activities, and many opportunities to read connected text (especially when the texts contain enough decodable words to allow students to apply the phonics information they are learning through explicit instruction). Both of these reviewers, known for their sympathies toward instruction in the code, are quick to add that rich experiences with language, environmental print, patterned stories, and Big Books should also be a staple of effective early reading instruction.[92]

Politicization of the Reading Research and Policy Agenda. From its beginnings, one of the great hopes of educational research (and those who conduct it) is that policymakers will take research seriously when they establish policy initiatives at a local, state, or national level. After all, the improvement of educational practice is the ultimate goal of educational research, and policy is our society's most transparent tool for educational improvement.

Historically, however, research has been regarded as one among many information sources consulted in policy formation, including expert testimony from practitioners, information about school organization and finance, and evaluations of compelling cases. In the past half decade, research, at least selective bits of research, has never been taken more seriously. Several laws in California make direct references to research. For example, Assembly Bill 1086 (1998) prohibited the use of Goals 2000 money for professional developers who advocated the use of context clues over phonics or who supported the use of invented spellings in children's writing. The federally sponsored Reading Excellence Act of 1999, which allocated US$240,000,000 for staff development in reading, requires that both state and local applications for funding base their programs on research that meets scientifically rigorous standards. The "scientifically rigorous" phrase was a late entry; in all but the penultimate version of the bill, the phrase was "reliable, replicable research," which had been interpreted as a code word for experimental research. As of early 1999, "phonics bills" (bills mandating either the use of phonics materials or some sort of teacher training to acquaint teachers with knowledge of the English sound-symbol system and its use in teaching) had been passed or were pending in 36 states.[93] In the early days of the current Bush administration, the goal of "evidence-based practice" was made even more explicit, with the phrase "scientifically based reading research" appearing more than 110 times in the Reading First portion of the No Child Left Behind Act of 2001 reauthorizing Title I.[94]

Policymakers like to shroud mandates and initiatives in the rhetoric of science, and sometimes that practice results in very strained, if not indefensible, extrapolations from research. This has happened consistently in the current reading policy arena. Two examples make the point vividly. First, California Assembly Bill 1086, with its prohibition on context clues and invented spelling, represents an ironic application of research to policy. The irony stems from the fact that many of the advocates of a return to code emphasis, such as Marilyn Adams, read the research as supporting the use of invented spellings in the development of phonemic awareness and phonics.[95] Second, the mandate in several states calling for the use of decodable text (usually defined as text consisting of words that can be sounded out using a combination of the phonics rules taught up to that point in the program plus some instant recognition of a few highly frequent sight words) is based on the thinnest of research bases. The idea is that children will learn to use their phonics better, faster, and more efficiently if the texts they read permit facile application of the principles they are learning. Although it all sounds very logical, there is precious little research evidence to support the systematic and exclusive use of decodable text.[96] This lack of evidence, however, does not seem to have deterred advocates who, on the phonics issues, championed scientific evidence as the gold standard for policy implementation.

Professional groups have entered the policy fray in recent years. For example, the American Federation of Teachers (AFT) has endorsed a particular set of programs as scientifically validated to produce excellent results. Interestingly, each of the programs on their endorsed list is committed to early, systematic, explicit phonics instruction in a highly structured framework. The AFT influence is evident in some other professional movements, such as the Learning First Alliance.[97]

When research moves into the policy arena, one of two outcomes are most likely. If the research is widely accepted by members of the profession from which it comes, widespread acceptance and implementation usually follows. This often occurs in medical, pharmaceutical, or agricultural research. If widespread consensus on what the research says about practice is not reached, then research-based policy initiatives are likely to sharpen and deepen the schisms that already exist, and the entire enterprise is likely to be regarded as a war among factions within the field. The latter scenario appears to characterize the reading field.[98]

Interestingly, the debate, accompanied by its warlike metaphors, appears to have more life in the public and professional press than it does in our schools. Reporters and scholars revel in keeping the debate alive and well, portraying clearly divided sides and detailing a host of differences of a philosophical, political, and pedagogical nature.[99] Teachers, by contrast, often talk about, and more importantly enact, more balanced approaches. For example, several scholars, in documenting the practices of highly effective, highly regarded teachers, found that these exemplary teachers employed a wide array of practices, some of which appear decidedly whole language in character (e.g., process writing, literature groups, and contextualized skills practice) and some of which appear remarkably skills-oriented (explicit phonics lessons, sight-word practice, and comprehension strategy instruction).[100]

Producing Measurable Results. Evaluation has always posed a conundrum for whole language supporters. First, some oppose the use of any sort of externally mandated or administered assessments as a matter of principle, holding that assessment is ultimately the responsibility of a teacher in collaboration with a student and his or her parents. Second, even those supporters who are open to external forms of accountability, or at least reporting outside the boundaries of the classroom or school, often claim that standardized tests, state assessments, and other external measures of student accomplishment do not provide sensitive indicators of the goals of curricula based on whole language principles. Most appealing would be assessments that are classroom-based and individualized in nature, with the option of aggregating these sorts of data at the classroom and school levels when accountability is required. During the 1990s, many felt that the increased emphasis on performance assessment and portfolios would fill this need.[101] In an age of high expectations, explicit standards, and school- and classroom-level accountability, none of these options is a good fit with the views and desires of policymakers and the public. Both of these constituents seem quite uneasy about the quality of our schools and our educational system, so uneasy that leaving assessment in the hands of our teachers seems an unlikely outcome. It is not at all clear to me that the proponents of at least strong versions of whole language can, or will be willing to, hold themselves accountable to the sorts of measures that the public and policymakers find credible.

A Shift in the Prevailing Model of Professional Development. Fast on the heels of the entry of scientifically based reading research into the professional discourse came a new vision of professional development. The models of teacher reflection and prerogative dominant in the early 1990s were replaced by training models that championed the development of the knowledge and skills required to implement scientifically based reading research. This led to implementation models that put a premium on monitoring for quality control and fidelity to programs touted as "scientific."[102] Earlier models emphasizing reflection and teacher inquiry shared a commitment to research as the basis for practice, but any similarity ends there. In the teacher inquiry models, research is used to inform practice, and practice is expected to vary from teacher to teacher and situation to situation. In the models emerging at the turn of the century, research is used to determine practice, and the expectation is that practice should vary minimally from teacher to teacher and situation to situation.

Who Holds the High Ground? One other factor, both subtle and speculative (on my part) seems to be an undercurrent in the rhetoric of the field in the first years of the 21st century. Whole language has always privileged the role of the teacher as the primary curriculum decision maker. Teachers, the argument goes, are in the best position to serve this important role because of their vast knowledge of language and literacy development, their skills as diagnosticians (they are expert "kidwatchers"), and the materials and teaching strategies they have at their disposal. And, in the arguments against more structured approaches, this is exactly the approach whole language advocates have taken: "Don't make these decisions at the state, district, or even the school level. Arm teachers with the professional prerogative (and corollary levels of professional knowledge) they need in order to craft unique decisions for individual children." Although this may seem a reasonable, even admirable position, it has recently been turned into an apology for self-serving teacher ideology.[103] The counter argument suggests that the broad base of privilege accorded to teachers may come at the expense of students and their parents. Thus, those who advocate a strong phonics-first position often take the moral high ground: "We are doing this for America's children (and for YOUR child!), so that they have the right to read for themselves." Even if one opposes this rhetorical move, it is not difficult to appreciate the clever repositioning on the part of those who want to return to more phonics and skills.

Taken together, these factors created a policy environment in which whole language was unlikely to flourish as the mainstream approach to teaching reading and writing. In the final analysis, however, I believe that the reluctance to own up to the "measurable results" standards was the Achilles heel of whole language. If whole language advocates had been willing to play by the rules of external accountability, to assert that students who experience good instruction based on solid principles of progressive pedagogy will perform well on standardized tests and other standards of performance, they would have stood a better chance of gaining a sympathetic ear with the public and with policymakers. And, as long as the criteria for what counts as evidence for growth and accomplishment are vague or left to individual teachers, the public could question the movement and wonder whose interests were being served by an unwillingness to commit to common standards.

Looking Ahead: Will We Benefit From the Lessons of History?

So where has this journey taken us? And, where will it take us next? We are, as Regie Routman has suggested, at a crossroads.[104] Many recent developments suggest that we are retreating to a more familiar, more comfortable paradigm of basic skills, in which phonics, skills, and controlled text dominate our practices. Other developments suggest that we are on the verge of a new paradigm, a hybrid that weds some of the principles of whole language (integrated instruction and authentic texts and tasks) with some of the traditions of earlier eras (explicit attention to skills and strategies, some vocabulary control of early readers, and lots of early emphasis on the code) in an "ecologically balanced" approach to reading instruction.[105] The most cynical among us might even argue that we are just riding the natural swing of a pendulum that will, if we have the patience, take us back to whole language, or whatever its child-centered descendant turns out to be, in a decade or so. Before making a prediction about the direction the field will take, let me play out the first two scenarios, phonics first and balanced reading instruction.

One Alternative for the Future

If those who have advocated most strongly for a return to phonics and a heavy skills orientation have their way—if they are able to influence federal, state, and local policy as well as the educational publishing industry—we will experience moderate to substantial shifts on most, but not all, the criteria I have used to measure changes in reading pedagogy over the last 40 years (range of materials, range of pedagogical practices, role of teacher, role of student, and underlying theory of reading and reading acquisition). As I read their views about policy and practice, the greatest changes will occur at the very earliest stages of learning to read: kindergarten and grade 1. They suggest explicit instruction on phonemic awareness and phonics, with a strong preference for decodable texts in the early grades. When it comes to writing, literature, response, and comprehension, they seem quite content to cede curricular authority to the practices that emerged during the 1980s and early 1990s, those associated with whole language, literature-based reading, and process writing.[106] Thus, looking broadly at the entire elementary reading curriculum (the range of materials and the range of pedagogical practices), things might, on the surface, look similar to the early 1990s, with some retreat to the 1980s, especially in terms of skill and strategy instruction.

But, beneath that curricular surface, major changes would have occurred. For example, the role of the teacher and the learner would have reverted to what they have been throughout most of the 20th century. The role of the teacher would be to transmit the received knowledge of the field, as reflected in research-based curricular mandates, to students. Students would eventually be regarded as active meaning makers, but only after they had received the tools of decoding from their teachers. The greatest changes of all would have taken place in the underlying model of reading and reading acquisition. The simple view of reading (RC = Dec * LC) would have returned in full force, and the job of young readers would be to acquire the decoding knowledge they lack when they begin to learn to read.

A Second Alternative

If those who are pushing for ecological balance prevail, the field will experience less dramatic shifts. A balanced approach will privilege authentic texts and tasks, with a heavy emphasis on writing, literature, response, and comprehension, but it will also call for an ambitious program of explicit instruction for phonics, word identification, comprehension, spelling, and writing. A balanced approach is likely to look like some instantiations of whole language from the early 1990s, but recalibrated to redress the unintended curricular consequences outlined earlier in this chapter. Major differences between a balanced approach and the new phonics are likely to manifest themselves most vividly in kindergarten and grade 1, where a rich set of language and literacy experiences would provide the context from which teachers would carve out scaffolded instructional activities to spotlight necessary skills and strategies, for example, phonemic awareness, letter-sound knowledge, concepts of print, and conceptual development. Thus, instruction, while focused and explicit, would also be highly contextualized.

Beneath the curricular surface, balanced approaches seem to share slightly more in common, at least on a philosophical plane, with whole language than with new phonics approaches. The teacher is both facilitator and instructor. The teacher facilitates learning by establishing authentic activities, intervening where necessary to provide the scaffolding and explicit instruction required to help students take the next step toward independence. The student is, as in whole language, an active meaning maker from day one of preschool. Reading is a process of constructing meaning in response to texts encountered in a specific context, and the emergent literacy metaphor, not the readiness metaphor, characterizes the acquisition process.

An Ecologically Balanced Approach

If my personal bias has not emerged, let me declare it unequivocally: I favor the conceptual map of the ecologically balanced approach. There are several reasons for favoring this stance. First, my reading of the research points to the balanced curricular position, not to the new phonics position, both at a theoretical and a pedagogical level. I do not see much support for the simple view of reading underlying the new phonics; readers do construct meaning, they do not find it simply lying there in the text. Regarding pedagogical research, my reading requires me to side with Chall's view that while some sort of early, focused, and systematic emphasis on the code is called for, no particular approach can be singled out. Even the recent report of the National Reading Panel took exactly that position. And, while I readily accept the findings of the phonemic awareness research, I do not read them as supporting drill and practice approaches to this important linguistic understanding; to the contrary, highly embedded approaches, such as invented spelling, are equally as strongly implicated in the research.[107]

Second, an ecologically balanced approach is more respectful of the entire range of research in our field. It does not have to exclude major research paradigms or methodological approaches to sustain its integrity.

Third, an ecologically balanced approach also respects the wisdom of practice. It is no accident that studies of exemplary teachers, those who are respected by their peers and nurture high student achievement, consistently find that they exhibit a balanced repertoire of instructional strategies. Teachers who are faced with the variations in achievement, experience, and aptitude found in today's classrooms apparently need and deserve a full tool box of pedagogical practices.

Finally, an ecologically balanced approach respects our professional history. It retains the practices that have proved useful from each era but transforms and extends them, rendering them more effective, more useful, and more supportive of teachers and students. And, it may represent our only alternative to the pendulum-swing view of our pedagogical history that seems to have plagued the field of reading for most of the 20th century. A transformative rather than a cyclical view of progress would be a nice start for a new century. It will be interesting to evaluate in another twenty years, with the lens of history at our disposal, which path we have followed.

ENDNOTES

1. The work reported herein was supported in part under the Education Research and Development Centers Program PR/Award Number R305R70004, as administered by the Office of Educational Research and Improvement, U.S. Department of Education. However, the contents do not necessarily represent the positions or policies of the National Institute on Student Achievement, Curriculum, and Assessment or the National Institute on Early Childhood Development, or the U.S. Department of Education, and endorsement by the federal government should not be assumed. An earlier and more complete version of this essay, titled "Reading in the Twentieth Century," appeared in Good, Thomas (Ed.). (2000). *American education: Yesterday, today, and tomorrow* (Ninety-ninth yearbook of the National Society for the Study of Education, pp. 152–208). Chicago: University of Chicago Press. Adapted with permission.

2. Austin, Mary C., & Morrison, Coleman. (1963). *The first R*. New York: Macmillan.

3. This account is from Chall, J. (1967). *Learning to read: The great debate* (pp. 13–15). New York: McGraw Hill.

4. Smith, N.B. (1986). *American reading instruction* (p. 276). Newark, DE: International Reading Association.

5. Smith, N.B. (1986). *American reading instruction.*

6. Bond, G.L., & Dykstra, R. (1997). The cooperative research program in first-grade reading instruction, *Reading Research Quarterly, 32*(4). Entire issue.

7. The reporting of data for students through grade 2 did not receive the fanfare that the first-grade report did, an outcome which I find unfortunate because it was, in many ways, even more interesting. It showed stronger effects overall for code-based approaches, and it revealed the most provocative of all the findings in this entire enterprise—the project effect. The project effect was this: Using analysis of covariance to control incoming performance, students were better off being in the poorest performing approach in Project A than they were being in the best performing approach in Project B. This raises the whole issue of impact of contextual factors on reading achievement. See Dykstra, R. (1968). Summary of the second-grade phase of the cooperative research program in primary reading instruction. *Reading Research Quarterly, 4*, 49–70.

8. If focus were on the impact of these studies on research rather than the practice, these issues would occupy more of our attention. In a sense, the First-Grade Studies created an opening for other research endeavors; indeed, the directions that reading research took in the mid-1970s—the nature of comprehension and the role of the teacher—suggest that there were groups of scholars ready to seize the opportunity.

9. When large-scale experiments returned in the early 1990s, it was not the Department of Education, but the National Institute of Child Health and Human Development (NICHD), that led the renaissance. For accounts of the development of the NICHD effort, see Lyon, G.R. (1995). Research initiatives in learning disabilities: Contributions from scientists supported by the National Institute of Child Health and Human Development. *Journal of Child Neurology, 10*, 120–127; or Lyon, G.R., & Chhaba,V. (1996). The current state of science and the future of specific reading disability. *Mental Retardation and Developmental Disabilities Research Reviews, 2*, 2–9. It is also worth noting that one of the likely reasons for the demise of Method A vs. Method B experiments is that scholars in the 1960s were looking for main effects rather than interaction effects. Had they set out to find in this work that methods are uniquely suited to particular populations, they might not have rejected them so completely.

10. The impact of Chall's book, particularly the phonics recommendation, was documented by Helen Popp (1975). Current practices in the teaching of beginning reading. In John B. Carroll and Jeanne S. Chall (Eds.), *Toward a literate society: The report of the Committee on Reading of the National Academy of Education.* New York: McGraw Hill.

11. In an unpublished research study, researchers found two- and three-fold increases in the number of words introduced in the first-grade books for the popular series published by Scott Foresman and Ginn. Hansen, J., & Pearson, P.D. (1978). *Learning to read: A decade after Chall.* Unpublished manuscript, University of Minnesota.

12. The teacher's manuals of the Ginn 360 program provide the most notable example of this new trend. See Clymer, T., et al. (1968). *Ginn 360.* Lexington, MA: Ginn.

13. Mastery learning can trace its intellectual roots to the works of Benjamin Bloom and John Carroll: Bloom, B. (1968). Learning for mastery. *Evaluation Comment, 1*; Carroll, J. (1963). A model of school learning. *Teachers College Record, 64*, 723–732.

14. For an account of criterion-referenced assessment as it emerged during this period, see Popham, J. (1978). *Criterion-referenced measurement*. Englewood Cliffs, NJ: Prentice-Hall.

15. Deno, S.L. (1985). Curriculum-based measurement: The emerging alternative. *Exceptional Children, 52*, 219–232.

16. Bloom, B. (1968). Learning for mastery.

17. During the 1970s, the most popular of these systems was the Wisconsin Design for Reading Skill Development, followed closely by Fountain Valley. Systems like these remained a staple in basal programs in the 1980s and 1990s and were still available as options in most commercial programs as late as 2002. For an account of the rationale behind these systems, see Otto, Wayne (1977). The Wisconsin Design, A reading program for individually guided education. In H.J. Klausmeier, R.A. Rossmiller, & M. Saily (Eds.), *Individually guided elementary education: Concepts and practices*. New York: Academic Press. For a critique of these programs during their ascendancy, see Johnson & Pearson, "Skills Management Systems."

18. This is not to say that there were no challengers to the conventional wisdom that emerged in the middle of the century. To the contrary, the alphabetic approach, now dubbed "synthetic phonics," survived as a force throughout the period, as did the language experience approach and a few assorted alternatives. See Chall, *Learning to Read*, and Mathews, *Teaching to Read*, for accounts of these programs.

19. It should be noted that a major child-centered reform movement, the open classroom, was creating quite a wave in educational circles and elementary schools throughout the United States in the early 1970s. It is hard, however, to find any direct impact of the open-classroom movement on reading instruction. However, one could make the argument that the open-classroom philosophy had a delayed impact in its influence on the whole language movement in the late 1980s.

20. Some portions of the text in this section were adapted in Pearson, P.D., & Stephens, D. (1993). Learning about literacy: A 30-year journey. In C.J. Gordon, G.D. Labercane, & W.R. McEachern (Eds.), *Elementary reading: Process and practice* (pp. 4–18). Boston: Ginn. (Sections adapted with the knowledge and permission of the coauthor and publisher.)

21. To assert that Chomsky laid the groundwork for an essential critique of behaviorism as an explanatory model for language processes is not to assert that he drove behaviorism out of psychology or education.

22. For an account of this view of language development, see Brown, R. (1970). *Psycholinguistics*. New York: Macmillan.

23. Goodman, K.G. (1965). A linguistic study of cues and miscues in reading. *Elementary English, 42,* 639–643; and Goodman, K.G. (1967). A psycholinguistic guessing game. *Journal of the Reading Specialist, 4,* 126–135.

24. Smith, F. (1971). *Understanding reading: A Psycholinguistic analysis of reading and learning to read.* New York: Holt, Rinehart, & Winston.

25. In all fairness, it must be admitted that this contribution was not exclusively Smith's. As we shall point out in later sections, many other scholars, most notably David Rumelhart and Richard Anderson, championed constructivist views of reading. It is fair, however, to say that Smith was the first scholar to bring this insight into the reading field. Rumelhart, D. (1980). Schemata: The building blocks of cognition. In R.J. Spiro, B.C. Bruce, & W.F. Brewer (Eds.), *Theoretical issues in reading comprehension.* Hillsdale, NJ: Erlbaum. Anderson, R.C. & Pearson, P.D. (1984). A schema-theoretic view of basic processes in reading comprehension. In P.D. Pearson, R. Barr, M.L. Kamil, & P. Mosenthal (Eds.), *Handbook of reading research.* New York: Longman.

26. Smith, F. (1983). Reading like a writer. *Language Arts, 60,* 558–567.

27. During this period, great homage was paid to intellectual ancestors such as Edmund Burke Huey, who as early as 1908 recognized the cognitive complexity of reading. Voices such as Huey's, unfortunately, were not heard during the period 1915 to 1965 when behaviorism dominated psychology and education.

28. Walter Kintsch and Bonnie Meyer wrote compelling accounts of the structure of exposition that were translated by others (e.g., Barbara Taylor and Richard Beach) into instructional strategies. See Kintsch, W. (1974). *The representation of meaning in memory.* Hillsdale, NJ: Erlbaum; Meyer, B.J.F. (1975). *The organization of prose and its effects on memory.* Amsterdam: North Holland Publishing; and Taylor, B.M., & Beach, R. (1984). The effects of text structure instruction on middle-grade students' comprehension and production of expository text. *Reading Research Quarterly, 19,* 134–146.

29. The most complete accounts of schema theory are provided by Rumelhart, D., (1980) "Schemata: The Building Blocks of Cognition," and Anderson & Pearson, (1984) "A Schema-Theoretic View of Basic Processes in Reading Comprehension."

30. Bartlett, F.C. (1932). *Remembering.* Cambridge, UK: Cambridge University Press.

31. It is not altogether clear that schema theory is dead, especially in contexts of practice. Its role in psychological theory is undoubtedly diminished due to at-

475

tacks on its efficacy as a model of memory and cognition. See McNamara, T.P., Miller, D.L., & Bransford, J.D. (1991). Mental models and reading comprehension. In R. Barr, M.L. Kamil, P. Mosenthal, & P.D. Pearson (Eds.), *Handbook of reading research* (Vol. 2, pp. 490–511). New York: Longman.

32. For early accounts of this perspective, see Baratz, J., & Shuy, R. (1969). *Teaching black children to read.* Washington, DC: Center for Applied Linguistics; and Labov, W. (1972). *Language of the inner city.* Philadelphia: University of Pennsylvania Press.

33. Baratz & Shuy (1969). *Teaching black children to read.*

34. See Bloome, D., & Greene, J. (1969). Directions in the sociolinguistic study of reading. *Handbook of reading research* (Vol. 2, pp. 395–421).

35. Rosenblatt, L. (1936/1978). *Literature as exploration.* New York: Appleton Century Croft. Rosenblatt, L. (1978). *Reader, text, and poem.* Carbondale, IL: Southern Illinois University Press.

36. Rosenblatt (1938) credits the idea of transaction to John Dewey, who discussed it in many texts, including *Experience and Education.* New York: Kappa Delta Pi.

37. A very interesting, even provocative attempt to understand comprehension processes appears in Thorndike, Edward L. (1917). Reading as reasoning: A study of mistakes in paragraph reading. *Journal of Educational Psychology, 8,* 323–332. The classic reference for using tests to reveal the psychological infrastructure of comprehension is the first published factor analysis of reading comprehension by Davis, F. (1944). Fundamental factors of reading comprehension. *Psychometrika, 9,* 185–197.

38. Robinson, H.M. (Ed). (1968). *Innovation and change in reading instruction* (Sixty-seventh yearbook of the National Society for Study in Education, Part II). Chicago: University of Chicago Press.

39. Dolores Durkin published a revealing study in 1978 documenting that what went on in the name of comprehension was essentially completing worksheets and answering questions during story discussions. She saw almost no instruction about how to engage in any sort of comprehension task—no modeling, no demonstration, no scaffolding. Durkin, D. (1978). What classroom observations reveal about reading instruction. *Reading Research Quarterly, 14* 481–533.

40. Among the most notable efforts at the Center were the classic works on reciprocal teaching: Palincsar, A., & Brown, A.L. (1984). Reciprocal teaching of comprehension fostering and monitoring activities. *Cognition and Instruction, 1,* 117–175; Raphael, T.E., & Pearson, P.D. (1985). Increasing students' awareness of sources of information for answering questions. *American Educational Research Journal, 22,* 217–236; and explicit comprehension instruction as a

general approach in Pearson, P.D., & Dole, J. (1988). Explicit comprehension instruction: A review of research and a new conceptualization of instruction. *Elementary School Journal, 88*, 151–165; Pearson, P.D. (1985). Changing the face of reading comprehension instruction. *The Reading Teacher, 38*, 724–738. This focus on comprehension and reasoning while reading continues today at the Center with the work of Anderson and his colleagues.

41. The work of Scott Paris and his colleagues is exemplary in the area of metacognitive training and comprehension monitoring. Paris, S.G., Cross, D.R., & Lipson, M.Y. (1984). Informed strategies for learning: A program to improve children's reading awareness and comprehension. *Journal of Educational Psychology, 76*, 1239–1252.

42. Michael Pressley, working in conjunction with a group of professionals in Montgomery County, Maryland, developed a set of powerful comprehension routines that, among other things, extended the four strategies of reciprocal teaching (questioning, summarizing, clarifying, and predicting) to include more aspects of literary response (e.g., personal response and author's craft). The best resource on this line of pedagogical research is a 1993 volume of *Elementary School Journal*, edited by Pressley, along with the following articles, one of which is from that volume: M. Pressley et al. Transactional instruction of comprehension strategies: The Montgomery County, Maryland, SAIL Program. *Reading and Writing Quarterly, 10*, 5–19; M. Pressley et al. Beyond direct explanation: Transactional instruction of reading comprehension strategies. *Elementary School Journal, 92*, 513–555.

43. K-W-L, an acronym for a graphic organizer technique in which students chart before and after reading what they know, what they want to know, and what they learned, is an interesting phenomenon, because while it has attracted a great deal of curricular attention in basals, articles for practioners, and staff development materials, it is hard to find much research on its instructional efficacy. See Ogle, D. (1986). The K-W-L: A teaching model that develops active reading of expository text. *The Reading Teacher, 39*, 564–570.

44. Isabel Beck and Margaret McKeown have spent several years in collaboration with a network of teachers perfecting this engaging practice, which focuses on how and why authors put text together the way they do. The net result of this routine is that students learn a great deal about how to read critically (What is the author trying to do to me as a reader?) and about author's craft (How do authors structure their ideas to achieve particular effects?). See Beck, I., McKeown, M., Hamilton, R.L., & Kucan, L. (1997). *Questioning the author: An*

approach for enhancing student engagement with text. Newark, DE: International Reading Association.

45. Chall, in the 1991 edition of *Learning to Read*, documented this important increase in basal comprehension activities.

46. Chall devotes a section to individualized reading in her 1967 description of alternatives to the basal (pp. 41–42), but has little to say about it as a serious alternative to basal, phonics, or linguistic approaches. In that same period, it is, undoubtedly, Jeanette Veatch who served as the most vocal spokesperson for individualized reading. She published professional textbooks describing how to implement the program in the classroom, for example, *Individualizing your reading program* (1959). New York: G.P. Putnam. In the middle 1960s, Random House published a "series" of literature books that were accompanied (in a pocket on the inside cover) by a set of vocabulary and comprehension activities that look remarkably like basal workbook pages. The Random House materials remind one of the currently popular computer program, Accelerated Reader, which is similarly designed to manage some assessment and skill activity to accompany trade books that children read on their own.

47. Anderson and his colleagues reported several studies documenting the impact of book reading on children's achievement gains: Anderson, R.C., Hiebert, E., Scott, J., & Wilkinson, I. (1984). *Becoming a nation of readers.* Champaign, IL: Center for the Study of Reading.

48. Atwell, N. (1987). *In the middle: Writing, reading, and learning with adolescents.* Portsmouth, NH: Heinemann. While it is difficult to locate data to document these claims about Atwell's particular influence, the rise of literature in the middle school has been documented by changes in the teacher survey portion of the National Assessment of Educational Progress of Reading.

49. James Hoffman and his colleagues painstakingly documented these sorts of changes in the basals of the early 1990s. Hoffman, J.V., McCarthey, S.J., Abbott, J., Christian, C., Corman, L., Elliot, M.B., Matheme, D., & Stahle, D. (1994). So what's new in the "new" basals. *Journal of Reading Behavior, 26*, 47–73.

50. For a complete account of the Book Club movement, see McMahon, S.I., & Raphael, T. E., with Goatley, V., & Pardo, L. (1997). *The book club connection.* New York: Teachers College Press.

51. Two classic books by Donald Graves were influential in leading the process writing movement at the elementary level, as was Lucy Calkins' (1986) classic, *The Art of Teaching Writing.* Portsmouth, NH: Heinemann; Graves, D. (1983).

Writing: Teachers and students at work. Portsmouth, NH: Heinemann; and Graves, D. (1984). *A researcher learns to write.* Portsmouth, NH: Heinemann.

52. Perhaps the most complete current reference on integrated curriculum is a new chapter in the third volume of the *Handbook of Reading Research.* Gavelek, J.R., Raphael, T.E., Biondo, S.M., and Wang, D. (in press). Integrated literacy instruction. In M.L. Kamil, P. Mosenthal, P.D. Pearson, & R. Barr (Eds.), *Handbook of Reading Research* (Vol. 3). Hillsdale, NJ: Erlbaum.

53. In Chapter 10 of Huey's 1908 book on reading, two such programs, one at Columbia and one at the University of Chicago, were described in rich detail. It is Dewey's insistence that pedagogy be grounded in the individual and collective experiences of learners that is typically cited when scholars invoke his name to support integrated curriculum. Huey, E.B. (1908). *The psychology and pedagogy of reading.* New York: Macmillan. (Revised 1912, 1915)

54. See Graves (1983) for an explication of his views on writing, and, for an account of how reading and writing support one another in an integrated language arts approach, see Hansen, J. (1987). *When readers write.* Portsmouth, NH: Heinemann.

55. Frank Smith and Robert Tierney and P. David Pearson carried this metaphor to the extreme. All three used the reading "like a writer" metaphor in titles to papers during this period: Smith, F. (1983). Reading like a writer. *Language Arts, 60,* 558–567; Tierney, R.J., & Pearson, P.D. (1983). Toward a composing model of reading. *Language Arts, 60,* 568–580; and Pearson, P.D., & Tierney, R.J. (1984). On becoming a thoughtful reader: Learning to read like a writer. In A. Purves & O. Niles (Eds.) *Reading in the secondary school* (Eighty-third yearbook of the National Society for the Study of Education, pp. 144–173). Chicago: National Society for the Study of Education.

56. Donald Holdaway's (1979) *The Foundations of Literacy,* summarizes this perspective and work.

57. The notion of significance here is intended to capture its impact, not its validity. Even those who question its validity would have difficulty discounting its influence on practice.

58. A rich account of the curricular antecedents of whole language and other progressive and critical pedagogies is found in Shannon, P. (1990). *The struggle to continue.* Portsmouth, NH: Heinemann. See also Goodman, Y. (1989). Roots of the whole language movement. *Elementary School Journal, 90,* 113–127. The phrase, "the child as curriculum informant," comes from Harste, J., Burke, C., & Woodward, V. (1984). *Language stories and literacy lessons.* Portsmouth, NH: Heinemann.

59. One cannot possibly name all the important leaders of the whole language movement in the United States, but surely the list will be headed by Ken Goodman, Yetta Goodman, and Jerry Harste, all of whom wrote important works explicating whole language as a philosophical and curricular initiative.

60. In the third edition of *Learning to Read*, Chall makes the case that phonics instruction increased during the 1970s and began its decline in the middle 1980s, at the time comprehension became a dominant research and curricular issue. She also notes a further decline in phonics instruction in basals, based on the work of James Hoffman et al. (1994). So what's 'new' in the new basals. On this issue, one should also consult Goodman, K.G., Shannon, P., Freeman, Y., & Murphy, S. (1988). *Report card on basal readers*. Katonah, NY: Richard C. Owen.

61. My understanding of the primary focus of the opposition to basals is that whole language advocates regarded basals as a pernicious form of external control on teacher prerogative, one that would lead inevitably to the "de-skilling" of teachers. In 1988, several whole language advocates and supporters wrote a monograph documenting what they took to be these pernicious effects (Goodman, Freeman, Shannon, & Murphy, 1988).

62. See Hoffman et al. (1994). So what's 'new' in the new basals?"

63. Perhaps the most compelling sign of the backgrounding of skills was their systematic removal from the pupil books. In the middle and even late 1980s, basal publishers featured skills lessons in the pupil books on the grounds that even teachers who chose not to use the workbooks would have to deal with skills that were right there in the student materials. By the early 1990s, as I noted earlier, they were removed from the student books.

64. One must keep in mind that I am discussing changes in published materials, not necessarily changes in classroom practice. Whether teachers changed their actual classroom practices in a matter consistent with, or at least proportional to, the basal practices is difficult to determine given our lack of broad-based data on classroom practices. One suspects that the pendulum swings of actual classroom practice are never quite as wide as the swings in the rhetoric of policy or even the suggestions in published materials.

65. Pearson, P.D. (1992). *RT* remembrance: The second 20 years. *The Reading Teacher, 45*, 378–385. This analysis documents the increasingly dominant force of whole language, literature-based reading, and process writing in the discourse of elementary reading and language arts instruction.

66. Perhaps the best documentation for the resistance to, or at least a more critical acceptance of, whole language practices comes from studies of exemplary teach-

ers who, it appears, never bought into whole language lock, stock, and barrel, but instead chose judiciously those practices that helped them to develop rich, flexible, and balanced instructional portfolios. See Wharton-MacDonald, R., Pressley, M., & Hampton, J.M. (1998). Literacy instruction in nine first-grade classrooms: Teacher characteristics and student achievement. *The Elementary School Journal, 99*, 101–128.

67. A recent analysis of the basals adopted in the early 1990s in California suggests that the vocabulary load of many of these basals was so great that most first graders could gain access to them only if they were read to them by a teacher: Martin, L.A., & Hiebert, E.H. (in press). *Little books and phonics texts: An analysis of the new alternatives to basals.* Ann Arbor, MI: Center for the Improvement of Early Reading Achievement, University of Michigan.

68. In the late 1970s, Marie M. Clay coined the term *emergent literacy* to signal a break with traditional views of readiness in favor of a more gradual view of the shift from novice to expert reader. See Clay, M.M. (1966). *Emergent reading behavior.* Unpublished doctoral dissertation, University of Auckland, New Zealand.

69. In my own case, it was the disdain that whole language seemed to spawn regarding the explicit teaching of skills and strategies, especially those that promoted the meaning-making goals of the movement: comprehension and metacognitive strategies.

70. Hiebert, E.H., & Taylor, B.M. (Eds.). (1994). *Getting reading right from the start: Effective early literacy interventions.* Boston: Allyn & Bacon. The researchers describe several research-based interventions that balance skills instruction with authentic reading.

71. Interestingly, a recent piece in *The Reading Teacher* makes exactly this point about the comprehension strategy instruction of the 1980s. See Dowhower, S.L. (1999). Supporting a strategic stance in the classroom: Comprehension framework for helping teachers help students to be strategic. *The Reading Teacher, 52*, 672–688.

72. Smith, "Learning to Read like a Writer," makes just this point.

73. For a compelling account of this "no text" phenomenon, see Schoenbach, R., Greenleaf, C., Cziko, C., & Hurwitz, L. (in press). *Reading for understanding in the middle and high school.* San Francisco: Jossey Bass. In this account, the staff developers and teachers of a middle school academic literacy course document the role of text in middle school as well as attempts to turn the tide.

74. Similar arguments have been made for the reform movements in mathematics; for instance, that the reforms got ahead of the professional knowledge base. The

results of the reform movement in mathematics have also been similar to the fate of the whole language movement. See Good, T., & Braden, J. (no date). *Reform in American education: A focus on vouchers and charters.* Hillsdale, NJ: Erlbaum.

75. In 1989, a Special Interest Group with the apocryphal label, Balanced Reading Instruction, was organized at the International Reading Association. The group was started to counteract the unchecked acceptance of whole language as the approach to use with any and all students and to send the alternate message that there is no necessary conflict between authentic activity (usually considered the province of whole language) and explicit instruction of skills and strategies (usually considered the province of curriculum-centered approaches). For elaborate accounts of balanced literacy instruction, see McIntyre, E., & Pressley, M. (1996). *Balanced instruction: Strategies and skills in whole language.* Boston, MA: Christopher-Gordon; Gambrell, L.B., Morrow, L.M., Neuman, S.B., & Pressley, M. (1999). *Best practices in literacy instruction.* New York: Guilford; Pearson, P.D. (1996). Reclaiming the center. In M. Graves, P. van den Broek, & B.M. Taylor (Eds.), *The first R: Every child's right to read.* New York: Teachers College Press.

76. Pearson details many of these concerns and arguments in "Reclaiming the Center."

77. As early as 1965, Kenneth Goodman had popularized the use of miscues to gain insights into cognitive processes. The elaborate version of miscue analysis first appeared in Goodman, Y., & Burke, C. (1969). *Reading miscue inventory.* New York: Macmillan.

78. For an index of the rising momentum of qualitative research in the early 1980s, see Guthrie, L.F., & Hall, W.S. (1984). Ethnographic approaches to reading research; and Bloome, D., & Greene, J. (1984). Directions in the sociolinguistic study of reading, in *Handbook of Reading Research.*

79. As a way of documenting this change, examine *Handbook of Reading Research*, Vols. 1 (1984) and Vol. 2 (1991). Volume 1 contains only two chapters that could be construed as relying on some sort of interpretive inquiry. Volume 2 has at least eight such chapters. For an account of the historical patterns in non-quantitative inquiry, see Siegel, M., & Fernandez, S.L. (2000). Critical approaches. *Handbook of Reading Research* (Vol. 3).

80. Beginning in the mid-1980s and continuing today, the pages of *Educational Researcher* began to publish accounts of the qualitative-quantitative divide. It is the best source to consult in understanding the terms of the debate.

81. For an account of the evolution of this line of inquiry, consult Lyon, R. (1995). Research initiatives in learning disabilities: Contributions from scientists supported by the National Institute of Child Health and Human Development. *Journal of Child Neurology, 10*, 120–126; and Lyon, R., & Chhaba, V. (1996). The current state of science and the future of specific reading disability. *Mental Retardation and Developmental Disabilities Research Reviews, 2*, 2–9.

82. The most highly touted pedagogical experiment supported by NICHD was published in 1998: Foorman, B.R., Francis, D.J., Fletcher, J.M., Schatschneider, C., & Mehta, P. (1998). The role of instruction in learning to read: Preventing reading failure in at-risk children. *Journal of Educational Psychology, 90*, 37–55. The NICHD work, in general, and the Foorman et al piece, in particular, have been cited as exemplary in method and as supportive of a much more direct code emphasis, even in the popular press (e.g., *Dallas Morning News*, May 12, 1998; *Houston Chronicle*, May 17, 1998; *Minneapolis Star Tribune*, August 5, 1998)

83. Much, for example, is made in this new work of the inappropriateness of encouraging young readers to use context clues as a way of figuring out the pronunciations of unknown words. The data cited are eye-movement studies showing that adult readers appear to process each and every letter in the visual display on a page and, most likely, to then recode those visual symbols into a speech code prior to understanding.

84. Allington, R., & Woodside-Jiron, H. (1998). Thirty years of research in reading: When is a research summary not a research summary? In K.S. Goodman (Ed.), *In defense of good teaching*. York, ME: Stenhouse. These writers document the manner in which Bonnie Grossen's manuscript, which is an alleged summary of the research sponsored by NICHD, was used in several states as the basis for reading policy initiatives: Grossen, B. (1997). *30 years of research: What we now know about how children learn to read*. Santa Cruz, CA: The Center for the Future of Teaching and Learning. Web document: http://www.cftl.org/30years/30years

85. Classic references attesting to the importance of phonemic awareness are Juel, C. (1991). Beginning reading. In R. Barr, M. Kamil, P. Mosenthal, & P. David Pearson (Eds.), *Handbook of Reading Research* (Vol. 2, pp. 759–788). New York: Longman; and Adams, M. (1990). *Beginning to Read*. More recently, it has been documented in Snow, C., Burns, S.M., & Griffith, P. (1998). *Preventing reading difficulties in young children*. Washington, DC: National Academy Press.

86. See Juel, C. (1991). "Beginning Reading."

87. See Juel, C. (1991). "Beginning Reading"; and Adams, M., *Beginning to Read*.

88. The work of Linda K. Clarke (1988), "Invented versus traditional spelling in first graders' writings: Effects on learning to spell and read," *Research in the teaching of English*, *22*(3), 281–309; and Pamela Winsor and P. David Pearson (1992). *Children at-risk: Their phonemic awareness development in holistic instruction* (Tech. Rep. No. 556). Urbana, IL: Center for the Study of Reading, University of Illinois, are most relevant on the issue of the various curricular routes to phonemic awareness development.

89. Nowhere is the rationale for the mandate of early, systematic phonics more clearly laid out than in the report of the National Reading Panel that appeared in April of 2000.

90. In Summer 1995, one entire issue of *American Educator*, *19*(2), was devoted to the phonics revival. Authors of various pieces included those who would generally be regarded as leaders in moving phonics back to center stage—Marilyn Adams, Isabel Beck, Connie Juel, and Louisa Moats, among others. One piece by Marilyn J. Adams and Maggie Bruck (1995, Summer), "Resolving the Great Debate," *American Educator*, *19*, 7, 10–20, is one of the clearest expositions of the modern phonics first position I can find. A second issue was also devoted entirely to reading (Spring/Summer, 1998, Vol. 22, No. 1 and 2).

91. See Connie Juel, "Beginning Reading"; and Gough & Hillinger (1980).

92. One of the reasons for the continuation of the debate is that few people seek common ground. Researchers who come from the whole language tradition, were they to read Adams and Juel openly, would find much to agree with about in the common privileging of Big Books, writing, invented spelling, and the like. They would not even disagree with them about the critical role that phonemic awareness or knowledge of the cipher plays in early reading success. They would, however, disagree adamantly about the most appropriate instructional route to achieving early success; phonics knowledge and phonemic awareness are better viewed, they would argue, as the consequence of, rather than the cause of, success in authentic reading experiences.

93. These and other reading policy matters have been well documented in a series of pieces in *Education Week* by Kathleen Manzo Kennedy (1997, 1998, 1999). See No. 99.

94. 107th United States Congress (2002). Public Law 107-110. No Child Left Behind. Washington DC: Government Printing Office.

95. Marilyn Adams (see *Beginning to Read*, and Adams & Bruck, "Resolving the Great Debate") has consistently championed invented spelling.

96. Allington, R., & Woodside-Jiron, H. (1998, Spring). Decodable text in beginning reading: Are mandates and policy based on research? *ERS Spectrum*, 3–11.

These researchers have conducted a thorough analysis of the genesis of this "research-based" policy and concluded that it all goes back to an incidental finding from a study by Juel and Roper-Schneider in 1983. They could find no direct experimental tests of the efficacy of decodable text.

97. Learning First Alliance (1998). Every child reading. Washington, DC: Author.

98. The war metaphor comes up time and again when the debate is portrayed in the public press. See, for example, Levine, A. (1994, December). The great debate revisited. *Atlantic Monthly.*

99. Manzo, Kathleen K. (1997, March 12). Study stresses role of early phonics instruction. *Education Week, 16,* pp. 1, 24–25; Manzo, Kathleen K. (1998, February 18). New national panel faulted before it's formed. *Education Week, 17*(23), p. 7; and Manzo, Kathleen K. (1998, March 25). NRC panel urges end to reading wars. *Education Week, 17*(28), pp. 1, 18.

100. Several studies are relevant here: First is the work of Wharton-McDonald and Pressley, cited earlier. Also important is the work of Pressley, M., & Allington, R. (1998); and Taylor, B.M., Pearson, P.D., Clark, K., & Walpole, S. (2000). Effective schools and accomplished teachers: Lessons about primary-grade reading instruction in low-income schools. *Elementary School Journal, 101*(2), 121–165.

101. See Pearson, DeStefano, & García (1998), for an account of the decrease in reliance on portfolio and performance assessment.

102. The clearest instantiation of this approach occurred in California where professional development-based on scientifically based reading research was transformed into law (AB 466). AB 466 required professional development funds from the state of California to be spent only on the state adopted materials, which were defined, prima facie, as based on scientific reading research. California State Legislature. (2001). Assembly Bill 466. The Mathematics and Reading Professional Development. Sacramento, CA: Author.

103. An interesting aside in all the political rhetoric has been the question, Who is de-skilling teachers? As early as the 1970s, whole language advocates were arguing that canned programs and basal reader manuals were de-skilling teachers by providing them with preprogrammed routines for teaching. Recently, whole language has been accused of de-skilling by denying teachers access to the technical knowledge needed to teach reading effectively; see McPike, E. (1995). Learning to read: The school's first mission. *American Educator, 19,* 4.

104. Written from a somewhat centrist whole language position, Regie Routman provides a compelling account of the political and pedagogical issues we con-

front in the current debates. Routman, R. (1996). *Literacy at the crossroads* Portsmouth, NH: Heinemann.

105. The *balance* label comes with excess baggage. I use it only because it has gained currency in the field. Balance works for me as long as the metaphor of ecological balance, as in the balance of nature, is emphasized, and the metaphor of the fulcrum balance beam, as in the scales of justice, is suppressed. The fulcrum, which achieves balance by equalizing the mass on each side of the scale, suggests a stand-off between skills and whole language—one for skills, one for whole language. By contrast, ecological balance suggests a symbiotic relationship among elements within a coordinated system. It is precisely this symbiotic potential of authentic activity and explicit instruction that I want to promote by using the term *balance*.

106. Adams and Bruck, "Resolving the Great Debate"; Adams, M. (1990). *Beginning to read: Thinking and learning about print*. Cambridge, MA: MIT Press; Fletcher, J., & Lyon, G.R. (1998). Reading: A research based approach. In W. Evers (Ed.), *What's gone wrong in America's classrooms?* Stanford, CA: Hoover Institution Press.

107. See the earlier cited studies by Clarke and Winsor and Pearson, as well as the review of phonemic awareness in Adams, M., *Beginning to Read*. See also the report of the National Reading Panel.

ANNOTATED BIBLIOGRAPHY OF
HISTORICAL REFERENCES IN READING

Compiled by Richard D. Robinson and Jennifer Wilson

University of Missouri-Columbia

The following is a selected list of references related to the history of reading education. Each was written following the last edition of *American Reading Instruction* published in 1986. No attempt was made to be comprehensive in this bibliography but rather to include those publications we felt were representative of the field of historical research in literacy.

Brandt, D. (2001). *Literacy in American lives.* Cambridge, UK: Cambridge University Press.

> Brandt discusses how people learned literacy behaviors in the past and the context in which it occurred. The influences of such contextual topics as economics, rising standards, generational differences, ethnicity, work and social relations, and social equity are discussed in terms of literacy development.

Brooks, G., Pugh, A.K., & Hall, N. (1993). *Further studies in the history of reading.* Cheshire, UK: United Kingdom Reading Association.

> This resource contains an important series of papers on the history of reading instruction. Of particular importance in this book are the questions asked about current research in historical literacy as well as suggestions for further research in this area.

Cavanaugh, M.P. (1994). *A history of holistic literacy: Five major educators.* Westport, CT: Praeger.

> This book provides a foundational look at holistic instruction through five prominent historical educators: Francis Wayland Parker, John Dewey, Rudolf Steiner, Hughes Mearns, and Laura Zirbes. A brief biography of each educator is presented, followed by chapters describing their views on such issues as children as learners; teaching reading and writing; structures of schools; roles and responsibilities of teachers, students, and parents; and evaluation.

Coleman, J. (1996). *Public reading and the reading public in late medieval England and France.* Cambridge, UK: Cambridge University Press.

This book is an ethnographic study of 175 years of public reading. The focus here is on how people read and looks at literacy through public and private behaviors. Coleman shows that group listening to books was found not only among the impoverished and uneducated, but also by the wealthy and highly educated. She concludes that the behaviors of group listening lasted long after many have previously thought.

Cranny, A.G., & Miller, J. (1987). History of reading: Status and sources of a growing field. *Journal of Reading, 30,* 388–398.

This is an important article on various aspects of the study of the history of reading. This discussion notes the current status of this field both in terms of its support in the academic community as well as the types of courses being taught in the history of reading. Of particular note for researchers is the extensive annotated bibliography.

Cunningham, J.W. (2000). How will literacy be defined in the new millennium? *Reading Research Quarterly, 35,* 64–71.

In an attempt to predict the future issues of literacy, this article provides five essays based on the past and present trends in reading education. Historical aspects of literacy education are discussed in context and add support to future predications.

Davidson, C.N. (1989). *Reading in America: Literature and social history.* Baltimore: Johns Hopkins University Press.

This collection of lessons is an excellent introduction to the history of the book. Chapters include discussions on early reading materials such as chapter books, gender issues as they relate to literacy instruction in colonial New England, and literacy and the mass media.

Graves, M.F., & Dykstra, R. (1997). Contextualizing the First-Grade studies: What is the best way to teach children to read? *Reading Research Quarterly, 32,* 342–344.

This article gives a concise timeline of the important dates in reading education in order to provide context for the First-Grade studies. It begins in the 1700's with a discussion of spelling and follows reading education to the phonics controversy of 1997.

Harris, W.V. (1989). *Ancient literacy*. Cambridge, MA: Harvard University Press.

> This is a scholarly discussion of reading in the ancient Greek and Roman empires. A noteworthy feature for reading researchers is the extensive bibliography of references related to reading and writing in the ancient world.

Kaestle, C.F. (1990). Introduction. *History of Education Quarterly* (Special issue on the history of literacy), *30*, 487–491.

> Reading education developments in a number of international settings such as England, Japan, Scotland, Spain, and Wales are discussed in this issue. For those who wish to compare and contrast national programs of reading instruction, this is an important reference.

Kaestle, C.F., Moore, H.D., Stedman, C., Tinsley, K., & Tollinger, W.V. (1991). *Literacy in the United States: Readers and reading since 1880*. New Haven, CT: Yale University Press.

> This book is unusual in the field of historical reading research in that it not only reports on the historical development of reading from 1880 to date but also provides a rich and detailed interpretation of these reading activities. This book defines the terms reading and illiteracy and addresses the question, What were the specific behaviors of readers during a particular time period? in the context of the social conditions at the time. For those interested in the effects of reading on various U.S. social practices, this is an important resource.

Manguel, A. (1996). *A history of reading*. New York: Viking.

> This book is a personal history of the author's many and varied encounters with print, which he then uses as an introduction to the study of the history of reading. Although this book was written for a broader audience, it does provide a good overview of the history of reading instruction.

McAleer, J. (1992). *Popular reading and publishing in Britain 1914–1950*. Oxford: Clarendon Press.

> This book looks at three publishing houses and their policies in order to help describe the reading behaviors of the masses. The commercialization of reading is looked at through the trends of the genres, time spent reading, cost of books, etc. McAleer also looks at the trends of adult and child literacy and goes in depth on how publishers stay in close contact with their clientele in order to instill their own values on their readers. The strength of

this book is the depth of context that is provided in the discussion of child and adult reading habits.

Michael, I. (1987). *The teaching of English from the sixteenth century to 1870.* London: Cambridge University Press.

This book is considered by many to be the standard reference work on the historical development of English as a curriculum subject. Subjects such as oral and written expression, literature, and linguistic skills are covered in detail. Special emphasis is given to the methods instructors of the past used in teaching these subjects. Of particular note for reading researchers is the historical bibliography of more than 1,700 references, making this book one of the most important resources in the study of the pedagogical history of language instruction.

Michael, I. (1993). *Early textbooks of English: A guide. Reading.* Reading, UK: University of Reading, Reading and Language Information Centre.

This short monograph is an important reference for those interested in studying the early history of reading education in Great Britain. References included in this scholarly volume are from the period 1530 through 1870 and represent most of the important titles in the field of reading from this period. The extensive annotations give details for each volume, not only as to author and publication but also the influence of the particular book on the history of reading. Also of great value is a discussion and bibliography of modern works on the study of the history of reading. This is a foundation reference for researchers who are interested in the roots of reading.

Monaghan, E.J. (1988). Literacy instruction and gender in colonial New England. *American Quarterly, 40,* 18–41.

This article discusses the teaching of reading skills in colonial America and includes descriptions of what parts of society were instructed in various reading skills as well as what methods were used. The influences of religion, politics, and economics are detailed as to their effect on various aspects of language instruction. Of particular importance is the author's discussion of several continuing research problems associated with historical reading research, such as evaluating literacy levels based solely on the ability of individuals to correctly sign their names.

Monaghan, E.J., & Saul, E.W. (1987). The reader, the scribe, the thinker: A critical look at the history of American reading and writing instruction. In T.S. Popkewitz (Ed.), *The formation of school subjects: The struggle for creating an American institution* (pp. 85–122). Philadelphia: Falmer.

This essay discusses the historical background related to the teaching of reading and writing, noting the disparity in favor of reading education for much of this period. Both social and political reasons for this dominance of reading instruction are discussed. The recent increased interest in writing at all levels also is documented.

Moore, D.W., Monaghan, E.J., & Hartman, D.K. (1997). Values of literacy history. *Reading Research Quarterly, 32*, 90–102.

This is an enlightening discussion of the values of the study of literacy history by three noted language historians. The authors address many of the vital questions in this discipline, both in individual statements and in dialogue with one another. This article contains an outstanding list of related references on the topic of the study of historical reading.

Mosenthal, P.B. (1988). Understanding the histories of reading. *The Reading Teacher, 42*, 64–65.

Mosenthal discusses the three ways in which the history of reading is viewed: definition, cause and effect, and ideology. He argues that until the goal of reading is determined the history of reading will continue to be an important area of research.

Nelms, W. (1997). *Cora Wilson Stewart: Crusader against literacy.* Jefferson, NC: McFarland.

This biography of one of America's innovative women focuses on Cora Wilson Stewart's work in Kentucky as well as her later literacy efforts. The book provides context that sharpens our understanding of Stewart's philosophies of education, specifically adult literacy. Nelms follows this dynamic national and international figure through her life, highlighting her accomplishments through pictures, diary entries, and letters as well as historical characteristics of the day.

Olmert, M. (1992). *The Smithsonian book of books.* New York: Random House.

This book is representative of a growing genre today on the topic of "the book." Chapter titles include "Scrolls and Scribes," "Illuminating the Dark Ages," "The Gutenberg Revolution," and "Bookmaker's Craft." This is an excellent introduction to the study of the many facets of the book as both a means of communication as well as an art object.

Petrucci, A. (1995). *Writers and readers in medieval Italy: Studies in the history of written culture*. London: Yale University Press.

This book, translated by Charles M. Radding, is a discussion of various aspects of literacy culture. There are ten essays in this book that look at readers and writers. The essays cross a multitude of topics including how books were meant to be used and how they actually were used, publishing by lay persons and professionals, and the very beginnings of book production.

Raven, J., Small, H., & Tadmor, N. (Eds.). (1996). *The practices and representation of reading in England*. Cambridge, UK: Cambridge University Press.

This book of essays attempts to answer the questions of what people read, how they read, why they read, and what it meant to them. Topics range from twelfth century pedagogy to eighteenth century libraries, the art of writing during the Renaissance to orality and literacy in provincial England. This book emphasizes the belief that by studying the history of reading an in-depth understanding of the culture in which reading is found can be obtained.

Robinson, H.A., Faraone, V., Hittleman, D.R., & Unruth, E. (1990). *Reading comprehension instruction 1783–1987: A review of trends and research*. Newark, DE: International Reading Association.

With its focus on reading comprehension, the authors of this book have provided a wealth of resources that provide a window into the history of comprehension instruction. Early textbooks and instructional materials are analyzed as well as contemporary instruction. The authors use this knowledge to provide the readers with future implications.

Robinson, R.D. (1989). Reading teachers of the past—What they believed about reading. *Reading Improvement, 26*, 231–238.

This article details the opinions of reading teachers of the past, from as early as 1660, concerning their definitions of reading, classroom goals, organization of reading instruction, and ways of dealing with problem readers.

Robinson, R.D. (2000). *Historical sources in U.S. reading education: 1900–1970*. Newark, DE: International Reading Association.

This annotated bibliography is divided into 15 sections reference works selected as being the most useful and relevant to the study of the history of reading education.

Robinson, R.D. (2002). *Classics in literacy education: Historical perspectives for today's teachers*. Newark, DE: International Reading Association.

This volume brings together the writings of eight classic reading educators of the past whose writings are most relevant for today's teachers of reading.

Saenger, P. (1997). *Space between words: The origins of silent reading*. Stanford, CA: Stanford University Press.

This scholarly book is a discussion of the influence of word separation as being an important element in the development of silent reading during medieval times. This is a vital resource for those interested in early developments in the use of silent reading. Of particular importance to reading researchers is the extensive glossary and reference sections of this book.

Sarroub, L., & Pearson, P.D. (1998). Two steps forward, three steps back: The stormy history of reading comprehension assessment. *Clearing House, 72*, 97–105.

This article looks at assessment of reading comprehension from the 1970s to the mid-1990s. The authors follow assessment through these 25 years and offer a critical look at the "progress" that was made during this period.

Stahl, N.A., & King, J.R. (2000). A history of college reading. In R.A. Flippo & D.C. Caverly (Eds.), *Handbook of College Reading and Study Research* (pp. 1–23). Mahwah, NJ: Erlbaum.

This is an extensive review of the history of college reading instruction with particular emphasis on the primary resources needed to do research in this area. Of particular note to literacy researchers is the detailed discussion of the philosophy of historical literacy investigations as well as information on the effective use of appropriate methods for the collection of this type of data.

Sullivan, D.P. (1994). *William Holmes McGuffey: Schoolmaster to the nation*. Cranbury, NJ: Association University Presses.

This definitive biography answers questions about William Holmes McGuffey, and about the impact and contemporary significance of the McGuffey Readers. Included in this book are letters from McGuffey himself as well as pictures of family members and memorabilia.

Note: Some of the information in this bibliography was taken from *Historical Sources in U.S. Reading Education: 1900–1970* (2000) published by the International Reading Association.

Nila Banton Smith, 1889–1976

Nila Banton Smith was totally dedicated to her academic and professional career in reading instruction. A prolific reader and writer, she stayed on top of the research and trends, enabling her to rise quickly in the field of reading instruction and remain among its leaders. "A lifelong teacher and administrator...she never lost touch with the classroom, the student, or the teacher" (Courtney, 1986, p. v).

Smith was born in Altona, Michigan, in 1889. In 1908, she graduated from Carson City High School and began teaching. She completed teacher preparation at Mt. Pleasant Normal School (now Central Michigan State University), and continued teaching in the Michigan school system in 1911. In 1926, she earned a bachelor's degree summa cum laude at the University of Chicago and was elected to Phi Beta Kappa.

While teaching at the elementary school level in the Detroit school system, she became Supervisor of Reading, and subsequently, Supervisor of Research from 1928 to 1933. To further her academic career, Smith earned a master's degree in 1929 and a doctorate degree in 1932, both from Columbia University. Amidst her doctoral studies, she spent a year as Chair of Education at Greensboro College in North Carolina. Smith's doctoral dissertation, *An Historical Analysis of American Reading Instruction*, was published as a book, *American Reading Instruction*, by Silver Burdett in 1934. Subsequent revised editions in 1965 and 1986 were published by the International Reading Association.

Smith's career in academe advanced rapidly as she served as Dean of Education at Whittier College, California, from 1933 to 1937, where she wrote *Adventures in Teacher Education*. This tenure was followed by two years at Indiana University in Bloomington, Indiana, and in 1939 to 1947, she served as Professor of Education at the University of Southern California (USC), where she also authored the basic reading series Learning to Read. During a tenure from 1948 to 1963 at New York University, from which she formally retired, Smith founded the New York University Reading Institute and authored the basal reading program Reading Instruction for Today's Children.

Smith also served as a distinguished professor at Glassboro State College, New Jersey, from 1963 to 1968; at San Fernando Valley State College, California, from 1968 to 1969; and USC, from 1969 to 1976. Upon her return to USC, she funded several projects, including the Nila Banton Smith Reading Improvement Laboratory where graduate students specializing in reading could view equipment, materials, and videotapes of classroom lessons. Perhaps this is where she had her greatest influence—with her graduate students, to whom "she was a vibrant, inspiring teacher...able to point the ways to apply modern research and psychology to classroom needs" (Robinson, 1958).

A generous supporter of the International Reading Association, Smith served as its president from 1963 to 1964, and received the Association's Citation of Merit. In the late 1960s and early 1970s, she was instrumental in purchasing the property in Newark, Delaware, where the Association's headquarters is now located.

The death of Nila Banton Smith in Los Angeles on December 13, 1976, ended a life devoted to improving reading instruction. A memorial service was held at USC on January 8, 1977, at which colleagues Millard Black, Constance McCullough, Irving Melbo, Grayce Ransom, and H. Alan Robinson spoke in her memory.

SOURCES

Courtney, L. (1986). *American reading instruction*. Newark, DE: International Reading Association.

Courtney, L. (1986). Introduction. *Nila Banton Smith, 1889–1976: A bibliography*. Newark, DE: International Reading Association.

History of Reading News, 2(1), April 1977, p. 1.

Robinson, H.A. (1958, May). Pioneers in reading VII: Nila Banton Smith. *Elementary English, 35*, 331–332.

INDEX

Note: Page numbers followed by *f* indicate figures; page numbers followed by *t* indicate tables; and page numbers followed by *n* indicate numbers in Selected Bibliography.

A

ABC BOOKS, 7–8, 12–13, 16
ABELL, ADELAIDE M., 177
ABILITY GROUPING, 174–175, 272–274
ACTIVITY PROGRAMS, 186, 227–238
ADAMS, MARILYN, 462, 464
ADULT READING INSTRUCTION: 1925-1935, 239; 1950-1965, 292, 300–301, 346–347
AFRICAN AMERICANS: sociolinguistics and, 440
AFT. *See* American Federation of Teachers
AIMS AND OBJECTIVES OF READING INSTRUCTION, 10–13; 1776-1840, 33–37; 1840-1880, 70–71, 77; 1880-1910, 114–115; 1910-1925, 154–156; 1925-1935, 186–193; 1935-1950, 253–254, 267; 1950-1965, 287–288, 295–297; for activity program, 230–231; Chall on, 420
ALDINE READERS, 139–141
ALEXANDER, CALEB, 60
ALEXANDER, THOMAS, 245
ALLEN, JAMES, 423
ALPHABET(S): alphabet-phonetic systems, 90, 92–107, 120–121; early, 3–4; emphasis on, 63; initial teaching, 363–364, 366–367; precursors of, 1–6; verses, 22
AMERICAN FEDERATION OF TEACHERS (AFT), 464–465
AMERICAN PRECEPTOR, 47–49
AMERICAN SELECTION OF LESSONS IN READING AND SPEAKING, 44
AMERICAN SPELLING BOOK, 41–44, 43*f*
ANDERSON, CHARLES J., 169, 180, 194
ANDERSON, IRVING H., 301
ANDERSON, RICHARD, 445, 475*n*25
ARNOLD, SARAH LOUISE, 109–110, 115, 137
ARTLEY, A. STERL, 341–342
ATWELL, NANCIE, 445
AUDITORY DISCRIMINATION, 270
AUSTIN, MARY C., 303, 305, 326, 387–389
AYER, JEAN Y., 209

B

R

RACE ISSUES: and reading instruction, 292–293

RATE IN READING. *See* speed

RAVEN, J., 492

READABILITY, 279

READERS, CHARACTERISTICS OF: 1607-1776, 18–20; 1776-1840, 38–39; 1840-1890, 80–107; 1890-1910, 126–145; 1910-1925, 162–169; 1925-1935, 199–214; 1935-1950, 257–261; 1950-1965, 303–305

READINESS FOR READING, 241–244, 258; controversy over, 329–330; versus emergent literacy, 481*n*68; research on, 239, 278

READING CARAVAN, 322

READING EXCELLENCE ACT, 463

READING FOR INTEREST, 261–262, 322

READING FOR MEANING, 323

READING: HOW TO TEACH IT, 109–110, 115

READING INSTRUCTION: 1607-1776, 9–32; 1776-1840, 33–68; 1840-1880, 69–107; 1880-1910, 108–147; 1910-1925, 148–184; 1925-1935, 185–246; 1935-1950, 247–286; 1950-1965, 287–390; 1967-2002, 419–486; beginnings of, 1–8; bibliography on, 487–493; future of, 468–472. *See also* aims; materials; methods; research

READING-LITERATURE SERIES, 141–144

REAL LIFE READERS, 200–201

REALISTIC MATERIAL IN READERS, 168–169, 197, 208, 304

RECREATORY READING, 198, 231–232

REESE, DORA, 300

RELIGIOUS EMPHASIS (1607-1776), 9–32

REMEDIAL READING. *SEE* DISABILITY IN READING

REPETITION OF WORDS IN READERS, 28, 42, 101, 104, 135, 204–205, 261, 305

RESEARCH IN READING INSTRUCTION: 1880-1910, 145–146; 1910-1920, 175–176; 1925-1935, 185–246; 1935-1950, 277–280; 1950-1965, 344–345, 372–378; politicization of, 463–465; in Sixties, 422–429; and whole language movement, 459–463

RICHARDSON, FREDERICK, 141, 144

ROBINSON, H.A., 492

ROBINSON, HELEN, 280–281, 372–373, 385–386, 415

ROBINSON, R.D., 492–493

ROBINSON, RICHARD, 487–493

ROGERS, JOHN, 17, 20–22

ROMANES, GEORGE JOHN, 177

ROSENBLATT, LOUISE, 442–443

STREPHOSYMBOLIA, 240
STRICKLAND, RUTH, 356–357, 359
STRONG, NATHANIEL, 23
STRUCTURAL ANALYSIS, 269, 333
STRUCTURAL EMPHASIS: whole language movement and, 456
STUDY READERS, 200
STUDY SKILLS. *See* content fields
SUBSTRATA FACTOR THEORY, 380–381
SULLIVAN, D.P., 493
SUMMERS, EDWARD G., 344–345
SUMMY, ETHEL, 200
SUPERVISION IN READING: 1925-1935, 244–246; 1935-1950, 283–286; 1950-1965, 386, 388; beginning of, 184
SUPPLEMENTARY READING MATERIALS, 118–119, 161–162, 197–199
SUZZALLO, HENRY, 200
SWINTON'S PRIMER, 142*f*
SYLLABARIUMS IN EARLY READING BOOKS, 7–8, 17, 22, 25–27, 29–30, 42, 53, 80
SYNTHETIC METHOD, POLLARD'S, 124–126

T

TABLETS, 3–4
TADMOR, N., 492
TANYZER, HAROLD J., 366
TEACHALL READING COURSE, 369
TEACHER PREPARATION: 1910-1920, 183–184; 1925-1935, 244–246; 1950-1965, 383–390; whole language movement and, 458, 466–467
TEACHERS' MANUALS, 90, 159–160, 301–303; 1925-1935, 196–197; 1935-1950, 256–257; in Sixties, 428
TEACHING OF READING, 117–118, 154, 157
TECHNOLOGICAL ERA (1950-1965), 287–295
TELEBINOCULAR, 282
TERMAN, LEWIS M., 190, 194
TESTS: 1910-1925, 148, 151–152, 173–174; 1950-1965, 306–307, 338; and disability, 180; standardized, research on, 175–176
THAYER, GIDEON, 92–93
THEISEN, W.W., 153
THOMAS, C.J., 147
THONET, EVELYN V., 200
THORNDIKE, EDWARD L., 148, 203, 476*n*37
THORNDIKE SCALE, 148